Who is that Weirdo Dancing in the Corner?

Who is That Weirdo Dancing in the Corner? by Spaceman Africa

Published by Spaceman Africa © All rights reserved

The moral right of the author has been asserted. All rights reserved. Without limiting the rights under copyright restricted above, no part of this publication may be reproduced, stored in or introduced into a retrieval system, or transmitted, in any form or by any means (electronic, mechanical, photocopying, recording or otherwise), without the prior written permission of the copyright owner of this book. The views of the author belong solely to the author and are not necessarily those of the publisher or the publishing service provider.

Notice that we do not use the heading 'Print Version' here because that is only needed when we have both print and ebook details here (eg. in the ebook editions).

1st Edition 2018, paperback.

ISBN: 978-1-925764-21-5

Publishing services by: PublishMyBook.Online

A catalogue record for this book is available from the National Library of Australia.

Who is that **Weirdo** Dancing in the Corner?

The Travel Diaries of Spaceman Africa

Spaceman Africa

29th August 2002

"Hi, I'm ringing on behalf of Sean Lewis." Jeremy continued, "Yes, well, you know how he travelled to Dublin for the weekend?"

"Yes," replied the employment agency consultant.

"Well, he was involved in a car accident on Sunday and died this morning."

It's not every day you fail to show up for work and one of your mates phones your boss to tell them you're dead. But, that's what happened when I found myself on a bender with some mates in Donegal, Ireland, when, really, I should have been at my warehouse job in London. At the time of the call, I was alive and well enjoying a few beers in the pub with some local women we'd met the night before. I was having too good a time to return to work. It was this bender that was the death, all be it fake, of Sean Lewis and the birth of Spaceman Africa.

Two months earlier, in June of 2002, I had returned to live and work in London after nine months away in Australia and the US. I found a job through an employment agency, working with Harvey Nichols in Greenford. My job was a typical picker/packer position. I picked orders of food and drink products and then packed them in boxes to be transported to stores throughout the country. I enjoyed the job. It was easy; it was a short ride from home; I was becoming good friends with the other workers, and the supervisors had explained their plans to have me moved to an easier position, working in the wine section. After having been there a few weeks, they produced a roster that extended for six months until January 2003. I remember feeling weird having my future mapped out like that. I liked to move from place to place a lot; who were they to say what I'd be doing in six months? I needn't have worried. To this day, they still think I'm dead.

When the changeover of the two rosters occurred, it worked out in my favour, and I ended up with a week off. I had friends from the States coming over to visit Ireland that same week, so I organised to go over and spend the weekend with them in Dublin. My mate, Jeremy Brown (not real name), who was living in Belfast, was also going to join us.

We all met at our hotel in Dublin, and even though some of us were meeting for the first time, we all got on great. My friends and I were big drinkers, so the weekend in Dublin was somewhat of a blur to me, but I do remember some of the absolute craziness we got up to.

Because Jeremy and I had been to Dublin before, we left the others to do their own thing during the day. We'd all meet up again in the afternoon and then go out together at night. One day, when the others were at the Guinness Factory, Jeremy and I were in a pub drinking, as you do, and Jeremy was explaining how it's possible to change your name and obtain a deed poll on the internet. As a laugh, he once bought a deed poll, changing his mate Pete's name to Edgar Stuart without telling him. Can you imagine Pete's surprise when the deed poll arrived in the mail? So, I said, "If it's that easy, why don't we change our names?"

And so, it was decided; we were going to change our names. But what's the point of going to all that trouble to change your name if you're going to change it to something common, like Paul Smith? So, we decided on unusual names, but nothing sprung to mind. Weeks later, Jeremy came up with the idea I change my name to my bracelet. I had a bracelet from South Africa that in different coloured beads read S. AFRICA. Jeremy suggested I be Stanley or Siegfried Africa. I said, "Fuck that. I'll be Spaceman Africa."

Spaceman was my nickname years earlier when I worked at the Shepherd's Bush Empire in London. And Spaceman starts with 's'. So, on 25th October 2002, I went to the internet café, Revelations, in Shaftsbury Square, Belfast, with a few friends and changed my name on the internet. The deed poll arrived by mail, a few days later. In the meantime, my partner in crime decided to change his name to Crazy Horse Invincible.

So, I e-mailed my friends about my name change. Some of their reactions were quite funny.

G'day All,

just a quick message to let you know that this week I changed my name by deed poll to Spaceman Africa, so if you could all refer to me as that from now on, I'd be most grateful. Hope to hear from you all soon,

Laugh Spaceman

Some of their reactions were quite funny. My friend Paddy, from South Africa, asked if I had lost my marbles and suggested now that I was a spaceman, I would have to watch out for Mulder and Scully: X Files Investigators. My buddy, Fosters, who I knew from London, was straight to the point, "What on earth are you on about son?" My friend Tracy, from Canberra, had a similar question, although she used the word hell instead of earth. "Hello, I love you with all my heart, but what the hell are you talking about?" My mate, Graeme, from Washington DC, assumed dementia had set in.

As you may have guessed, my name is Spaceman Africa. I was born in Sydney, Australia, May 1974, and at the age of four was relocated to the Canberra area, Australia's capital city. I grew up there as a wee lad; I went to school there and worked a few jobs after that but nothing serious. I took the weekends seriously though and enjoyed getting on the piss with my friends and experiencing moments of pure hilarity.

We used to write an account of our antics on the bottles of Southern Comfort we devoured each night.

In my late teens and early twenties, music was a big part of my life. I played the guitar and tinkered on the piano a bit, but my favoured instrument was the bass guitar. Originally, I learnt the guitar, but after the scores of gigs I went to once I was over 18, I saw some bass players whose presence on stage was suave and smooth. They played an important role in the rhythm of the band but stood back, out of the spotlight, happy to play the supportive role. The bass player is kind of like the guardian of the band, standing back and keeping their cool, whilst the guitarists parade around like chickens with their heads chopped off. This character type suited my personality and so it wasn't long before I gravitated to the bass. Plus, the bass sound is just cool anyway, not to mention a lot of chicks play bass.

I played in a few bands with different friends, and one of the more interesting groups I played in were Insomnia, an all-male, five-piece rock band. Phill on vocals worked for the Government but wasn't allowed to tell us what he did, as it was confidential. Mick, on guitar, sold toilets for a living; Richie, also on guitar, was a Paralympian, and Tom on drums was a dealer. Whenever stuck for conversation with Tom, I just asked when his next court hearing was coming up. Richie often travelled overseas to compete in various power lifting championships and trials. There was talk that Phill and I would join him on a trip to the States in '96, but nothing ever came of it.

The truth is, up until that point. I'd never had any desire to travel overseas, except, maybe, to New Zealand. But, now, in my early 20's, it was becoming a common endeavour amongst my peers to hop on a jet plane, armed with a working/holiday visa, and head to the UK. The UK is a popular destination for Australians because of the possibility to work and the language there is English. The idea of myself doing the same started to gain momentum. I read travel books and spoke to my cousins who had spent time in London. The stories of adventure in faraway lands and the descriptions of foreign cultures were both factors in changing my mind about travelling. Plus, if I'm honest, I thought my social standing on the ladder of coolness would certainly skyrocket if I became a globe-trotter.

I was single at the time; I had a cleaning job of no importance and, so, with nothing tying me to Canberra, in 1997, at the age of 22, I decided to take the exciting and scary step into the unknown and fly to London. I had a four year working visa, through my Grandmother, on my Dad's side, who was born in England. Other than a bus ticket for a one month trip around mainland Europe, I didn't have any plans at all. I wanted to go to Ireland at some point, but otherwise, I just wanted to get drunk, meet some women and have a good time.

Little did I know, the adventure I desired would be found in spades. Whilst hitch-hiking in Germany, I would be propositioned by a horny truck driver. I was going to rub shoulders with Madonna backstage at a Björk concert. For some extra cash, I was going to volunteer to be a human guinea pig for medical experimentation, and whilst passed out drunk at Barcelona airport, I would have nearly everything I owned stolen from me. Yep. Good times lay ahead. It's a common belief, international travel, especially solo and long-term, is a great way of 'finding yourself'. That wasn't my goal. I wasn't even thinking about that at the time. However, self-insight, self-awareness and growth were coming my way, whether I was searching for it or not, as you'll see.

Essentially, this book is an elaborate diary, a record of some of the experiences and wonderful people I encountered over ten years. This is a journey of exciting thrills and funny misfortune. I hope you enjoy the ride.

Information of note: I was born with a tremor condition, called Essential Tremor Disorder, which affects my hands and voice. When drunk, the shakes disappear. Hung over, the shakes are twice as bad. My eyesight is also mediocre. I wear glasses due to being born with a lazy left eye, and at the age of nine, I suffered a detached retina. Do you remember your mother telling you as a child not to throw stones or someone will lose an eye? Well, I'd have to agree with her on that one. Throwing stones with one of the neighbourhood kids, I was hit in the eye, and three operations later, my eyesight in my right eye is still rather average. You'll learn more about me as we go along.

1997

12 February 1997

My Dad drove me to Sydney airport, and we arrived to find check-in queues miles long. I found my queue and, bonus, I was third in line. I guess flying with the lesser known airline, Egypt Air, had its advantages. Being my first international check-in, all the security questions were new to me.

"Did you pack your own bag, Sir?"

"Yes."

"Are you carrying something for somebody else?"

"Yes."

"What is it?"

"I don't know."

My cousin had given me a wedding gift to give to his newly married friends, who were living in London. I hadn't bothered to ask what was in it. The check-in attendant wanted to know and told me to open the gift. My relationship with my cousin was on an acquaintance level. I had no reason not to trust him, though. But, shit! Was my trip into the big wide world about to end before it started by getting arrested for smuggling? There could be rare eggs of the Baw Baw Frog in the box for all I knew. I nervously opened the box to find I was a devious smuggler of champagne flutes. So, with nothing to worry about, except getting the flutes to London in one piece, I checked in my bags. Dad gave me his customary fist-bump-to-the-shoulder goodbye, and I was on my way.

The plane was monstrous, much bigger than anything I'd ever been on previously. I'd never been on a plane before that had two aisles. I felt like I was looking at something from out of the movies. I was super excited. I had a window seat, and with the view outside and all the in-flight entertainment to enjoy, I didn't have time to read any of the books I'd taken with me. There was one book I had that I was too chicken-shit to read anyway. My flat mate, Dan, had given me a book to read specifically on the plane, but I was worried if other passengers saw me reading it they would get upset. So, I never did end up reading *The World's Greatest Air Disasters* until a few weeks later when my feet were firmly on the ground.

During a brief stopover in Cairo, once again, I had a bit of drama. After putting my bag through the x-ray machine, security saw something they didn't like. I emptied the contents of my bag and security grilled me, "What is that?" One officer pointed to my harmonica. I picked it up and gave them all a rendition of "Stairway to Heaven", which may or may not have sounded anything like the Led Zeppelin song. Happy with my explanation, security waved me through before I had a chance to dazzle them with more of my untapped skill. On the flight out of Cairo, I looked at the ground out the window. From 35,000 feet, it looked the same as when I looked out the window flying between Canberra and Sydney. It just didn't sink in that I was flying over Africa.

I arrived in London, and to my surprise, it was sunny. I managed to navigate the London Underground to the Kensington area, in London's west, and checked into O'Callaghan's Hostel on Holland Rd. The first few days were a bit scary. I didn't say more than a few words to anyone. I felt so small in such a big, intimidating city. But it didn't take me long to find my feet, and after four weeks, I'd quickly found some casual work, made some friends, and found myself on the right side of the hostel manager. Occasionally, he went out and put me in charge, and I worked behind reception. I got paid to sit and watch TV, basically. When the rent went up, somehow, in a drunken speech, I persuaded him to let me stay for the old price. I became good friends with the Ethiopian shopkeepers in the local supermarket. I also spent those first weeks exploring all the famous London landmarks. I shopped at various markets, went to museums, got drunk at various pubs, visited distant relatives in Surrey, and caught up with friends from home who were also in London, including a day trip to the seaside town of Brighton, south of London, with a former work colleague.

I liked London. It was exactly like I'd seen on TV—black cabs, red double decker buses, pubs on every corner. Some of the people were friendly, and some pushed and shoved past you on the street. I certainly wasn't the only Aussie in London. There was a shitload of Australians, as well as Kiwis and South Africans. Walking down the street, I often said to myself, "Shit man. I'm in London," and then smiled in amazement. It was weird. London's official language is English, but when staying in a youth hostel, English is one of the least languages spoken. Plus, all the shops are owned by immigrants, so they don't speak English that well, either, so I was forever asking people to repeat themselves. I didn't have any thoughts of long term plans at this stage. I was simply hanging out in London open to anything and everything.

But the most significant thing to happen occurred only two weeks after I arrived. I walked down the stairs in O'Callaghan's to the basement with my newfound friend, Paul - a tall, ginger haired, peep-show employee from Seattle. There, I saw two girls chatting and sitting on the floor. Paul had met them earlier, and he introduced me to them. Hanna and Julia were both from Germany and were over for a two-week holiday. They were super friendly. One night, the girls invited me to join them to go to Heaven, a famous gay nightclub in Charing Cross, Central London. It was quite a fun night out and I really bonded with Hanna.

Hanna was 20, tall and slim, with long, dark hair and really attractive. She had a playful and caring nature about her, and we were really hitting it off. I blew my chance that night to kiss her. As the club was closing, Julia had gone to collect her jacket, leaving Hanna and I alone, but I missed my opportunity because I was too busy staring at all the freaks lining up for the cloak room. However, the attraction was there. The next night, walking back from the pub, down Holland Rd, I made my move, and, success, we kissed in the street under the glow of the street lights. It was a real delight spending time with Hanna over those two weeks. We explored some of the sights, and she taught me various German phrases, whilst at night, we socialised with the other hostel residents.

Julia was cool, but she seemed a bit distant towards me, maybe because I'd stolen her travel partner from her. She says that wasn't the case, and things changed when Julia hooked up with Gary. Gary was a cool Irish guy, also staying at O'Callaghan's, who worked at a pub in central London—O'Neill's, Woodstock St—where we soon became regulars. But life is funny. My relationship with Hanna didn't last long, but Julia and I became good friends, and we're still good friends to this day, more than twenty years later.

It was exciting being away from home and travelling by myself. No one knew me, so I could behave however I wanted, and no one knew if I was acting out of character. I had a sense of freedom and invincibility and did things I normally wouldn't do back home. I felt unaccountable for my actions and that I could get away with a lot more.

The girls went home to Germany... at their second attempt. We got to spend an extra night together because they missed their bus home first time around. The plan was, I would go to Germany about a month later and stay with the girls for a while. In the meantime, I was going to go on the now defunct Eurobus, a bus tour around Europe. It was something I'd organised before meeting Hanna; otherwise, I would have followed her to Germany straight away.

Not to worry, my long-time school mate, Brian, would be joining me on the trip, as would two of his old work mates, Jon and Natasha, who I'd already met a few times. Travelling with Brian was fun and easy. He was slim, faired hair and wore glasses. We shared the same sense of humour, and he'd travelled a lot before. Jon was a big lad. He was good company, as well, except he was a 'soft talker'. I often struggled to hear what he was saying, and Natasha was a cute little blondie. I don't know why she even came. She didn't get involved in anything.

Eurobus travelled around Europe on a designated route stopping at many various cities along the way. Passengers had the choice to get off at any stop, do their own thing, stay for a night or more, and then catch the next bus coming through to the next desired destination. You could travel around the circuit for different lengths of time. We were on the road for four weeks, and there were many stand out moments.

First stop, Paris. Just beautiful. My first taste of mainland Europe, and I was having a ball—so many sights, so many famous landmarks, and so many attractive women with sexy accents. We went to the *Pierre La Chaise* cemetery to see Jim Morrison's grave; we smuggled a bottle of tasty French wine up the Eiffel Tower and watched the sunset, and spent an hour on top of the *Arc de Triomphe* watching the chaotic traffic below. We were hoping to see a car accident on the roundabout but no luck.

Unexpectedly, we had a good time when we stayed in

a small village, called Kirchdorf, in Tirol, Austria. Across from our hostel was a cheap supermarket that sold cases of beer for just under $13AUD. We pigged out on food, too, after starving in Paris due to it being so expensive. We started drinking at 3pm with others from the bus, and later that night, a whole gang of us went out to a bar in St. Johann and got remarkably drunk on flugels (vodka and raspberry, from memory). Surprisingly, the bar played Australian music and had Australian road signs on the walls. The usual sign, 'There are no kangaroos in Austria' was there, too. We met some of the local girls, and I practised what little German Hanna had taught me. Upon leaving the bar, we found it was snowing, and we danced down the street as the snow-covered village looked so picturesque.

Next morning, Brian and I, along with Amber, a Kiwi lass on our tour, made a snowman. I also did a face plant trying to toboggan down a hill, much to the amusement of those watching. I didn't find it so funny.

I'd already had one attempt at sliding down the small embankment with some success before talking up the experience to Brian and Amber.

"You gotta see this," I asserted.

I took a long run up with the idea I'd build some speed and then place the toboggan on the ground in front of me, launch myself onto it, landing on my chest, and then slide down the 2—3 metre slope. It didn't quite work out that way. I ran as fast as I could and then placed the toboggan in the snow a metre short, thinking I'd slide the rest of the way from there to the slope. My experience with snow was minimal, and I didn't realise the snow was too powdery to slide on. Brian loves telling the story of how he saw me take a run and dive onto the toboggan, and the toboggan stopping dead when I placed it in the snow. He watched in suspense as I continued to hold on to the stationary toboggan, whilst the rest of my body continued to propel forward. I then went face first into the cold, wet snow. Brian says he saw my head disappear with only my long hair visible, fanned out in the snow, and my arms stretched out behind me, my body coming to a stop right before the edge of the slope.

Oh, Jesus, Mary and Joseph, it hurt. It was quite a rude shock. It wasn't what I was expecting at all, and I winded myself. I knelt on the ground, hunched over in pain, struggling to get my breath back. Brian and Amber were struggling to breathe properly, as well. They were pissing themselves laughing and found it a real effort to ask about my welfare. My breath returned, and I decided to have another go, but this time, I was determined to get it right. Like fuck I did. I was quite sheepish after that and didn't join in anymore reindeer games, choosing instead to have some time to myself to recover. I lamented how lucky I was not to be wearing my glasses as I would have broken them ... and my face.

Moving right along, Venice was beautiful with its canals, its maze of narrow lanes (it was so easy to get lost), and the large squares surrounded by grand architecture. The lack of motor traffic added to the beauty, and a highlight was when we took a ride in a gondola.

On the way from Venice to Rome, our bus broke down at a large roadside *Autogrill*. Some of us, Brian and myself included, bought some cheap wine and started drinking, sharing jokes, and just having fun. Brian and I danced to the music coming from the bus stereo, and then we started to mingle with others in the car park. We found a monk, who politely declined our request to bless our bus. Brian and I were quite loud and drunk, and everyone was happy we passed out asleep when the bus finally got going again.

In Rome, the tour took us to a campsite about half an hour outside of Rome. Strangely, there were emus roaming around the site. Fuck, it was cold. We stayed in huts that had thin canvas walls. It may as well have been Glad Wrap, the fat lot of good they did to protect us from the cold. I went to bed with a sleeping bag plus four blankets. Brian had seven blankets.

In Rome, the four of us were on high alert as we'd been warned by our tour guide to be extremely vigilant of highly skilful pick-pockets. It appeared we hadn't been the only ones warned as I saw other tourists wearing their backpacks on their fronts. We went to St Peter's Basilica. We went through the tomb, climbed to the dome, and saw a panoramic view of the city. Afterwards, we walked, visiting a lot of the ruins, the Colosseum, Circus Maximus, and the Forum. We went to the Vatican and saw the Sistine Chapel. It was amazing. There was something to look wherever you turned. It was hard to take it all in, and some of the paintings looked 3D, as if they were jumping out of the wall at you. No, I wasn't on drugs.

After getting lost, we arrived late in Barcelona. The hotel at the tour drop-off point was fully booked, so we had to fend for ourselves and find a place of our own. We rung around and found two different places. So, six of us, with backpacks, went walking through the dodgy-looking, narrow alleyways of the Gothic Quarter, lined with loads of bars and crowds of people. We became lost and asked some police to show us the way. All this was at 11:30 at night—a bit scary.

Brian, my usual partner in crime, was bedridden with a nasty cold he'd caught from our time in Rome, and he passed out in our room. Jon and I went to a few bars and ran into the guides from our tour. We drank loads of *Sangria* and didn't call it a night until 5am.

The next day, I hung around our hotel area in the Gothic Quarter; I saw the city's main thoroughfare, *Las Ramblas*, did a bit of window shopping, and went to a bar or two.

With Brian still not feeling well, and God knows what the others were doing, I went out by myself. I found a bar near our hotel that sold jugs of *Sangria* for about $6AUD, compared to $19AUD the night before. At the back of the bar, through some curtains, was a small, heavy metal bar. It was awesome. The people there sang along to all the songs in English. There I met a girl, called Yolanda, and she took me to a disco on Las Ramblas, where I met some of her friends. We all had a great night drinking, and it could have been an even better night if not for bed logistics. Yolanda and I got on very well, but I didn't even have a bed to myself, let alone a room. I'd drawn the short straw and was sharing the double bed in our room, with Jon, I think, and unfortunately, Yolanda lived out of town.

After a few brief stopovers along the way, our bus took us to Brussels. The gang and I decided we'd much rather stay in Bruges. We felt Bruges would be more interesting and relaxed, and it's only an hour's train ride east of Brussels. That's only if you catch the right train, of course. The hostel we'd booked in Bruges had a cheap restaurant downstairs, and upon check-in, the first beer was free. After close to 24 hours on the bus, we were looking forward to getting to the hostel and downing that first beer. But, somehow, we caught the wrong train. We only realised our mistake when the conductor came to check our tickets. Dejected, we got off the train, went back to Brussels, and finally arrived in Bruges two hours after we set off from Brussels the first time—twice as long as it should have taken. That first beer went down in seconds. Bruges, a small medieval town, was beautiful with canals, cobble stoned streets, and century old buildings. Being Belgium, we naturally indulged in many different beers and chocolates.

Our next stop was Amsterdam, and after two days there, I vowed I was definitely going to visit again. On our first day, we took a canal cruise around the city and learnt about the leaning houses and the different waterways. We went to the Sex Museum and saw displays and artwork, covering anything and everything about sex since it was invented. At night, Brian and I went for a walk through the red-light district, and for some unknown reason, we couldn't find the famous windows. How that's possible, I don't know.

Amsterdam is easily assessable by foot, so the next day, we walked around the city taking in the sights. We checked out one or two coffee shops. Because the others weren't smokers, and because I was too intimidated, as I knew fuck all about the different types of weed or hash available, our smoking experience was passive, to say the least.

In the early evening, Brian and I went to a live sex show: *Top Quality Dirt & Filth*. Watching our pennies, we went early so as to get in for the day rate. We witnessed some naked women dancing, a couple having sex, and various guys being pulled up on stage and stripped, whilst being embarrassed by a stripper performing some sort of sex party trick on them. Brian and I hid behind our complimentary beer and managed to avoid being called up on stage.

Once again, we found ourselves walking the red-light district at night (funny that), and this time, we found the windows. They were everywhere. How we missed them the night before I'll never know. We spent some time window shopping and taking in the atmosphere of the area. One hooker tried her best to get my custom, but I couldn't afford it even if I'd wanted to. I showed her my empty wallet to prove I had no money, only for her to steal the glasses off my face and then run inside to the back of her room. I chased after her into an adjoining room to find Brian, of all people, with another hooker, who, also, wouldn't take no for an answer. They finally let up, and we left with all our belongings. Before leaving for Berlin the next day, we went to look at the Torture Museum. Oh man, there have been some evil and painful torture devices in the past. Some displays made the eyes water, I tell you.

After a shitty night drive on the bus, where we froze and got little sleep, we arrived in Berlin at 7am and headed out on foot to our hostel. Along the way, we asked some local lads for directions and got a extremely animated answer. Arms were waving and pointing in all directions, and almost every word was stressed. The look of, "Oh my God, what's going to happen here?" on Brian's face was priceless. An hour and a half later, we arrived at our hostel, ready for bed. But no rest for the wicked, nor a backpacker with only two days in a city. That afternoon, in the rain, we went for a walking tour and saw the Brandenburg Gate, Checkpoint Charlie Museum, and what was left of the Berlin Wall.

I noticed I'd lost my wallet. *Scheiße*. I had to buy a new bus pass and organise new bank cards. Luckily, my friends were able to support me until we were back in London, where I could get back on my feet again. That night, it also bucketed snow. At about twelve o'clock, I was out walking, retracing my steps, hoping to find my wallet, and I was absolutely covered in snow. It was awesome, one of those, "If my friends could see me now" moments. I also contemplated trying to get a piece of the wall, but in the end, I couldn't break off a piece.

From Berlin to Prague the snow followed us. Prague was great, although absolutely freezing. Whilst exploring, we often walked into shops to have a look around just to get in out of the cold. The Old Town was architecturally eye-catching. Things like the Charles Bridge, the Old Town Square, and the Prague Castle had so much detail. And at night, when lit up, they were so beautiful. Walking back to our hostel at night, up a large mountain, we had a great view of the city. Just as we'd been told, we found Prague to be cheap. Food, alcohol, clothes, and crystal were incredibly cheap. But because of my lost wallet, and using money lent to me by my friends, I wasn't able to spend much. The buildings weren't the only things that were eye-catching. The Czech women were stunning, so well-dressed and lovely pale skin.

The only real noteworthy thing of Munich was when we went to the *Augusteiner Braustuben* Beer Hall. There were the four of us, plus an Aussie couple and two Aussie girls, and we were all sampling the different beers available. I was drinking *Radler*, which was going down very nicely. It had an amazingly smooth taste. My wonderment was quickly deflated when I learnt Radler was beer mixed with lemonade. Ah, well. A few of us, including me, left a bit early as we were souveniring (stealing) various stein mugs and glasses with the beer hall insignia on them. The rest of the group followed not long after but were stopped at the door by a waitress. They told the waitress one of her colleagues had collected the glasses. Not quite believing them, the waitress went back inside to check their story, whilst everyone else did a runner. I saw all this whilst hiding in a used car yard across the road. It was quite funny once the heart rate and adrenalin levels calmed down.

It was getting towards the end of our trip, and I lost all enthusiasm to do anything but drink and laze about. I was looking forward to going back to London for a few weeks and then to Germany to see Hanna. In Basel, Switzerland, we had a look around town and did some window shopping. I spent most of the time lazing around the hostel, playing ping-pong and watching cartoons. Brian had bought the scripts to the Stars Wars movies, so Brian, Jon, and I learnt lines from the movies and acted out various scenes outside a church. It's really fun when you're drunk.

Arriving back in London, I felt like I was returning home. I knew my way around, people spoke English, and

I had friends there. After the tour, the four of us went our separate ways. However, I did catch up with Brian again, and we spent a day visiting all the streets featured on the Monopoly board and had our photo taken at each one. We even went to the police station on Vine St, where the police kindly took our photo, whilst throwing us into the back of a police van. Luckily, we didn't need a 'Get out of jail free' card for them to let us go.

Otherwise, I spent most of my time in the East End. Gary, who I knew from O'Callaghan's months earlier, was sharing a flat with two Irish women near Bethnal Green and had let me crash on the couch. I remember some fun relaxing days drinking in Victoria Park with the Irish lasses and more sessions at O'Neill's, Woodstock St. During this time, it was my birthday, as well. It fell on a Saturday, and I had a big night out with Gary and his mate, *Ádhamh*, another Irish lad. The plan was to wake up early again the next morning, Sunday, and go to church, but Gary couldn't manage to get out of bed, so it was just *Ádhamh* and me.

Now, we didn't go to just any church; we went to The Church. In the industrial wasteland behind King's Cross station, on Sunday mornings from 9am—12pm was the best spreading of the gospel I'd ever experienced. The Church is a party with comedians, strippers, music, and copious amounts of alcohol held inside a warehouse. The drinking system was quite an eye-opener. One had to buy a ticket for a drink and then present the ticket at the bar, which only had cans of lager. I'm guessing this system was a way to get around liquor licencing laws. They weren't selling alcohol; they were selling tickets. And so, people bought tickets in bulk and then got their drinks in bulk. There were lots of guys walking around with large plastic bags full of beer cans. Most of the guys and gals there were Aussies, Kiwis, and South Africans. It took a while for *Ádhamh* and me to hit our stride. We were feeling a bit fragile from the night before, but after a few drinks, we were back in the swing of things enjoying the entertainment. I kept thinking, 'Whose idea was this?' It was a great way to spend a Sunday morning. I imagine it's common for hard core party goers to party all night and then head to The Church without having slept. Some people certainly looked the worse for wear. My favourite bit was the final act, where women from the crowd were encouraged to get up on stage to dance ... and take their tops off. Happy birthday indeed.

After two and a half weeks, I'd recovered from my lost wallet. I had sorted out some replacement bankcards, and I was off to Germany. The plan was to go to Bonn and stay with Hanna and see what developed from there. Whilst I was travelling around Europe, I'd spoken to her on the phone many times, and things were good between us. I was thinking of using Bonn as a base whilst taking short trips around Europe and, at the same time, falling madly in love with Hanna. I quickly learnt, when travelling, plans change.

Before Bonn, I wanted to go to a rock festival in Nuremberg, called Rock Am Ring, and to get there, I caught a bus from London to Munich. The ferry from Dover to Calais broke down, and 21½ long and tiring hours later, I arrived in Munich.

I arrived in Munich to t-shirt and shorts weather. Three weeks earlier, when I was there, it had been snowing. From Munich, I'd be able to get a train the 160km north to Nuremberg for the festival.

I found travelling solo and independently, as I now was, to be very different from travelling with friends on an organised tour. Travelling with friends gave me the confidence to make new friends. It also meant I didn't have to try to meet others if I didn't want to, because I was already travelling with some members of my fan club. Travelling solo meant being alone, unless I made an effort to meet others. It forced me to make the effort as there weren't friends to fall back on. There was also the different style of travel. Independently meant doing everything myself, which was sometimes daunting and hard work, but I could do things when and how I wanted. Back in the late 90's, that meant working with guide books and using public telephones. There were no smart phones nor easily accessible internet back then. Travelling with an organised tour allows you to relax more as the leg work is done for you, but you're sometimes restricted as to what you can do and where you can go. I quickly developed a liking for travelling independently.

I made it to Nuremberg and stayed in a large old farmhouse, part of Nuremberg Castle, which had been converted into a youth hostel. There was a great view of the castle and the old town from my dorm window. The old town, with the castle and large town square, cathedral, monuments, and statues from the 11th century onwards, were remarkably impressive. Walking around was like being back in time, except it was hot. Damn hot. So, whilst the surroundings were from centuries ago, walking around in shorts and a t-shirt, I didn't feel completely absent from the 21st century. I would definitely go back to Nuremberg given the opportunity.

I was lucky to meet some cool people. I met some young Germans at the hostel from Chiemsee, a small place east of Munich where the story of Hansel and Gretel is set. At the festival, whilst queuing for beer, I asked a bystander in my best German what the price of beer was. He replied in perfect German but with an English accent. I asked, "Do you speak English?" and that's how I met Bob and Jimi, two Englishmen living and working in Germany. I spent my time at the festival alternating among the Germans I'd met at the hostel, the Englishmen, and just wandering around by myself.

It was a jam packed three days of sun, beer, and music. All up, I saw the bands: Kiss, Live, Texas, Supertramp, Reef, Bush, Supergrass, and Aerosmith. What a weekend. I had a great time, but for the first time since I left Australia, there were moments of drunken emotion where I felt lonely. I wasn't homesick, but I missed my friends. I wanted my friends to be with me at the festival. I remember even phoning my housemate, Dan, back in Canberra during the second day of the festival. The loneliness passed, though. My feelings changed all the time.

I went to Freiburg in the Black Forest. It had a surprisingly lively vibe for a small town, and I even tried to get a job there, but with my very limited German, I had no luck. The Black Forest was thrilling and relaxing at the same time. I caught a train to the nearby town of Titisee and went for a walk. The weather was overcast, just how I like it when walking through bushlands, and there was fog covering some of the higher peaks. The forest was dense and wonderfully green. I felt there were forests in Australia as equally impressive, but being the Black Forest made the experience special.

From Freiburg, I caught a train through the Black Forest, past Lake Constance, and further east on to the edge of the Bavarian Alps, finally stopping in Kempten where the Englishmen I met at the festival, Bob and Jimi, lived. Bob had mentioned he thought he could get me some work labouring, and I was welcome to go and stay with him.

My whole reason for coming to Germany was to hook up with Hanna. I'd become really fond of her and had been telling people she was my girlfriend. But this was to be my first lesson of a holiday romance. A romance on holiday should be left on holiday. A lesson that took me many attempts to learn. Of course, there are exceptions to the rule, but my observations have taught me that things change, and things aren't the same between two people when they return to the stresses of daily life.

I'd phoned Hanna a few times on my travels, and whilst she said she'd be pleased to see me, I got the impression she couldn't care either way. She'd returned home from London to her routine life, so the fun we had together in London became a distant memory and was just that, fun. It was now early June and almost three months since I last saw Hanna. That's too long to expect someone to wait for you if your only time together was a two-week fling. I hadn't done myself any favours by travelling wherever the wind took me. Had I gone straight to Bonn after the Eurobus trip, things may have been different. I just assumed we'd pick up where we left off in London. I was making my way to Bonn but just taking a few detours along the way. Perhaps, this non-urgency to get to Bonn led Hanna to believe I wasn't keen on her. So, sensing that Hanna's feelings for me had waned somewhat, I decided to see what would become of setting up camp in Kempten.

May 1997

Kempten was a new chapter of my holiday/life. With a population of around 61,000, Kempten was hardly a thriving metropolis, but I didn't care. I wanted to experience living in a small town in Bavaria, getting to know the locals and the language, and the fact I knew two locals, Bob and Jimi, gave me a head start.

Bob and Jimi were both from England, had been living and working in Germany for a few years. Both in their 30's, the guys were mates from back home but were very different people. Bob was average height and slim with an out of style flat top hair-do, whilst Jimi was tall and solid and often shaved his head. Bob liked Germany and Jimi didn't.

They both worked in construction in different places around the country.

I got on best with Bob, at first. I can't remember how it happened, but even though it was Bob who invited me to stay, I ended up staying with Jimi. I think it's because, when I arrived and phoned the guys, Bob didn't answer his phone, but Jimi did. So, I stayed with Jimi, which was weird, really. Jimi had a flat that was basically a two-room bed-sit, one of the rooms being the bathroom. The other room had a small open kitchenette in the corner, and the rest of the room was living space with a balcony outside. Bob had a much larger flat with proper separated rooms. It would have been much more convenient had I stayed there with him.

It didn't surprise me work never eventuated, me being a foreign alien and all. I decided to stay, though, because the guys went to work up north in Osnabrück for three months, returning only now and then on weekends. Jimi said I could stay in his flat as long as I wanted. "Fuckin' prima," as Jimi would often say. There I was, in the south of Germany, with a flat to myself, living rent free for up to three months, and on the weekends, I could get on the piss with the boys, or I could take trips to visit friends and other parts of the country. I could also learn and practise my German with the locals, whilst out shopping or in the bars. Not only that, but Jimi had Sky TV, so I was able to watch TV in English, anything from the latest movies to the Aussie drama *Heartbreak High*.

Spending so much time alone in the flat, I thought a lot about my life, the future, and this travelling caper, and my diary entries became highly philosophical.

12th June 1997

It's four months today since I left Australia. It hasn't exactly flown by; it seems ages ago since I first arrived in London. Time does move quickly though when you're kept busy. It doesn't seem six weeks ago that I finished Eurobus, yet sometimes, it feels longer. The two weeks I've spent here in Kempten have gone quickly. And have I enjoyed the last four months? Ja, bestimmt (Yes, definitely). I'm at the stage now where I've been travelling for a while, and I've become blasé about where I am. I have to keep reminding myself how lucky I am to be here and have the opportunity to travel through Europe. Four months ago, I never would have predicted being where I am now and having done what I've done, and when travelling alone, you learn things about yourself and the trouble with that is, you don't always like what you learn. Then what? Do you then accept that side of yourself and just avoid any situation that brings out that side of you? Or do what I only just now have decided is the answer? That is, try to change it. Because there is no such thing as 'that's not me', 'it's not in me to do such and such'. I've learnt how afraid and boring I can be. I came travelling for sex, drugs, and rock & roll. While Kempten is cheap and gives me plenty of time to learn German, I think I might be wasting my time here. The way I see it, I'll be back home a year from now, and I still have a lot I want to do—here and in life. But can I have my cake and eat it, too?

I always looked forward to when Jimi came back for the weekend. It was good having someone else in the flat and a drinking partner to go out with. Other weekends, I took advantage of the German rail's cheap weekend ticket and visited other towns and cities, such as Heidelberg. After some weeks in Kempten, I decided to go and explore more of the country. Using Jimi's as a base, I left most of my things at his place and took with me a few changes of clothes in a small backpack and let life take me where it will.

I stopped off in Mainz to try to meet up with a German guy I'd met in the Freiberg hostel. I rang him but didn't understand what the person was saying on the other end of the line. To save money on accommodation, I decided to spend the night on the street. I never knew how hard it would be. I just thought I'd find a park bench and crash out. I'd seen many people do it in London. There, people just chose random shopfronts to set up their cardboard beds and go to sleep in a sleeping bag.

I had two schools of thought about where to sleep. One: sleep in a crowded area where, if anything was likely to happen to me, there would at least be witnesses and, with any luck, having witnesses around would deter anyone from coming near me. Two: sleep in a hidden area away from everyone so no one was likely to find me and hassle me. But if someone did find me, I was on my own because no one else would be around to help me. So, there were pros and cons for both locations. At first, I tried a small city park, but I was put off by the rowdy drunk people on their way home from a night out. I moved to a waiting room at the train station, where I found others trying to sleep. So, I joined them, in out of the cold.

5th July 1997

I woke the next morning unharmed and with all my belongings. That's always a bonus. It wasn't to be the last time I'd sleep rough. Next stop Cologne. I kept myself awake on the train as the view of the Rhein in the early hours of the morning, with clouds around the mountains, the sun breaking through, and the occasional castle overlooking the river, was fantastic. Bonn is only 25 minutes by train from Cologne, and I was nervous about seeing Hanna again. But when I got to Cologne, I thought I'd get it over and done with and called Hanna straight after I'd checked into a hostel. When I called, the vibe from Hanna wasn't too bad. It was Saturday, and I expected her to have plans for the evening, but maybe she'd see me for a few minutes on Sunday. That might have been the case, but Julia was with Hanna. Julia was super excited to hear from me and invited me to a music festival, the *Rheinkultur*, which was on that day. After the call, I thought this might not be such a bad thing after all.

When I met the girls at Bonn station, it went well. They were asking me questions and were impressed with the amount of German I'd learnt. When we got to the festival and met their friends, Hanna pretty much kept her distance and didn't talk to me unless I initiated the conversation. Julia surprisingly was the friendly one. In London, we hadn't been that close, but here, she was always talking to me, really excited to have me there. This is when I really started to get to know Julia. She's very intelligent, loves to chatter, and has a good sense of humour. She was 20 at the time, short and slim, and with long, brown, straight hair, truly German looking. J She loved snogging guys and knew how to move on the dance floor.

She was more than willing to come up to the front of the mosh pit with me. We came away wet and covered in mud as it was pouring rain. The festival was so fun. Despite the awkwardness with Hanna, I had a great time. I drank heaps and met some friendly and interesting people and learnt some more German. Hanna's and Julia's friends were way cool. Most of them were male, and I was watching closely to see which one might be Hanna's boyfriend. Each one took their turn putting their arm around her and holding her hand. I think they were all just good friends. In the end, Hanna went home with Julia, and I went to a party with the guys.

Whilst I felt a bit uncomfortable at times or left out, I thought, in retrospect, meeting at the festival was the perfect circumstance in which to see the girls again. They had others to talk to, so that meant I didn't have to talk much. I was drunk, so when I did talk, I wasn't too boring, and I didn't have to spend all my time with them. I spoke to their friends and often struck up conversations with strangers.

8th July 1997

After a few more days in the area exploring Cologne, I went to Amsterdam for a few days. This time, I went to the Heineken Brewery. The brewery held tours in the morning only, and it cost a small donation to get in; two guilders, I think it was. The tours were 45 minutes long with free drinking afterwards. I went to the 9:30am tour with an American rockabilly/skater guy I met at the hostel where I was staying. The tour groups were quite full, and whilst some people pretended to be interested in the making of the beer, others made it clear they were just interested in the free samples at the end. It was funny watching elderly tourists drinking early in the morning. Whilst enjoying our free drinks, we met two more lads from our hostel—two brothers from Brisbane, Australia.

After the brewery, all four of us spent the rest of the day exploring the city. We came across the Mushroom Museum. I'd taken acid plenty of times, but I'd never had the opportunity to take mushrooms before. Keen to partake in some of Amsterdam's more decadent pursuits after such a tame first visit to the city, I bought a bag of Hawaiian mushrooms. The others bought some, too, but saved them for later. I took some straight away. Despite making a good start towards drunkenness, I stopped drinking to experience fully the effects of the mushrooms.

It was a sunny day, which is enough to put someone in a good mood anyway, and I was in great spirits. I found the littlest things amusing and enjoyed all the bright pastel colours. The others, who had mushrooms experience, checked in with me every now and then to see if I was all right, often asking what I was laughing at.

We hung out in Vondel Park, a large park in the city with plenty of walkways, trees, water features, and grass banks to lie down and take in the sun. On a sunny day, there was always plenty of bare flesh around the park. I felt so euphoric. It was another if-my-friends-could-see-me-now moment.

It wasn't all bliss, however. Two days earlier, I'd had my glasses stolen off my face by an African guy, because I wouldn't buy some coke off him. It was my fault, as I'd been hanging out with drug dealers in the red-light district trying to get some ecstasy. This guy had seen me on my way home late at night. He approached me and wouldn't take no for answer. I said I couldn't afford it. He gave the common response, if I can afford the airfare to Europe from Australia, then I must have a lot of money. Eventually, in frustration, he grabbed my glasses from my face. He had a big friend with him, too, so I wasn't getting my glasses back. Not that I would have had a go if he were alone. He was quite big himself. I was going to have to wait until I got back to Kempten, where I had a spare pair, before I'd be able to see properly again.

The rest of my time, I explored the city drinking and smoking in different coffee shops. I overcame the problem of not being a weed or hash connoisseur by buying pre-rolled spliffs, rather than a bag of gear. All that smoking didn't do my shakes much good. Holding the spliff and trying to light it was quite an exercise.

My stay in Amsterdam marked ten weeks in Germany and, of course, a few days in Holland. After this visit,

I felt like I could now say, *been there, done that*, as far as Amsterdam was concerned. I'd been pretty stupid, though, in my eagerness to indulge in some illicit substances. As a result, I was without my glasses, which made life somewhat difficult; reading train timetables was a chore. Young, dumb, and trying to get some.

I caught a train to Hamburg. On the train, I met a Pakistani guy, called Jamal. He'd picked up from my bad German that I wasn't a native. When I told him I was from Australia, that was it; I'd set him off. He wouldn't shut up about cricket after that. It was getting close to midnight as we were nearing Hamburg station, and Jamal asked where I was staying. I told him I had nothing organised and planned to sleep at the station and find somewhere in the morning. He said the station was dangerous at night and full of drug addicts. He suggested I stay with him in his flat for the night, and he'd show me the next day where a youth hostel was. However, come the next day, he said, "Ah forget it. You can stay here."

It was great staying with Jamal. Jamal was about 34 at the time. Originally born in Pakistan, he'd been living in Germany for 15 years. He lived on the 13th floor of a block of flats, overlooking the main thoroughfare called *Grindelberg*, and from the lounge room, there was a great view over the city. There was a great view of Hamburg's telecommunications tower. We were up just as high. Although unemployed, Jamal was a chef by trade and cooked some great curries whilst I stayed with him. He showed me around the city, and he helped me with my German. He showed a great sense of humour and everything was translated into cricket terminology, e.g., when we had to run to catch the bus, he called out, "Quick single."

Jamal was also captain/coach of the Hamburg cricket side. It wasn't long before he took me along to a training session. The team was mainly made up of ex-pats from the sub-continent now living in Hamburg. I was a champion backyard cricket player when I was young, but this was the real deal. I was playing with the big boys.

I didn't really want to interfere with their training, so I started by fielding in the outfield. This is when the fun started. Perhaps, I was too far away from the action, because I couldn't see the fuckin' ball. I had trouble seeing without my glasses. Quite often, the ball was hit in my direction and flew straight past me before I even knew about it. The others, not knowing of my blindness, thought I was some sort of retard, the way I stood motionless whilst the ball was coming straight at me. I got bored of all this and sat down in a chair ... in the outfield. I'd given up all hope of stopping the ball and resigned myself to the fact I was basically just playing fetch. This didn't go down well with the Asians. Cricket is like a religion to people from the sub-continent, and they take it extremely seriously. They spoke to each other in their native tongue, and I could sense they were talking about me. Jamal later told me they were saying, "Look at this guy. Has he no respect for the game?"

They asked Jamal, "Where did you find this guy?"

He replied, "I just met him on the train."

Despite my lack of respect for the game, Jamal and I remained good friends.

I headed back to Kempten and stopped off in Bonn along the way. This time, I stayed with Julia at her parents' house in Bad Breisig. I met her parents and her brother, Julius, who were all very welcoming and took us to lunch at a café overlooking the Rhein. Julia and I also went to the flea markets and to a rave party under a bridge. Julia let me drive her car through Bad Breisig. It was my first time driving on the right side of the road, and I wasn't too good at it, either. It takes some getting used to. Julia's mother made the most of having a young, fit man about the house and put me to work, painting some furniture. It has been a great source of amusement ever since and is often brought up in conversation whenever I'm visiting Julia. My favourite memory of painting the furniture was speaking to Julia's mother in German. I didn't know the word for birthday, so I had to improvise. I said, *"Die Tag wann mann kommt aus die Mütter,"*—The day when one comes out of the mother

The Horny German Truck Driver
21st July 1997

The next day, Monday, I was on my way back to Kempten. With my savings low and being a weekday, the cheapest way to make the trip was to hitchhike. Julia made me a sign in German, saying I was an Australian looking for a ride, hoping the Aussie link would make people stop. Armed with the sign and a map from Julia's father, they drove me to a rest stop on a nearby motorway, where I could start to look for someone to give me a ride. It's illegal for vehicles to stop on the autobahn, so to hitch a ride, you have to find one at rest stops. There were a few ways to go about getting a ride. One was to approach people and to ask to travel with them or another was to stand near the exit of the rest stop and hold up a sign as people drove past in the hope they'd stop.

I'd made good progress in the morning. I hadn't had to wait long for a ride each time I was looking. Different friendly people had driven me as far as they were going in my direction, and come lunch time, I was at a large busy truck stop with petrol station, shops, and restaurant. After about half an hour of trying the sign method with no luck, I decided to try the direct approach. With my limited German, I walked through the car park asking around.

I noticed a truck drive past and pull up. I saw the driver hop out, and I decided to ask him. Instead, he came over to me and asked if I needed a lift. Hell, yeah. I noticed his fly was undone and just thought the idiot had forgotten to do it up when he last went to the toilet. If only that were true.

So, we were on our way down the autobahn, and I quickly noticed a porn mag sitting on the dash. The truckie looked at me and said I could have a look if I wanted to. I had a browse and after a few minutes, he asked me if I liked the magazine. I smiled and kept looking. Not long later, he asked if it was making my dick hard. WHAT? That's a bit fuckin' personal, I thought. He revealed it makes his dick hard when he looks at the mag.

What you have to realise is all this was in German. I was struggling to get my head around the language, as well as the fact I was being propositioned by a male German truck driver. He started to rub the bulge in his trousers, and it suddenly dawned on me why his fly was undone.

This guy was about 5'72" (in height, not length), quite lean, and slim and had short brown hair and a porno-star moustache. With him excited and his fly undone, I could see he was wearing bright pink underwear. What was that all about? He said something like, once he's hard, he likes to have sex or to wank. Do I need to know this, I thought? He kept saying the word *mush*, whilst mimicking the wanking motion. I concluded that mush must mean wank. He kept touching himself. I thought he was going to have a wank right there and then, in front of me, as we were motoring down the autobahn.

To add to my this-must-be-a-dream mindset, he said, "50 Deutsch Mach." I nervously asked what was 50DM. He said a few words including the word mush. I innocently thought he was saying he pays 50DM to have a wank. I thought, what an idiot; everyone else does it for free. But then he kept mentioning it, and I realised it wasn't a statement but a question.

What you must realise is that all this was in German. I was struggling to get my head around the language, as well as the fact I was being propositioned by a male German truck driver. I hid behind the language barrier and pretended not to understand. Fuck this pretending shit. The truth was I didn't understand. 50DM was to pass hands, but that's all I knew. Who was to pay who? Who would have to do the mushing to whom? Would there be more than mushing? Oh fuck, get me off this truck.

I continued to play dumb, afraid of his reaction if I turned him down. Would he turn violent if I said no? Travelling down the highway at over 100km/h with nowhere to run and with no control over where the guy was driving me, what could I do? Admittedly, there wasn't a lot he could have done to me whilst driving the truck, but at the same time, I was a passenger, just along for the ride, literally and figuratively.

Well, this could have gone on forever—him asking for some sort of sexual favour and me pretending not to understand. Maybe that's what I should have aimed for until we got to the next stop. In the end, I just said no; I wasn't interested.

Expecting the worst, once again, the truckie's behaviour came from left field and surprised me. The guy became all normal. He started asking me if I was studying in Germany or just travelling around. He asked me about Australia and other places I'd visited. That didn't stop me from asking to get off at the next stop, even though the guy was going in my direction a lot further.

I sat down at the stop for a second to collect my thoughts. I asked myself, "What just happened there?" Unfortunately, I couldn't get the picture of the truck driver, touching himself through his pink underwear, out of my head.

I later managed to get a lift to the nearby town of

Augsburg where I caught a train the rest of the way to Kempten. I arrived in Kempten and went straight to the pub and had Bob and Jimi in stitches telling them about the horny truck driver.

I was back in Kempten for the week. It was good to see Bob and Jimi again, literally, as I was now reunited with my spare pair of glasses. I arrived back at Jimi's flat to find a pile of letters from friends and family back home. I was almost out of money, and my love for alcohol wasn't helping. The plan was to look for work in Hamburg. Hopefully, with Jamal's connections, I'd be able to find something. Otherwise, it was back to London.

27th July 1997

I got all my shit together and said good bye to Jimi, Bob, and Kempten. I was totally grateful to Jimi for letting me stay, rent free, and entrusting me with the place whilst he was away. That showed a lot of trust on his part. My time there had allowed me to experience life in a small German town for a few months, as well as being able to use it as a base whilst I travelled the country. Jimi and Bob spoke of plans to go to Australia for a few months over Australia's upcoming summer period. The idea was they'd come and visit me in Canberra. Never happened. I sent them the odd postcard over the following months, and I even spoke to Bob on the phone once, but no plans were made to meet in Australia. A year or two later, I'd lost Bob and Jimi's phone numbers, so I phoned their local pub and spoke to the governor there, Klaus, who knew me well. Klaus said Bob still lived in Kempten, but Jimi had moved back to England.

Occasionally, over the previous few months, but particularly at this time, I felt down and sorry for myself, and the thought occurred to me a few times of hopping on the next flight back to Australia. I felt so lonely sometimes, even when surrounded by people. Reading letters of my friends back home having a great time without me only added to my depression. Was the honeymoon period coming to an end? Was this a bout of homesickness catching up with me? Back home, I had a large circle of friends and acquaintances that I was familiar with and that were familiar with me. Here, I was riding solo, and whilst I met some awesome people, there wasn't that same connection or history that I shared with my friends back home. The theory I could be whoever I wanted because no one knew if I was acting out of character or not was bullshit. Whenever in new and unfamiliar territory, I inevitably slipped back into my default setting of being introverted. My inability and/or fear to talk to others didn't help. That's why I drank so much, because life became a whole lot easier when all my insecurities were washed away by the booze. Life was a lot more exciting, too. Homesickness was something I was to experience periodically over the years

4th–13th August 1997

I travelled back to Hamburg by train, avoiding any horny truck drivers. Jamal was kind enough to let me stay at his flat again, and I hoped to find work and make Hamburg my home for a while. I loved Hamburg. It was a great playground for me to get up to mischief and being a large city provided more opportunity to find work.

And what a playground it was, too. Hamburg is home to the *Reeperbahn*, a street in the St Pauli district lined with restaurants, nightclubs, and bars. Oh, yeah, let's not forget the strip clubs, sex shops, brothels, and sex museum, too. Street prostitution is legal there at certain times of the day. The women line the street, and if a man walks past, the women walk a few steps out to greet him, and as he walks on, the women return to their position near the building walls. It looked quite funny, like a Mexican wave of sorts, as the women moved out and then back again and so on down the line of girls until the man was out of reach. There is also *Herbertstraße*, a small alleyway running parallel to the Reeperbahn, which has women in windows like those in Amsterdam. It was in the Reeperbahn, too, that the Beatles played in the early 60's, before they made it big, resulting in many legendary stories of their antics, both on stage and off.

When I was first in Hamburg, I asked Jamal about nightlife. He pointed me in the direction of the Reeperbahn from out his apartment window. Nice one. I headed off and didn't return until after five the next morning. I did a lot of bar hopping around the place and drank like a motherfucker. It was this night I took cocaine for the first time. I bought a small, white ball from an African guy off the street. It was white and could have been a mint for all I knew. With a belly full of piss in me, I thought it a good idea to go ahead with the deal, despite the trouble I had in Amsterdam. I took the ball and sat in a nearby school playground. I unwrapped the cloth covering of the ball and found a light-brown powder. I'm guessing it was about half a gram's worth. Whoosh, straight up my nose.

"*Woaaaa*. Fuckin' hell. What was that?"

Not having snorted coke before, I snorted with all my might, and it felt like my nostril had been singed. It certainly did the trick. I was wide awake now and felt sober again and in the mood to drink much more. Coke affected, I was able to knock the drinks back so easily and became so drunk that, in the wee hours of the night, I succumbed to the advances of one of the women on the street. The end result of that was an animated argument over the method used to reach the desired result, $500 cash stolen from my wallet and having to give a police statement in German. Don't do drugs, boys and girls.

Jamal, aware of my need to phone home occasionally, told me of a friend of his who had a magic phone card. It worked just like any other public telephone phone card, except when the credit ran out, you could reinsert the card, and it was at full credit again. Jamal was able to borrow the card for a week and, man, we went to town on that thing. He phoned family in Pakistan and America whilst I phoned all sorts of family and friends, both in Germany and back in Australia. I phoned friends I normally wouldn't call, due to my small calling-Australia-budget, which usually dictated that I only made calls to immediate family. I also took the opportunity to make a few business calls and sort out my tax return.

I learnt of a saying through the backpacker community that says, don't drink and dial. It refers to phoning home when drunk, advising it's not a wise thing to do. You run the risk of making a real dick of yourself, waffling on, talking shit to people such as parents, who perhaps you've worked hard over the years to hide the fact you enjoy a drink or twelve. It doesn't get any better when you wake the next day with that unwelcome feeling of dread and regret, struggling to remember what bollocks sprouted out of your mouth the night before. Or even worse, remembering what you did say and cringing with embarrassment whenever you're reminded of the conversation.

I didn't heed the suggestion. Being an eight-hour difference between Germany and the east coast of Australia meant I often called anywhere between 1 and 5am after a big night out on the town. It was brilliant. Being drunk meant I was remarkably chatty to say the least, and with unlimited credit, I was able to talk for ages. And, yes, I suffered to varying degrees the side effects of drink dialling.

I remember everyone being really amused about the magic phone card. Every now and then, I had to interrupt the conversation and say, "The credit's about to run out. I'll call you back." The card had 60DM credit, and whenever it ran out, I took the card out and inserted it back into the phone, and another 60DM would appear. Jamal and I looked at the card to see if we could make our own. There was adhesive tape stuck over the computer chip. But when we tried to replicate it with our own card, the public phone claimed it was invalid. We didn't want to play with the magic card in case we ruined it, so we decided to let the card keep its mystique and just accept that the card was, indeed, magic.

I spent a lot of time in Hamburg looking for work at restaurants, mostly in Altona. I thought a restaurant was likely to pay people under the table, and a kitchen hand needn't have to know how to speak German. Once again, though, they weren't prepared to hire someone without a work permit.

Well, the money was coming to an end, and after four great months in Germany and with little hope of finding a job anytime soon, it was time to head back to London. There, I'd be able to work legally and understand the language. Jamal and I decided the cheapest way to get to London was to ride the trains using other people's weekend tickets to Aachen on the German/Belgium border. At the time, a weekend ticket in Germany was a set price and valid for up to five people. So, it was possible to hop on the train without a ticket and just find a person with a ticket who was willing to let you ride with them. When the conductor came around, you just said, "I'm with him/her." It was funny. All the tourists bought tickets, whilst all the locals just travelled on other people's tickets.

Jamal used to live in Aachen and said that, once there, I should make my way to a bar called the *KellerDom*. There, I would find someone who would take me to Belgium. Then the plan was to hitch to Ostend on the Belgium coast, catch a ferry across to Ramsgate, England, then make my way to London. And that's what I did. It took me three days but I arrived at Victoria Station on a sunny, September day, feeling excited about what the future might hold in the next chapter of my overseas adventure.

9th September onwards 1997

"You don't sound Australian; I thought you were English or something."

One cool thing to happen when I arrived back in London was a lot of people couldn't pick my accent. Some people thought I was a German speaking English. Others thought I was British or even Canadian. Hearing German for the last four months had obviously affected my accent. I left Germany in love with the place and would have stayed there, had I not run out of money or had I found work there. I loved the language, the beer, the beautiful countryside, and the thriving nightlife in the cities. The people I met were so friendly; perfect strangers opened their doors to me and welcomed me in. I was resolute on returning one day.

Back in London, over six months since I first arrived, I found myself drawn to Olympia again, in London's west. From a flyer I'd been handed in Victoria Station, I went and stayed at the Sinclair Hotel, on Sinclair Rd, one block west of Olympia Station. My original haunt, O'Callaghan's, was just on the other side of the tracks, one block over. The place was actually a hostel, as opposed to a hotel, with the kitchen and common room in the basement and dorm rooms on the other four floors. It didn't take long for me to meet some of the other guests, and wouldn't you know it, some of the long-term residents were from Canberra.

It was somewhat different settling into London again. This time around, I was moving in, so to speak. Previously, I'd just been passing through or hanging out, but this time, I'd be joining the rat race and immersing myself into the London culture. I had the advantage, though, of knowing how things worked, where things were, and how to get there. With accommodation sorted, the next thing I needed was a job. Despite my lack of funds, I was in no hurry to start work. I spent valuable job hunting time lying in the sun on Shepherd's Bush Green, doing nothing. I managed to drag myself to a few pubs around the Bush and asked for bar work, but nothing promising came of any of it.

Lying in the sun one afternoon, I decided to ask for work at the Shepherd's Bush Empire. The Empire is an old theatre converted into a concert hall. My cousin, Andrew, had worked there during his time in London, and he had given me a contact name before I left Sydney in case I ever considered looking for work there. I dismissed the thought back then; I didn't want to follow in my cousin's footsteps. I wanted to carve my own path and succeed on my own, without relying on family connections. But now, faced with homelessness, I found myself at the box office window asking for work. I was introduced to Simon, the acting bar manager, and he explained there was a position available as a bar aide/cleaner. "I'll take it." And there started my tenure at the Shepherd's Bush Empire. Little did I know the immense impact working there would have on my life. Events of that time still influence my life today.

The Empire has four levels with seven bars, including one backstage, and it was my job to stock these bars during the day, pack away any stock deliveries, and prepare the cellar for the evening. Come nightfall, during the concert performances, it was my role to wander around to all the bars and keep them stocked up with anything they might be running low on, change empty beer barrels, and check the toilets periodically and keep them clean as best I could.

September was traditionally quiet at the Empire. There were only one or two gigs a week. This meant little work for me, which made it hard for me to keep my head above water to begin with, but I stuck with it, as I was assured, come October, the Empire would be flat out until Christmas.

So, with little money coming in, I spent most of my time at the hostel getting to know the other long-term residents. None of us at the hostel were flush, and for our evening entertainment, we used to drink 3litre bottles of cider that cost just a few quid from the local off-licence. The bottles were about 7% alcohol, but it was the name that was the real laugh: *Applemania*. The guy who ran the 'offie' got to know us well.

After sitting on the front stairs drinking for an hour or two and all charged up, we usually rounded up whoever we could, and we ventured into Shepherd's Bush to the Walkabout Bar. The £1 shots of schnapps got us all excited. The Walkabout was an Australian themed bar situated next to the Empire. It was one of many Walkabout bars situated throughout the UK. It has since closed down. The inside was decorated with clichéd Australian paraphernalia all over the walls, Aussie tucker on the menu, and Aussie rock anthems playing continuously. This provided great conversation opportunities when explaining words like dunny (toilet) to the foreign chicks. I enjoyed going to the Walkabout at this time. I was always there with a big group from the hostel; we were always exceedingly drunk and in good spirits; the drinks were cheap, and there were plenty of non-Australian ladies there, too. I wasn't particularly interested in the Aussie girls. I didn't travel all that way to hook up with someone from back home.

In the sobriety of the day, I mainly kept to myself, too unconfident to relate to people without the assistance of booze. After a few weeks, I was truly down. I felt alone and was heading straight into a miserable English winter. I rang my mate, Dan, back in Canberra for his birthday, which made matters worse. I spoke to him and a load of friends there, celebrating, and they all voiced how much they missed me. That didn't help at all. I just remember feeling I had no one I could talk closely to.

It didn't last too long, though. The parties continued at the hostel, and Julia had moved to London, as well, to do some study. She was staying in Stoke Newington in the far north-east, but we caught up quite regularly whenever we could.

I also started to do a few shifts at the Empire. My first shift was just a meet and greet and a tour of the place. I met the venue manager, Matt. He was the contact my cousin had given me to ask for work. I didn't mention anything to him about my cousin, though. I was somewhat intimidated by Matt. He was quite tall, had broad shoulders, long hair, and often dressed all in black. He, also, used to wear a lapel two-way radio, like the British Police do. I likened his presence to that of Darth Vader. Although, sometimes, he wore some outlandish coats and hats, as well. He was cool, though—strict but fair. He was in his late 30's / early 40's and was from Melbourne, Australia, originally.

The bar manager, Simon, was a cool dude, too. He was English, but not your typical shaved head, football-loving, lager lout. Simon's passion was music (the good stuff, not the shite pop music that was so popular in the charts). He had long hair and is only eight months older than me. He'd worked in many pubs around the Bush and was quite the authority on alcohol. He was very welcoming and friendly towards me, and we spent many a lunch time in the pub, enjoying a pint or two during a break from work. He was always encouraging and seemed to be happy with my work.

Usually with us was Bruce, the head barman. He was a few years older, from South Africa, and had long hair, too. Man, I had certainly come to the right place. I was one of seven dudes with long hair. Bruce was the one I worked with directly in the beginning when doing the daytime duties. He was a big drinker, and by all accounts, quite the ladies' man. He introduced me to the art of drinking a bottle of beer in minutes. We often had a beer or two from the store room when putting away the deliveries, which we had to drink quickly to avoid getting caught.

The first gig I worked was a performer called Johnny Mountain. I don't remember any of his performance; I was more focused on learning how to do my job. I went all right, but I was a bit shy at getting behind the bar. I wasn't used to being behind the bar, any bar, and in the beginning, I approached the bar from the punter's side and asked the staff if they needed anything. After a few gigs, I quickly lost that inhibition, mainly through necessity, as on the busier nights, I couldn't get through the crowds to the bar, so I started to walk behind the bar to speak to the bar staff.

For the second gig, I showed up for work in the afternoon and was standing around the stage door with a few others. The doors to the elevator opened, and this kool kat, black guy came out and said hello. He was super friendly to me. It wasn't until Bruce (head barman) asked for his autograph that I realised it was Ben Harper.

Oh man, did he put on a great show. I certainly remember the happy vibe from that night; he played some awesome, electric slide-guitar. It was a full house, and most of the dreadlocked crowd were standing in their seats moving to the music. I had a good night and thought I could easily get used to the perk of seeing cool acts for free. It wasn't always a pleasure, though; performing the next night was Billy Ray Cyrus.

There was only one gig over the 18 days that followed Billy Ray Cyrus, and I spent a lot of time with the hostel crowd. It was never a dull moment, with a lot of drinking and drugging, listening to music, playing chess, and watching movies. We were an interesting lot: Dave from Canada, 20-something, greatly intelligent, wrote poetry; he reminded me of what I imagined Jim Morrison to be like, judging from the books I'd read about The Doors. Dave was also the primary drug supplier in the hostel; Tim and (another) Dave were young mates from Canberra with British ancestry travelling together doing the 'London thing'; they were a lot of fun. I got on well with them. Elodie from Sydney was young and affable. We had fun one night tripping on acid. We found some stars on the footpath around the corner from the hostel on Blythe Rd and signed our names on them as if it were the Walk of Fame on Hollywood Boulevard. Elodie also found a book called *Bridget Jones's Diary* on the street, which no one had heard of back then. She kept it and read it and told me about the regular use of the phrase 'major fuckwitage', which became our catch phrase for a while; Sa'eed, from northern Africa somewhere, had some funny, interesting stories and was another provider of drugs to the hostel. We had some good times tripping around the place; Pedro, from Italy, was a quiet, unassuming guy, partly because he didn't speak English very well and partly because he was always stoned. Some of his mates came from Italy to stay at the hostel for a while, and they were crazy. They smoked so much and used to do so in the most inventive ways, and many, many more: Sam (Israel), Annika (Sweden), Sassa (Sweden), Wendy (Australia), Peter (South Africa), two funny Scottish guys (Scotland), Ben (Australia), that ever-present Turkish man (Turkey), the tall, weird, night reception man (from another planet).

The receptionist I was interested in, though, was Maria

José. She was a beauty from Argentina. She was 28, a bit chubby (don't tell her I said that), and looked a bit like Cher, especially around the cheeks. She worked the reception in the evenings and lived in the hostel. I first met her when I walked through the front doors, and she was sitting on the steps reading a book. As I got to spend more time with her, I realised how cute she was and that she had an endearing sense of humour. I got close to her by asking her to teach me some Spanish, and we both shared a love for grunge music.

After a fortnight or so, I was walking with her from the shops back to the hostel, and I made a somewhat optimistic move and kissed her. She was taken completely by surprise and sped off quickly back to the hostel, talking out loud in Spanish, claiming not to speak English. I laughed and thought, well, that went well. After that, I kept my distance, and a few days later, she started chasing me. Unlike her, I didn't play so hard to get.

October 1997

Once work started up again, on the 7th, it was action all stations. I only had a handful of days off over the remaining twelve weeks of the year. Some of the gigs worth bragging about were: Whitesnake, Front 242, KMFDM, The Australian Pink Floyd Show, Gary Newman, Björk, Jewel, The Corrs, Ben Folds Five, Foo Fighters, Beth Orton, and The Cure.

Living in a hostel and working at the Empire provided me with a large circle of friends. I heard stories of people moving to London and finding it difficult to make friends. I had my family of friends at the hostel, plus there was about 40 casual bar staff on the books at the Empire. Because I worked every gig and part of my job was to coordinate with the bar staff, I got to meet them all. After each gig, I looked forward to the staff drinks around the main bar, where we gathered to relax after a busy night.

Amongst the group was Stuart or, as he was affectionately called, Jesus. Not because he was a god or because he performed miracles, but simply because he looked like Jesus, i.e., long, straight, brown hair, and a goatee. Stuart had a great sense of humour, which was evident by a pair of trainers he used to wear. The print on the sole was of teddy bears with erections. He was English, about my age, and he and Simon, the bar manager, were good mates.

Another was Bryce. He was from South Africa and had been in London for a few years. Oh, man, he could talk. He was two or three years older than me, loved a drink, and we got along well.

Although he had things running smoothly, Simon was only the acting bar manager, and a new bar manager was hired, a guy called Kieran. He was English, friendly, middle-aged … and an alcoholic. An alcoholic and a bar manager didn't make for a good combination. It certainly made work interesting, if not particularly trying on Simon and me having to pick up the slack.

Simon took the opportunity to tell me he appreciated the great job I was doing at the Empire. Apparently, the guy that did my job before had a rather lackadaisical approach to the job, which, of course, made me look good. I only had to do a decent job to be viewed as doing a top job. A number of the staff thanked me for the job I was doing, too. However, I did work hard. It was the norm for me to work a 50—60 hour week. The fact that I enjoyed the work helped, as did getting along with my supervisors. My working relationship with Simon was the best I'd ever had with a boss. I could be myself around him, without fear of jeopardising my position, unlike previous jobs I'd had. And we were friends outside of work, too.

November 1997

At the beginning of November, there were some new bar staff. I was giving the walls of the level one dress circle an extra coat of paint (not a good hangover cure, I learnt), when Monica was being shown around the building. She was Japanese-American from Maryland, around my age, and wonderfully outgoing. It was always fun to hang out with her; we had a similar temperament and, over time, became good friends.

Sitting in the Firkin one day, Bruce introduced Simon to a guy named Barry. Barry used to work at the Firkin with Bruce and was now looking for work, so Simon gave him a start at the Empire. I found Barry to be really funny, but most people didn't like him. He looked like a young Robert De Niro. He used to speak a lot of rubbish, but I just accepted that as who he was. We could both speak German at an elementary level and we often spoke to each other in German just to be different.

On Friday 7th, Howard Marks did a pre-recorded spoken word show about his drug smuggling—something different. After the show, a few of us from the Empire went out to U4Ria, a club out the back of the Captain Cook pub in Acton. We were drinking and dancing when Bruce (head barman) called me over. I thought he asked me, "Where's the ecstasy?" meaning, who in the club was selling it. I didn't know but made light of the situation. I said, "Good question," and feigned frustration as I posed the question in the general direction of the dance floor.

"Oi. Where's the ecstasy?"

Bruce said, "No. *Want* some ecstasy?"

I was like, "Yeah, alright."

He gave me a pill, called a pink crown. I swallowed it and continued drinking and carrying on. I'd taken ecstasy a few times in the past, but it never really had an effect on me. I was dancing on the stage with Barry when I started to feel fuzzy. I felt euphoric and profoundly warm and compassionate towards everybody ... and I couldn't stop dancing. I felt wonderful and had an awakening, "So, this is what all the fuss is about." I realised then why people were so into ecstasy pills. I looked at the other people around the room in a new light and wondered who might be in the same state as me. I later learnt Barry was only alcohol affected, but he was dancing with as much animation as I was. In the past, I was never sure if the pill had had an effect on me or not, but there was no question this time. I couldn't keep still for the next three days. I'm not kidding.

Another thing to happen the night of Howard Marks was I broke my glasses. I wanted to look cool, so I'd taken off my glasses and put them in my pocket. Who'd have thought they'd break, hey? I couldn't afford the £100 price tag for a new pair; I was living from week to week. To get by, I used to carry my left lens around in my pocket, and whenever I needed to read anything, I pulled it out and held it to my eye, like a photographer looks at their prints. I got quite a few looks of disbelief from people when they saw me pull out my monocle. My favourite was at work, when I signed the invoice from stock deliveries; I used to say I was checking the fine print.

At work, Bryce bestowed the nickname Spaceman on me. I thought the name referred to me being a weirdo, a space cadet. I learnt, years later, it was in reference to me appearing from out of nowhere. The Empire is a grand theatre with seven bars on four levels. For me to get around to them all as quickly as possible, I took short cuts through side stairwells and behind the back of the stage. I used to drop in on the bars without being seen and show up as if I'd been beamed in like a spaceman.

I'll just go on a quick tangent here. One of my favourite tricks to play was to stand around the stage door area and watch people get into the lift. As the doors were closing, I'd wave good bye to them. Then, when the doors were fully closed, I'd race up the stairs to the second floor where, inevitably, the lift would be stopping. Once I got there, I'd stand there in a casual manner, as if I'd been there for ages, and then delight in the look of surprise on the people's faces when the doors opened and they saw me standing there.

I quite liked the nickname Spaceman. As I said, I thought it was a reference to my eccentric behaviours, so I played up to it. I'm someone who delights in being original and unique. I am quite happy doing my own thing. During the period at the Empire, I used to wear a black, ladies' beret. I was talking to Bryce one day and told him, the true story, about the hostel not having any hot water, so I had a shower in my clothes to keep warm. He laughed and started singing the Babylon Zoo song 'Spaceman'. So, whilst the name may have originated from appearing unexpectedly, I believe it developed to imply being unconventional. The name took off, and there were a large number of people who didn't know my Christian name and only knew me as Spaceman.

Mid-November, Björk played two sold out nights at the Empire. Wow, she put on a great show. She has such big lungs for a tiny woman. Her stage set-up was interesting. She had a strings-section sitting behind see-through partitions. Unfortunately, I missed most of the first show, dealing with a burst pipe in the downstairs toilets.

Maria was keen to see Björk play and Matt, the Empire manager, was kind enough to put her name on the guest list for me—that was big brownie points for me with Maria. Another VIP in attendance was Madonna. The Beastie Boys were also rumoured to be there, but I don't know if that was true. There was a lot of excitement amongst those in the know of Madonna's presence. I knew she'd be going to the after-show party backstage, so I made sure I was near the stage doors after the gig, so I could see her make her way to the backstage bar. Sure enough, she walked past with her entourage. My first impression was, "Gee, she's tiny."

Everyone was getting in on the act. Our doorman, Nick, had taken it upon himself to escort Madonna and her male companion from the dress circle to the backstage bar and was trying to act all suave and important, but just looked like a ponce. I followed the entourage backstage and then stood at the end of the bar, about two metres away, as I gawked at her, along with about half a dozen other people.

Serving behind the bar was the loveable Marie, from Australia. She wasn't aware that music royalty was in the room. She just saw two punters at the bar and went ahead with serving them. After a closer look, she recognised the guy was someone she knew from her gym. They said hello and greeted each other with a friendly kiss. Marie, being the sociable lass that she is, then turned to the woman next to him, put her hand out for a handshake, and introduced herself, "Hi. I'm Marie."

"Hi. I'm Madonna."

Marie stopped dead in her tracks as the reality of the situation became apparent.

"Oh, sorry. I didn't recognise you."

"That's alright."

Madonna had some weird thing going on with her hair. It was a combination of blonde and burgundy. That, coupled with the fact she was shorter than one would expect, it was understandable that someone wouldn't recognise her.

About a week later, Simon and I were in The Walkabout having lunch with Simon's mate, Chris, who I was meeting for the first time. I didn't say much. I just left the two mates to catch up; it didn't occur to me to join in on the conversation. I started reading a story from an Aussie newspaper about the recent death of Michael Hutchence. Chris struck up a conversation with me about INXS. Although Chris was English, his wife, Mouse, was from Melbourne, and he was very savvy on a lot of Australian topics. He was another with long-hair. He was a big lad, in his 30's, and he rode a Triumph motorbike. He grew up down the road in Fulham and had lived in Shepherd's Bush for over ten years. He enjoyed a pint down the pub with his mates, and that was all we needed in common. We grew to become good friends.

By the end of November, I was fully ensconced in the London rat-race and way of life (if one exists). I was fortunate to live, work, and socialise all in one area. I was enjoying the variety from one day to the next, the large assortment of people I was meeting and mixing with, and I felt pleased with myself for having landed on my feet so successfully.

There was no doubt winter was coming. The weather was grim, and it started to get dark around 4:30pm. Not that that dampened my spirits; it wasn't much different to winter in Canberra. I always felt the shitty weather made the pubs more enticing with their fire places and large comfy lounges and alcohol for sale. I lost count the number of times people asked me why I had left the beautiful weather of Australia to come to Britain. My usual response was, "I obviously didn't come here for the weather, did I?"

I was also enjoying the recreational drugs scene. I'd experimented with drugs back home in Canberra, but they were so much more available and cheaper in the UK. I embraced them with open mouth and nostril. I established a friendship with a dealer who I'd visit every Friday, which was my payday, and buy some supplies for the weekend. Like an African game hunter, my attention was on the big five. Although, these were animals of a different kind: pills, coke, speed, acid and hash, in addition to my constant diet of alcohol.

After a few months, I grew to disdain the Walkabout and the cringe-worthy London-Australian culture as a whole. I found their stick-with-one's-own mentality to be lacking in purpose and open-mindedness. My objective was to immerse myself in anything and everything outside of Australian culture. But, I grew to realise we all travel for different reasons. There's no right or wrong way.

Through my busy work schedule, I was spending more and more time with the Empire and Firkin crowd and less time at the hostel. As a result, Maria and I were spending less time together. Over the previous three weeks, I didn't see her for longer than five minutes. I would have loved to have spent more time with her; I was really into her, but she had become distant towards me. As a consequence, I felt hurt, and in an attempt to get back at her, I became detached, but I only succeeded in hurting myself. Her visa to stay in the country was about to end, and she thought it was highly likely she'd be going back to Argentina. So, her behaviour was just a self-preservation mechanism to prevent being hurt.

In a bid to spend some time with her and have a proper talk, I stayed up all night one Saturday, so I could see her first thing Sunday morning. Maria worked reception Sunday mornings, which was generally a quiet time with little for the receptionist to do. It worked out well; we got to have some time together without any interruption. What didn't work out so well was the state of the relationship. Maria couldn't commit to a relationship under her current circumstances, and it was decided, quite harmoniously, we'd let each other go. In the end, Maria decided to stay on in the country, but that meant she was now an illegal immigrant, and within a week, she had left the Sinclair Hotel.

December 1997

On the 5th, after another Howard Marks show, the Empire's Stage Manager, Jim, was looking for someone to go with him for a night out on the town. I was up for it, and we went to the Electric Ballroom in Camden. It was Friday night, which meant the club night was Full Tilt—alternative/Goth/industrial/punk music—my kind of crowd. I loved perving at all the hot Goth and industrial chicks. It was a pretty good vibe there, and the place was quite large. There were two floors and a balcony area upstairs from which you could see the main dance floor below, and another small room with a dance floor that played grunge music. There was, also, another small little room that played punk music that wasn't easy to find; it was hidden in one of the corridors upstairs.

We met Simon and Jo there (my boss and his girlfriend). They hung with us for a while, but then they disappeared. Jo knew the venue manager, so we assumed they'd gone to see him. So, it was just Jim and me, and it was on this night we first established a close rapport with each other. Jim and I had spent time together before in groups but never just the two of us. Jim was a lot of fun and adventurous, which surprised me. The man I saw at work was a serious man in his late 30's, but tonight, he was letting his hair down. Not that he had any hair; he usually had his hair shaved quite short. He was English, quite intelligent, and had a clever sense of humour. The more we got to know each other, the more it was apparent we had similar personalities.

This night just seemed to fly by, which is often the case when one is flying on drugs, such as I was. The music was kicking and the beer was going down so quickly. The club possibly had some sort of gay bent, because in the men's urinals, there were mirrors positioned so you could see each other's dicks as you were pissing. I met this guy putting on makeup, and I asked him if he could make me up, too. I was hoping to look Gothic, but I'd asked the wrong guy. This guy made me up to look like a woman; I had the brightest red lipstick on. Anyway, not to worry; I didn't give a fuck. I covered my mouth until I found Jim and then took my hand away.

"Look what happened to me," I announced.

The club was closing, and we joined the throng of freaks on the street looking for a cab. We went back to Shepherd's Bush. Neither of us was ready to call it a night, and we walked past the Firkin, hoping there was a lock-in we could gate crash. The pub was well and truly closed for the night; the only sign of life were the cleaners. But, as we were walking past, we noticed a side fire-escape door was ajar. Well, we took that as an open invitation. We knew, sometimes, the live-in staff had parties upstairs, so we thought we'd check it out.

To get to the stairwell leading upstairs, we had to walk through the pub first, past the cleaners. Jim was hilarious; he walked in with a brass neck as if he owned the place and turned the tables by checking that the cleaners weren't intruders. Once we established the cleaners were meant to be there, we then went upstairs. We got up there to find the girls just going to bed. Illona, a friendly Aussie chick, and Pauline, a Kiwi girl, affectionately known as Kitchen Pig, based on her job at the pub, shared a room together. Jim and I went into their room to drum up enthusiasm for some party action, but they were having none of it. They were somewhat surprised we were there, but they were happy for us to crash on the floor if we wanted. I was still buzzing, and the thought of calling it a night was none too appealing.

Illona asked me, "Would you like a sleeping bag, Spaceman?"

"No, thanks! I'd like a dance floor."

However, I had to resign to the fact that it was game over, and, in the end, I did settle down to sleep. Jim, meanwhile, was talking with Pauline. Jim had recently come out of a long-term relationship and was still coming to terms with it. He formed a bond with Pauline through ordering soup every day in the pub. Jim's feeling towards it was just a rebound fling that was never destined to last long. Pauline, on the other hand, was quite infatuated with the relationship. Jim took this opportunity to break it off with her. The way he did it was classic. He said to her, "I'm into blue and purple at the moment, and you remind me of orange." That's brilliant. What can one say to that?

The Sinclair Hotel was doing my head in; I'd had enough of the crowd there. I was spending more and more time with Jim, and when he suggested I move in with him about a week before Christmas, I didn't hesitate. He lived in a flat on Holland Rd, of all places (O'Callaghan's Hostel is also on Holland Rd). I found most flats in London had some sort of quirky characteristic. This one was no different. To get to the kitchen and bathroom, you had to walk through Jim's bedroom. It meant I had to be quiet in the mornings when stumbling to the dunny, but otherwise, it wasn't a problem. My bed was in the lounge room. It was a rather sizeable room, and I had one side. It was an unusual arrangement, one that only two people that got along well could make work, and thankfully, it worked. Jim made me feel incredibly welcome and was very kind in sharing his space with me.

The Christmas/New year period was one of the best.

Wednesday 24th: Jim and I walked to Portobello Road in Ladbroke Grove, a hip little neighbourhood close to Notting Hill Gate. We met up with some others at the Market Bar for some drinks. Jan, who I'd met two nights before, was there. She was an English, blonde beauty in her mid-30's, and lived in the flat above Jim. Surrounded by her own circle of friends, I could see a warm-hearted side to her nature. Also there, was a woman called Tessa. She was a friendly and quite attractive English woman in her late 30's, too, but rather quiet on this night as the conversation was dominated by others in the group. It was a delightful night out, meeting new people and enjoying their company. I was going to see a lot more of them in the future.

Thursday 25th: Christmas Day started at Jim's. Before I headed off to Simon's flat, Jim suggested I go upstairs and wish the crew (Jan, Tessa and others) a Merry Christmas. I did so, and the girls thought I was the nicest fellow. Thanks, Jim, for that one.

It was wet and miserable outside as I walked to Simon's place up the Goldhawk Road. As I passed the Firkin, some of the female staff came running out to wish me a happy Christmas. They invited me inside, but I had to get going. Leading up to Christmas, I didn't have any plans and thought it might be an utterly boring, quiet day, but come closer to the day, more and more options had popped up.

It was a great relaxed day at Simon's. There was a good bunch of people there, such as Simon's girlfriend, Jo, Stuart and his wife, and Simon's flat mate, and friends. Simon cooked lunch, and it was fantastic. The drinks flowed and so did the laughs.

Late in the evening, Jim came around for a while before we headed back to Holland Rd, where the party was still going upstairs in Jan's flat. At the party, I complained of a sore back, and Jan ordered me to lie on the floor as she gave me a relieving massage. The party died down, and people went home or went to bed, whilst Jan continued to give me a massage. When she finished, I thanked her; I felt a lot better. I then went back downstairs to Jim's flat.

I walked in and he said, "What are you doing here?"

I joked, "You said I could live here."

"Couldn't you tell Jan was flirting with you?"

For the second time that day, Jim suggested I go upstairs. Again, I did so, and … well, you can guess the rest. Thanks, Jim, for that one.

There was nothing on at work until New Year's, so over the next few days, Jim and I continued our drinking spree and we got up to some silly stuff. Coming home drunk from a big night out, we found a glove and put it high up on a tree branch from the bridge on Addison Gardens, just around the corner from our flat. Remarkably, the glove stayed there for over 18 months and was a reminder whenever we walked past of the fun and games we got up to during the early part of our friendship.

New Year's Eve at the Empire was like a military operation. It felt like we were preparing to go into battle. The evening's show was a DJ club night from 9pm until late the next morning: 3 or 4 am. A full house was expected; it was going to be busier than any other night we'd experienced. Being New Year's Eve, the punters weren't coming for a tea party; the bars were going to be invaded; it was going to be a war in the trenches.

Simon and I arrived mid-afternoon, stocking the bars with as much arsenal (alcohol) as there was room for. Only the auditorium and level one would be open, which helped, as there would only be four bars operating. In the evening, the infantry arrived (barstaff). The best of the best had been conscripted for the expected savage skirmish, including a few recruits especially enlisted for the occasion. We assembled at 20 hundred hours at the makeshift operations base in the backstage bar to outline the evening's battle plans. General Matt made an appearance to rally the troops; Simon gave instructions, and I did too, about reloading when out of ammunition (when the bar was out of ice), to which Bryce started singing 'Spaceman'. There was no time for disciplinary action now; he'd have to be court marshalled later.

It was almost time for the venue doors to be opened. Soon, the enemy would be landing on the beaches, the bars besieged with aggressive revellers who would take no prisoners. We were ready. Bring it on!

OK, so maybe we weren't ready. The enemy surprised us with a heavy attack on the cloakroom. We had been expecting some action on that part of the battlefield, but not to such a large extent. I was called off my post to help in the situation. A makeshift cloakroom was set up on level three and was manned by Simon's mate, Chris (who you might remember I met in the Walkabout) and me. Chris and I were bombarded for the first two and a half hours. We worked like motherfuckers and managed to hold off the advances of the enemy troops. When it finally calmed down, I did a sweep of the auditorium bars to survey the action on the front line. The people waiting at the bars were four or five deep, ordering pint after pint. The world of war-draught was in full swing. The workload was full-on; we were taking plenty of hits but hadn't suffered any casualties. Simon and I were running around like crazy men.

I took a beer each up to the cloakroom for Chris and me. Matt dropped by to check on us and, he too, brought up some beers. Come midnight, I was down in the trenches behind the main bar. A five-minute armistice had been imposed from the stroke of midnight. There was a bottle of champagne on each bar for the staff to get into for the celebrations. During the ceasefire, the crowd was going off; everyone was cheering; there were streamers deployed, and there were hugs and handshakes between both sides. When the bars reopened, the hostilities began again.

I took some more beer upstairs for Chris, who was unable

to leave his post and had seen the New Year all on his lonesome. At least the collecting of coats would be staggered, as people left gradually over the next few hours, unlike when they all arrived at once. As the night wore on, the conflict shifted towards chemical warfare, H_2O to be precise. The run of beer and spirits had slowed down, and the call for water was in high demand. We performed many a raid on the store room to replenish water supplies at the bars. I worked like a dog, as the intense workload didn't let up all night. On my travels around the combat zone, I spotted Jim at the lighting desk, having a great time operating the party's light show.

I complained to Simon my back was killing me. All the heavy lifting of beer barrels and cases of beer over the last few months had taken its toll. Simon played medic and issued me some combat gear. He had a weightlifting belt he gave me to wear. It was a thick, leather belt that helped to keep the back straight. It certainly helped. Just like any war, the use of drugs existed amongst the ranks. To make life interesting, at about 2 or 3am, I took a pill and some acid.

The night finished and the club closed, around 4am, I think. The opposing troops made their retreat; everyone could take a breath again and slow down to a more casual pace. We had survived the War on Leisure and began the clean-up effort immediately. Normally, I'd be right in the thick of it during the clean-up process, but I just couldn't get my head around it. The drugs had kicked in, and I was too fuzzy to take up arms.

This show was to be my last tour of duty, as I was calling it quits, annoyed with the inadequacy of Kieran's management and the knock-on effect it had on making my job more difficult. So, my last shift at the Empire, and come time to clean up, I was M.I.A. Not that anyone noticed or cared. It was just me that felt like I was skiving off. Matt tapped me on the shoulder and asked if he could have a private word. I thought, shit! Darth Vader's going to choke me, using the power of the dark side, for being off my head. Instead, he gave some cash as a reward for the hard work I'd put in during the night. Wow, was a pleasant surprise.

With the battle won, then came the spoils. Simon kept the stage-left bar open, and we partied like it was 1998. I was absolutely flying and having a lot of fun behaving in an outrageous manner. By this stage, most people were wrecked, and I needed little encouragement. I donned my trademark beret and red scarf. I'd also commandeered American Monica's pink coat as I paraded around the place getting my photo taken with everyone. My catch phrase became, "Have you seen my belt?" as I lifted my shirt, like some perverted flasher, and showed off my naked torso and large weightlifting belt. Jim got on to the music desk and provided the soundtrack for what was a thoroughly enthusiastic party.

The party ended at around ... I don't know, I'm just guessing, 7 or 8 o'clock. We left the Empire as our eyes struggled with the light of day. Welcome to the New Year.

1998

A cool story from early January was when I met a fellow Aussie in a bar. I was waiting for a friend at the Beaconsfield Pub just around the corner from the Sinclair Hotel. It was called the Frigate & Firkin back then. This pub is in a quiet back street; it's not a well-known famous pub tourists flock to whenever they're in London. You go there because you live or work in the area or because you just happen to stumble across it.

Anyway, a young guy standing next to me at the bar heard me order and recognised I had an Australian accent. He said G'day and asked where I was from. I told him Australia.

"Yeah, me too," he replied. "Where abouts?"

"Canberra."

"Wow, me too. That's amazing. Which part of Canberra are you from?"

"Curtin."

"Bullshit. That's where I live."

I was excited, too. This was amazing. The population of Curtin is only about 5,000 people, and here we were, meeting in a small pub off the beaten track, on the other side of the world. He asked me which street I lived in.

"Carruthers Street."

"Fuck off. That's my street."

We were both blown away—incredible.

I later told Jim the story, and he thought it was amazing, as well. I played it down, though, saying, "Yeah, but, Carruthers St is a long street."

Jim just laughed and said, "You idiot."

Jim and I arranged to have one of our signature nights out at the Electric Ballroom. Amongst others, Monica, from the Empire, and Nick, also from the Empire, joined us, and I invited Julia, as well. She'd just returned to London after having gone home for Christmas and New Year. We met up in the Halfway House pub, near the Camden tube station. Julia was running customarily late. Julia had been to the Sinclair and met that crowd, but she hadn't met anyone from my Empire circle.

She finally arrived, and Jim flirted with her immediately. He chastised her for being late, but in a cocky/funny way. Julia was somewhat shocked but attracted at the same time. She later told me she thought, "Who does this guy think he is? Gee, he's cute." We moved on to the Ballroom after that and had an entertaining night with the industrial Goths.

Jim was classic. Between flirting with Julia, he'd periodically buy drinks and give them to the girls in the cloak room. Of course, they adored him for it, and later, the rest of us came to adore him for it, too. When the club closed, and it was time to leave, there was a long queue at the cloak room, but Jim just walked straight to the front and was able to get our coats immediately. Nice one, mate. This is something he did regularly whenever we were at the Ballroom. Jim's advances had worked, and Julia ended up staying at our flat the whole weekend.

February 1998

Friday the 6th was going to be my last night in London for a while and some of the gang came out and partied with me at the Electric Ballroom. When I got back home to Jim's flat, it was about 3:30 in the morning. I had to catch a bus a few hours later, and I hadn't even packed for the trip yet, so I decided to stay up, rather than get some sleep. I was tripping hard and couldn't have slept anyway. Jim, Julia, and Jan stayed up with me and struggled to stay awake as they sat watching my antics getting ready to leave. I was in such a muddled state; I didn't think I was ever going to get my act together in time to catch my bus. But, I managed it, and I said my goodbyes to three people who were very sad to see me go. It wasn't easy leaving. I arrived at Victoria Coach Station and hopped on my bus to ... Preston. "Preston? What are you going to that shithole for?" you may ask, and a valid question it is, too.

7th–22nd February 1998

Back in December, Michael J. Fox approached me to see if I was interested in an assignment in Russia. I was to accompany him and two others to Moscow and then St Petersburg. I'd be required to participate in some horseplay and monkey business, some vodka drinking, and endeavour to make a connection with the native women. The trip was to take place during February, when Russia would still be very much in the grip of winter. This would sort the men from the boys. Returning with a Russian bride was up to the individual, but I was instructed to bring back some Russian dolls. Michael briefed me on the other operatives who would be in attendance. I knew them and was confident they'd be up to the task. I told Michael to count me in. I then set about learning some Russian.

Did I say Michael J Fox? I meant, Brian, my mate from school, who you might remember from such adventures as Eurobus. In some inexplicable way, Brian reminds me of Michael J Fox. Brian had returned to the UK after more than six months back in Australia. He'd found a deal on offer from Lufthansa Airlines that, for £280, two people could fly return to Moscow from London Heathrow. Brian wanted to know if I was keen. Definitely. I mean, who goes on holiday to Russia in the middle of winter? I certainly never envisaged going to Russia. At the time, Moscow wasn't a common destination on the tourist trail, and that was a major selling point in me wanting to go. There would be no Aussie themed pubs in Moscow. I had no qualms about going in winter. Any mention of Moscow or Russia conjures up images of snow, vodka, and large fur caps. I wanted to experience the cold, harsh, and picturesque, snow-covered Russia I'd seen in the movies. Still being young at heart, there was no way we weren't going to pretend we were in a spy movie.

My trip to Preston was the beginning stages of 'Operation: Freeze our bollocks off in Russia'. Preston's a small city of about 114,000 in the north east of England, roughly 50km north of Liverpool. I went there to meet up with my fellow operatives, Dave (a lad from Canberra) and Brian. Dave was good value. He was a stocky lad and a mischievous smile or laugh was never far away. For the next two weeks, we were going to be living with Jon, of Eurobus fame, and his girlfriend, Tanya, in their council estate flat. We assembled there to work and save money in preparation for our trip to Russia, and what a preparation it was, too. Oh man, where do I start?

Jon and Tanya had kindly offered to let us stay in their flat and confirmed we'd be able to get work with them. Brian slept in the lounge room, whilst Dave and I shared a room. The room was completely bare—no furniture, no carpet, no wallpaper, nothing—so Dave and I set up a tent in the room, and we both slept in there. It was hilarious. It looked so funny. We were totally comfortable, and it helped to keep us warm. We often kept each other up, talking and laughing about our favourite moments from *Seinfeld*.

Monday arrived, and it was business time. It was time to get to work and start earning and saving. Oh, man, what a shock to the system. Jon and Tanya worked for some guy, who acted as an intermediary to provide workers at supermarket factories in the area. We were separated to begin with, but by the second day, all five of us were working in a factory operated by Asda (supermarket chain), packing vegetables. We had to rise at six in the morning, which wasn't easy, considering it was the middle of winter in the north of England. Jon and Tanya had a car, and we had to drive about 40 minutes to the factory. The staff there wore white lab coats with white caps. They looked rather respectable but we, being outside hired help, had to wear a burgundy coloured overcoat with a matching cap, similar in style to the cap a Private wears in the army. Although, we looked more like prisoners of war from a World War II concentration camp.

I'd never really paid much attention to leeks in the past, but now, I knew all about them. The five of us were on the leek production line. Leek, as in the vegetable, had to be cut to size to fit a small plastic container, then packed in the container, wrapped in plastic, then labelled with the company logo and price tag, packed in crates and loaded on to pallets, then wheeled out the back for delivery. It was easy enough but not the most enjoyable of environments. The room was a large, cold, sterile place. It was good we could talk to each other whilst working, and there was a radio playing, which provided some music relief over the noise of the conveyor belts. The radio station was a typical commercial network that repeated the same half a dozen songs over and over. We used to play a game on our way to work, where we'd predict what songs were going to be played on the radio that day. It wasn't difficult to get it right. But otherwise, it was a somewhat depressing place.

Whilst our motley crew consisted of the United Nations, the Asda employees were all English folk from the area. Some of them were friendly but, in general, they didn't associate with us. There were quite a few attractive women amongst them, which provided some visual pleasure during our otherwise monotonous day. It would have been nice to chat to them, but it was unimaginable they would be interested in someone who looked like a POW. Not only that, but they thought we were gay.

I'm told the people from the north are a conservative bunch, and we found that to be true. The Asda staff didn't know what to make of me—a male with long hair. The fashion was for men to have extremely short hair. Another prejudice we exposed was their homophobia. Towards the end of a long day with the leeks, Brian was suffering from sore shoulders. I gave his shoulders a quick 30 second massage to help relieve some of the pain. As I was doing it, Brian looked over at two older women working nearby and smiled at them as if to say the massage was soothing or that he was lucky to be receiving a massage. The women looked on in horror. Obviously, that kind of interaction between two men wasn't the fashion, either, up in the north. The women's look of disapproval didn't escape our notice, and we were sure word of our 'immorality' was going to be spread around the factory awfully quickly. We decided to have some fun with it. From then on, we played up to the rumours; we deliberately pretended to be gay in plain view of everyone in the factory. I remember one lunch break, skipping to the cafeteria and pinching Brian on the bum as I went past. We had to keep ourselves amused somehow.

That first week in Preston marked one year since I'd left Australia. I reminisced about the last 12 months and evaluated what I'd done and where I was going. I'd enjoyed myself, had lots of adventures and amusing stories to tell. I'd had a few misfortunes, as well, but I accepted them as par for the course. I thought about my plans after Russia and what I might do. There were a lot of places I was keen to go, and I could relate to the adage, 'There's so much to do and so little time and so little money.' My main goal, though, was to go to Ireland.

23rd February–8th March 1998

If first impressions count for anything, then Moscow made us feel amazingly special by putting on a fireworks display on our arrival. As we walked down *Prospekt Mira*, one of Moscow's main roads, treading ever so carefully so as not to slip and fall flat on our arse from the ice on the ground, the night sky lit up with colourful explosions. In some small way, it felt like we had entered a war zone as we walked through the neighbourhood of old Soviet concrete buildings covered in snow with sounds of gunshots and high-pitched, loud whizzing and humming echoing off the buildings. The scene looked right out of a World War II movie.

Upon checking-in at our hostel, we learnt the fireworks hadn't been put on solely for us (what a shame). February 23 in Russia is commonly referred to as Men's Day. The day is a celebration of men, in general, and all Russian women celebrate the special men in their lives. Still, it was a great reception to arrive to, and the fact the three of us are men, we can say, in a loose way, the fireworks were for our benefit.

The fun began earlier on our Lufthansa flight, drinking booze and speaking German. I was particularly excited and anxious. The main concern for us was how we were going to get through immigration and navigate our way on public transport to our hostel with such an extreme language barrier. Not only could we not speak the local lingo, but with Russian being constructed from the Cyrillic alphabet, we couldn't even read and pronounce words, which is sometimes necessary when asking for directions. I mean, how do you pronounce a back to front R? Or any of these letters: Я, Ф, Ж, Й.

We were fortunate to have a guide book that had translated Moscow's place names into English, which helped somewhat. Dave and Brian did most of the navigating as I was still operating without glasses. Whilst in Preston, we had spent time learning, from a book and audio tapes, various Russian phrases and the numbers up to ten. We could give greetings, say please and thank you, and knew how to order a beer.

I was rather nervous when we arrived at immigration. This was Russia, the great superpower. The immigration officials didn't look friendly, and there were guards everywhere ... with guns ... big ones. Anxiety turned to tiredness as we queued for an hour to have our passports inspected. We managed to make our way through immigration and onto a bus to our hostel. It was around 7pm, and the weather wasn't as cold as I'd expected. Looking around, things definitely looked like I had imagined: snow, Lada cars, and fur hats.

Hostels weren't too common in Moscow in '98, and we stayed at Traveller's Guest House Moscow near the Prospekt Mira metro stop, just a few kilometres from the Kremlin. The hostel was up on the tenth floor of a 12-storey residential complex, consisting of a few rooms and an office that offered travel services. The three of us had a room to ourselves, and during our week there, the only other guests we encountered were two German lads.

That first night, after we'd checked in, we wandered down the road looking for somewhere to eat. The first place we came across was ... McDonald's. Hey, what can I say? Sometimes, convenience wins out over the authentic local culinary experience.

Our first full day in Moscow, and we just had to go and

see the famous landmarks. To get there, we took the metro. Oh, man, what a service. Up to this point, my city metro experience included the London Underground, Germany's U-Bahn, and Sydney's CityRail service. None of them compared to this. First, it was so cheap. It cost the equivalent of 20p for a journey anywhere on the network, unlike London, which charges more if you travel through numerous zones. The next compelling characteristic was the barrier-gate. To enter the metro, one needed to buy a token and then place it into a slot at the gate, which then removed a barrier, allowing the person to move through. This was a pretty anxious moment, because the barriers didn't stay open for long, and if you didn't pass through the gate quickly enough, the barriers slammed shut, crippling your legs and, in some cases, ruining any chance of parenthood. Making the mad dash through the gate was always an adventure. We held our breath and bolted through the barrier, arching our backs and propelling our bums forward. If we were lucky, we'd escape with only the fright of our lives as the barrier crashed shut behind us. If we were too slow, or we weren't paying attention, we'd end up with the hard plastic like barriers slamming our legs, leaving us just short of being a paraplegic.

The London metro is called The Underground, but the Moscow Metro is more than underground; it's a few levels below that—it's under-underground. Moscow's metro is said to be one of the deepest subway systems in the world and has the longest escalators in Europe, the longest being 84 metres. Once the leisurely ride down the escalator was complete, we then entered the metro station and were faced with what can only be described as an art museum. The metro stations were filled with murals, mosaics, sculptures, and ornate chandeliers. 20p for travel and art? Wow, the price was definitely right. If you missed your train because you were too busy taking in all the visual delights, then it was no great loss as a train came along every three minutes. 20p for travel, art, and an efficient train network? Now that's just showing off.

We went to Red Square and saw the famous St Basil's Cathedral with its multi-coloured domes. The Cathedral looked magic, especially all lit up at night, like something out of a fairy tale. Having seen many Cathedrals over the last 12 months, this was, by far, my favourite. The inside consisted of small, dimly lit chapels and maze-like corridors with the walls covered in light floral designs. Legend has it, on completion of the church, the Tsar ordered the architect to be blinded, so he could never reproduce another cathedral like it.

Brian and I wasted no time assimilating with the locals and bought a famous Russian fur cap each, for a cool $10 USD. The correct name for the cap is *ushanka*, meaning ear hat. The hat has ear flaps that can be tied up on top of the cap or tied around the chin to keep the ears, cheeks, and chin warm from the cold. Ours also came with a tacky soviet badge on the top, which I was later advised to take off by a local, as it wasn't a popular symbol.

Day two, we had already arranged to meet with a Russian contact. Her name was Olga, and we were to meet her on the metro. There was no espionage involved, just a friend of a friend offering to show us around town. My London mate, Jim, was in Moscow a few years earlier touring with a band and met a local girl who he put us in touch with. I rang her in the morning, and we arranged to meet at one of the train stations. I picked Olga out of the crowd immediately. She was short with straight black hair and had the facial features of a Mongolian. If I remember right, she was about the same age as us, give or take a few years. Her English wasn't perfect, but it shat all over our Russian. Pleasantries aside, she took us on a bit of a tour.

We went to Red Square and to Lenin's Tomb, which serves as the resting place of Vladimir Lenin, Russia's historical figurehead. We went inside to see his wax-like, embalmed body on display. Entrance was free of charge, and we had to keep quiet and keep moving past the display, in one door and out the other. There was no photography or videotaping inside allowed, no smoking and no wearing hats. There were plenty of armed guards around to settle the issue if you had a problem with any of the rules.

From there, we went to the Kremlin. Kremlin is a term given for the fortified stronghold of a city. The Moscow Kremlin, situated next to Red Square and overlooking the Moskva River, includes four palaces and four cathedrals within the surrounding Kremlin walls and towers. The complex serves as the seat of the Russian government and official residence of the President. The government buildings and palaces weren't open to the public, but we had a look inside the cathedrals and walked around some of the grounds.

Afterwards, we went inside the GUM department store, partly to have a look around, but mainly to get in out of the cold. We came to Russia in winter, because we wanted to experience the stereotypical Russian cold weather. Well, we got it. It was freezing cold, and the wind was a killer. It was -15°C, but with the wind, it was a lot colder; it was painful. I was half expecting my fingers and toes to be black when I took off my gloves and boots. I made the mistake of leaving the hostel that morning not fully rugged up. I still had another jacket I could have been wearing.

After this day, we took turns going outside in the morning and gauging the weather conditions and then reporting back to the others the number of layers recommended. I went out one morning, and it felt like a much milder day than usual, so I told the lads we didn't need to wear our entire wardrobe. We had a nice comfortable day, and in the evening, we found out the day's maximum temperature had been -9°C. It was funny how, after what we'd already experienced, -9°C now felt warm to us.

The GUM department store is located right on Red Square and is a work of art. Stretching over 200 metres long, GUM looks like a palace from the outside with the interior featuring elegant and ornate architecture, topped off with a glass ceiling. For the Sydneysiders amongst us, think the Queen Victoria Building. The complex features approximately 200 stores of posh, high-end fashion. The place was more for window shopping than actually buying anything, as the prices were off the charts.

As I said, GUM was a warm escape from the harsh weather outside. This meant the women took off their overcoats inside, and we could see their figures. The young Russian women were in a class of their own and had beautiful, smooth, pale skin, despite the extreme low temperatures and cold winds.

Olga had to work that evening—she taught English—and she left us to our own devices. Whilst she may have been a bit crazy, she was amazing. She knew so much about the history of the people and the buildings. We said goodbye and arranged to meet the next day; we then went CD shopping.

Struth Bruce; the CD's were so cheap. We payed from £1.80 to no more than £2.50. We deduced the CD's were copies, but you have to remember this was 1998, long before burning a CD at home was so easy and common. Once we realised they sounded just as good as an original, we went nuts; we were like kids in a candy store. There were a lot of CD's that didn't even exist, such as best-of-compilations. Because of the price, we bought some CD's based on just one song. There were kiosks everywhere selling these cheap

CD's, usually above ground, around the metro stations. You could almost buy anything outside of a metro station from fresh produce to puppies. I bought a few videos including, *From Dusk till Dawn*, which I'd never seen before but heard was worth watching. There was usually war memorabilia for sale, as well as souvenirs, knick-knacks, cheap tobacco, and alcohol.

Kiosk/newspaper stands all around the city sold alcohol; the national beer was *Baltika*, which we definitely had our fair share of. They came in large 500ml bottles, over 5% alc/vol, and there were different coloured labels to choose from, each one a different type of brew. I sampled them all before sticking with the lager. Olga told us of a common practice of mixing beer and vodka together, which we also tried. She called it a green snake. It went down well, I must say, unlike the paint-stripper-esque type beer I bought one morning, called Amsterdam, that was 10% alc/vol. I took a few sips, and it was gross. I wasn't prepared to put up with it when there were plenty of other palatable beers available so cheap. I gave the Amsterdam away to a homeless guy, who couldn't thank me enough.

The vodka was something awesome as well. As with the beer, the vodka bottles had different coloured labels signifying different blends. We discovered the green label was our favourite—a tasty herbal mix.

We met with Olga the next day and wandered around the city. We went and had a look at Gorky Park, a funfair-amusement park, situated along the Moskva River. There wasn't much going on there, except for ice skating; none of the rides were operating. We then moved on to the Modern Arts Museum and then looked at yet another cathedral. We were bored shitless and decided to get something to eat. Olga took us to a fancy pizza place that was way too expensive. She must have thought, being Westerners, we were rich. We left the pizza place and she took us to a pie shop. This was more our style. The pies were small bits of meat wrapped in pastry about the size of a scone. They were so delicious, especially when washed down with strong raspberry vodka. We made a note of that shop for future reference; it was an easy meal on the go. Our staple diet, though, was hot dogs. There were hot dog stands littered around the city and at most metro stations. We went to the hot dog stand at *Prospekt Mira* so often, the old woman learnt our preferences and made us what we wanted without us having to specify.

Olga was especially helpful in buying us tickets. We struggled with the language if any conversation was required. If it was a short, simple exchange with closed questions, then we were usually able to get by. Sometimes, tourists were charged extra, as well, so it was handy having a local negotiate the price for us. Olga helped us with our train tickets to St Petersburg and with tickets to the circus, the one and only, Moscow State Circus.

On the day of the circus, I remember we were just the three of us, without Olga, hanging out in a park near the Kremlin. For some reason, morale was low. I can't remember why; I'm guessing something hadn't gone our way. As we were standing there bummed-out, three girls walked past and they made reference to my beret being a lady's hat. They were right. A lot of women in Moscow were wearing the same style hat as me, only I wore it in a baggier fashion. Anyway, it was enough to start a conversation with the girls. They were Russian but spoke English quite well. One thing led to another, and two weeks later, we took them back to England as our new Russian brides. Yeah, not quite. We moved the conversation to a bar over a few drinks and morale perked right up, I must say. Beer and babes do it every time. We even considered blowing off our circus plans, but in the end, we chose the clowns over the chicks.

We left the girls and took the metro to *Vernadsky Prospekt*, the location of the circus auditorium. We were in great spirits by this stage, and I don't know about the others, but I was a wee bit drunk. The circus was quite thrilling, with unbelievable acrobatics and skilled animal tricks. It was a good night's entertainment as we watched in awe along with the other 3000+ crowd members.

As far as night entertainment went, we usually went the cheap option, choosing to buy beer from the kiosk rather than go out bar hopping. We read with great interest the nightclub reviews in an English newspaper we found in our hostel. There were a wide variety of clubs, all offering something different, but many of them, supposedly, run by the mafia. One review stated, if you asked the wrong woman to dance, you could expect to get shot. The review that really stood out was for the Hungry Duck. Touted as the most famous and infamous club in Moscow, the club was popular for its Ladies Night. Hundreds of women would show up and take advantage of the free drinks whilst being worked up into a drunken frenzy by male strippers. Later in the night, the men were let in and debauchery followed. This hedonistic environment caused some problems. It wasn't uncommon for fights to break out, shots were sometimes fired, there were many police raids and subsequently the club was forced to close in 2001. Looking back, I don't know why we didn't go there. Hahaha. Apparently, another version reopened in 2012.

We spent some evenings drinking in the hostel playing cards. Sometimes, Olga was with us, too. Brian bought a pack of cards with some cool Russian symbols on them that we used for our card games. The first game we played was poker, and it took us a few games before we realised how good everyone's hand was all the time. We looked through the deck and found there weren't any cards below 8; there were only 28 cards in the deck. Trust us to not be playing with the full deck.

Red Square was a popular hangout spot for us in the evenings, as well. With St Basil's Cathedral all lit up and snow gently falling, it was an inspiring place to be, one of those, "If my friends could see me now ..." moments. Dave and I lay on the ground of Red Square and spread our arms and legs to make pretty snow angels, as well as getting our bums wet.

For a bit of sport, we also hung out in the lobby of the classy Ritz Carlton Hotel, which was where all the wealthy tourists stayed. The lobby was also where working girls congregated to drum up business.

Our regular playground of choice, though, was on the metro. We liked to buy a couple of beers and go riding around on the trains, searching for girls and mixing with the locals. We had a ball. 20p for travel, art, an efficient train network, and a place to meet women? Rock on.

Whenever the train stopped at a station, we used to run around like idiots from one carriage to the next, looking for people we thought might be outgoing and sociable. There were definitely a lot of colourful characters. One time, the three of us were on one carriage, Dave and Brian were talking to two girls, whilst I was chatting with a married couple. Our frivolity was contagious, and the guy pulled out a bottle of vodka and shared it with us. I was being silly and doing somersaults in the air by holding the railings on the carriage ceiling, which got a lot of attention. I stopped, though, when I noticed a guy sitting nearby had something moving under his jacket. I looked closer, and it was a little monkey. I tell you, it was never a dull moment.

Walking along Prospekt Mira after a night of metro mingling, Dave and I staggered back to our hostel, where

Brian was already settled. We were quite drunk and struggled to stay upright. It was hard enough to keep from falling when we were sober, let alone drunk. After the snow had fallen and been trodden on, it turned to sludge and then froze, forming ice, which made the footpaths extremely slippery. I know I fell on my arse a few times. Anyway, we were minding our own business, when suddenly, a car pulled up beside us. Shit! It was the *Militsiya*—Moscow's civilian police force. The Moscow Militsiya had a bad reputation for racism, physical attacks, unjustified detention, and other rights violations. Brian had learned about the misdeeds of the Militsiya from somewhere and had warned us to never give our passports to them; otherwise, they might keep them, and we'd be screwed.

With that information at the forefront of our minds, we went over to see what the Militsiya wanted. Being the polite and well-mannered (and drunk) guys that we are, we offered them some of our Pringles and M&Ms, but they didn't seem interested. The officer closest to us, on the passenger's side, stuck his head out the window.

"Passports."

Passports? Ah, we knew the correct response to that one. "Nyet."

The officer pointed a gun at us.

"Passports."

We knew the correct response to that one, too. We handed over our passports and prayed they'd look kindly on us and let us go. And thankfully, that's what they did. The Militsiya gave our passports back, and we were free to skate back to the hostel. Perhaps, being Australian worked in our favour, because most Russians just assumed we were Americans when they heard us speak English.

Guns were incredibly common in Russia ... and visible. Most public places like shops, train stations, tourist landmarks, and banks had guards standing watch with big machine guns. It was sometimes unnerving, lining up in the bank, with the guard spinning and playing with his gun, because he was bored out of his mind.

Our week in Moscow had been amazing. We were going to spend a day or two there again before we were due to fly back to England. In the meantime, we were going to St Petersburg.

If ever we felt like we were spies in a James Bond film, it was on the train to St Petersburg. We took the overnight train and had a four-berth cabin to ourselves. It was way cool. The picture was perfect; there were Russian guards and, of course, everyone was speaking Russian. The scene around us was straight out of a classic spy/war movie. Looking out the window, one could see large fields of snow, and every so often, small villages with cosy looking *dachas*. A food and drinks trolley came around, and we were able to munch on some snacks and relax with some beers. The icing on the cake would have been if we found out Casey-fucking-Ryback was on board the train.

The bunk beds were quite comfortable, but I didn't get much sleep, well, not as much as I would have liked, anyway. It wasn't any great annoyance, though; I was able to stare out the window and watch the countryside go by and hear the gentle clatter of the train over the tracks. It was no annoyance, that is, until we were abruptly woken at 8am when the train pulled into St Petersburg. We were all a bit uncommunicative that morning as we disembarked the train and set about finding our way to the hostel.

Our hostel in St Petersburg was the Hostel Holiday on *Mikhailova* St near *Finlandsky* Station. If Finlandsky Station sounds familiar, it could be you remember it from the Pet Shop Boys song 'West End Girls', where it gets a mention. The hostel was comfortable; we had a room to ourselves, and the heating was adequate. It needed to be, too; it was super fuckin' cold outside. Any dissatisfaction we may have had with the hostel's facilities, we needed only look out the window to see we didn't have it all bad. Behind the hostel was a prison.

After checking-in, we decided to head out and have a look around the city. Still tired from our overnight train journey, we agreed we weren't going to do any sightseeing that day, rather just wander around and take it easy. Sightseeing can be surprisingly exhausting, sometimes. So, we left our cameras behind and walked to the metro.

St Petersburg's metro was just as elegant and efficient as Moscow's, with clocks on each platform counting down the time until the next train, usually no longer than four minutes. One thing I'd never seen before were walls along the platform's edge, next to the tracks, with doors that opened when the train arrived. The doors of the train lined up with the doors of the platform and passengers passed through both to get on or off the train. I assumed it was designed to stop people from getting on to the tracks.

Despite our wish to avoid the tourist spots, we still headed to *Nevsky Prospekt*, the city's main thoroughfare. We didn't realise much of the city's attractions, as well as the majority of the city's shopping and nightlife, were located on or around Nevsky Prospekt, until, we stumbled upon one attraction after another, and without our cameras. The sights were abounding: the huge neoclassical *Kazan* Cathedral, *Eliseyev* Emporium, the Art Nouveau Bookhouse, half a dozen 18th-century churches, the *Rastrelliesque Stroganov* Palace, a monument to Catherine the Great, an enormous 18th-century shopping mall, the Russian National Library, and the *Anichkov* Bridge. We had to return the next day and do it all again to get some photos. At least with the second time around, we were able to save time as we knew where to go and what sights we wanted to take shots of.

I was surprised to see the Church of the Saviour on Spilled Blood looked notably similar in design to St Basil's Cathedral in Moscow. Built 300 years after the church in Red Square, the design of the Church on Spilled Blood, as it's known to the St Petersburg locals, was heavily influenced by the design of St Basil's. St Basil's is an iconic, easily recognisable landmark of Moscow and Russia, but I wasn't aware of the Church of Spilled Blood at all. It had the same onion shaped domes as its Moscow counterpart, in blue, green, and white colours. In some respects, I liked it more than St Basil's. In the early morning sun, as the dew from the cold night melted, the church glistened and sparkled, giving the impression it was alive.

The surprise I experienced seeing the Church on Spilled Blood was nothing compared to the surprise all three of us experienced at the Peter and Paul Fortress. Built in the 1700's, the fortress is located on a small island by the bank of the *Neva* River. The fortress covers several hundred square metres and consists of many notable buildings, including the Peter and Paul Cathedral. We explored the grounds, looking at the various structures and monuments, and noticed a path leading to the river. We decided to go check it out and get a close look as the river was completely frozen over.

We walked out onto an embankment and surveyed with amazement the thick block of ice that was the river. We could hear it crackling and moving and didn't dare attempt to walk on it. We then became aware of some noise coming from behind us and to the left. We turned around ... and, geez Louise; there were a couple of dozen people standing in the sun against the fortress wall ... in their underwear. It was a sunny day, with a clear blue sky, but it was still absolutely freezing. I had many layers of clothing on, and I was still cold, yet these people were out in the biting, fresh air, sun baking. Some of them did have overcoats on that were open, exposing the front of their near naked bodies to the sun. A few of them had reflective boards, shining the sun at their faces to get that all-over tan. We couldn't believe it; it was hilarious. I imagine they don't get a lot of sun in the winter, so they make the most of it. They were probably gathered there as the sun beating down on the fortress wall provided them with some warmth. Still, it's not something I would do (too often). I'd probably try it at least once. Not on this day, though. Just looking at them made me feel cold.

Whilst Moscow looked and felt Russian, St Petersburg was more of a Western city and looked European. In some circles, it holds the nickname The Venice of the North, referring to its many rivers and canals. One example of the city's Western influence was the presence of Carols, a fast-food chain and franchisee of Burger King. Carols was a regular feed of choice for us; it was cheap and convenient.

One afternoon, whilst enjoying the inelegant ambience of Carols, we met an American guy living in St Petersburg, married to a Russian woman. I'd seen him a couple of times, out and about earlier that day, and then he said hello to me, in English, in the bathroom of Carols. He introduced himself as Gus. We had a brief chat, and then I went and sat back down with my two amigos. Gus came over afterwards, asking if he could join us and relax in the presence of other English speakers. I gathered he'd been in St Petersburg for some time, and I knew from my experience in Germany how tiring it can be to concentrate all day when immersed in another language. He was a big, tall lad, but a friendly, gentle giant and offered to act as our tour guide and show us around some of St Petersburg's treasures. We were cool with that. Gus could speak enough Russian to get by, so as well as company, he'd be helpful in translating for us.

Gus came with us to the Hermitage Museum, one of the largest and oldest museums in the world. The museum consists of five historical buildings, including the Winter Palace. The collections number over 3 million, displayed in 400 halls of the museum. The collections contained artworks, sculptures, and artefacts from many eras and places, but we took fuck-all notice of the exhibits, preferring to follow two good-looking Russian girls around the museum. However, I will say, the Winter Palace did look stunning—highly classy.

Anyway, back to the girls. One was a gorgeous and slim brunette, whilst the other was a tall redhead. If ever, in our deluded spy fantasies, we thought we'd make good secret agents, that belief was quickly discarded when it became obvious to the girls we were following them. They knew that we knew that they knew we were following them, but they pretended that they didn't know. They whispered to each other and were giggling at us. They needn't have whispered; we wouldn't have understood them. We followed them right out of the museum. With Gus' help, we approached them and asked if they'd like to join us for a drink. Naturally, we took them to Carols.

They were friendly and charmed by our attention. We did our best to be interesting and keep them interested, which isn't easy when having to communicate through a translator. But we must have been doing something right, because they were happy to hang out with us. Gus had to leave, so we made the most of his bilingual abilities whilst he was still available and had him arrange another meeting with the girls for the next day. Mission accomplished; we had a time and place organised to meet them again. Gus headed off to meet his wife, but that wasn't the end of it for us. We went with the girls to an American styled bar and had an entertaining night communicating with sign language and drawings.

Unfortunately, two into three doesn't go. Whilst Dave and I both had periods of apathy towards the girls, Brian was love struck with the brunette girl. He told her she was the most beautiful woman he'd ever met. But whilst there was just the two of them and three of us, nothing was going to happen romantically. With any luck, they'd bring an extra friend with them tomorrow when we were to meet again. But come the next day, they didn't show. Whether it was a miscommunication or they blew us off, we don't know.

In the basement of our hostel, there was a small shop that sold drinks and snacks and had tables and chairs for people to sit and congregate. One evening's festivities started here with staff from the shop and hostel. We were drinking beer and vodka and getting along well with our Russian friends. I was playing chess with one guy, and we were able to communicate through our combined knowledge of German. Brian was getting along with one of the girls there, who could speak English quite well. The drinks were going down well, and everyone was in good spirits. The session was fun, but our friends wanted to take it to another level. The manageress of the hostel said she also ran a nightclub, and she invited us all out to continue the party at the club. One of our male friends assured us we'd be safe if we went with them, and he pulled out a gun, which Dave described as a mini-canon. Dave and I were up for it, whilst Brian wanted to stay behind and try his luck with the English speaking Russian girl.

So, Dave and I went with our new friends to this nightclub. As it was run by the hostel manageress, they gave us the impression they'd look after us financially with free entry and a few free drinks. But when we got there, not only did Dave and I have to pay to get in, we had to cover the others as well. Not to worry; I was pretty pissed and in a carefree, playful mood. The women left us to it as they went to work behind the bar, whilst Dave and I hung out with the two comrades from the hostel. It was quite a decent sized place, with a large dance floor and places around the sides to chill out. I don't remember it that well; I remember it was dark, and I remember it being moderately full.

I was absolutely flying and adopted my dance floor approach technique that seemed only to come out during times of total obliteration. When I saw a girl dancing that I liked, I just walked straight up to her and started dancing in front of her, right in her face. My arms were moving all about the place, in an exaggerated psychedelic way, as if I was a wizard casting a spell. It's a failsafe method when trying to attract the ladies; they love it. Well, no, not really. Usually, the girls get freaked out and make their escape. The problem with doing it in Russia was, if a jealous boyfriend got upset, he wasn't going to use harsh language; he was likely to shoot you. Perhaps, even more so in St Petersburg, as it's known as the crime capital of Russia. Dave was by my side throughout the night, looking out for me, as we moved about the dance floor. I remember approaching a lot of girls; some of them were open to my personal space invasion, some of them not.

Dave and I were enjoying ourselves so much that we were oblivious to the social protocol going on around us. It was only towards the end of the evening we became aware of it. We noticed only the women were on the dance floor, whilst all the men just stood back and watched, standing near the wall and using the counter to rest their drinks on. I don't know what that was all about. No one ever confronted us about it.

I remember meeting these two girls, and I was quite infatuated with one of them. We spent quite a bit of time together, and I gave her a toy troll as a gift. The girls enjoyed our company, but there would be no east meets west on this occasion, if you know what I mean. We left the club with our two comrades and walked back to the hostel. I was still considerably drunk and skipped down the street, amazed and delighted with the fact I had very few layers on and yet didn't feel cold. With jeans and just a shirt and jacket, I felt almost naked compared to the assortment of coats and jumpers I usually had on. After a very notable and exciting night, we made it back to the hostel in one piece and without any bullet holes through us. I like nights that end that way.

Brian had spent his evening chatting with the young Russian girl, but was cock-blocked by the jealous, armed guard at the hostel. The guard wouldn't leave the two of them alone and had his machine gun at the ready the whole time. The young girl told Brian the guard was stupid, but whilst he was toting a machine gun, Brian was going to show him total respect. Not wanting to get shot, Brian tried to build some rapport with the guard and started a conversation with him about football. The girl got pissed off she wasn't getting all the attention, anymore. So, it was a frustrating night for Brian.

We had another thrilling overnight train trip back to Moscow. We arrived Saturday morning and had until Sunday evening before we flew back to London. Olga and I spent quite a bit of time hanging out, just the two of us. She took me to her flat to show me where she lived and to meet her parents. She was an only child and lived with her parents in a small flat, consisting of a main room, one bedroom, and a small kitchen and bathroom. The flat was one of hundreds in a high-rise building block out in the suburbs away from the city centre. They were your standard issue dog-boxes and looked distinctly industrial. There weren't any tourists out there.

As we were walking up to the block of flats, Olga slipped on the ice and took a big fall. Man, it would have surely hurt. She showed no pain, though, and soldiered on. I met her parents, who were really lovely. They made sure I was well-fed by giving me a very filling and tasty meal.

Olga and I had formed a close bond during our time together. The other guys thought she was a bit loopy and liked to tease her a bit. As she was a friend of my mate, Jim, I was compassionate towards her. She kindly accompanied us to the airport so we wouldn't have any problems with the language. The three of us had been shopping to find Olga a gift as a thank you present for her help and kindness. We couldn't believe our luck when we were looking through the cuddly toy section of a store and found a koala with an Australian flag. It was a perfect gift to give her. After Russia, Olga and I kept in touch occasionally with phone calls and letters. About 12 months later, I lost her contact details, and the contact between us stopped. Neither of us had email back then.

We checked-in for our flight with no problem, but the real concern was getting through immigration. For some reason, we were under the impression the CDs we'd bought were illegal. I don't know what I was thinking, but for some reason, I thought the best thing to do would be to stash my CD's in the multitude of pockets I had in my overcoat. There were about 14 CDs, and they were so obvious. My overcoat went through the x-ray machine and the immigration officials just waved me through. There was no problem at all. Looking back, I can't remember what was going through my head to make those decisions. It seems irrational now, but I'm sure there was some thinking behind it.

So, after two awesome weeks, we flew out of Russia on March 8th, which, coincidently, was Ladies' Day. Russia had been a truly thrilling and unique experience. Over fifteen years later, the three of us still cite it as one of the best trips we've ever done.

After the trip, we went our separate ways. I headed back

to London, whilst Dave and Brian continued to Leighton Buzzard where Dave's family lived. Dave remained there indefinitely, living and working, whilst a few weeks later, Brian returned to Australia.

March 1998

Jim kindly let me resume my residency at his flat. I contacted Simon, and he was more than happy to have me back at the Empire doing my old job. It was as if I'd never left. Kieron the alcoholic bar manager had been given the sack after New Year's.

That was true regarding my external circumstances, but on the inside, I was different, and as a result, my friendships weren't quite the same, especially between Jim and me. A few people mentioned I had come back with an attitude. I don't know about that, but after Russia, I definitely felt I was drinking a lot more, if that was possible, and with more intensity. Jim and I were still mates, but there just wasn't that strong bond we used to have. Jim and Julia were still seeing each other, and they gave me a large magnifying glass as a gift to help, whilst I still didn't have a pair of glasses.

One Saturday night, I was allowed an early mark from work, and I went with a group of about a dozen people to a dance party in North Woolwich, on the other side of London. The group consisted of Firkin staff and some kool kats that drank there. Bryce was there. He'd left the Empire and was now working at the Firkin. He assured me the great trek across London would be worth it just for the music alone. He turned out to be right. There were loads of cool people there, and the venue had a balcony out the back overlooking the river Thames. The trance music was kicking, and the drugs were doing their job, too. This was the night of the famous bottle of punch full of acid trips that was shared around the party.

But what I remember most about the party was hanging out with a French chick, called Emmanuelle (also, Manny or Manu). I first met Manny at a Firkin lock-in months earlier. We'd mixed in the same circles since but hadn't spent any time with each other one-on-one. We were both single at the time, and there was something truly graceful about the way she danced that captivated me. She also looked the goods. She was slim with long blonde hair, although on this night, she had purple streaks through it. And she used to wear these cool, long, baggy, grey cords that added to her allure. We were both off our heads and had a great time together, moving about the venue, dancing, and talking about the weird and the wonderful. Nothing developed on this occasion, but the wheels had been set in motion.

April 1998

About a week later, Asian Dub Foundation did a gig at the Empire. Simon had kindly put Manny's name on the guest list for me. This was the night I was going to make my move. I was going to do my best to show her the royal treatment. Standing at the dress circle bar, I said to Manny, "What shall we have tonight—a pill or acid?" She gave a look of ecstatic pleasure. We took both. There was no doubt in my mind we were going to get it on.

Asian Dub Foundation's electronic music was a great soundtrack to our journey into another reality. I took Manny up to level three, which was empty on this occasion, so we had the whole place to ourselves. Level three was nicknamed, The Gods, because it was so high up. We had a great view looking down on the stage from high above, and we danced like there was no tomorrow.

Unfortunately, I had to snap back into the mainstream reality. I was meant to be working. I made an appearance back down at the stage door, and Simon was on to me. He asked, "Where have you been?" He said he appreciated I was trying to seduce Manny, but I had a job to do. I'd let Simon down on this night. This was a departure from my usual reliable work ethic. Simon told me to help in the clean-up and then I could go; he'd take care of the after-show party. I told you he was the best supervisor I'd ever had.

I went to the auditorium and helped in the clean-up. I told the security Manny was with me, and so they let her wait for me on the stage-left steps. One thing Manny and I connected on was we both had an imaginative sense of humour when we were tripping. The punters going to the after-show party had to go past Manny on their way to the backstage bar. Manny took it upon herself to check everyone had the correct pass to go backstage, and amazingly, everyone stopped and showed it to her. It was so funny.

Manny and I went back to Jim's flat and had a three hour, maybe longer, candle-lit bath. Jim's bathroom was painted lots of different colours and was the perfect setting for us two tripping daisies. No doubt, our bathroom occupation was an inconvenience to Jim if he needed to go to the toilet. Thankfully, we had easy access to the toilet upstairs in Jan's flat.

And so began a festive, somewhat dazed, relationship between Manny and me. The relationship's honeymoon period was night after night, rave after rave, of flying higher than the clouds. We were having a great time. To begin with, Manny got a job at the Firkin, so she was right in the thick of the action and with our two social circles combined, we were able to party all the time.

At the Empire, at this time, Simon was bar manager and I was his aide, whilst Nick, formerly the doorman, was employed as the assistant bar manager. He was an English geezer in his 30's, a good sense of humour, and we got along well ... outside of work. At work, I found him to be lazy and under the thumb of his ego, obsessed with the prestige of the job. He got an exceedingly short haircut one day, and I kept teasing him about it; I thought he looked like a thief. He asked why I didn't tease Jim, as his hair was even shorter than Nick's. Jim, who was close by, leaned over and said in a frightening voice, "Because, whilst you look like you might rob someone, I look like I might kill someone." Classic. Jim came out with the best one-liners sometimes. I was laughing over that one for weeks.

We had a young Aussie guy start at the Empire. He was originally from Malawi and had dark skin and dreadlocks. He was quite short, cute and loveable. Nick joked that he was the kind of guy you'd like to put in your pocket and take home to keep; he was that adorable. And so, Nick gave him the name Pocket Rasta and that became his nick-name (pun intended), which stuck. We called him Pocket for short.

Everyone loved Pocket, and he was a lot of fun to be around. He and I became good mates and spent a lot of time together outside of work. Pocket and Manny got along very well, too. They were both deranged.

May 1998

By this time, I was spending most nights at the Firkin. By this I mean, sleeping upstairs in the staff digs with Manny. Jim wasn't happy with me and her hanging around his flat all the time, off our chops. Fair enough, too. There's nothing worse than being with people who are drunk and drugged up, whilst you're straight. The worst part was this was in his home, the place where one normally goes to escape the stresses of the outside world. His only respite was when we were out socialising. But even that was no great comfort, for he knew when we came home, we'd be totally baked and fried. The early days of Jim and I going out partying together had long gone. Jim preferred isolation and to sit in and watch TV. He was rather tolerant of Manny and me, despite the fact he didn't like her, and he didn't agree with the path I was going down.

Whilst he may not have made any snide comments, his vibe was rather cold. His relationship with Julia was more often than not quarrelsome, and I was caught in the middle. Both of them complained to me about the other. I did my best to play Switzerland in the whole affair, but I, mistakenly, told Julia one day something Jim had said. She went straight to Jim and confronted him about it, which was a body blow to our friendship. Jim didn't confide in me for a long time after that, when in the past, we'd been very open with each other.

One day, I gave Jim my rent money, and he wouldn't accept it. I only vaguely remember his reasoning behind it, but, ultimately, it resulted in me moving out. We were still mates, but it was just better I move out. As I said earlier, the flat's design dictated that, if two people lived there, they needed to get along. We got along a lot better after I moved out.

I moved my gear to Manny's room upstairs in the Firkin, which was handy being right next door to work. Officially, I wasn't meant to be there; the rooms were for staff only. I think the manager knew I was staying there, but he and I got along well, and he didn't do anything to have me removed. I kept out of sight whenever possible.

Towards the end of May, I was becoming more and more disgruntled with working at the Empire. I wasn't happy with the lack of management from the management and their lack of communication with the staff. Too many times, the diligence of some conscientious workers covered for the complacency of the management, and nothing ever changed because things always came together on the night, and so the head brass weren't even aware, or they didn't care, there was a problem. I didn't voice my grievances, because I didn't feel my opinion was important. Who was I to say how things should be run? Instead, I became rude and bitter and too big for my own boots. My anger boiled over one night, and I took it out on the duty manager that happened to be working that night. I can't remember her name now, but the poor woman copped the brunt of how I felt about all the management there. Simon said, "You're not happy here anymore, are you?" and with that, we worked out my departure. My last gig was Errol Brown a few days later, and then Pocket took over my job.

Well, it was fun while it lasted. The Empire had given me so much. I had many great experiences, met so many cool people, and made some good friends, many of which I'm still in touch with today. The Empire had been my social life as well as my job. Had it not been for Simon, I would have lost my job a lot earlier on a few occasions, for drinking on the job, or being drunk on the job, or for being M.I.A occasionally (I was usually on the dance floor). Simon stood up for me when my neck was on the chopping block, and I always managed to be given another chance, thanks to him. So, thanks, Simon. Thank you, linesmen, thank you, ball boys, and thank you, Shepherd's Bush Empire.

The Empire certainly left its mark on me—a scar on my chin. One club night, a 70's disco night, called the Love Bug, I was there off-duty and extremely drunk. I was dancing with Nick's girlfriend, and she was spinning me around, and I fell flat on my face. I was in a black out at the time and have no memory of this. Apparently, the pounding thud of my face hitting the floor could be heard over the music. Thankfully, I was as drunk as I was, because I didn't feel any pain. I just got straight back up and continued dancing. The scar is still visible on my chin today.

Errol Brown, of Hot Chocolate fame, played on the 30th. It was a slow night, as less than 800 people (the auditorium's capacity) showed up. When the show ended, I didn't hang around. I went to the Firkin, and that was the final curtain on my Empire career. Not that I was overly upset; I was going to take off soon, anyway. Less than a week later, I was on a plane with the American lass and fellow Empire workmate, Monica, jet-setting our way to Amsterdam. Before we left, though—HIP, HIP HOORAY - after seven months of using my left lens like a monocle, I bought a new pair of glasses. Once again, people and objects had sharp edges.

June 1998

Some thought it odd that I was taking off on a jaunt around Europe with a girl who wasn't my girlfriend. Monica and I had talked about going away together long before Manny and I had hooked up. Monica was a very enthusiastic, sociable person, and I knew she'd be good fun to travel with. We'd organised a three-week holiday and bought rail passes to get around once we were there. First stop was the land of dykes and tulips.

We flew to Amsterdam, and on my suggestion, we stayed at the hostel above Durty Nally's Irish Pub on *Warmoestraat*. I'd had a good experience there, last time, I was visiting. This time around, it wasn't such a pleasant experience. On the first night, we were kept up by two guys in our dorm tripping on mushrooms. I don't know what they were thinking. To begin with, all was quiet as the two lads went to bed to get some sleep, and then about half an hour later, they started to become totally animated. Obviously, the mushrooms had kicked in. I don't know why they went to bed after having eaten some mushrooms. Anyway, they were extremely noisy in their alternate universe, and we didn't get much sleep. As a result, we moved the next day to The Globe, a much nicer, cleaner place, overlooking a canal. We were much happier there.

As well as hanging out in Vondel Park, we strolled around the city enjoying its beautiful neighbourhoods. We visited the Anne Frank House and stopped in at a canal boat full of cats. It was a relaxing few days, and we'd be back, as our last night of the trip would be in Amsterdam again.

We caught an overnight coach to Hamburg and arrived the next morning as zombies. We hadn't slept well, and we said little as we moved in slow motion. I phoned my cricket buddy, Jamal, and we went and crashed at his place. It was great seeing Jamal again and being back in Hamburg. Jamal, once again, was greatly hospitable, making Monica and I feel welcome. It had been nine months since I left Hamburg bound for London, but I slipped right back into the swing of things as if it had only been last week that I left. It was akin to a homecoming for me, and I was excited to be back in Germany on familiar territory with the opportunity to speak German again.

This time around, though, like in Amsterdam, I was well-behaved, because I was travelling with Monica. She enjoyed a good party as much as the next person but tended not to hang out in shady, dive bars like I was prone to do. We did visit the Reeperbahn but didn't get up to much other than visit the Erotic Art Museum.

The next stop was Copenhagen. We caught the train and had to take a ferry from the mainland of Germany to the Danish islands where Copenhagen is. Copenhagen was new and exciting, as neither of us had been there before. We found a great, environmentally conscious, little hostel run by young, mohawked punks in their 20's.

We did quite a lot whilst we were there. There was some great architecture around the place—looking very palatial—as well as many parks. The city was particularly bicycle friendly with a large network of bicycle lanes. Throughout the downtown area, the city provided public bicycles. For a small deposit, you could take a bike from one terminal and then return it at any other terminal around the city. This was the first time I'd seen such a system, but it's quite common in European cities today.

We checked out a lot of the Royal buildings and the stables. Monica is into horses. We went and had our photo taken by The Little Mermaid statue, based on a tale by Hans Christian Andersen. It was surprisingly smaller than I expected; it sits on a rock in the harbour, just over a metre high.

We visited a place where the employees were allowed to drink on the job. I was going to be looking for a job in a few weeks; maybe it was worth considering handing in my résumé. It was the Carlsberg Brewery, and we went on a surprisingly entertaining and informative tour of the site. The tour guide told us, in the mid-1800's, the employees were allowed to drink as much of the product as they wanted whilst carrying out their duties. Then, at some point, this was limited to 12 beers per person, per day. I mean, even that's generous. Can you imagine the foreman breaking the news?

"There's good news and there's bad news. The good news is, you can still drink on the job. The bad news is, you can't have more than 12 a day."

Ha. Even for an alcoholic, that's not the end of the world. Anyway, that rule only lasted for a short time.

"The bad news is, the drinking limit has been changed again. The good news is, it's back to unlimited."

The good news for us was some drinks were included at the end of the tour.

We had a chance to be big kids again at the famous amusement park, Tivoli Gardens, opened in 1843. Apparently, it's the second oldest operating fun park in the world, second only to *Dyrehavsbakken*, opened in 1583, also in Denmark. Having been around that long, we hoped the fun rides had been serviced over the years and were safe. We went on the Demon, which was one of your more modern rides. We got thrown about, hung upside down, and spun in all directions ... fast. It took a while to regain my walking skills after that. We arrived as it was getting dark, and at night, the park looked awesome, lit up like a Christmas tree.

I didn't have the largest amount of savings for this trip, so while Monica went to Berlin, I stayed with Jamal in Hamburg and took advantage of the free accommodation. I had a good time with Jamal again, enjoying his home cooked curries and attending cricket practise. With Monica out of the picture, I let loose for the first time on the trip and had a big night out in the Reeperbahn. I was pretty tired by the time I made my way back to Jamal's flat. I fell asleep on the train and woke up on a different train. I don't know how that happened.

At my next destination, three people came to meet me at the train station. I was in Bonn so, not surprisingly, Julia was there to meet me. She was home again for the summer break from her studies in London. Also, there was Monica who'd arrived earlier from Berlin. The third person was Jim from the Empire. I did know he would be at the station, but it was somewhat surprising when he decided to come to Germany, as he normally didn't venture far from Shepherd's Bush. I was excited. Here I was on holiday, in Germany, with three of my favourite people.

We all stayed with Julia at her parent's house in Bad Breisig. We had an awesome couple of days together, relaxing by day and dining out by night. The best time, though, was a party we went to in a small hut in the forest. It was wonderful. Especially seeing all the friends I'd made from the previous summer. For a while, Jim was DJing. He mixed Led Zeppelin with Björk; it worked really well. There was a period of about twenty minutes, where Jim had the party really pumping. I was dancing right beside him and it felt like old times between us: that bond that two people share when having a good time together that we used to have during the early days when we used to get up to mischief.

From one forest setting to another, Monica and I travelled deep into the Black Forest to a small village, called Triberg. We arrived at the station and, the lazy arses that we were, we caught a taxi the short distance to our hostel. Well, you would too if you had a big, heavy backpack to carry and you saw the steep mountain we would have had to walk up to get to the hostel.

We went exploring on some of the trails around the area. The vegetation was so lush and green; there were trees everywhere. Whoever called it a forest wasn't kidding; the place was beautiful. Triberg is home to a series of short waterfalls, plunging 163 metres from the Gutach River, promoted as the highest waterfalls in Germany. There was a boardwalk that climbed up the mountain following the course of the cascades one could get a good vantage point from.

Triberg also has the world's biggest Cuckoo clock, and many of the stores along the main drag were selling an extensive variety of the clocks in all sorts of designs. Monica bought an enormous cuckoo clock, possibly the second biggest in the world, as a gift for her mother. Thankfully, the store made deliveries. There's no way Monica could have carried it around with her in her backpack.

The next stop was chocolate and cows. We travelled south to Zurich, Switzerland, and paid a visit to the Lindt factory, where we devoured the free samples, and we bought a box each of their oh-so-good chocolate.

Whilst we were in Zurich, the city centre was littered with fiberglass sculptures of cows, decorated and painted by local artists in various themes. This concept later became known as Cow Parade and has since featured in many major cities around the world. I came across it a few times in my travels over the years; I remember London had it in 2003. All in all, I quite liked Zurich. It had a groovy, alternative, arts vibe about it.

We caught the overnight train from Zurich to Vienna. We arrived having had fuck all sleep. The train was cold, and we were all woken up in the middle of the journey to show our passports when we crossed the border. We arrived at Vienna's main station and wanted nothing more than a bed to sleep in. Unfortunately, we hadn't booked anywhere to stay. We were tired and irritable with no motivation to sort out what we were going to do. I remember we just sat in the station, lifeless, for ages. I was thinking how nice it would be if Monica could organise the accommodation for once, and I could just take it easy whilst someone else did all the leg work. Monica's German was non-existent, so it was always up to me to do the ringing around. We ended up at an old monastery converted into a hostel.

Once again, Vienna failed to impress me. I really need to go there and have a local resident show me around because, despite being a wonderful city architecturally and there being some beautiful parks, the two times I've been there, I found the place to be rather boring. What little I remember was, we walked around the city centre, we visited the cemetery where Mozart is buried, and we bought some beer cheese, which when we opened it, stunk so badly.

With a few days to go and low on funds, Monica and I parted company again, and I headed back to Bonn to stay with Julia. The day before we were due to fly back to London,

Monica and I met up at The Globe Hostel, in Amsterdam. It was our last night, and we were up for some fun. We befriended a young American guy, who was staying in the hostel, and the three of us went out together. We took some mushrooms, and I had one of the most intense experiences I've ever had on hallucinogens. We walked around the different neighbourhoods; colours were so much brighter and sounds so much sharper. People whizzed by on their bicycles, and half a dozen exact images followed behind them. Time was distorted as minutes sometimes felt like hours. After many hours, we went back to The Globe and hung out in the bar there. Our American friend entertained us with some animated dancing; it looked like he had eight arms. We sat out the back overlooking the canal, and a wave of relaxation came over me. It happened to Monica at exactly the same time. She looked at me and said, "Wow." We'd ridden the peak and had just come out the other side. The experience was a lot milder from then on.

The next day, back in Shepherd's Bush, I walked into the Firkin, and Simon from the Empire was at the bar ordering a drink. He said, "Hey, good to see you. When did you get back?"

"Now. This is me getting back … right now."

I asked if he'd seen Manny, and he pointed to a table behind me. I turned around, and Manny saw me at the same time. It was one of those moments from the movies, where two friends/lovers run slow motion through a field of sunflowers towards each other to give each other a big hug. It had been a delightful holiday, and it was good to be back. I'd missed Manny. I'd missed her company and her quirky idiosyncrasies. There was a song out at the time, by French house-music band, Stardust, called "Music Sounds Better with You", which expressed perfectly how I felt about partying with Manny. Partying without her just wasn't the same.

In September, I found myself in a pub I'd never been to before. I'd never been treated to such service before, either. Drinks were on the house. It's not every pub you go to that the barman says help yourself to the beer tap, but that was the case when I went to *Le Petit Marly*.

Manny and I took some time off work and travelled to stay with Manny's parents in France. They lived in a small village of about 6,000 people, called Liancourt, an hour's drive north of Paris. They lived in a lovely, three-story house, where Manny had grown up. It's a dream of many a man to marry a woman whose Dad owns a brewery. Kevin Bloody Wilson sings about it in his song, 'Do You Fuck on First Dates?' Manny's Dad didn't own a brewery, but I'd say he went one better. On the ground floor of their house, the house I'd be staying in for two weeks, Manny's parents ran and owned … their own pub. Hallelujah!

Webster's online dictionary defines the word holiday as: 1. Leisure time away from work devoted to rest or pleasure; 2. A day of exemption from labour. Well, my friends, you couldn't get any more 'holiday' than this. My time was devoted to rest and pleasure, and there was definitely no labour on my part. A typical day consisted of me rising at whatever time my body chose to awaken. I then said hello to Manny and her mother, Muriel, who were downstairs running the pub, cooking lunch in the kitchen for the pub customers. I'd make myself at home upstairs in the TV room and watch movies in English on the cable channels all day, whilst enjoying some cold beers. At lunch time, I'd be served—upstairs, I didn't have to move at all—a wonderfully filling, delicious, cooked meal of meat and vegetables. In the evening, Didier would arrive home from his day job and relieve the ladies from their work. Muriel would rest and take over from me in the TV room, whilst Manny and I mingled with the customers in the pub. Or, sometimes, we'd go out and visit Manny's friends.

Muriel was short, overweight, friendly and a little bit crazy—always animated whether she was laughing at something or complaining about something. She spoke no English whatsoever. Didier was tall and slim. He was the joker, the class clown. He was quite intelligent and, as I mentioned before, Didier's English was minimal, but he made me feel truly welcome when he was able to say, "The beer tap ... help yourself." It was a kind gesture, especially as he knew how much I liked a drink. But, I didn't take the piss. I only helped myself to a couple of drinks in the evenings. The rest of the day, I drank bottles Manny and I had bought from the supermarket.

It really was an enjoyable two weeks. I found everyone to be exceedingly friendly. Manny's parents were very hospitable and generous. Manny's friends were all very friendly towards me, too. It didn't take me long to get in the habit of kissing the women four times—twice on each cheek. None of them were confident enough to practise speaking English with me, so Manny always had to translate. She did well, too, considering how drunk we got. My French was limited to only a few basic phrases, such as, "*Stella Artois, s'il vous plait.*" All the customers I met in the pub, too, were friendly and keen to meet me and share in having a drink.

The name, *Le Petit Marly*, was inspired by a pub they went to once, called *Le Grande Marly*. They liked it so much they chose to name their smaller pub after it. The one not-so-great thing about the house/pub was the toilet. The only toilet was downstairs in the pub. There was a urinal for the guys, but for everything else, there was a Turkish styled toilet, which, basically, is a toilet used by squatting, rather than sitting, over a hole in the ground. I know what you're thinking; Yes, it did have a flush.

1999

January–March 1999

"Guess what?"

"You're getting married."

I had a call from my brother, Neville, in Canberra. I found out he was getting married later in the year. Actually, I guessed it. It was the craziest answer I could think of, and it just happened to be right. He expressed his wish I be the best man. That required me to return home, so I booked a flight back to Australia for the end of March ... and Manny was coming with. I don't know why I chose March. Looking back, it may have been better to have stayed for the European summer, rather than go home to winter, having just experienced one.

With our impending departure to Australia, we went back to France, so Manny could spend some time with her family and organise a visa to Australia which was a real mission. After filling out all the forms, we spent hours at the Australian Embassy in Paris getting her application processed. It took forever before we got to the front of the queue to submit the forms. We'd originally applied for a one year working visa, but because of France's nuclear testing in the Pacific, working visas weren't issued to the French. We did alright, though. Manny got a six month, multiple-entry, tourist visa, valid for one year. That meant, for one year, every time she entered the country, she was given another six-month stay. Even if she were to enter the country a week before the one year was up, she'd still be granted a six month stay. Effectively, she could stay in Australia for close to eighteen months. She wasn't permitted to work though.

After two years in Europe, I finally got to visit Ireland.

Before I left Australia, Ireland was one of the places I was most looking forward to visiting. I just never got around to it. And what a time to be going, too. We went at a time when there was a little day of celebration which attracted one or two people. You may have heard of it; it's called St Patrick's Day. Manny had never been to Ireland before, either.

We booked a four-day coach tour for the 15th—18th from London taking in the sites of Dublin and its surroundings. It wasn't going to be the romantic wandering of the Irish countryside I had envisioned when I dreamt of going to Ireland, but it was going to be great *craic*, anyway.

We had an early morning departure from Victoria before setting off on the tour. Looking around, I noticed the tour was a mixed bag of guys and gals in their 20's, which I thought would make for a good party vibe. We arrived at our accommodation in Dublin in the early evening. It was a little bit away from the city centre but a clean and inviting three-star hotel. We had a comfortable double room with all the mod-cons. That first night, we spent the evening at the hotel bar and restaurant, being entertained by a ginger-haired duet, playing live fiddly-diddly music—how Irish.

Our first full day in Ireland started with a heavenly buffet breakfast at the hotel—a great way to start the day. Our itinerary consisted of a tour around the city on the coach, a tour to some regional sites outside of the city, a visit to the Guinness Brewery, which involved a self-guided tour and some complimentary Guinness. We would then be free to explore the city as we wished. Manny and I only lasted an hour.

During the city tour, the coach passed the Guinness Brewery, which our guide mentioned we'd be visiting later. There were two guys up the front of the coach, who asked if they could get off and go to the brewery straight away. The guide said they could, but the coach wouldn't be waiting for them; they'd be missing out on the rest of the day's activities. They didn't seem to mind; they jumped off the coach without hesitation. Manny wasn't interested in any city tour. She suggested we get off, too, and we did.

I'm not a fan of drinking stout beers, but I was on this day. We did the Guinness Brewery tour, which finished in a bar, and with our admission ticket, we got a complimentary half-pint of the black stuff each. Guinness is said to taste better in Ireland; I've heard other people say that's bullshit. My mate, Jim from the Empire, was one. He drank Guinness all the time and claimed there was no difference in the taste. Jim didn't even think letting the Guinness settle was necessary. He always ordered his Guinness to be poured in one straight pull.

I don't like drinking coffee or eating coffee flavoured desserts for that matter, and the taste of stout, to me, tastes similar to coffee. I don't know about Ireland having the best Guinness, but on this occasion, I was able to tolerate it and even enjoy it. Being in Ireland and getting into the spirit of St Patrick's Day probably had something to do with it. I haven't touched the stuff since.

In the bar at the Guinness Brewery, we joined the two guys from our tour for a drink. They were both students in the south of England, yet one was German, whilst the other one was ... French. You wouldn't know it to look at him or hear him speak, but anyway, we got to know them over a few pints, and we got along well. The Frenchman's name was Gerry, and I can't remember German man's name. Let's call him Orlando Bloom. There was a little resemblance to the movie star.

We'd tasted the blood by this stage, so the four of us left the brewery in search of other pubs that could give us a taste of the Dublin ambiance. We ended up in the Temple Bar Pub, with the red and black exterior that features on most postcards of the area. The Temple Bar is also the name of the lively nightlife area where the pub is located. It's a popular place in central Dublin, with many narrow cobbled-stone streets full of pubs and clubs with plenty of loud music echoing from the different venues.

It was rather quiet in the pub when we arrived. We found a suitable table for the four of us and relaxed with another pint each of Guinness. After about our second pint, a three-piece band set up right next to us and started to entertain the lunch time crowd with some traditional Irish music. It was great; we had front row seats. The bar filled up, and the atmosphere was rowdy and jolly. Manny was having a ball, not least because she was quite fond of Guinness, plus the happy vibe in the pub. It was a special experience. I was enjoying it, too. Music sessions in the pub were one of my motivations for wanting to go to Ireland. I had been looking forward to the drive through the countryside on our coach tour, but I was glad now we'd bailed and gone drinking instead. Being so close to the band, we got involved in some banter with the guys, and they played some of our requests. We later moved on from there and drank in the many other pubs around the Temple Bar, but we vowed to go back the next day to see the trio play again.

The next morning, the coach dropped us off in the city, and we were free to do our own thing. We paired up with our mates, Gerry and Orlando, again. We went and joined the crowds along College Green, one of the many streets in which the parade would meander through. We got there early and were able to get a pretty decent vantage point. The crowds were 12 deep, and people climbed and stood on whatever was available, e.g., statues, bike racks. It was a sea of green as far as the eye could see. We waited quite a while, just standing there in the crowd, waiting for the parade to come along, but we didn't want to leave and lose our spot.

We thought if we did leave, the parade was bound to come along. So, we waited ... and waited ... and waited for about an hour or two.

It was worth the wait. The colour and the spectacle were magnificent. It was a dazzling display of elaborate floats, street theatre troupes, artists, dancers, and marching bands. The parade continued on and on as it snaked its way through the city streets. After a while, we all felt we'd seen enough of the parade and we could cross it off our 'to do' list. It was lunch time, and we went in search of a drink. We found one pub, but it was so full you could hardly move. The thing I noticed, though, was the parade was being televised live in the pub. Shit. All those hours standing on our feet, and we could have been in the pub watching the parade. On the positive side, it meant we started on the sauce later. It would have been no good peaking early; we had a big night ahead of us.

We went back to the Temple Bar Pub to see the band from the day before. The pub was chockers, and as you can imagine, exceptionally lively with everyone in good spirits. The band put on a great show, as we all shouted along to the songs whilst enjoying the sweet, sweet taste of beer.

The rest of the day and night we spent exploring the city and its pubs, singing and dancing in each one. We wandered out of the Temple Bar and checked out all the goings-on on Grafton St and the nearby pubs. Everywhere we went, there were loads of people, cheering and carrying on, people from all walks of life. My impressions were that Dublin was a miniature version of London, only Irish.

We came across some other revellers from our tour bus. They were showing the effects of a whole day drinking. One guy, in particular, was a mess. It was a good illustration of what we could have been like had we started drinking earlier. Manny and I ran out of money late in the evening. We'd had some great craic, so we left the others whilst we went back to the hotel.

It was a great experience, and I could now say I'd been to Ireland. Yet, I hoped to go back one day to see the rest of it, its green rolling hills, rugged mountains, wee villages, and friendly country folk. But that would have to wait, because in just under two weeks, Manny and I would be on a plane to Australia.

The major undertaking we had to attend to was saying goodbye to everyone. We were like a band on a farewell tour, doing gigs and making appearances around the place. The Firkin organised some staff drinks as a farewell for Manny. The Australians there didn't instil any confidence in Manny by questioning her decision to go to 'boring' Canberra. Although, one guy provided some hope; I don't think he was even Australian; he said, "Yeah, I've been to Canberra. It's a cool place."

Our last Friday night in the country, and we had a few jars in The Bushranger, where we ran into some familiar faces. We also went and paid a visit to our buddies in Kensal Rise. They were all there. We had a good, drunken night catching up with Julia, Monica, and Co. It was hard to say goodbye.

Sunday afternoon, we went by Jim's place before going to The Kensington Pub around the corner, for a small get-together. I was glad to be in The Kensington. There were a lot of memories drinking there, right back to the days of staying at O'Callaghan's when I first arrived in London. Simon and Jan showed up (my Empire boss and Jim's upstairs neighbour). They were a couple now and had been for around six months. Tessa, Jan's friend, was there, too.

Jim didn't stick around long. He only stayed for a few rounds. As he said his goodbyes, I gave him a hug and thanked him for his friendship. He left and I cried like a baby. I couldn't stop either. Any thought of farewelling my mate triggered me off again. We had been rather close, and despite some periods of disagreement, we still had a strong regard for each other. As a parting gift, I gave Jim a framed photo of me, standing on the bridge of Addison Gardens, with our famous glove still fixed in the tree. It was still there, 15 months since we placed it there, coming home from a big night out.

Once the bawling was out of the way, we went on to have an entertaining afternoon. Manny pulled out the drugs we had left over from the weekend, and that livened things up a lot. We all had strikingly big smiles on our faces after that.

Tuesday, it was time to rock & roll. With all our goodbyes done, we caught the tube to Heathrow and hopped on one of those big, flying machines. We flew with Japan Airlines and took advantage of the complimentary wine for most of the first leg. There was a seven hour stop-over in Tokyo, which we tried to sleep through before our connecting flight to Sydney. The second leg wasn't so fun. The facilities on the plane were old, and we didn't drink; otherwise, we would have disturbed the woman sitting in the aisle seat next to us when we got up every 20 minutes to go to the toilet. The nine-hour flight dragged on as we sobered up and struggled to get any sleep. It was at this time I was looking forward to arriving in Sydney the most. After 25 months away, returning home couldn't come fast enough.

Australia
31st March 1999

The first thing to hit me, and it was like being hit in the face, was how Australian, Sydney airport was. The Aussie accent was unmistakeable and could be heard everywhere. It was a bit too full on for me. With time, I'd get used to it.

The Australian currency was the other thing I had to adjust to: the different notes and coins, saying dollars, instead of quid. Another thing were the different beer sizes, schooner instead of pint. And then there was the slang. I'd embraced certain English slang, and it had become a part of me; I spoke it without thinking. Now, I had to lose it or risk not being understood, you know what I mean, like? The one that was always questioned was 'cash point' (ATM). I'd say, "I need a cash point," and people would ask, "What are you on about?"

Needless to say, the last two years had a big influence on me, and I wasn't going to lose it overnight. However, the novelty of being back was fun, if not a little weird. It meant, though, when it came to adjusting to life in Australia, Manny and I were in it together.

April 1999

I don't remember suffering jet-lag to any great degree. We were staying with family in Blacktown, in Western Sydney. I remember our one year anniversary, on the 4th. Manny and I were up early to make the most of the day, and we went sightseeing in the city. Manny wasn't aware of any of Sydney's famous landmarks. She'd never even heard of Bondi Beach. I could have taken her to Parramatta and told her it was Sydney City, and she would have been none the wiser. Over a few days, we saw the Sydney Opera House, had our photo with the Sydney Harbour Bridge, caught the ferry and went swimming at Manly beach, went to The Rocks, went to Kings Cross and took advantage of the net cafés offering $3 unlimited access, ran into someone we vaguely knew from Shepherd's Bush, went swimming at Bondi Beach, and saw the filming of a TV soap on the beach.

Weeks later, we sat down to watch TV and tuned in just in time to see the episode we had seen being filmed on the beach and, to our great surprise, we saw us in the background. It was high-fives all around when we saw that. Had we switched on five seconds later, we would have missed it.

Despite officially being autumn, the weather was beautiful—sunny and warm. It had been a long time since we'd experienced weather this good. Even the UK's summer of '98 wasn't this good. We revelled in it.

Friends made the comment that I hadn't changed very much. As much as I thought the last two years had been unproductive career wise or planning for the future, I did feel I had changed. I mean, I still looked the same and dressed much the same way; I still had long hair. My belly had reached new limits, but the rest of my figure was much the same. However, I felt I'd changed on the inside, changes that weren't so immediately noticeable. I felt I'd matured and had a greater awareness of the world. I couldn't have had the experiences I had and not have changed. I replied that I'm a different person to different people, and I had simply just slipped back into the persona I am when around any specific individual.

After a week or so in Sydney, we travelled to Canberra. My younger brother AJ, and his girlfriend, Bec, were kind enough to drive us the three hours south to the nation's capital. The beauty of this trip was our brother, Neville, wasn't aware I was back in the country. I wanted to surprise him. AJ told Neville he'd be in town and arranged for Neville to meet him at the Jolimont Centre bus station. I was looking forward to seeing his face when we showed up, expecting to see one brother and then, to his surprise, seeing two.

We pulled up at the Jolimont Centre, and we could see Neville's car. We didn't see him anywhere, so we went inside and sat in the lounge waiting for him to show up. He appeared and AJ stood up to meet him. Neville was glad to see him. I stood up, but AJ was blocking Neville's view of me. As I stepped out from behind AJ, I could see the look on Neville's face change. It went from a warm smile, to a look of confusion and then to a look of aggravation when he realised what was going on. He was annoyed I hadn't told him I was coming back. Had he known, he wouldn't have had the electricity turned off in my flat the week before. Otherwise, he was over the moon to see me.

We all went and had brunch at Gus' Café. After we filled our bellies, AJ and Bec left and made the return trip back to Sydney. That really was nice of them to drive us all the way to Canberra and then turn around and go straight home again. That's six hours of their day on the road. Thanks, guys.

OK ... so, back in Canberra, after more than two years away, now what? I was excited and itching to see everyone again and to visit my favourite drinking holes. First things first, though, after Gus's, Neville took us to his house to meet his fiancée, Belinda. She'd heard a lot about me from Neville, who had painted me out to be a super-extraordinary person. She was somewhat anxious about meeting me, and I'm sure she had aspirations of making a good impression when the day came that we would finally meet. I'm almost certain meeting me on a Sunday morning, without any warning, having just gotten out of bed, was not how she envisioned the meeting taking place. Not that it mattered (to the rest of us), we all got on well. Belinda was a school teacher, a few years old than me and so a good five or six years older than Neville. I think the two first met through mutual friends in the pub. With introductions over, we went to the pub, too.

We went to Filthy McFadden's in Kingston. My good friend and former house mate, Dan, was at the pub, too. Party on. Dan made the comment that, despite not having seen each other in so long, it felt like it was only just the other day we were hanging out together. I agreed. Whilst I'd been away, I'd kept in touch by letter and with the occasional phone call (drunk dialling), so because of that regular contact, it was hard to comprehend it was a couple of years since we'd seen each other. I've found this to be the case throughout my travels. When meeting any good friend again, no matter what time has elapsed, it's easy to pick up the relationship where it left off at the same level of familiarity, as if it were only just last week, for example, the two of us caught up, even if there'd been no email or phone contact in between.

Returning home to the flat on Carruthers St, was like going back in time to 1996. There had been occupants in the place whilst I'd been away, but so many of my belongings were how I had left them. Many of the old posters were still up on the walls; some of the old furniture was there, old clothes in the cupboard, and photos from '96 were in my desk drawer. It was fun for a second, an opportunity to walk down memory lane, but then it was confusing and uncomfortable. I didn't want to be back in '96. So much had happened since then. I'd moved on and wanted to keep it that way. It didn't take long to rearrange things in the flat and for Manny to give it a woman's touch.

After arriving in Canberra, we did the opposite of when we left London. We did a tour, meeting and greeting family and friends, saying hello rather than goodbye. We had a night out at the ANU, one of my favourite bars, and was able to catch up with a lot of acquaintances from the old days. It was fun reacquainting myself with Canberra and getting a warm welcome from family and friends.

You may have heard the expression, 'Nothing's changed, yet, everything's changed'. That's how I felt being back in Canberra. On the surface, things looked much the same as when I last saw them. People may have still been at the same house, doing the same job, hanging out with the same crowd, but underneath it all, they, too, had changed and grown. New friendships had formed and old ones discarded. They, and Canberra, had an extra two-year history from when I last saw them and, at times, I felt like an outsider when recent history was recounted with great enthusiasm. Sometimes, in conversations, I'd get lost, as there was a presumption from other people I had knowledge of certain events, but I didn't know what they were referring to, because I'd been away.

I've heard the saying, 'It's better to leave than to be left behind,' and I can certainly agree with that. Many times, when parting company with a close friend, despite a heavy heart, at least I had some comfort knowing I was off on another adventure. For the person staying put, it was business as usual minus a good friend. Whilst I'd never give up the experiences I had or the opportunity for further travel, there is a flip side to the coin. There were times when I felt it's better to stay than to go and come back. I thought it was better to have evolved with the people and its surroundings, rather than returning to find you have some catching up to do. A good analogy would be watching a TV series. You watch the program from week to week and you become fully immersed in the story and its characters. You miss the show for a couple of months and then, when you tune in again, it takes some time to pick-up on what's going on: some new characters have been introduced, unlikely alliances have been made, and that hot actress you fancied has left the show to pursue a music career. However, it's still better to be in the leaver's position as they had the brilliant holiday, and with time it's possible to settle back into the swing of things and become up to date with what's been going on.

I also found no one was really interested in what I had

been up to. When they asked, "How was your trip?" all they wanted to know was it was good. If I went into any detail, they switched off, which is understandable; they couldn't relate to it. However, the horny German truck driver story grabbed everyone's attention.

July 1999

"Fuck this shit. I'm never hopping on a plane again. Flying and I are *finished*."

That was the claim I made and had every intention of sticking to, until I remembered I was on a plane to Fiji at the time. Seeing as Fiji is an island, unless I wanted to charter a boat across the Pacific or swim home to Australia, I was going to have to catch a flight back.

As part of Manny's visa requirements to leave the country every six months, we decided to spend a week in Fiji. We arrived at Sydney airport and did all the check-in malarkey. We waited impatiently for the call to board the plane. A week away on a tropical island, leaving the middle of winter behind us, couldn't come fast enough.

Soon enough, we were boarding the plane and sitting in our seats. The usual preparations were taking place for take-off as we started to taxi onto the runway. The plane moved into position, waited briefly for the all-clear, and then, the familiar feeling of being pushed back in our seats as the plane charged down the runway. Those twenty odd seconds careening down the runway can take forever sometimes. Just when it felt like the plane should be taking off, the brakes came on, the wing flaps opened, our seatbelts stopped us from moving forward, and the plane was well and truly still on the ground.

All the passengers looked at each other confused as the plane taxied back to the terminal. The captain announced over the PA there had been a problem with the take-off system. We were back at the terminal, and we could see out the window, men working under the plane. Time passed and passengers spoke of other experiences of long delays sitting on the tarmac.

Just to go on a tangent here, my friend Julia has this great story of when she was on a flight from Frankfurt to London and the plane was delayed. She and her fellow passengers sat in the plane for hours without going anywhere. Julia struck up a conversation with an Italian lad sitting nearby. Just as it looked as if the long delay was coming to an end, and the plane might be on its way, Julia asked the Italian,

"What are you doing in London? Have you been there before?"

"London? I'm going to Rome."

"But this plane goes to London."

The Italian asked someone else; "London," was the reply. Julia told me of the absolute panic that came over this guy's face as he realised he was on the wrong plane. So, the plane was delayed even longer as they had to get the Italian off.

Getting back to our flight to Fiji, we didn't have to wait long before the captain came back over the PA to inform us of what was going on. Now, I'm not the bravest of flyers, and I find taking off the scariest part. I heard once, it's the most dangerous part of flying. So, I, too, had a look of panic on my face when the Captain announced:

"Ladies and Gentlemen, engineers have been working to fix the problem. We're not sure if the problem is fixed, but I've decided we're going to take off anyway."

My God! Who the fuck says that to a plane full of people when their safety is in your hands? I translated it to mean, "We have a problem, don't know if it's been rectified, but let's risk our lives anyway." It's like saying, "I don't know if I packed our parachutes properly, but let's jump and find out."

The announcement raised more than a few eyebrows amongst the passengers. Children can be so honest and funny sometimes. I said sometimes. I didn't find it funny at all when a boy sitting nearby asked his father,

"What happens if we take off and we fall back down to the ground?"

The boy gave a demonstration with his hand in case we didn't understand the implications of falling to the ground. A valid question I thought. One I wanted to ask the Captain. Daddy just dismissed it, "Oh don't be silly, Son."

So, without the all-clear from the engineers, the plane was, once again, preparing for take-off. As we sped down the runway, I was twice as nervous as usual and held on tightly to my armrests. It didn't help that the plane was shaking like a motherfucker and making all sorts of noises. My imagination ran wild. I was worried the plane my not hold together. I've caught many flights in my time and have a good idea of the usual noises a plane makes, but I didn't recognise the loud grinding noises that could be heard. The plane managed to take off this time, although, I wished it had stayed on the ground. The plane was still shaking and rattling during our ascent and then, just to add to my fear of the plane falling apart, the big screen that shows the in-flight entertainment fell off the wall. Scared witless, this is when I declared never to hop on another plane again.

Once up at cruising altitude, the rest of the flight went quite smoothly. I calmed down and, once again, looked forward to spending a week on an island in the Pacific. There were the odd periods of turbulence causing Manny, on one occasion, to spill her orange juice all over the in-flight magazine, leaving a big orange stain. I was so happy to be alive when we landed at Nadi airport.

Manny and I spent a completely relaxing week in the

sun. From good food and drink, to friendly locals and travellers, to snorkelling and sunbaking, to cheap shopping, we had a fun, relaxing escape from the rat race back home. A highlight was spending a few days on Beachcomber Island, a small island that takes just seven minutes to walk one lap around its shore.

The week was over, and it was time to catch our flight home. At the airport, I declared, "After this *next* flight, I'm not flying again." Manny and I were a bit apprehensive, especially as there had been a Fijian domestic flight, crash land in the mountains during the week. We boarded the plane, and for some reason, we had the same seats we had on the outbound trip. We sat down, and Manny pulled out the in-flight magazine and AAAAAAAAAAAAHHHHH!!!!!!! We were on the same fuckin' plane. There, on the magazine, was the same orange juice stain from when Manny spilt her drink during the flight over.

We made it back to Sydney, grateful to be alive and with plenty of stories to tell our friends. It was 16 months later before I hopped on a plane again. It was pointed out to me later the captain knew what he was doing. If the take-off system hadn't been repaired, the plane would never have left the ground. Of course, I knew that.

September–November 1999

Finally, we were mobile. I bought a Toyota Hiace van, long wheel base, with the intention of us travelling around the countryside in it. It took a bit of time for me to get used to the column shift; otherwise, it was great. It had so much room in the back, with a double seat that could be folded down, creating more room. I loved sitting high up in the driver's seat and able to see out over the traffic. Immediately, it gave us more freedom to get around town, and for me, I could sleep in a bit longer now I didn't have to catch the bus to work.

Burning Gas Bottle
December 1999

Our next trip was an adventure into the unknown. With no set timeframe, we went cruising down the NSW south coast and over the border into Victoria, stopping finally in Melbourne. We'd been there for four weeks, living out of our van. We had a little gas burner, which we boiled water on so we could have noodles, canned foods, and coffee. The gas bottle was from the '70's; I commandeered it out of the junk in my aunt's garage. So, one day, when it ran out of gas, we had to buy a new bottle because no one would refill our ancient bottle. In the end, we spent $50 on a new bottle, plus we had to buy an extra fitting, as our single burner wouldn't fit the new bottle without it.

Later that day, we pulled up at Carlton Gardens, an inner-city park, to boil water for some coffee, and the fuckin' gas bottle caught on fire. The new attachment we'd bought had two outlets, and the one we weren't using must not have been closed properly and was leaking gas. Actually, I don't know why the fuck it caught fire, except for the obvious reason ... I put a match to it.

All I knew was I had a burning gas bottle in the back of our van with flames about half a metre high. I swiftly grabbed the bottle and put it out onto the footpath, and whilst I was looking for water, the gas bottle, which by this stage had some mean looking flames, fell over and rolled under the van.

PANIC.

I thought the whole fuckin' van might blow up. Like a flash, I ran to the driver's door and put the van into neutral and pushed it down the hill away from the flaming danger. I didn't want to start the van in case starting the engine with the fire underneath it caused an explosion.

I threw some water on the gas bottle, but I didn't have enough to put it out; it just kept burning. We couldn't turn the gas off, as the fire was too large and too hot to put our hands near. My arm hairs got singed trying. We tried to smother the flames with a towel and some sand, but the flames were too strong.

Meanwhile, this old hippie passing by started to give us a ten minute lecture on the safeties of camping. "Too fuckin' late," I thought. He had no advice as what to do about an out of control gas bottle.

We couldn't just get out the marshmallows and sit around the fire waiting for the gas to burn out. It was new and had ten hours' worth of gas left in it. By this time, the bottle was just lying in the gutter burning away, and I thought it was time to call the fire super heroes.

We had just bought a new mobile phone, but I hadn't worked out how to use it yet. So, here I was walking around with a phone in my hand, asking passers-by if they had a phone. I felt like I was walking around with my dick in my hand the way people were looking at me. In the end, I threw one of our blankets on the fire to smother the gas bottle and flames started to shoot out from under the blanket at my legs. That was fun. But I fought back and completely choked it of oxygen, and the fire died. "Die, you fucker" I yelled as if I had just stuck a knife into a voodoo doll. I don't think I yelled that at all, but that's how I felt.

The fire was out, and I sat down with black ash over my hands, and I wiped my sweaty brow in time to see two big fire trucks, with their sirens blaring, coming down the street to make the whole matter even more embarrassing. All this happened in a little park in the city, about two minutes from the CBD. We had lost $50, but we could have lost our van or even ourselves. I thought we might get in trouble from the firemen, but they were just concerned that we were OK. They suggested we go around the corner and buy a coffee instead.

It's hard to explain in words how fuckin' scared I was when all this was going on. It didn't help when I saw the fear in Manny's eyes. The whole incident from start to finish was a long 25 minutes.

We bought a new gas bottle… again. Every time I went to light it and the sudden burst of flames occurred, like when you're lighting a gas grill or oven, I jumped back and my heart would skip a beat. One morning, a week or two later, when I was leaving work, the radio in the van caught on fire. But that's another story.

Radio on fire story

I was in Melbourne working nightshift at a plastics factory. One morning, when I'd finished for the night, I hopped in my van and started 'her' up. I turned my head around to see if all was clear as I reversed out. When I turned my head around to face the front, the whole fuckin' cabin was full of smoke. I couldn't see a thing. Oh great, another fire in the van. Except this time, it was the van itself. Oh shit! In Hollywood, cars blow up really easily, so I flew into panic mode. I didn't want the van blowing up because that would just suck losing the van. But, also, because I was living out of it at the time, it was my home. Oh yeah, and I almost forgot, the most important reason, my girlfriend Manny was fast asleep in the back.

I turned off the engine and quickly ran around to the sliding door to see if I could find something to put the fire out. I shouted to Manny "Wake up!!! There's a fire in the van." There was no chance she was going to get, "Morning, rise and shine", or "Hi honey, I've made you breakfast in bed." I can only imagine what it would be like to be woken up with someone shouting, "Fire."

There was another guy in the car park sitting in his car that had arrived early for his shift and was just getting a few more minutes sleep before he had to start. He told me later he'd opened his eyes to see my van full of smoke, and he wasn't sure if he was dreaming or not.

Manny's not really a morning person, and she stayed in bed, probably still half asleep and not aware of what was going on. I returned to the driver's side with a 3-litre bottle of water to see the smoke clearing. It was then I could see what was burning. The fuckin' radio decided it was going to take up smoking. The wires for the radio weren't connected but were still live. They'd come loose and were touching metal. So, when I started up the van, they started burning and burnt themselves out after a few seconds. So, there was no real danger, no real need to panic, and in the end, I didn't have a good excuse for not making Manny breakfast in bed. I guess we weren't in Hollywood.

Melbourne
3rd December 1999

Before the gas bottle incident our arrival in Melbourne was quite exciting. This was a big deal. I'd heard nothing but how cool Melbourne was ever since I started to take an interest in cool things. It's considered the top spot for the arts, shopping, entertainment, and style, with loads of restaurants, bars, cafés, and nightlife and is often referred to as the cultural capital of Australia. It has many cultural attractions, such as museums and galleries, festivals, public/street art, music, film, and fashion. One of the things I was particularly interested in was Melbourne's highly regarded live music scene. A lot of cool bands came out of Melbourne.

Melbourne has a reputation for being particularly laid back, cool, and relaxed, and it held a lot of mystique for me. I'd heard and seen bits and pieces of it on TV and, now, it was going to be our playground for the foreseeable future. I'd equate it to someone from the country arriving in the big smoke for the first time, excited by the bright lights. We were there to try our luck in the big city, as it were. Plus, we knew a few people there: some acquaintances from The Fringe & Firkin pub in London. but, more importantly, our Empire buddy, Pocket, and his girlfriend, Afra. Another good friend from the London scene, Crazy Dave, was also in town doing the backpacker thing. I believe it was at this point Manny viewed her Australian experience as just starting to get interesting.

We came in from the south. We just followed the signs to the city, and once we hit the outer suburbs, I could see the CBD in the distance and just headed for that. It was like in the Westerns when a stranger wanders into town on his horse taking in all the surroundings. Our eyes were wide open, observing the hive of activity. Sharing the roads with trams was a new experience and took some getting used to. On a few occasions, I almost ran over people hopping off the tram, because I didn't realise I had to stop and give way. Also, the 'hook turn' was a complete novelty: moving to the left when wanting to turn right. Who came up with that idea?

We got to the CBD, parked the van, and then set out on foot. It was a warm Friday afternoon; the end of the working week had arrived, and an air of excitement at the approaching beer o'clock filled the air. Our first heading was for the backpacker's hostel on Franklin St, where Crazy Dave and his girlfriend, Fiona, were staying. The backpackers was a huge complex with a café and travel agency. There were foreigners everywhere and travel posters and literature all around. We got there to find Dave and Fiona were out, but we left a message and then headed to the nearest pub. I remember being excited from that first beer, combined with the vibe we picked up from the backpackers; it felt like we were in the thick of the action again, amongst our own kind. It felt like we'd awakened from our six-month slumber in Canberra, and now, the party was about to get started.

We, later, met up with Dave and Fiona and had a jubilant reunion. They had been in Melbourne for a few weeks and were long-term residents at the hostel. This proved handy for Manny and me. From hanging out with the guys regularly, we got to learn the hostel procedure, and so we were able to sneak in and use the showers frequently. The shower blocks at the beach were another place we took advantage of.

We got to know our way around quite well from driving everywhere. It wasn't until weeks after we arrived we went for a ride on a tram. We became familiar with suburbs I'd heard of many times and got to see them first hand, e.g., Fitzroy, Carlton, Collingwood, Richmond, St Kilda. I wouldn't know them now, but at the time, I knew all the street names of the CBD and in which order they came.

We soon came to establish ideal spots to stay, depending on our circumstances and location. We stayed at quiet parks that had toilets and running water for us to do our cooking and washing up. If at the end of the day, we were in the west, we'd stay down by the bay in Williamstown or Altona. If we were in Clifton Hill, we'd stay nearby in North Fitzroy. If we went to the beach to cool off after a hot day, we had a few places around Port Melbourne we liked. At other times, we just parked wherever we went out drinking and stayed there the night.

During the winter months in Canberra, we'd had some

friendly conversations with Pocket on the phone. He was the cheerful, funny guy we knew from London, and we spoke about us, one day, visiting him in Melbourne. We were happy to travel to Melbourne anyway, but the prospect of seeing Pocket again had been a big motivation in our decision to go there. When we got to Melbourne, though, he was M.I.A. We couldn't reach him on the phone nor at the address we had for him. So, the grand visions we had of going to Melbourne and reviving the wild times we had with Pocket in London never eventuated.

Christmas Day was a scorcher. Manny was really confused about the weather. Being from the Northern Hemisphere, Christmas to her meant cold weather. She had a hard time feeling it was Christmas. Not that that took away any of the enjoyment from our day. We went to the supermarket and bought a cooked chicken, pasta salad, cold beer, and spent the day on the beach. It was a day of firsts for Manny: Christmas in summer, Christmas on the beach, and getting sunburnt on Christmas Day.

For New Year's, we didn't really have anything planned; the lack of money was an issue. Manny had a job as a waitress in Clifton Hill and decided to work at the restaurant. She knocked off at about 11pm, and we caught our very first tram into the CBD. A co-worker and her friend from the restaurant came with us. They were dickheads, so we quickly lost them.

This was the big one. The one we'd all been waiting for, the end of the 1900's and the beginning of the magical, futuristic, year 2000. We headed down to the Yarra River for a good vantage point for the fireworks. Man, the crowds were full on; as expected, there were people everywhere. There was an air of excitement like no other. People were incredibly rambunctious and hysterical. We stood shoulder to shoulder with thousands of others on St Kilda Rd near

Flinders St Station. Federation Square was still being built at that stage. The fireworks were quite impressive, with the launch sites spread out around the Southbank.

All eyes were focused on whether the Y2K bug was going to cause mayhem with computer programs once the date ticked over to midnight. The problem was a result of abbreviating a four-digit year to two digits and possible program errors when the date went from 99 to 00. There were reports of random computer failures around the world, with some websites reporting the date as 01/01/19100. However, there weren't the catastrophic events that had been suggested in some circles of the media. Planes didn't fall out of the sky. The funniest thing to come out of the whole hullaballoo was a joke I received by email. It said: "K-Y Jelly is bringing out a new product for the new millennium. It's called Y2KY and will allow users to stick an extra two digits in their date."

2000

After three months in Melbourne and living in the van, I'd had enough. I wanted to go back to Canberra. The novelty of living in hot, untidy, and cramped conditions had long worn off. Continually living in each other's pockets wasn't helping the relationship either; we often argued with each other. However, Manny wanted to stay. She liked the Melbourne way of life and enjoyed having a job. I put up with it for about another week before we decided to leave.

I felt happier straight away. We didn't head straight home; we took the scenic route, and it felt like we were on holiday again. From Melbourne, we headed south-west and took the Great Ocean Road, one of the world's most scenic drives. The road follows the spectacular coastline, stretching 243km. It winds its way along close to the beach edge and up along breathtaking clifftops, offering a great view of the ocean. It's better to be a passenger on this drive, so you can take in the stunning scenery. As the driver, I had to keep my eye on the windy road.

We did stop at a few places. We went and checked out Bell's Beach to see if it was actually the beach used to portray Bell's Beach in the Hollywood movie, *Point Break*. Looking at it, I thought it was, but I found out later the Bell's Beach scene in the movie was shot on a beach in Oregon, USA. We also stopped to check out the rock groups Loch Ard Gorge, The Grotto, London Bridge, and The Twelve Apostles, except this wasn't a music festival.

Along the Great Ocean Road, there are several well-known limestone and sandstone rock formations, created by the harsh weather conditions and erosion from the ocean. This formed caves in the cliffs, which then became arches, which collapsed, leaving rock stacks up to 45 metres high. Many of the formations have been given names; the most famous of these is The Twelve Apostles. The Twelve Apostles are giant stacks that rise from the ocean around 100 metres offshore. At sunrise and sunset, they offer particularly impressive photo opportunities as they change colour from darkness to a bright yellow in the sun. You should check them out online.

After the Great Ocean Road, we headed north to the Grampians National Park. We found some great little hideaways off the beaten track that were peaceful and relaxing. We would have loved to have continued further into the park, but we were low on petrol and worried about running out of fuel in the middle of nowhere. From the park, we headed north-east and hooked up with the Hume Highway, which would take us most of the way to Canberra.

March 2000

Back in Canberra, we quickly slipped back into our old routine. It was nice to be living with some mod cons again, like running water, a fridge, and a shower. I went back to my previous job at Toll Logistics as a picker/packer, and we were able to get back on our feet again, financially, pretty quickly.

Our old routine of arguing continued, as well, and we both thought it was a good idea we end our relationship. Of course, once we did, the pressure was off, and we got along really well. Manny still had four months available to her on her visa if she wanted. However, when coming to Australia, she'd bought a one year ticket with the return date for the end of March, which she saw no reason to change now. That meant she only had a few weeks left in Australia before she'd be off, and with about ten days to go, we went to Sydney.

I guess it's better late than never, but Manny was able to get in touch with Sue, one of her good Australian friends, whom she knew from Shepherd's Bush and was now in Sydney. We were invited to an engagement party where more people from the Shepherd's Bush circle would be. We went to the engagement party. We walked into the room, and it was like walking into the Fringe & Firkin class of 1997 reunion. It was a real blast, if not somewhat surreal, to see some of the old crowd again. It felt a bit funny seeing them in Sydney when we were so used to seeing them in London. I was so glad I'd had a haircut, so it looked like I'd changed over the years and didn't look like the same old grunge kid I did in '97. I was really happy for Manny that we had this special time with all the old friends before she was due to go home.

The morning of Manny's departure had come. We had to get up rather early, about six-ish, and the plan was to drive to the airport in the van. Along with the usual anxiety of getting to the airport on time, we had two more ingredients added to the mix. The first was the van had been playing up. Some mornings it wouldn't start, not even try to turn over, nothing, dead. And then some mornings, it wasn't uncommon for it to start first go. What would it be today? The second concern was, once we got the van started, which way was it to the airport? We were staying in Lane Cove, 9km north of the Sydney CBD, whilst the airport was in Mascot, 7km south of the CBD. That meant we had to navigate our way through the city during the morning rush hour. Sydney's labyrinth of tunnels and one-way streets are a challenge at the best of times and even more so when you're not familiar with them, like I wasn't. We were able to get a map and some directions to get to the airport in advance. Hopefully, that would be enough to get us there on time.

All preparations had been done. We woke on time, and Manny was all packed. We had the map, and we were ready to go. All we needed now was the van to start and then not to get lost. How fitting our last moments together be a suspenseful, exhilarating endeavour. Were it characteristic of our usual activities, we would have been making the journey off our faces on booze and drugs. Somehow, it just didn't seem appropriate on this occasion. We were going to experience a natural adrenalin rush of euphoria and ecstasy if we pulled this one off. Get lost and miss the flight, and the feelings would lean more to the negative end of the scale and a few drinks might be needed to deal with that 'excitement'.

However, having built the suspense, I can tell you, we got to the airport no problem. The van started, and we didn't get lost. I saw Manny off at the departure gate, and after two intoxicating years (I mean that in every sense of the word), she boarded her flight, and we parted ways. We parted on good terms, and I planned on going back to Europe, one day, so we intended to keep in touch.

I walked back to the van. I felt weird, to say the least. I felt somewhat lost without my partner in crime, and it took some getting used to, to only have to account for myself.

My early days in London, 1997. This was a day out visiting the different sites that feature on the Monopoly board.

My close friend Julia from Germany. We met within a week of me arriving in London and we're still close friends today, over 20 years later. This shot is taken in The Kensington Pub, close to Holland Rd, London.

My Pakistani cricket buddy, Jamal, and I having fun in his flat in Hamburg. We remained friends despite his cricket team-mates saying I had no respect for the game.

My boss at the Shepherd's Bush Empire, Simon, and I pulling faces at the Empire New Year's Eve club night, 1997. We were good mates outside of work, too.

My mate Chris, who I met through Simon, and I working the cloak room at the Empire New Year's Eve club night, 1997. Chris was very kind to me over the years, letting me stay in his flat in Shepherd's Bush whenever I needed a place to stay.

This is my mate, Jim, and I acting like idiots at the Empire New Year's Eve club night, 1997. You can see the weightlifting belt I wore that night. Jim and I were tight mates for so long. I cried when I said goodbye to him when I left London for Australia, 1999.

L—R: Jon from the Eurobus trip; Dave from the Russia trip; Brian from the Eurobus and Russia trips; and myself. Here we are dressed in our factory work clothes. We thought we looked like POWs. Shot taken in Preston, England, 1998.

Shepherd's Bush Green—the park in the west London district of Shepherd's Bush. Shepherd's Bush was my home in London. There was a time in 1997 where I lived, worked and socialised in Shepherd's Bush.

Manny, my French girlfriend 1998—2000. One thing Manny and I connected on when we first hooked up was we both had an imaginative sense of humour when we were high on drugs.

The van Manny and I travelled around Victoria in. On two occasions, we had a fire scare. Once from a gas bottle and the other time when the van radio wiring caught on fire.

2001

A Drunken Odyssey
November 2000

"What's your reason for going to Paris?" asked Darren.

"Sex," I replied.

Surprisingly, Darren the travel consultant was poker-faced and proceeded to check his database for cheap flights. Moments later, he couldn't compose himself any longer and burst out laughing, shaking his head in disbelief.

"That's the first time someone has given the answer sex as their reason for travel."

And on December 5th, I hopped on a plane to London and returned to Shepherd's Bush, my old stomping ground, after 20 months away.

London

"Where the fuck is everyone?"

I caught the Airbus from Heathrow to Shepherd's Bush, with grandiose thoughts that my arrival would be similar to a winning, national, sporting team returning to their home country. Whilst I wasn't expecting a media presence or a ticket tape parade, if I'm honest, I probably was expecting everything to be the same as when I left, the same people, doing the same things in the same places. It was a weird mindset, which I suffered from many times. As I was away living life, travelling to new places, and experiencing new things, part of me envisaged the people and places I left behind to keep going as they were, without changing, developing, or growing, until I got back. Of course, that was never the case.

As the bus drove down Goldhawk Rd, towards Shepherd's Bush Green, the first difference that stood out was my old 'home away from home' was no longer the Fringe & Firkin but now an O'Neill's pub.

I can't remember if I'd told my friends I'd be arriving or if it was my plan to surprise them. I do remember I hadn't arranged any meet up of any kind. It was mid-morning, and I dropped by Holland Rd to see if my old mate from the Empire, Jim, was in. There was no answer at the door. I tried the upstairs neighbour, Jan, and same result. I walked to the Kensington Pub and rang Jim from the public phone outside. There was no answer, and I left a message. I booked a bed for the night at a B & B on Russell Road and thought, whilst I was in the area, I'd drop in and see my Ethiopian mate, Jhone, who worked at Londi's near the Crown & Sceptre, but he wasn't there either. "Where the fuck is everyone?" I started to think everyone had disappeared.

Later in the day, I managed to track down Jim—woohoo—and he invited me to live with him again. Nice one—it was like putting the old band back together. That night, Jim and I met up with Julia at one of our old favourite spots—the pub in Woodstock St, Central London. It was good to be back.

At the time, I had extremely short hair compared to the below-the-shoulder length hair I had when I used to live in London. I didn't like the look of it too much and wore a baseball cap, which meant I was quite unrecognisable to all my friends. I was on the wagon, too, and drank lemon squash when in the pub—another reason not to recognise me. It also meant any of the old dodgy Bush weirdos, whom I didn't want to associate with, didn't recognise me either, so I didn't have to sit and listen to their bullshit. Over the following weeks, I slowly caught up with all my old friends. I felt so thrilled to see them all again and rekindle the friendship.

In the first part of January, Manny came to London to visit for the weekend. I told Jim she was coming over, and I was about to tell him I'd organised a hotel room for her stay, and that I wouldn't be in the flat during that time. As I was telling him, though, I could see the fear come over his face. He was obviously worried about her staying at the flat. So, halfway through telling him, I changed direction and asked him if it would be alright if Manny stayed at the flat whilst she was in town. Oh man, I was in stitches. I laughed so hard. Jim wasn't Manny's biggest fan, and he was shaking his head before I'd even got out the entire question. It was hilarious. Oh, the look on his face. I just couldn't resist teasing him like that.

I met Manny on the Friday afternoon at High St Kensington tube. Here we were, together again, in London, where it all began. We had dinner at a restaurant and then went to the Bushranger pub, where some of the Bush celebrities were drinking: Simon, Jan, Jim, Tom, and Julia. It was a good little get-together and provided a good time for Manny's return visit to the Bush. Julia's brother, Julius, was there too, also on a brief visit, which was pretty cool.

Saturday evening, Manny and I were rather tired, and we could have quite easily spent the evening sitting in our hotel room watching telly. However, we'd agreed to go to the nightclub The Fridge with Julia and Julius, so we dragged our weary asses down to Brixton, where we met up with them. Once we were there, though, Manny and I really got into it. We took half a pill each and started drinking and dancing like we were on drugs—oh, hang on. Julia and Julius are always full of energy on the dance floor and were good fun to dance with. We all had a marvellous time, and afterwards, Manny and I went back to our hotel for some great sex. We started again the next morning, but we were interrupted by the receptionist reminding us we had to check out.

We did a tour of some of our old haunts in Shepherds Bush before we went to the airport. We were late to the airport, and had a stressful dash to the check-in desk, but Manny still made her flight. I kissed her good bye, and we've never seen each other again since.

I spoke to her once or twice on the phone over the next few months but we soon lost touch. Ten years on, in 2011, I spoke to her father, Didier, who said she was doing well. She's now married with two children and living in Lisbon, Portugal ... I think. I couldn't understand very well what Didier was saying in French.

I'm glad we had a memorable last hurrah together. Whenever I think back to our two years together, a big cheesy grin appears on my face. I often wonder what she's up to nowadays.

Towards the end of January, my whole circumstances had changed. With the Christmas/New Year season over, the job I had at Marks & Spencers had finished. This coincided with Jim asking me to move out of his flat. He just wanted his own space; we didn't have a falling out or anything. I went with Julia, who was looking at a bed available in a house in Kensal Rise, whilst I was going to look at one for myself in Queen's Park. The bed at Queen's Park fell through, but there was a second bed available at Kensal Rise, so Julia and I ended up both moving in. With a change of address came a new job, and I scored work in Neasden, for a computer hardware company, Elonex, assembling computers.

My time was now taken up adjusting to my new home life and job. It had been a long time since I'd lived in a share house, and including me and Julia, there were seven people living in the flat ... and I was the only male. I had a lot of fun telling my male friends I lived with six women, and I enjoyed all the acclaim that came with it, but realistically, I thought it was unlikely I'd end up bedding any of the girls.

They all had boyfriends, anyway. I thought if I did, though, I wanted it to be good because word was bound to spread about my performance. However, I knew from experience groups of women living together could be volatile, so I was hoping to play the role of Switzerland in this house of United Nations.

I could only boast about being the sole man in a house of women for two weeks because, after that, one of the women moved out, and an Australian guy and his Puerto Rican girlfriend moved in. The other girls included two Brazilians, a Spaniard, and an English lass. The flat was two levels, had four bedrooms, two bathrooms, a kitchen, and lounge room. I shared a room with Julia and Helen, the English girl. Helen was super friendly. I felt comfortable around her, and, except for a tendency to watch TV whilst others in the room were trying to sleep, she was a good roommate. She was in her early 20's and had a job as a party host/clown/magician for children's parties. She used to practise her routines on me whilst I pretended to be a four-year-old.

Julia on the other hand, what a bitch! I couldn't stand her. Ahhh, just joking. We were close beforehand, but living together brought us even closer together. Amongst the sometimes-hectic activity in the flat, we had each other to turn to when we needed someone to confide in. I remember, one day, I fucked off work and spent the day with Julia in the park talking about anything and everything. We became partners in crime and dressed up in disguise at the farewell bash for our friend Monica, who you might remember I travelled around Europe with for a few weeks back in '98. I dressed up like someone from Spinal Tap. I wore leather pants with a velvet jacket and a long burgundy wig, whilst Julia dressed in a floral shirt and tied her hair up and wore a short wig in the style of a bob. She looked so different; she looked like Velma from Scooby Doo, minus the glasses.

I met a young French guy whilst working at Elonex, who told me of a clinical trial that paid the participants £10,000. This really sparked my interest. I knew of the existence of clinical trials; they were a popular way of earning money amongst the backpacking community. For a few days or weeks, whilst in hospital, it's possible to volunteer as a human guinea pig and partake in new pharmaceutical trials and walk away with a couple of thousand quid in the pocket. Normally, it would take months to save up this amount of money.

The trial the French guy spoke of involved a trainee doctor removing your little toe and then sewing it back on, all in the name of practise and experience for the trainee. I would have done it, but I never came across anyone that had done it or knew of where it was done. It was more of an urban myth than real. But still, volunteering for a trial was something I was going to look into.

Things at home were going well for a while. It was a real party/raver house, and we all went out clubbing a few times together. Helen was a master at spinning poi balls and gave the other girls lessons on how to do it. There was usually someone in the lounge room practicing with the balls.

I got along well with Cristina. She was about 24, from Madrid, and could play guitar; I taught her how to play a few songs. She was quite a cutie, and we both had a soft spot for each other; shame she had a boyfriend—a New Zealander. Oh, what a dent to the pride to lose out to a New Zealander. Not that it was an issue; I had been spending a lot of time with Tessa, anyway. Tessa, you might remember, was someone I met back at Christmas time of '97. She's a good friend of Jan who lived upstairs from Jim. The two of us regularly mixed in the same circles and our friendship was on an acquaintance level. However, at Monica's farewell a few weeks earlier, we had a fun time together and at the end of the night we went home together. It must have been my Spinal Tap look that attracted her to me. Hahaha

We realised that despite having spent all that time in each other's company over the years, we didn't know that much about each other. That changed as we spent a great deal of time together. In early 2001, Tessa was 42 (I was 26). She was English but originally born in Tanzania, one of two identical twin girls. She was short, slim with long brown hair. She's quite a caring, gentle person with an open mind and delightful sense of humour.

In Kensal Rise, the house group dynamics were continually changing. The flat was one of hundreds like it around London—a share house with lots of transient travellers coming and going. At the time, though, there were only people coming. A few of the girls' boyfriends moved back in after having been travelling for a while, and the flat became a predominantly Latino clique, one Julia and I didn't feel part of. I got along with them all individually, in particularly the girls, but, as a group they were closed off to everyone else. Add this to my social fear and insecurities, I didn't always feel at home, in my own home. I often avoided going home after work and spent my weekends with Tessa.

Julia wasn't a happy camper either, and relations between her and the Brazilian girls were tense—we referred to them as 'The Brazilian bitches'. She picked up a job working behind the bar at the Frog & Firkin in Ladbroke Grove, and we both hung out there a lot. There were quite a lot of interesting locals there, and Julia got quite a lot of male attention, which she enjoyed. The Frog was a great escape for Julia, and she acquired a large new circle of friends.

By the end of February, the house had swollen to 20 people. A group of mainly Australian surfers had returned from a trip away and were dossing on all available space around the flat. They were only there for a week or two, though, thankfully.

I didn't see the point of hanging around in London where I'd been there, done that, so I decided to go to Scotland for a while. A couple of days before I left, when meeting Tessa in Convent Garden for a few drinks, I noticed I didn't have my glasses. There was no sign of them at the flat, and they weren't handed in at the bus 'lost and found' so it was a mystery. It meant the only way I could see was with my prescription sunglasses, which was fine during the day, but at night, I was lost.

16th March 2001

I arrived in Edinburgh at about 8 pm. I knew the address of the hostel I'd booked, but I didn't know how to get there. I knew it was across the road from the castle, but where was the castle? At night, every little church, castle or supermarket is lit up, and without my glasses, I didn't know the difference between a place of worship and a place of war. Solution? Cab. Only £2.28, too; not bad. Safely checked in at the hostel, I went to the toilet/shower block on my floor to which there was only one door. I expected, after this door, there would be another two doors—male and female. But after the first door, I was already in the toilet and shower block and the place was full of girls. What the fuck? Where's the men's? The girls didn't bat an eyelid upon seeing me. "Mmmmmm" I thought. A closer inspection of the fine print on the door revealed they were unisex toilets. It would be another week before I had a new pair of glasses.

I was staying at Castle Rock Hostel, which was huge; it was once a hospital, apparently. It was in the perfect location, right in the Old Town close to the Royal Mile, the main thoroughfare, and the nightlife of the Grassmarket and Cowgate, and only a stone's throw away from the famous Edinburgh Castle. When I checked in, the receptionist took one look at me and said, "I'll put you in the Virgin room." I didn't know whether to be offended or not. Was I being labelled a virgin or was I being given the royal treatment and placed in a room full of young, subservient, virgin women? Well, it wasn't the latter. The jury's still out as to whether it was the former. All the rooms in the hostel had a name, and within each room, all the beds had names related to the room name. I was in The Virgin Room and my bed was Records. The other beds in the room were Airlines, Jesus, Madonna, Brooke Shields, Cliff Richard, Sandra Dee, and Immaculate Conception. The room was for males only.

My first full day in Scotland and it was, literally, four seasons in one day—there was sun, rain, snow, and wind. In the morning, I did a hop-on, hop-off bus tour around the city and got the low down on Edinburgh's sordid history, which was captivating. Edinburgh was once rife with grave robbers, stealing the corpses to make money from the internal organs.

The first couple of days were quite lonely for me. The hostel was full of Aussies, Americans, and Canadians, mainly. I looked to meet people, but I didn't find the opportunity or have the nerve. The long-time residents all seemed to have their own little groups and weren't advertising for newcomers. As a result, I spent those first few days alone just wandering the city and sitting in pubs writing post cards. It was dejecting going to bed early and being the first 'Virgin' to call it a night. On more than one occasion, I went to bed just as another guy was getting up.

However, it wasn't all self-pity; early to bed meant early to rise. Every morning was sunny, and I would look out the bedroom window over at the castle, which always put a smile on my face. Usually, by the end of the day, it was cold and snowing, which I loved. There was something enchanting about walking the cobblestoned streets at night, whilst it was snowing, in a city that dated back to medieval times.

On the night of day four, things really shifted for me. I decided to go on a walking tour that claimed to visit a cemetery with poltergeist activity. I met Dave the local guide. He was an entertaining guy, late 20's, with short, spikey, dark hair and his mannerisms reminded me of my former Empire boss, Simon. I also met a guy from Kansas, whose name was Joe. He was tall, slim with ginger hair. He was with his brother, Jake, and their mate, H. They were staying at Castle Rock, as well. They were really friendly dudes.

The tour, with roughly 20 people, took us to various locations around the Old Town. Dave acted out the many stories about Scottish history, all the while, talking up the frightening experience of the cemetery tomb still to come. The tour culminated in a visit to the Greyfriars Cemetery, which was said to be the haunt (pun intended) of the Mackenzie Poltergeist, the restless spirit of Bloody George Mackenzie buried there in 1691.

Dave told us stories of other tours where people had felt strange sensations whilst in the tomb, such as feeling suddenly cold, whilst others experienced injuries such as bruises and cuts that they had no recollection of getting. He told us of a little boy who was crying and his mother looked at him to see scratch marks down his face, also, of a big, tough Australian rugby player being scared shitless, and of one guy fainting, prompting everyone else to run out of the tomb screaming. The cemetery has featured on the television show *Scariest Places on Earth*.

Sir George Mackenzie, whom the Mackenzie Poltergeist is named after, was the governor of the prison in the 1600's and persecuted the Scots Presbyterians, known as Covenanters who refused the King's orders to change religion. His nickname of Bloody Mackenzie came from the sheer delight he took in sentencing the Covenanters to hang from the gallows. Mackenzie wasn't actually buried within the prison grounds but most of the paranormal activity has occurred there—the final resting place of many of his victims. The poltergeist only started in 1998 when a homeless man broke into and ransacked Mackenzie's tomb in the Greyfriars Cemetery. Since then, the Mackenzie poltergeist has wreaked fear and harm, and over 500 ghostly attacks have been reported by those visiting the tomb.

When we reached the gates of Greyfriars Cemetery, Dave gave everyone the option of pulling out. Some girls from Texas decided they weren't going any further and left. We walked through the cemetery and saw a few graves with metal grates over them to prevent grave robbers. We walked through to the locked gate of the Covenanters Prison. Dave's tour company was the only tour group allowed access to this part of the cemetery.

We walked to a tomb towards the back of the yard, and I was a little apprehensive. Dave lead us into the tomb, which was the size of a large bedroom. We all huddled together in suspense. I was standing at the back of the tomb, the furthest point from the tomb entrance. Dave was whispering, checking-in with everyone to see if anyone was feeling anything out of the ordinary.

"AAAARRRGGGHHHHHH!"

All of a sudden, people started to scream. The unexpected shouting caused me to jump with fright. Being at the back, I hadn't seen a guy come screaming into the tomb wearing a scary mask. Apparently, he was the manager of the tour company. For a few seconds, I thought some real paranormal shit was going down.

After we all settled down and checked our pants, we headed to the pub outside the cemetery gates for a few calming drinks. No one found any unexplained cuts or bruises on their bodies. After a while, it was just the Kansas lads and me, talking with Dave, and we were so intrigued by the story of the poltergeist that Dave took us into the cemetery again. We were still on edge, despite having had a few beers, but, unfortunately, there was no sign of the poltergeist this night. I say unfortunately because I was very keen to experience some supernatural activity.

I met up with the Kansas lads again late the next day in the hostel common room. This was the beginning of my social circle opening up and my drinking skyrocketing. Joe Kansas introduced me to some guys who had just arrived at the hostel. I met Stewy, from Ottawa, Canada. He was a truly genuine guy. He had a great sense of humour, was a big rugby fan, and loved a drink.

"Fuckin' hell, it's Harry Connick Jr."

Well, actually, no, it wasn't, but Adam from Texas sure looked and sounded like him. He was tall and slim and even had the same dangly, styled fringe as Harry. And, oh man, was he brash! He was one of those stereotypical Americans, who was cocky, arrogant, and ignorant. I really liked Joe Kansas; he wasn't the stereotype, and actually, he took the piss out of Adam and quickly disassociated himself from the Texan.

Joe was pumped and said he was going on the poltergeist tour again. It hadn't occurred to me to do it again. It was only £5; "Count me in." I was really hooked on the possibility of experiencing the ghostly phenomenon, and in fact, we all went: the Kansas trio, Stewy, Texas, and me.

Tonight, we had a different tour guide. Her name was Cara; she was gorgeous, think Katie Melua but with tidier hair. She gave a good tour and did well to put up with our Texan friend. The vibe was calmer on this tour and, at times, even funny, thanks to the wisecracks of Stewy and Texas. It was a particularly cold night, and Cara said, "Let's keep moving so we warm up."

Stewy was like, "I'm from Ottawa. This is like a balmy, spring evening for me."

Cara was playing out an old historic story with a volunteer from the group as she feigned to chop off the person's finger. Texas said, "If she cuts off his finger, this'll be worth the five quid." We all cracked up. The solemn moment had been burst. We went to the tomb in the cemetery again, and again, there was no poltergeist action. This time, though, I was ready for the tour manager's scary prank.

Like the previous night, we finished in the pub. We all made sure to sit at the same table as Cara. Texas was loud and obnoxious, which we could see was annoying Cara, but she handled it well. Texas left and then we all started to bag him out, just so Cara knew he wasn't our friend and so she knew she was more than welcome to bag him out, too.

Group email: Wednesday 21st March

Greetings.

I can't stop going to a haunted cemetery every night to see if I can be attacked by a poltergeist. So far, no luck. But that does mean, at least, no stains to clean out of my pants.

On Wednesday, the Kansas trio left for a three-day bus tour around the Highlands. They'd be back for one more night after the tour had finished. I went on the walking tour again, this time solo. Dave was the guide again, and it was another eerie night. Dave was a skilled guide and he was able to build up the suspense better than Cara. It was said the poltergeist can sense fear and that's when it strikes. I didn't know how true that was, but Dave had had more freaky shit happen on his tour than any other guide, and it might have been for that reason.

When we got to the tomb, I made sure I was the first at the entrance. I wanted to take a photo of inside the chamber to see if any weird apparitions showed up in the photo once it was developed. I quickly took the photo and the flash went off, causing some people to cry out in fright. Disappointingly, there was no evidence of an unfriendly entity (there was no evidence of anything supernatural in the photo either when I got it developed). However, as an experiment, Dave said he was going to go back later and put a toy ball in the tomb to see if it would be in the same place the next night. I expressed I was interested in returning to see the results, and Dave said I could go on the tour for free—sweet.

Thursday night I was at it again, walking the trail of terror to the haunted cemetery. I went with a couple of cans, so I'd be a bit drunk and feeling brave. That way, the poltergeist would attack someone else, because I wouldn't be showing fear. "Anyway, it should know me by now," I thought. Before we got there, Dave said he'd put the ball somewhere in the middle of the tomb. We arrived to find the ball right in the centre, but then, it may just have rolled there. Dave wasn't sure if that was the exact spot he'd left it. So, the experiment didn't show anything.

The next couple of days were a lot of fun. I got to know many of the other guests at the hostel. A couple of times, we went out clubbing as a large group and had a lot of fun. I made friends with some of the other lads in the Virgin room. I drank like a man possessed—perhaps, the poltergeist *had* affected me—and I usually started drinking from the moment I woke up.

Friday was a cause for celebration. I went to the opticians and picked up my new pair of glasses. I could see again. YIPPEE! It hadn't exactly been sunglasses weather, so I'd been operating without full strength vision for the last nine days. I actually had two new pairs. It was a 2-for-1 offer,

Sunday, a whole gang of us from the hostel went out to The Globe, a bar hosting an open mic night. Having been drinking all day, and all the other days, I suddenly didn't feel well. I left the pub, and I was all over the place. I was hardly able to walk, and I threw up when I made it back to the hostel.

I woke the next morning feeling like shit. I thought it was time to take a break from the booze. I had been at it non-stop for a good while. Water became my drink of choice, which raised a few eyebrows in the hostel from those that knew me. A few of them had never seen me without a beer in my hand.

I went to bed early as I was tired and still felt a bit rough. But, I didn't get much sleep at all. I hadn't noticed before how uncomfortable the bed was; I usually passed out quickly from being so drunk. When on my back, no matter how I lay, my lower back hurt, and for some reason, I really felt the cold this night. The window in the room was always open, because of Mr. Virgin Airlines, even when it was cold and snowing. He amazed me by sleeping without a shirt on, and if the window was closed when he was going to bed, rather than be concerned that obviously someone might be cold, he would open it again. I can only guess he didn't feel the cold or maybe he needed the fresh air to escape the smell of eight pairs of smelly socks. Normally, I'd be dead to the world, and it wouldn't worry me, but this night, when he came in and threw the window wide open, I explained to him I wasn't well and asked if we could have the window closed tonight. He compromised and lowered the window halfway. Better than nothing, I guess. I put more clothes on, but that didn't help.

It took me three days to recover. They weren't my three

favourite days. Each night, I was freezing cold, no matter how much clothing I wore or blankets I had. My sleep was awfully unsettled, and I had full-on dreams with hallucinations. At one point, my bed was full of spiders. Often, the dreams were quite frightening as someone or something would threaten to attack me. I was often woken by my own groans. I can only imagine what the other Virgins thought if they heard me.

Weird? Well, actually, I'd just experienced my first full scale horrors. The 'horrors' is a term to describe alcohol withdrawals. The shakes, night sweats, nightmares, a fried brain, totally wired 24/7, I had them all. The pains in my back, I came to realise, were my kidneys crying out. The dreams seemed so real because the scene for the dream often started in the bed I was sleeping in.

Sleep was made all the more difficult, too, by the fact one of the Virgins was a snoring machine. God, he was loud. And who the fuck called it the Virgin Room? During these nights, Mr Virgin Airlines, again, indulged in some of the old 'in and out' with an American lass. How's a man meant to sleep when he can hear a woman having an orgasm?

At the end of the week, feeling a lot better, I headed off on a MacBackpackers tour around the Highlands. The tour was by bus, for five nights, stopping off at various sites along the way. The pickup point was conveniently at Castle Rock. Our tour guide for today was a guy by the name of Osh. He was quite a character. From what I understood, usually the driver and tour guide were one and the same, but Osh had his own driver, which left him free to put on an entertaining show ... and so he could drink.

He did put on a good show, too, and I'm not talking about the show under his kilt. Although, we did catch a glimpse of that during a photo op when Osh sat down with his legs spread, inadvertently showing us all his 'Scottish caber'. He was extremely passionate and funny and the genuine article. Unlike the Scots who get their kilt out only on formal occasions, Osh was wearing a well-worn, full-length number in which the upper half could be worn as a cloak draped over the shoulder or brought up over the head as a hood. He gave us a lesson in Scottish history and an education on Elvis. We were a group of about ten, and Osh had us singing Elvis songs and doing various actions along to the music.

We had a stop at a whisky distillery, which included a free dram. Apparently, we were supposed to sip it and savour the flavour. Woops. I downed it in one. As was customary on all the tours, a bottle of whiskey was passed around the bus to assist in creating a lively, jovial atmosphere. The distillery must have given us a taste for it, because one bottle wasn't enough. We had to stop off and get some more. Osh said he hadn't encountered needing more than one bottle before. Our group was a mix of Brits, Aussies, and Kiwis, and mainly females. But surprisingly, the girls were into the whiskey just as much as the guys. One English guy was into it a bit too much and became rather obnoxious. Even his mate was displeased with him, as was the rest of the bus. We went through six bottles by the time we arrived at Inverness, the location for our first stop-over. We checked-in to the hostel and then all went to the pub.

This trip was where I regained my drinking legs. Having spent the previous four days detoxing, I was now in good shape. There was some live music at the pub, and I got up and danced with Rachel, a Kiwi lass from our group. We ended up having a highland fling, if you know what I mean.

Next day, the tour headed for the Isle of Skye. Our obnoxious English passenger was quiet and sheepish today. The countryside was littered with beautiful scenery and awe-inspiring mountains. Osh told us the history and folklore of the different surroundings we passed through. We stopped at Loch Ness to have a look around. I was surprised at how big the loch was; it's about 52km2. I didn't see a monster anywhere, but I did see some freaks swimming. It was cold enough out of the water; it must have been freezing in it. I guess, as some sort of badge of honour, they can now say they have swum in Loch Ness. We checked out a few castles along the way, including *Eilean Donan* Castle, which features in the movie *Highlander*.

The Isle of Skye, part of the Inner Hebrides, was beautiful. We stayed there for two nights and went on a tour around the island with one of the locals. She told us stories of fairies and myths. One picturesque area was said to be protected by fairies, and if anyone were to take anything from the area, they would be cursed. Our guide told us of a girl who dismissed the story as that of legend and took a small shiny rock from the area back home with her. Over the following months, she lost her job, lost her boyfriend, and suffered other instances of misfortune. She wrapped the rock up and posted it back to the island with a note explaining what had happened and from where she took the rock.

Other than St Petersburg, in Russia, this was the most northern I'd ever been, and although it was only March, it didn't get dark until quite late. The weather was cloudy with constant drizzle, but I liked it like that. It's how I imagined the Highlands to be—the majestic mountains surrounded by cloud and mist.

The drizzle continued at our next stop in Fort William, near Ben Nevis. Ben Nevis is the highest mountain in the British Isles, so quite naturally, I decided to climb to the top. HA, fuck that for a laugh. With the weather so poor and the summit at 1,344 metres, I opted for a walk around the base of the mountain. Even that was considered idiotic in the persistent rain. Rachel and I were the only two from our group to do it. There were plenty of stories of people having to be rescued from the mountain after becoming disorientated from bad weather moving in. One such guy, against all advice, went up the mountain in bad weather and had to be rescued. Once back down, he realised he had left his mobile phone up on the mountain, so he went back up to get it and had to be rescued again.

Instead of eating out at the pub, I joined Rachel and her sister, Rebecca, in buying some food at the supermarket and cooking dinner at the hostel. I helped in the cooking process with some stirring and serving. This turned out to be the only occasion in the whole nine months from January to September 2001 I did any cooking. The rest of the time I got take away, or someone else cooked.

The next leg was headed south to Oban, and along the way, we stopped off at Glen Coe. Glen Coe is a large spacious valley with spectacular scenery of the surrounding mountains. It was easy to feel insignificant in the large vastness of the landscape. On a dark, cold, windy night, I imagine it would be possible to feel like you're the only person on the planet.

On this leg to Oban, we had a different driver, who was also our guide. There were quite a lot more people on the bus, as well, who had come from the Isle of Skye and weren't stopping in Fort William. As we were driving along, the driver played a session of 'getting to know you'. Unaware of what the passengers who had travelled through from Skye had said, when I was asked what my favourite film was, I thought I was choosing a random good movie when I answered, "*The Shawshank Redemption.*"

Everyone let out a loud moan. Apparently, I was like the eighth person to say *The Shawshank Redemption*. I was really embarrassed and decided from then on nothing like that would ever happen again. I decided to choose an unlikely film to be my favourite, one that no one else was likely to choose. So, from that moment, and still to this day, whenever I'm asked what my favourite film is, I say *From Dusk till Dawn*. Fortunately, I do like the film. I just didn't choose it because I thought no one else is likely to confess to it being their favourite. I love the genre shift the film makes halfway through, leaving the viewer thinking, "WTF?"

In Oban, we had dinner in the pub as a group. The tour guide spoke about the long-time residents of Castle Rock Hostel, in Edinburgh, being generally aloof and unwelcoming to newcomers and, apparently, it was a point of contention at the hostel. I didn't feel so inept socially after that, knowing it wasn't just me that found the hostel to be cliquey.

Oban also involved a run-in with the police. It happens sometimes. A Kiwi guy from the tour and I met some locals in the pub. When the pub closed and everyone else from the tour went back to the hostel, we went with the locals on to another pub.

At 1:50am, Kiwi guy and I realised we had ten minutes to get back before the hostel closed its doors for the night. We ran but still arrived too late. We attempted to climb a roof of a neighbouring building so we could get in through the window of the hostel, but we were stopped by a passing policeman. He was pretty cool about it. He knocked on the back door of the hostel until someone woke up and let us in. It was the manageress, and she wasn't too happy to be woken up, but everyone saw the funny side the next day. All except Rachel and her sister, Rebecca, who was Kiwi guy's travel partner. Rachel avoided me during the day, until we got to Sterling, which was her stop, and we said good bye.

I was having a good day; I was drinking whiskey. Looking back, I think I was the obnoxious passenger on the bus this time. When we got back to Edinburgh, I was in need of a little lie down.

5th April onwards

After three weeks in Scotland, I returned briefly to London and the Kensal Rise flat. I was excited to see Julia again, but no more than she was. She was overjoyed to have me back. Things still weren't great for her at the flat, but it wasn't all bad. An Aussie lad, called Liam, was now staying in the house. Julia and Liam had started a romance, so now, she didn't feel so ganged up on anymore. She was also having a great time being part of the Frog & Firkin family and mixing with all the characters of the pub.

I managed to organise a screening for a medical trial in Belfast, Northern Ireland. It was my hope I'd be accepted on to the trial, and with the money, I could fulfil my long-held dream to travel south into the Republic. At the time I didn't have my passport. Back in February, I applied to the Immigration Office for an extension on my four year ancestry visa. The official line was that the application process would take six to eight weeks so I was still waiting to get my passport back. This meant I was confined to the UK. However, I was sure I'd be able to enter Ireland if I travelled overland from Northern Ireland.

May 2001

In Belfast, I stayed at the Ark Hostel near the architecturally impressive Queen's University. The hostel was the taxi driver's suggestion when I got off the ferry. It was a nice little place, converted from a house. Saturday was the beginning of my abstinence from alcohol, in readiness for my screening in two weeks time and for my own good. I stayed in Saturday night and watched *The Fugitive* on TV, whilst everyone else in the hostel went out.

Sunday, I went on a black taxi tour of west Belfast and

learnt about the Troubles. The Troubles is the commonly used term to describe the 30 year period of conflict in Northern Ireland between loyalists (predominantly Protestants) who want Northern Ireland to remain part of the UK, and republicans (predominantly Catholics) who want Northern Ireland to leave the UK to form a united Ireland. The tour took in the Falls Road in Catholic territory, and the Shankill Road in Protestant territory. West Belfast was the scene for a lot of the violence that occurred during the conflict. We stopped to see the scores of elaborate murals, memorials, and a 5+ metre high wall, known as The Peace Line, dividing the two neighbourhoods.

I found Belfast to be quite safe. The city centre was free of trouble; it was just certain neighbourhoods one needed to avoid, and it seemed to me the different factions fought amongst themselves more than against each other. Having said that, about a week after I arrived, three Australian tourists found themselves in the wrong place at the wrong time. They were walking through east Belfast, close to the main city railway station, during a time of tension between nationalist and loyalist residents, and they were attacked by a group of about 20 youths with iron bars. One of the three was in serious condition from an ear injury and required plastic surgery. I'd heard one of them was on the phone to his father back in Australia at the time of the attack. Can you imagine the concerned father talking to his son in Belfast and his son assuring him everything is OK, that Belfast isn't as bad as it used to be, it's quite safe now, only to be set upon by a gang of youths as he's on the phone?

As I was going to be in town for a while, I moved to a cheaper hostel. The Linen House had dorm beds available for £6/night. This hostel was a lot larger and located in the city centre. I spent my days going to the library, reading books, and writing in my diary. At night, I watched TV in the hostel basement and met the other interesting guests. Life was pretty cruisey for me at this time. I just needed to stay healthy, so I could pass the medical screening and get accepted for the trial. Taking part came with a long list of what to avoid in the days prior to the medical. This included alcohol, recreational drugs, certain medications, and any food or beverages containing caffeine, such as tea, coffee, cola, cocoa, and chocolate. Also, strenuous exercise was to be avoided, and I think I had to fast for eight hours beforehand. Poppy seeds were also on the list, as they often show up in a drug test as opiates, resulting in exclusion from the study. Grapefruit and grapefruit juice were no-nos as they have the potential to interact with numerous drugs, thus producing inconclusive test results.

15th–16th May

The day of the medical screening had arrived. Also arriving was a friend of mine from London, Alberto, who I met whilst working at Marks & Spencer earlier in the year. Alberto, originally from Asturias in Spain, was in his early 30's and living in London with his South African wife. He had a good sense of humour, and we got along really well. He and his wife, Storm-lee, had flown up from London to take part in the screening. Both had partaken in medical trials before, but never in Belfast. As for me, I had heard of medical trials before, but had never done one.

The screening process wasn't too taxing. I didn't have to strip and cough as a doctor held my balls. The first part involved reading information about the drug being trialled, the possible side-effects, the diet restrictions, the dates involved, the number of volunteers needed, and the monetary compensation once the trial was completed. I had to fill out a medical history and sign a consent form that all the information I'd provided was correct.

For this study, the new pharmaceutical to be trialled was cold decongestion medication taken in tablet form. The possible side-effects were things like headache, nausea, vomiting etc. If successful, I'd be in the clinic for five days, then released for five days and then return to the clinic for a further five days—ten days all up for a nice little cheque of £1500. For this study, they required 15 men and 15 women.

The payment for a medical trial is compensation for your time during the study. It's not 'danger money'. Signing consent to participate doesn't waiver your right to take action should something go wrong. I thought it was unlikely something would go wrong, and besides, the study was being conducted under controlled, supervised conditions in a hospital. Should I become ill, I'd already be under medical supervision. It's not as if I had any regard for my health all the times I necked ecstasy pills. Why would this bother me? I didn't see this as a risk at all.

I was more worried about concealing my tremor disorder. I could have disclosed it, but I thought it might exclude me from the study, if not this one, then other ones in the future. I was quite calm about it, though. Having been off the booze for several days, my nervous condition was in good condition. I gave a blood sample, had an ECG test, an examination by the doctor, and gave a urine sample. The urine sample was interesting. It wasn't just a case of pissing in a cup. No. I was required to give a mid-stream sample. The beginning and the end of the stream is the dirtiest, so I had to piss in the toilet, then quickly stop and go in the cup, then stop and shift back to the toilet for the remainder. I was particularly grateful my hands weren't shaking during this process.

All done, and Alberto, Storm-lee, and I went to the pub for lunch. They were both a bit dejected about the selection process for the trial. The next day, at 3:30pm, we had to ring the clinic to get our results for the medical examination, and like some competition on a radio station, the first 15 healthy callers of each gender would be accepted. Alberto and Storm-lee hadn't experienced this before at any of the clinics in London. Their experience was, if you passed the screening, then generally you were accepted on to the study. They weren't too optimistic about our chances. My attitude was, "We'll see what happens." They'd forked out money for return flights from London, just to be at the screening. It would be an expensive exercise if they weren't to get on to the trial. To add a bit of drama to the mix, one provision of the phone-in competition was that someone could ring in on your behalf. So, if any of us managed to get through, we could give the names of all three of us. It also meant you could have family and friends ring up on your behalf. There was no telling how many people would be trying to ring at 3:30.

Fast forward to the next day and the time came for the ring-in. I started ringing three minutes early. I figured it was worth a try. I was met with an engaged signal, but I put that down to it not being 3:30 yet. I kept ringing and after a few attempts, I got a ringing signal. At the check-up, the nurse said, if no one answers after four rings, that means it's engaged. I heard four rings and I thought about hanging up, but I decided, fuck it; it can't hurt to keep it ringing. On about the sixth ring, someone answered.

I gave mine, Alberto, and Stormy's ID number. I was informed we had all passed our medical and, consequently, were now on the study. Woohoo! I tried to phone the others in London, but their line was engaged. I guessed they were still trying to ring the competition line. It was harder to get through to them than it was to the clinic. They had all but given up by the time I got through to them. They were well happy when I told them we'd made it on.

The study didn't begin until the 27th, another eleven days away. I thought it was going to be a long wait until then. I wasn't sure how I was going to fill the time. I even considered going to the coast and staying in Port Rush for a while. This would be a completely different book if I had, for if I had, it's unlikely I would have ever met Crazy Horse Invincible.

17th May–26th May 2001

I had met a good bunch of people in the Linen House: Phil and Astra, an Australian couple; Kiwi Andrew, Spanish Andreas, Irish Rob, staff members Basel and Eileen, a South African couple, Chrissie and Kerrie, an English couple. But my Belfast experience changed completely the day I walked into the hostel and met a new guest. I'd actually seen this guy around the hostel the day before and my first impression was, "Gee, he takes a long time in the bathroom of a morning." On this occasion, he was sitting down, eating a plate of spaghetti bolognaise. I remarked, "That looks nice."

He replied, "There's more in the pot if you want some."

"Yeah, I think I will. Thanks for that."

I helped myself to a plate and got stuck into the spaghetti bolognaise. It tasted oh so good. I offered to do the washing up, and that's how I met Crazy Horse. Of course, his name was Jeremy Brown (not real name) at the time, and the scenario of him cooking spaghetti bolognaise and me doing the washing up continued for many years to come.

We got chatting in the kitchen about our respective situations. It turned out he was also doing a medical trial at Harris (name of clinic, also known as MDS) in an upcoming study. It was a different one to mine but would be on at around the same time. At some point, Crazy suggested we go to the Tavern next door for a pint. I thought, why not. So, over a pint or two, we got to know each other better.

Crazy Horse was tall and slim with dark hair and a strong English accent. Originally from Redcar in the north-east of England, he was in Belfast on a break from his studies and work in north London. He'd been to Belfast many times before and was quite knowledgeable on the history of the Troubles. He was fascinated by all British history. We hit it off by telling each other funny anecdotes of our travels and drinking careers. He's highly intelligent and has a playful sense of humour. I'd liken his character to that of the Australian radio personality, Hamish Blake. He's also very caring to people he likes.

And from this couple of drinks stemmed a bender which was to last the whole week. The Tavern became our regular morning drinking hole, and we invited anyone from the hostel who was willing to come along. It would often be our last point of call at night too, to buy a carry-out for some partying in the hostel TV room. The Tavern was a small place of Catholic persuasion and had some genuinely friendly staff and regulars in there. It didn't look so friendly on the outside, with a cage door at the entrance. To get in, you had to be buzzed in by the bar person, who could see you on their surveillance cameras. Apparently, they had a bit of trouble in the past with the wrong crowd coming in and causing trouble.

We were learning more and more about each other. I was learning a new vocabulary of slang words from Crazy Horse, whilst he learnt through my constant trips to the dunny, my bladder is piss-weak. We each learnt what the other one likes to drink. Crazy Horse drank Guinness and I drank lager, which, in this part of the world, was either Carlsberg or Tennent's. Quite often, we'd have a chaser, as well. Crazy liked to drink Pernod and lemonade, which I thought smelt disgusting. It had a strong liquorice flavour, which almost made me sick on occasions, and I drank Southern Comfort and coke, which Crazy Horse was fine with, but it's certainly caused plenty of people to be sick in its time. We had this weird drinking toast we used to say that just developed naturally:

Crazy: Cheers
Me: Up yours
Crazy: Get fucked
Me: Cheers

Having been to Belfast before and knowing the ins and outs of the conflict and thus knowing what to say, what not to say, which areas of town to say what, and what one could and could not say to whom, meant Crazy Horse felt confident in the company of anyone in any area of town. He took me to a few pubs on the Shankill Road he'd been to before. I met some full-on people in those places—extremely passionate about their cause. We ended up drinking with some of the young lads of the lower Shankill just on a vacant lot. They were all friendly, and we had a good time. I thought, "Isn't life interesting." Earlier that month, I was on a black taxi tour of this very area and the driver said he didn't want to stop because it was a bit dangerous, and here I was drinking in the very same spot with some of the local residents.

One thing about Belfast I wasn't a big fan of was having to watch what I said. This is just my experience, my feelings on the subject, but, drinking in both nationalist and loyalist pubs, I had to be mindful of what I said, depending on whom I was speaking to and in which pub I was in. I didn't want to mention I had a Catholic upbringing, for example, when I was hanging out on the Shankill, or mention I spent time on the Shankill when drinking in the Tavern. Being mindful of what you're saying, when you're boozed up, isn't the easiest thing to do.

27th May–June 10th, 2001

On the day of check-in for the medical trial, I was a wee bit anxious, more through fear of the unknown than worrying about what effects the drug would have on me, if any. Alberto and Stormy arrived and met me at the Linen House,

We made the walk up Lisburn Road to the clinic. It was like the march of destiny. There were a number of small groups of people walking up the road with overnight bags, obviously going to Harris. We walked inside, went upstairs, and joined the queue to have our bags searched and to receive wrist bands. We gave a urine sample and then chose a bed.

The set-up was an all in one large, long room. At one end, the entrance, there were lounges, a TV, tables and chairs, and a pool table. At the other end were small cubicles with two beds in each. The toilets and showers were off the main room, and the dining room and kitchen were upstairs.

There were some attractive women on the trial and some particularly attractive nurses, indeed. Most people were from Belfast, but there were also some from Dublin, Scotland, Australia, New Zealand, Canada, Poland, Spain, and South Africa. The next five days were filled with blood draws, urine samples, being dosed, watching movies, playing pool, listening to my Walkman, playing chess, and chatting with people.

For meal times, we went upstairs to eat dodgy hospital food, including some things I can't stand, like tomatoes, bananas, and milk. Everyone was given the same food, and we all had to eat everything that was on our plate, so any differences in our test results couldn't be put down to having different diets. The kitchen staff, however, did give the males larger servings than the females. Some of the lads found they were still hungry after having eaten everything, but I struggled to get through mine. Our medication contained pseudoephedrine, which can be used as a stimulant to increase one's state of alertness. Thankfully, I didn't have any trouble sleeping, but it did result in me having a loss of appetite. At times, I had to pass food to Stormy when the staff weren't looking because I just couldn't eat anymore.

When we took the medication for the first time, there was a group of suits in the small dosing room watching, along with the patient and nurse. I was nervous about my shaking, which just made me shake even more. As I placed the pill in my mouth and then took the cup of water from the nurse and held it to my mouth, my hand was really trembling. God knows what the suits were thinking when they saw me shake like that; none of them said anything. One of the nurses comforted me by saying something along the lines of, "There's a lot of pressure when people are watching, isn't there?" At a later dose, I told the nurse I don't like hospitals, and that's why I was nervous. By the second or third day, I was a lot calmer, and it was no problem taking the medication. Of course, the suits were no longer hanging around by then. In the first week of the study, I was in the group of patients who were dosed four times a day, including one dose at 2am. We were a dazed and confused lot queuing up at 2am, I tell you. On Friday, we had 22 blood draws. We started at 8am, and every half hour, we sat down and the nurse stuck a needle in our arm and took some blood. After a while, it didn't hurt at all.

There were some really likeable people amongst the group. The staff were complimentary about us, too, saying we were a well-behaved group. This was put down to the fact there were women on the trial. Quite often, the groups are all male, which apparently, can get quite rowdy. I became friends with a guy called Kenny. He was from the Belfast area and looked like a Caucasian Enrique Iglesias. He was quite intelligent and funny and had a kind nature. We played each other at chess and discussed the finer points of health and the supernatural.

Along the same lines, I got to know Stormy a lot better, too. She was a warm and cheerful person and used the spare time available to learn how to read tarot cards. Alberto and I had some epic battles in chess. I always won, of course. J Just kidding. Actually, it was pretty evenly matched.

During our five days off, it was a pretty quiet affair. Alberto, Stormy, and I stayed in the closer and somewhat more comfortable Ark Hostel. I stayed off the booze, even though I could have gotten away with having a drink during the first few days. The morning of the day we were due to go back in, I felt a bit crook in the guts and ended up vomiting. The night before, we had gone to the movies and saw the film *Pearl Harbor*. I don't know if I was sick from the medication or whether it was something I ate or maybe just my body's reaction to the poor acting in the film, but my spew was predominately popcorn, so I put it down to having eaten something dodgy. I kept this information to myself when being questioned during check-in later that day.

The second stint was much the same as the first, except this time, I only took the medication twice a day thus avoiding the 2am dosing. And like before, we had another day of 22 blood draws. Thankfully, I'm not squeamish when it comes to needles and giving blood; otherwise, I could have been in real trouble.

Sunday, we were released around 5pm, and a lot of us headed straight to the pub. Some of the nurses joined us, too. After being locked up for the last five days and off the piss for at least the last 17, we were all excited. Being in the pub and having a few drinks meant we were all mixing with each other and getting along famously, which wasn't always the case in the clinic. I got chatting with Rachael, an effervescent lass from Dublin. We had spoken a bit during the study, and now I learnt she was a psyche student. We had fun talking about the different characteristics and behavioural quirks we had observed of the other patients.

After two weeks away, I went back to the Linen House to find my circle of friends there had all moved into a house together on Eglantine Gardens, not far from the University. Irish Rob was the organiser of it. From what I understood, it was his name on the lease and everyone gave their rent money to him and he paid the agent. He invited me to move in, too. I'd even have a room to myself. I say room, but it was more of a dog box. It was the smallest of storage rooms about the size of a small bathroom. It was full of a lot of junk, and I slept on the floor with just an old blanket for covering and a jumper as a pillow. Not too comfortable but I was drunk most nights, which helped me to pass out and get to sleep.

It was quite a large terrace house: three floors with five bedrooms. 1. Phil and Astra (Australian couple). 2. Basel and Eileen (South African couple). 3. Chrissie and Kerrie (English couple). 4. Crazy Horse. 5. Rob.

When I was at the hostel collecting my stuff to move out, there was a message at reception for me from Rachael. We caught up that night for a few drinks at the Bot (Botanic Inn). We got on great guns and talked more about the trial. After we left the pub, we discussed what to do next. Being the alco that I am, I said I wanted to keep drinking. She invited me back to her place, but I said, "No. Let's go back to mine because there will be more alcohol there." We went back to Eglantine Gardens, and Rachael got to meet some of the gang. She had a few drinks and then she went home. I realised my mistake later. What a fuckin' idiot. I could have gone back to hers and slept with her that first night. Instead, I spent the next two weeks trying to get into her pants.

Living at Eglantine Gardens is when the routine of spaghetti bolognaise, for Crazy Horse and I, really developed. We had ours with jalapeños, kidney beans, corn, onion, parmesan cheese, and tomatoes. There was always enough to go around if others wanted to have some, too, but it wasn't for the weak. It was hot (spicy). Crazy and I liked it that way. I'd acquired a taste for hot food from eating curries with Jamal in Hamburg. I remember Kenny, one of the other patients from my medical trial, was over one night, really struggling with the spicy taste. He looked at us with a strained look on his face as if to suggest, "How are you guys able to eat this?" Not that we ate with impunity, mind you. We used to sweat like running taps. The toxins from all the alcohol we consumed were flushed out, and it always paid to have some tissues handy to cope with the continuous runny nose. Our booze of choice was usually accompanied with a glass of water at these times. We'd have it for lunch, dinner, and for a late-night snack. It became simply known as 'food'. If one of us was to say, "Fancy some food?" or "Let's have some food," it always referred to spaghetti bolognaise. Crazy Horse always did the cooking, and I did the washing up. Crazy is a good cook, and he enjoys doing it. I don't like doing it, and I'm quite happy to do the washing up, so it was a harmonious arrangement.

2nd–9th July 2001

Despite the fun and games of living at Eglantine Gardens, Crazy Horse and I chose to leave and live in a tent, instead. Only for a week, though; we weren't that deranged, although, it could be argued a tent was an upgrade from my poky storage cupboard. Our cheques from our respective medical trials had cleared, so we decided to hire a car and go for a wee drive around the countryside. We went shopping and bought a cheap tent, some sleeping bags, a disposable barbeque and, wait for it … some steaks. Yes, something other than mince and pasta. They say a change is as good as a holiday; we were self-indulgent and had both.

By the end of the week cruising around the country, amongst other things, we'd drank in the notorious Bogside Inn in 'Derry, been attacked by midges at an Omagh campsite and had been kicked out of a hostel in Sligo, still half asleep, because of a 9am check-out. Next stop was Westport, of County Mayo fame. This was where Crazy Horse and I parted ways. Was it something I said? No; the hire car had to be returned; Crazy was running low on funds, and he wanted to get back to Belfast for the 12th July Orange Order marches and the bonfire parties held on the 11th, whereas I was headed for the vibrant culture of Galway and its numerous festivals and celebrations.

10th–28th July 2001

The plan was to spend a few days in Galway and then continue on further south before eventually heading to Dublin in early August for a music festival, where I'd be joined by my friend, and yours, Julia. Yet, at the same time, I had no plan.

The sun was hot that day, my friends. I arrived to a blaze of sunshine and activity; Galway looked and felt alive. I spent the first few nights at Barnacles Hostel on the busy, pedestrianised Quay Street. With a few name changes along the way, the street stretches for 650 metres from Eyre Square down to the Spanish Arch. It's lined with shops, pubs, and restaurants; I'd come to the right place.

The first night, I spent getting acquainted with the place, and I visited a few of the pubs around the inner-city. It was July, so the Galway Arts Festival was in full swing. The streets and pubs were littered with performers and musicians creating an exciting atmosphere. I met a French guy at the hostel, and we hit the town together. I think his name was Jacques or maybe Rowan; I can't remember. For the sake of this story, let's call him Ace. It's not very French, I know. But, it's easy to remember. He was a nice guy. He'd just arrived in town and was looking to live and work in Galway. We went cruising around the different pubs, meeting girls and having fun. By day, we explored the city on foot looking at rooms for rent that might be suitable for Ace.

I really enjoyed Galway and its social scene. Everywhere, there was something colourful or quirky or unique and interesting. When I was on my own, I spent my time in pubs or sitting in Eyre Square with a few cans and listening to my Walkman. I went for a walk to the nearby seaside town of Salthill. It was a cold, windy day when I went and not much sign of activity, but usually, the town attracts lots of tourists. There's a long promenade there, overlooking Galway Bay with plenty of bars and restaurants. The other attraction is the clear blue sea and sandy beaches, which are popular with the locals and tourists all year round, regardless of the water temperature.

Ace and I were sitting in Naughton's pub on the corner of Quay and Lower Cross Streets. Well, I was anyway; Ace had ducked off to sort something out. And when I say I was sitting, I mean I was standing at the bar ordering a drink. As I was waiting for my pint though, I noticed a couple at my table, sitting in my place and moving my things out of the way. I went over and told them I'd collect my things in a minute. They were like "It's no problem." In Galway, it's common practice to sit at a table with strangers if there is free space, which was great. It usually meant you weren't strangers with them for much longer. It was a great way to meet new people, and that's what happened on this occasion.

Niall was in his mid-30's and from the midlands of Ireland. He had a white complexion and would normally have had ginger hair, except he had a beanie covering his shaven head. Tina was about the same age and from the Galway area. She was quite attractive with long blonde hair and large child bearing hips. Niall and Tina were once a couple but now had a best mates type relationship that fluctuated from cordial to the bickering of a married couple. They turned out to be really friendly, and Niall, in particular, had a great sense of humour, which I fed off, cracking jokes as well. I was glad when Ace returned so it looked like I had friends and wasn't a loner sitting in the pub. We all hit off, and Tina warmed to the French charm of Ace; we left Naughton's and painted the town red.

The next morning, I was sitting in Eyre Square sipping on a cure for my hangover when Niall spotted me and came and joined me. We got chatting and had a laugh about the night before. It was easy to be around Niall; he was a talkative chap and was willing to listen as well. We'd only known each other for less than 24 hours, but it was as if we'd been friends for years. One reason we got along so well was that we were both drifters. Niall had with him a sports bag with a few clothes in it, some books, and that was pretty much the extent of his belongings. He was very intelligent, too, and well-read.

Niall had some great stories. He spoke of his experience with Devil's Bit. As well as being a mountain in North Tipperary, it's also a cider. Niall and his mate had a crate of about nine, two litre bottles. On the label, it said the contents of the bottle had to be consumed within 24 hours of being opened. Niall wanted to get going and attend to other things, but his mate wanted him to stay. So he wouldn't leave, his mate opened all nine bottles of the cider. Well, Niall couldn't leave then. He sat down and joined his mate in what was a groggy 24 hours. Devil's Bit is 6%.

Another story was of an amazing experience Niall had in Canada. He was in one of the major cities, just bumming round, living from day to day. He ended up getting mugged by a gang of about four or five guys. Niall complied and handed over the few valuables he had. When the guys left, Niall became quite angry. He didn't own much, and now, these guys had taken what little he had. He went psycho and chased after the guys to get his things back. Long story short, he became friends with these guys and spent the next three days with them on the piss.

Niall left Galway to go to his home town, Athlone, and I thought maybe I should start thinking about leaving, too. I'd been in Galway for about a week or more. I had about three weeks up my sleeve before I had to be in Dublin to meet Julia, so I thought I'd do a bus tour around the country. Way, way, back in early '97, when I was in Sydney for a few weeks before starting my big travel adventure into the unknown, I bought a few travel passes. One was Eurobus, which I utilised a few months after I arrived in Europe. Another pass was a similar hop-on, hop-off styled bus tour that travelled around Ireland. As you know, I never actually got around to using it. The group operating the tour was a company called Slowcoach. The company still existed but under a different name. I thought I'd try my luck and see if they'd honour my ticket four years on.

I rang the office in Dublin, and surprisingly, they were cool with me exchanging my ticket for a new one. The guy I spoke to was a bit reluctant, at first, but he came around. He told me they had an office in Galway I could go to, to get a new ticket. I went to the office, got the new ticket, and I was set.

The tour I was interested in was a six-day tour starting in Dublin and heading anti-clockwise around the south going to Galway, Killarney, Ring of Kerry, Dingle, Cork, and then back to Dublin. I was told I could join the tour in Galway, but I wanted to start the tour with everyone else, and I didn't want to miss the first day of the tour, so my plan was to go to Dublin.

The night before I was due to leave for Dublin, I went on my own to a comedy night at Cuba, a club near Eyre Square. There were some entertaining comedians doing stand-up routines. I was sitting towards the back of the room—more for easier access to the bar than to avoid being picked on by the comedians. I saw a group of three—two girls and a guy—arrive and sit in one of the booths on the side. One of the girls had super-short, dark hair about 2mm all over, not too dissimilar to Natalie Portman when she shaved her head. I was quite attracted to her and continually swapped my gaze from the show to her. When the show finished, I decided to go over and talk to her.

I asked her if I could sit next to her (smooth, hey?). She didn't seem too excited by the prospect but grabbed her coat from the seat, giving me room to sit down. I thought the simple fact I had asked to sit next to her was enough to indicate I was interested in talking to her. After all, she was sitting in a two-person booth. However, she just sat there looking bored whilst her two friends were in the next booth. I asked what she thought of the show, and from there, we got chatting. As soon as she started talking, I picked she was from South Africa. Ironically, her name was Paddy.

She was in Galway on holiday for a week visiting her niece. I found out later, in Johannesburg, where she was from, strangers don't sit next to each other in a bar … at all. When she came to Galway, she was amazed to find strangers sitting with strangers in the pub. She quickly learnt that was normal, so when I came over and asked to sit down, she just thought I wanted somewhere to sit.

We were getting along well and having a good laugh. I went to the bar and offered to buy her a drink, but she said, "No thanks." I was a bit disheartened, thinking that meant she wasn't much of a drinker; maybe I'd have to curb my drinking a bit if I wanted to make a good impression. But when she finished her pint, she went to the bar to get herself one and offered to buy me a drink. In fact, Paddy loved a drink; she was into Bulmers cider. I discovered you don't accept drinks from strangers in Johannesburg in case the drink is spiked, and Paddy was carrying that philosophy with her in Galway.

Paddy and I were really hitting it off, and it wasn't long before we were passionately making out. Paddy's niece, Fay, was in the next booth, and she started to tease us. "Hey, you two, get a room." I had a bed in a ten-bed dorm at the hostel, but I didn't think that was suitable. I wondered if, perhaps, Fay had a room we could use where she lived. Turned out, she did.

Well, that was the trip to Dublin knocked on the head for the time being. Paddy and Faye thought it was hilarious when I said I had plans to go to Dublin to catch a bus to Galway. I spent most of the next five days with Paddy, seeing the sights and getting to know each other. Paddy was 32 and worked for the British Government in Johannesburg; we shared similar tastes in music, and she enjoyed going to the pub with her friends to watch South Africa compete in the rugby or cricket.

We went on a day trip together to the famous Cliffs of Moher, south of Galway, in County Clare. These spectacular sea-cliffs, which are 200m high, extend for 8km long. The first thing I noticed was that there weren't any safety barriers keeping people back from the cliff's edge to protect them from falling off. Not that we were complaining; we went to one part to take some photos. The wind was strong that day, my friends. To look over the cliff edge, we lay down on our stomachs so as not to get blown off our feet. One woman near us had her hat blown off, which went flying towards the cliff's edge. She went chasing after it and managed to catch it with a couple of metres to spare. I think I would have just let it go. No hat is worth risking a two hundred metre drop.

As part of Galway's arts festival, there were a lot of street performers, buskers, and theatre. Paddy and I had fun watching different performers, but, by far, the best were the four men living in the windows. "WTF?" I hear you ask. Well, it was really cool. There were four men living inside the city library on St Augustine Street, and like some sort of live reality TV show, you could go along and watch what the guys were up to through the windows. The windows stretched for about 30 metres, and the guys had their living quarters from one end to the other. Their 'house' was decorated like a hut from a tropical island with bamboo fittings and palm leave coverings. Think Gilligan's Island, and it was very much like that. They had a kitchen and dining area up one end, a recreation area complete with shower in the middle, and at the other end were hammocks for sleeping.

We went past on the odd occasion during the day, and the guys were just up to mundane activities, like sleeping or reading the paper, but in the evenings, they used to put on a show. We went one time, and they were putting on a real song and dance about having a shower. The shower consisted of the shower head and partitions surrounding the sides and western saloon styled doors that faced the windows. The partitions around the shower only extended from knee height to shoulder height, so we could see whoever was in the shower. There was some razzle-dazzle type music playing over a PA; one guy was in the shower moving to the music, and the others were dancing around like idiots.

Then the guy finished his shower whilst two others held a towel up in between him and the audience. Then they put on a whole tease show whilst he got dressed, and the others danced around, conveniently placing things in strategic positions, hiding his modesty—pure hilarity. What added to the tomfoolery was the larrikin nature of each of the guys and the silly expressions they had on their faces.

Paddy's last day in Galway was a little saddening. All holiday romances must come to an end, but there was some light at the end of the tunnel; I had to return to Australia in a month's time for my brother AJ's wedding and I hoped to visit Paddy in South Africa on my way home.

In the meantime, Galway remained my stomping ground. Niall was back in town, and he and I got on the lash again. On one occasion, we found ourselves walking the streets in the wee hours of the morning feeling a bit thirsty. The early-opener had our names written all over it. Two streets over from the library, on Dock Rd, there was a pub called Porrick's. I don't know if it's there anymore, but it used to open around 6am or something like that. It had a black exterior, and the door and windows closed off from the inside, so you couldn't see in. I don't know if the pub was opening illegally, but they liked to keep everything shut, even after they'd opened, until later in the morning.

We walked round to Dock Rd, and there were a few people outside waiting for the pub to open. One of them had a sense of humour. When we got inside, he was the first to order, and he asked for a cup of tea. The pub consisted of two rooms—one with the bar and another with a pool table. Niall played pool whilst I just watched, usually chatting to the other thirsty folk. By the time staff opened the doors and the window coverings around 9ish, I was in such a happy state. I was feeling euphoric from already having had a few drinks, and the sun was coming in through the large window, and there was a great view out over the water—awesome. The rest of the day was the usual fare: drinking and hanging out at the Spanish Arch, Eyre Square, and/or watching the men living in the library.

At some point, Niall left town. I hung around another day or two before the shenanigans of the last few weeks had caught up with me, and I needed a break. I felt surprisingly good, the morning of my departure out of town, considering the boozy night I'd had before. I only came to Galway for a few days, and 18 days later, I was finally dragging my butt out of there.

Witnness Festival
3rd—6th August 2001

The festival was quite amusing. My friend, Julia, arrived in Dublin Friday night. It was so exciting to see her again, especially in new surroundings. Saturday morning, we went out and bought a few supplies. Julia already had her camera out taking photos of street life, including a sign in a pharmacy shop window that read, 'support stockings'. We hadn't given it much thought before then, but when we thought about it, we agreed stockings probably could do with more of our encouragement and assistance.

We caught a bus to the festival sight and must have queued for about an hour before we got into the campsite. Not that that was any great stress. We made friends with the group of guys and girls behind us in the queue, and they were kind enough to help us carry some of our supplies every ten minutes when the line moved forward a few metres. We really felt sorry for them when we were close to the front of the queue, and they realised they were in the wrong line. Shit, hey! Whilst waiting, I could also hear the first acts performing, including Jimmy Barnes—the Australian Bruce Springsteen.

Once we were in the campsite, we had no trouble finding a place and setting up the tent. We then headed off to see what we could find. We got some food and then the fun began. It started absolutely pissing down. Everyone was running to the big dance tents to get out of the rain. When the rain eased a bit, Julia and I went dancing in it.

We went to the main stage and saw Muse. I'd heard their stuff on the radio a few times and thought they were just all right, but live, they were excellent. The singer gave so much energy, and Julia and I were up the front getting off on his vibe. Afterwards, we saw Alabama 3, Stereophonics, and Faithless.

At Alabama 3, we met these two Irish guys and shared a joke with them about them being from India. I'm not sure how it started. Because their accents were clearly distinguishable as Irish, I'm guessing, as a joke, one of us asked what part of India they were from. And they ran with it; one of the guys spoke in a really good Indian accent. Julia does a great Indian accent, as well, and so the two of them spoke the whole time as Indians. We hung out with them for a few of the bands. I was pleasantly surprised at how much I liked Faithless; they were way cool. They were on last and had a really good sound. They have some really, anthemic, dance songs that involve audience participation; fantastic.

We said good-bye to our new friends as they went home, and Julia and I went to our tent to find a lot of the inside soaking wet from the rain. We slept in wet sleeping bags, trying to get some sleep, while a lot of the campsite stayed up partying and making noise around us. We woke the next morning to find the sun shining.

I got up for a walk around the campsite and managed to buy some toilet paper, as ours was wet and useless. Toilet paper is like gold at these festivals as the porta loos usually don't have any in them, so it's best to carry your own with you. I went back to the tent and hung my wet sleeping bag and shoes out in the sun. Julia woke up a bit later, and pretty soon, our tent area looked like a shanty town with all the muddy ground and all the clothes hanging up everywhere. We managed to get most things dry, most importantly, the sleeping bags. We then set everything up in the middle of the tent on a ground sheet, so if it rained again, they would hopefully stay dry.

So, off we headed to the festival sight, ready for another day of drinking, dancing and dialogue. Our first mission was to find some breakfast. Once found (a delicious veggie burger), we sat on the grass in front of the main stage, drinking beer and listening to the bands. Life's tough, sometimes, innit? We saw Feeder, James, and Placebo. For Placebo, we stood up the front and had a bit of a jump around. The bass player decided he would play the gig in a nice one-piece red dress - very becoming.

It was about 6 pm now, the sun had gone, and the rain clouds had returned, but for the time being, they were holding off on dumping their water. After Placebo, we went to the dance tent and saw the Avalanches play a mixture of techno mixed with 80's, cheesy theme tunes. It worked quite well and was a change from the rock music. After a few songs of Paul Weller in one of the side tents, we went to the main stage to witness Ash. They were excellent. Once again, I thought they were nothing special beforehand, but seeing them live, I thought they were great.

I particularly had fun during Ash, because the people in the crowd near where we were standing were making human pyramids, not unlike the big human pyramids they make in Spain during some of their festivals. There were a few guys, arm in arm, standing in a circle, and people then climbed on to their shoulders, and then people onto their shoulders, until either the pyramid was a few stories high, or it collapsed, which is what usually happened. I didn't ever climb, but I stood around giving people who were climbing a leg up and trying to hold them steady. It was thrilling, all these strangers trying to work together and, sometimes, even succeeding, but always having fun trying.

After Ash, the festival was over, and we started to make our way back to the camp. On the way there, Julia commented on how we hadn't met anyone that day. I suggested we go to the meeting point and see who we could meet. Of course, the meeting point was a place for friends to meet up or for people who had lost their friends to meet up again. But we interpreted it a different way and used it as a place to meet new friends. I went up to a few people and said, "Nice to meet you, this being the meeting place and all."

Some weren't impressed; others gave a little smile and then walked off. But this one guy I met, Mark, from Dublin, fancied Julia so we stayed talking to him while he was waiting for his friends. His friends arrived, and they were from Belfast, of all places. They were super friendly, and I was chatting to them for ages about Belfast and drug trials at Harris. We all went back to their tent for some drinking and smoking. By this time, it had started raining again, and it was getting heavier and heavier. But we had a good time mixing with our newfound friends and the other people in the surrounding tents. Julia and Mark had disappeared, back to our tent I assumed.

It was starting to get late, and most of the booze had gone. I was feeling pretty stoned and was curious to know how our tent was holding up to the latest barrage of rain. I got back to the tent to find Julia and Mark there. They had only just arrived and had been running around the campsite, visiting other tents and talking to anyone and everyone. Julia got to meet plenty of people after all, plus had a snog with the good-looking Mark.

It was time to sleep, and now, there were three of us in a normally crowded two-man tent. Our belongings were relatively dry, most importantly, the sleeping bags. The three bodies kept the tent warm, and with the vast amount of alcohol we had consumed, we quickly fell asleep, only to be woken again at 7:30am by security telling everyone to pack up and go. I felt like getting up and telling them where to go, but I was too tired and just rolled over and went back to sleep. Luckily, they left our tent alone, and we managed to sleep until 9:00. I got up and went to visit our friends from Belfast, but their tent and every tent surrounding them was gone. They were the unlucky ones to be targeted by security.

I went back to our tent to start the cleaning up process to find, during the night, our tent was pretty much flooded. Everything in my bag was wet. The shorts and t-shirt I had on were the only dry clothes I had. I had left my muddy jeans outside overnight, and they were a mess, so they were the first casualty. I'd have to bite the bullet and let them go, so I threw them away. My shoes were just as bad, but I decided to keep them and wear my sandals. My sleeping bag was wet, but I rolled that away and kept it. My bag was looking decidedly empty without all the food, booze, and clothes I'd brought to the festival. There was some booze left, and Mark and I quickly got stuck into it to make the somewhat uncomfortable situation bearable. We would have drunk it no matter what the conditions, to be honest. We were making light of the situation and having a few laughs.

The second casualty was my sleeping mat. It had served me well and provided a dry patch to sleep on but, now, carrying it to wherever we were going, was in my opinion, going to be a liability. With the booze finished, we weren't having much fun and decided it was time to go. Julia had packed her bags and dumped whatever she didn't want and then we hopped outside of the tent to find it absolutely pouring. And now for the last casualty—the tent. When I'd camped at the Glastonbury Festival in '98 and it rained non-stop the whole time, my friends who had cheap tents abandoned them and saved themselves the hassle of carrying the wet, dirty, blobs of mud home. But I was borrowing someone else's tent and had to pack it up and take it home. I spent a week trying to clean the thing. But not this time. It was my tent, well, half-mine, and after three seconds of deliberation, I made the decision the tent was on its own and was going to have to make its own way out. If you think that was cruel, we then decided to make life even harder for the tent by throwing anything we could find at the tent to knock it over. I was throwing cans, bottles, and shoes but wasn't doing too much damage. Then, from out of nowhere, Mark came running up from behind me with a big steel barrier, normally used for crowd control, raised above his head and threw it on the tent, squashing it in an instant. In fits of laughter and amazement at how Mark was able to lift the barrier, we hopped on a bus back to Dublin.

I arrived at Dublin bus station wet, cold, and tired. We said goodbye to Mark. I went to the luggage storage place where I'd left my big backpack with stuff I didn't need during the festival, and I got changed into dry clothes, socks, and shoes. Oh, how sweet it felt to be dry and warm. Julia didn't have to be at Dublin airport until six. With some time up our sleeve, we went for a walk into the city. I remember we stopped for a pint at a pub near St Stephen's Green that had been host to the famous Irish folk band, The Dubliners, on many occasions. Julia made her flight to London. Me? I met up with Niall in Athlone.

I only planned to hang out with him for one day, as I had to head to London and meet up with some friends. Also, I was due back in Australia early September for my brother's wedding. My plan was to fly home via South Africa and visit Paddy, which I hadn't organised yet either. It wasn't until seven days later that I managed to say farewell to Niall.

We had to do a little business in Athlone before heading to Tullamore, where Niall was going to be house sitting a friend's house for the week. On our way, we ran into two drug dealers that Niall knew. We went to their place for a bit of a puff and some beers, and they were nice enough. But I just thought, here I am in Ireland, I've seen the Cliffs of Moher, been to the picturesque Wicklow mountains, and now I've hung out with some of Athlone's heroin dealers. You don't see that advertised at the Irish tourist office, I'm sure.

I spent the week with Niall in Tullamore. The house was a large three-bedroom place with garden and all mod cons. It was great to chill out here and take a break from hostel life and to regroup after the festival. I had my own room and a double bed and no early check-out—heaven. We spent every waking moment drinking (cider and Jamaican black rum). In just seven days in small town Ireland, we were barred from two pubs, we were known to undercover police (for drinking in public), and we were such regulars at the off-licence that we knew all the staff by name, and often, when they saw us coming, they had what we wanted ready, before we even asked for it. One woman even gave us discounts.

We sat around the house telling jokes and watching movies. We had a great time, oblivious to the outside world. We watched the battle scenes in *Hidden Dragon, Crouching Tiger* and *Henry V* with binoculars as to give the feeling of being right there in the action. We shared a lot of stories, and often, we'd go on great big tangents of captivating tales before getting back to the original thread. I thought that would make a great name for a band—The Tangents. I thought, halfway through a song, the band could go on a tangent and play another song before coming back to the original song. Then I realised this already exists. It's called a bridge.

On the Tuesday night, we went into this quiet pub, and there were a few locals watching the big screen, but we noticed there were two girls sitting by themselves up the back. We went and spoke to them and got on well. They were from out of town and were staying at a B & B. Then, Niall lost the plot and started to argue with them about how to speak Irish properly; this made me look very attractive to the girls. So, when the pub closed, one of them invited me back to their hire car to change my oil, if you know what I mean. She was an interesting lass. She liked to keep count. 8—2, to her, was the final score.

Come Friday, we had to hitch to Athlone to pick up Niall's dole money. After all the relaxation of the last few days, it was a real effort to get our act together and get to the dole office before it shut. We left it a bit too late, and we only got as far as Kilbeggan, about half way, before we realised we wouldn't make it to the dole office before it shut. The urgency to get somewhere at a particular time was stressing me out. When we called off the mission, I suddenly livened up.

We had a great ride back to Tullamore. We were hitching by the side of the road and a few hundred metres from us was another guy trying to get a ride. We noticed a car stop to give the other guy a ride. "Lucky bugger," we thought. Then the driver got out of the car and called to us, "I can take you two as well." Nice one. Niall sat in the back with the other guy whilst I sat in the front with our new best friend. Oh, and what a beauty she was too. She was young, blonde, attractive and wore a leopard print jacket and velvet trousers. Cool baby. And so, from Kilbeggan to Tullamore, we had a party in the car. Niall and I shared our booze, and the stereo was cranked up as we cruised down the road singing to 'Baker Street'.

The next day, I left Niall at the house, whilst I went out to a phone box to make a call. I spoke to a friend, who gave me some interesting information. I went back to the house to share it with Niall. "Mate, are you sitting down? Good. OK. Get this. Today ... is Sunday."

"OK."

"Do you know what that means?"

"What?"

"It means yesterday was Saturday. Even if we had made it to Athlone yesterday, the dole office would have been closed, anyway."

Niall burst out laughing, yet at the same time, I could see his brain ticking over trying to work out how that happened. We were oblivious to the time so much that we lost a day.

The next day, Monday, Niall and I went to the train station and said good bye to Tullamore. We sat on the platform and opened a can of cider each. Niall was feeling rough; he looked at the can and said, "This'll cure me or kill me."

I said, "Either way, you can't lose."

I was headed to Dublin and then on to London. Everyone must have been wondering where I was. Niall invited me to go to Athlone with him, first, so he could give me some money for all the drinks I'd shouted during the week. I knew, if I went with him, we'd end up on another adventure, and I really needed to get back.

I made it to London about a week later than I had planned. Friends of mine were wondering if I'd been deported or something. By this stage, Julia had escaped the 'bitch bullpen' in Kensal Rise and was now living upstairs at the Frog & Firkin. With only ten days in London before I was to fly out, there was no time for rest, and my friends and I partied hard. I had little sleep and lots of chemicals.

28th August–6th September 2001

During the night, I was woken by this growling noise that sounded like there was something just outside the front door. "What the fuck is that?"

"Lions."

I nearly shat myself. "What? Just outside?"

"No," explained Paddy. Even though they sounded close, they were about 2km away in an enclosure. Apparently, they can be heard up to 7km away.

Paddy and I were spending the night in a chalet at the Rhino and Lion Nature Reserve, about 40km outside of Johannesburg. The reserve covered approximately 1200 ha. Just as long as the lions were far away and there was an enclosure separating us, then I felt safe. Come the next day, I did not feel safe.

A guide took just the two of us on a tour of the nature reserve in an open roofed jeep. I was super excited as we drove up to the lion enclosure. I was curious to see the beasts that had been making all the noise the night before. They had sounded quite ferocious. We drove up to the gate. We won't be going in, I thought. But hang on. The gates were opening. We were driving in. What the fuck? My excitement turned to fear. Didn't this guy know there were lions in there?

"Don't worry," he said. "They were fed yesterday."

It was true. We saw the lions, and they were too lazy to do anything but lie in the sun. We drove over a wee crest, and Paddy spotted them first—Mr and Mrs Lion and two cubs. We saw their heads visible through the long grass resting near some trees about 50 metres away. Some excitement returned. They didn't pay us much attention at all. That was fine by us. We left the large enclosure and toured more of the reserve. The reserve boasts 600 head of game, representing 25 different species. We saw some rhino, zebra, ostrich, buffalo, buck, springbuck, wildebeest, wild dog, jackal, and cheetah. Truly amazing.

South Africa was so much fun. Jo'burg was quite different from anywhere else I'd been. The first thing I noticed was how dry the place was. Driving from the airport was an eye opener. The traffic was full of erratic taxi vans used by the black population. The vans were generally old and poorly maintained and full beyond capacity with passengers hanging out windows and doors. As well as that, there were blacks selling all sorts of products and services on the side of the road. At the 'robots' (traffic lights) you could get anything from food, to tools or car repairs. You could even get your hair cut if you wanted.

I was told by one of Paddy's friends, the police usually target specific things on certain days, e.g., If you get pulled over and you have guns on the dash board but the police are targeting car registration that day, then you're fine. However, if they're targeting guns, you're in a wee bit of trouble.

I stayed with Paddy at her parents' house (separate beds) and met her family and friends, who were all rather friendly. It was great to see Paddy again and rekindle our romance. Paddy was even happier to see me. She'd planned a week of activities and was looking forward to showing me around.

The weather the whole time there was warm during the day and cool at night because there were never any clouds. We went camping one weekend in Magliesburg and stayed in a *Rundavul*. We shared the campsite with some lively monkeys, as well. I experienced the Saffa braai. Braai is the local word for barbecue, and with South Africa's wide array of good quality meat, the braai is an incredibly popular social event. I don't know if it was just this time or if it's the usual method, but it took forever to cook the meat. Paddy's niece's boyfriend was our braai master this day and spent ages preparing the fire, then waited for what seemed forever until the grill was hot enough, and then we had a long wait as the meat was slowly cooked. I was fuckin' starving before we started the fire. It did taste good in the end, though.

We went and checked out Hartbeespoort Dam and stopped at the markets there. I saw a few Dutchmen walking around with guns in holsters hanging off their hip. Apparently, that's normal. Paddy bought me an Afrikaans beaded love letter, and I bought myself a beaded bracelet with the words S. AFRICA on it.

One cool thing we did was go to Sun City, a luxury casino and resort, situated in the middle of nowhere, about two hours' drive north from Johannesburg. We saw the utterly lavish and elaborate casino there, and we went swimming at the water park that had an exciting wave machine. It was good fun, despite the water being rather cold.

Speaking of casinos, we went to the new Monte Casino in Johannesburg. The complex was designed to replicate a Tuscan village. The interior was made to look like the streets of the village with the floor decorated like cobble-stone streets and the ceiling painted a dark, light blue to imitate the sky during dusk. The shops looked right out of Tuscany, complete with houses with clothes hanging out on the balconies. It really did feel like one was outside. And, dude, the beer was so cheap. I paid 75p for a pint ... in a casino, that's fuckin' unbelievable. I walked away from the roulette table having broken even, but my bar tab was another matter.

My ten days were up. I would have loved to have stayed longer, but I had a wedding to get to in Sydney. It wasn't easy saying good bye to Paddy. There were a few tears at the airport. Holiday romances, hey? Why do we do it? Well, I can think of a few reasons. I've met some people who are resistant to starting a relationship that has an expiry date, not wanting to get hurt. I tended to just jump in and deal with the heartbreak later.

September 2001

It was really weird being back in Oz. I thought it wouldn't take long for me to settle back in, but the first few days, I had to keep pinching myself I was in Sydney. Normally, on the road, hearing an Australian accent would arouse my curiosity, but here, they were everywhere. I made the usual mistakes: quid instead of dollars and asking for a pint instead of a schooner (375ml). Not only that, but for the first week, I was still operating on South African time. I was sleeping during the day and then staying up all night.

Because of the week in Tullamore, I was a week behind schedule, and my family was wondering if I was going to make it to the wedding, which would have been a problem, me being one of the groomsman and all. My brother, AJ, was happy when I rang and told him I'd arrived in Sydney. I stayed at my dad's house again. The morning of the 12th, I woke and walked into the lounge room. Everyone had gone to work, and the place was empty, except the TV had been left on. I was still in a daze, but the pictures on TV quickly grabbed my attention. Some planes had crashed into the Twin Towers in New York.

The wedding went like clockwork. AJ and Bec were pronounced husband and wife. I really enjoyed being part of the bridal party without any responsibilities. I didn't have to say a speech, so I was free to take advantage of the free bar tab. Cheers. I got to catch up with my other brother, Neville, as well, and meet his 14-week-old boy, John.

I returned to Canberra and to begin with, stayed with my aunt, in Duffy. I kept busy by catching up with friends and sorting out the routine things, like buying a car and finding a place to live. One night, I called for a taxi to take me to the city for a night out on the town. The taxi arrived; I jumped in and met my driver for the journey, Max. He joked his name used to be Maximilian, but he lost his million, so it was now just Max. He was a funny fucker. He originally came from Paraguay but had been in Canberra for over 30 years. He would have been in his 60's, I reckon. He was extremely chatty, and we talked all the way to town.

After a few hours at the casino, I was walking through the bus interchange when I heard a car horn. I looked around to see Max in his taxi again. I was in two minds as to whether to go home, but with Max there at my service, I decided to head home. We got chatting about my circumstances and my need for somewhere to stay. Max took us on a slight detour to a house in Sterling. It was about 2am and Max took me in the back door of this house, and we woke up the resident. And that's when I met my future landlord, Wally.

And, oh God. It was Wally by name and wally by nature. He was a funny guy, but unintentionally, 70 years old, from Uruguay, and his English was quite poor. He worked as a chef at The Vikings Club. He regularly used the services of hookers and went out every Monday night, with his top three shirt buttons undone, to the club Bobby McGee's to hang out with the 'chickens' (his word for women). He spoke in a super fast and excited manner—it was hilarious. On top of all that, he was a nice guy.

His house was a three-bedroom place, and he had two spare rooms, so one was mine if I wanted it. SOLD. I now had a place to live. Max lived in a caravan in the backyard. I was on a pretty good wicket: $70/week and it was almost as though I lived by myself, because both Max and Wally worked nights. I also had the perk of having my own personal taxi driver. Max gave me a lot of free rides around town when I was too drunk to drive myself, and other times, he gave me a healthy discount. Max spoke about seven or eight languages, maybe more, including Spanish, of course, and German. So, Max and Wally taught me a bit of Spanish, but when I was drunk, Max and I had conversations in German. Max also spoke Japanese and went to the Salt Lake City Winter Olympics in February 2002, as a driver/interpreter for some Japanese delegates. I really enjoyed living there and got on well with both the guys.

I caught up with most of my friends and had a few memorable nights out. I really caned the booze during this time and rediscovered vodka/Red Bulls. I liked how they got me drunk so much that I usually blacked out quite early in the night and didn't remember a thing until I woke up the next morning. One Sunday morning, with the help of the ol' trusty vodka/Red Bulls, one of my sexual fantasies came true. Scores of times, I've woken from a heavy night's drinking and been unable to remember what happened the night before and/or how I came to wake up where I was. Despite it being a cliché to wake up from a black out in bed with a woman … in Vegas and married, I still thought it would be a pleasant surprise to wake up to find a hot chick in bed with me.

I woke, and the first thing to arouse my interest was I didn't recognise the ceiling. I looked around, and I didn't recognise anything. I found myself lying in bed, naked, next to a naked woman. I had no fuckin' idea where I met her, how I met her, or how we got back to her house. I did vaguely remember some foreplay, but needless to say, I initiated some of the old 'in and out' after I woke up, just in case I'd failed to do so the night before. She did tell me her name was Louise, and she was married with one kid. She kicked me out soon after, because her sister was coming over. I'd been out the night before with mates at King O'Malley's, but when I spoke to them again, they weren't able to shed any light on how I met Louise. My fantasy came true, though; she was hot.

Email: 21st December 2001

Hello, fellow space cadets, and welcome to another Spaceman lunar log entry. Let the games begin:

Bondage Bob

"I live in my leather, No matter what the weather.
With whips and chains, I'll please with pain.
Let me give your arse a paddle, Let me try you with a saddle
Keep me always by your side You will always stay satisfied."

I've been a bit quiet lately, but I'll give you a short excerpt of my current Christmas shopping battle.

I arrived back in Canberra a few months ago for my brother's wedding and decided I would stay for the summer, which naturally includes Christmas. This Christmas, my brother Neville has invited me to his house for Christmas lunch, and it will be my first family Christmas in 7 years. Also invited, are his wife's parents and grandparents, her sister and sister's husband.

It's going to be quite a formal affair. But I've decided to liven things up a little with quite a provocative present.

My brother has a 7-month-old boy, called John Robert, so one must buy a present for the young man. Now, I like to be a little different from everyone else. I've spoken to a few people, and a few of them have taken the easy option and bought a cuddly toy for young JR. Not me, I thought. But the closer to the 25th, the more desperate I became, and yesterday, I found myself taking the easy way out and buying the young lad a stuffed bear.

But if I thought Christmas day was going to be uneventful, I changed all that with one purchase. I bought JR a small teddy bear ... dressed in ... bondage gear. Bondage Bob is his name, and he is dressed in leather undies, and he is tied up with leather straps. He even has a ball in his mouth, with leather straps around his head. I can't help but laugh thinking about the trouble I'm going to cause when the in-laws see what I've given their grandson. The bear even comes with a little tag with a poem, and you can read the poem at the beginning of this e-mail. I may never be invited to another one of their Christmas dinners again.

Email: After Christmas

As for Christmas dinner, my brother's wife, Belinda, cooked some great food. For starters, we had prawns and orange duck. For the main meal, we had some lovely turkey with roast potatoes and other vegies all covered in gravy. I love gravy. Belinda had been preparing the meal since lunch time the day before, and all nine of us enjoyed the food and stuffed our faces.

As for Bondage Bob, well, after we had all opened our presents, John woke up so he was brought out into the living room for him to open the mountain of gifts he had. And wouldn't you know it? Belinda asked me to go first. I took my gift over to John, who was sitting on Bronwyn's lap (Belinda's sister), and as they both unwrapped it, all the family's eyes (about ten of us) were on them.

The different reactions from people were hilarious. Some were laughing, and some had a look on their face as if to say, "What the hell is that?" Thankfully, everyone thought it was quite funny; Belinda's grandparents didn't even understand what it was all about, so in the end, no one was offended.

Later in the day, when other guests dropped in to say hello, the first gift they were shown was always the bondage teddy.

Thailand New Year's 2001

Back in March, my American friend, Monica, who I met through working at the Empire in London, (and we travelled around Europe together), had mentioned that Sally, formerly of the Empire, as well, would be DJing at a dance festival over New Year's on the island Koh Pha Ngan, Thailand. She asked if I was keen to go, "Definitely." So, it was decided we'd spend New Year's in Thailand and, in the meantime, try to round up a few friends to come along, too. I invited Tessa, my friend from London, who had been to Thailand before, and she was well up for it. Monica enlisted a few friends as well, so it was going to be a delightful little get together.

    I arrived in Bangkok after an uneventful 8-hour flight from Sydney. I enjoyed disembarking in Bangkok, whilst everyone else on board was travelling another 11 hours or more on to London.

    Thailand was amazing, unlike anywhere I'd been before, lots of noise, movement and smells. I was both excited and nervous. I caught a cab to my hotel—a big cheap 3-star place—and checked-in. What have we here? I got to my room and, surprise, it was a single room with a double bed, TV, private bathroom, air-conditioning, and a mini bar, and all for $37AUD. Luxury. Beats the hell out of a dorm room with nine other people or sleeping on the floor of a friend's house in a storage room.

I went up to my room, watched a bit of Asian MTV, and then went to bed with no idea of how I was going to get to my destination the next day. The next day, I got to my destination no problem. I just walked down the hotel corridor, took the lift to the lobby, asked the receptionist for some directions, and then before I knew it, I was walking through a set of big double doors into a hall and wallah—I'd made it; breakfast was served. As for reaching the island, I'd be taking the train and ferry.

On the train ride, I met up with some other people (Americans, French, and Korean) going to the festival. We stayed up drinking until we realised we had to get off the train at 5am, so we went to bed and managed to get a few hours' sleep. Little did I know I wouldn't be getting much sleep over the next three days.

By now, we were at the seaport town of Surat Thani, where we'd catch the ferry to Koh Pha Ngan. Whilst waiting for our transfer from the station to the ferry terminal, we found a café type place to have breakfast. My newfound friends and I all ordered beer, as you do. We met an Aussie guy, Tristan, sitting at the café who was headed to Koh Pha Ngan, too. He was just in the area and had heard there was a party on, so he thought he'd go check it out. He didn't have a ticket for the festival or any accommodation lined up, but was going for an adventure anyway. We coaxed him into joining us.

When we got off our transfer bus at the ferry terminal,

one of my new American friends asked me to hold the beat box, which was playing loud reggae music. I obliged, but I felt like a real dick when other festival goers looked at me. I knew that look. I'd given that look myself, many times in my life. That look of contempt when someone can be as so arrogant as to inflict their musical tastes on everyone else. For a brief moment, I had become the type of person I can't stand.

The drinking and party vibe continued on the ferry. The sun was out, there were lots of young kool kats from all over the globe, and I was in the thick of it. My social confidence was sky high, and I was chatting with everyone. I was excited about the good time at hand and the good time to come when I'd meet Monica and Tessa.

We arrived on the island about lunch time to the hustle and bustle of the ferry port. Koh Pha Ngan is an island in the Gulf of Thailand about 168km^2 and a population of over 11,000 people. It is famous for its full moon party at Haad Rin Beach and as a backpacker's destination.

This is where I parted with my newfound friends and promised to meet up again later at the festival. Aware that Tristan had no accommodation organised, I invited him to come with me. Tristan was a bronzed lad, in his mid-20's, travelling wherever the wind blew him and always keen to smoke some pot. Having travelled that nomadic style in Ireland earlier in the year, I was enthusiastic for Tristan to have a good time. Many times, in Ireland, some totally unexpected turn of events occurred from meeting various people that blew my mind. I wanted the same for Tristan and, despite not knowing what the hotel arrangements were, I was resolute Tristan would be joining our party whether others liked it or not (Gee, I was drunk).

We managed to find the hotel resort, where I found Tessa first and later Monica. I was excited about seeing my close friends again and in such an exotic location and for such a significant occasion. This excitement, coupled with my insistence of Tristan's presence, was perceived by the group members I was meeting for the first time as overbearingness and obnoxiousness. I didn't make a very good first impression. Woops. Things improved though, and Tristan did manage to organise himself some bed space.

I'd already been drinking since 5am, so come 9pm, when we all went (about eight or nine of us) to the New Year's Eve party, my memory was hazy. The party was a three-day trance music festival set in the lush vegetation of the island's forest. Happy days.

I became separated from the rest of the group, twice, and because I'd asked Tessa to look after my money (so I didn't lose it), I wandered around the festival for hours alone and couldn't even drink. It was hot, so I took off my shirt, and later, I realised I didn't have it anymore. I'd lost that too. I briefly ran into my friends from the train, but they were off on their own adventure.

After the sun came up, Monica found me, and she took me to where Tessa and Michael (Monica's friend) were dancing. Everyone else had gone back to the resort. After a few minutes of saying, "How was your night?" I grabbed my money from Tessa and went straight to the bar.

After a few drinks, the four of us decided to go back to the resort. Michael and Monica went back on motorbike, whilst Tessa and I decided to go down to the sea and walk back along the beach. When we got to the water, we went for a swim; the water was beautiful. When I hopped out of the water, I noticed my sandals were missing. Bollocks. Whilst we'd been swimming, the tide had come in and taken my sandals and were now floating away somewhere. I saw something that could have been a sandal floating about 50 metres from the beach, but I didn't bother to get it. I arrived back at the resort wearing only shorts, having lost my shirt and sandals, and having lost my friends during the night. Happy New Year.

Over the festival, we did a lot of dancing, swimming, eating great food, getting Thai massages, and lots of drinking. The weather was humid but not too bad. Monica and I managed to catch up with Sally, and we danced like motherfuckers during her set.

Monica's friends were really cool people; we were all about the same age and got along well. Some of them have since become my close friends. There was:

Vanessa, who was American but born in Canberra, of all places, and now based in LA. She was hot. Rebecca, who worked with Tessa and was backpacking around Thailand. She was a competitive synchronised swimmer. Brian and Michael, both from Gaithersburg, Maryland, grew up together. They'd known Monica for years. Brian lived and worked in DC as a journalist, and Michael worked as a finance guy in New York. Michael was charming, curious, and funny and liked to dance. Brian was confident and calm and could do a great impersonation of Michael dancing.

A day or two after the festival, we all went our separate ways. I had planned to meet up with Monica again in Bangkok, but we never got our act together. Tessa and I went and stayed at another resort on the island, where we just ate and drank, went shopping, and lay on the beach for two days. On the second night, we realised we were sharing our bungalow with a rat. Thankfully for me, I was leaving the resort for Bangkok the next day, but Tessa had one more night in the hut, and she said the rat made its presence felt again.

I caught the night ferry, and that was quite a pleasant experience. The deck was organised in rows of numbered pillows, and the number on your ticket corresponded with a pillow. Welcome to your bed for the night. I woke in the middle of the night needing to go to the toilet. It was pitch black, and everyone was sleeping. I hoped nothing happened to the ferry or we'd all be fish food.

The scenery on the train ride back to Bangkok was really interesting: mountain ranges and temples. I made it to Bangkok and caught a *Tuk Tuk* to Khao San Rd, a backpacker haven, and found a single room with no windows for 250baht ($12.50).

I went exploring and ended up meeting two crazy Dutchmen, and we got pissed as we amused ourselves watching the gorgeous hookers (who were really men) chat up unsuspecting males at the bar. I did a bit of looking around, went shopping at the markets in Pratunam; they were a maze of shops and alleyways and easy to get lost in all the bargains. I bought a few shirts, including one with Osama Bin Laden's face on it with the words "I did not do it." That was for my brother, Neville. He's the only crazy bastard I thought would wear it. I don't think he ever did.

I went to have a butcher's hook at the red-light district, Patpong, where there were even more clothes markets. I bought a watch that looked like a big spaceship had landed on my wrist. I found a bar with outdoor seating, so I bought some cans of beer for really cheap at the 7/11 and then sat outside the bar and did some people watching. Quite amusing.

Some local girls invited me to the bar, and I sat drinking and talking with them. I went with one of the lovely girls to a private hotel room for some adult fun. She wasn't the prettiest girl in the bar, but that's why I chose her. The really attractive ones were usually the men. I was anxious to get to the room and have the girl take her clothes off. Never have I been so excited to see a woman's vagina. I was relieved, to say the least, to find out she didn't have a dick.

We returned to the bar for a few drinks and played this funny little game with dice and numbered tiles. Anyway, it was time to get some sleep before the flight home the next day. No dodgy ping pong shows for me. Sorry to disappoint.

Wherever I went, I travelled by motorbike taxi. They're mad, those drivers. They don't let anything or anyone get in their way or slow them down. The ride from Patpong back to the guest house was the best. He was the fastest, by far, and the trip was a good half hour, so I had a lot of fun.

Bangkok was really cool for a couple of days. Any more than that, and I may have become bonkers. My flight home was enjoyable. I had my preferred aisle seat, a vacant seat next to me, then a young woman next to the window. We talked for the whole trip, stopping only for sleep. The exchange I had with this woman remains the best chinwag I've ever had with a fellow passenger on a plane. We chatted away as if we were old friends. Normally, I find chatting to other passengers to be awkward, so I generally keep to myself, but this was a refreshing change.

I arrived home and stayed at my dad's place. Not having slept for about 24 hours, I went to bed, and then three hours later, I was wide awake again. I didn't feel too good, though, and when we had dinner that night, I threw up after only a few mouthfuls. I assured Helen, my Dad's wife, it wasn't a reflection of her cooking but rather due to my diet in Thailand.

All up, it was a fantastic way to spend New Year's. We all decided to do it again somewhere the following year.

2002

April 2002

I was heading back to the UK because that's where I felt drawn to. I had received a new four year visa just before I left there in August. I considered my friends in the UK/Europe to be my closest friends. I loved the travel opportunities available on that side of the world and the culture at every turn. So, after eight months in Australia. I left for the UK via a two-month jaunt in the States. I was super excited to visit the country that I'd seen so much of in movies and television and it didn't disappoint. I learnt the art of tipping in bars in San Francisco, almost had a home invader land on me in bed whilst in Las Vegas on my birthday, had a woman invite me to have sex with her in a church in New Orleans, drove on the right side of the road in Washington DC without crashing and in a bar in New York, got caught up in some rowdy celebrations with the local Turkish community when the national Turkish football team winning a game at the World Cup.

Let's start at the beginning.

I arrived in San Francisco via LA only a few hours after I had left Sydney because of the time difference, and I stayed at the first hostel I could find: AAE S.F. European Hostel on Minna St, located in the South of Market area. I got fuck all sleep on the plane. It was over 24 hours since I'd slept, but I was too excited to sleep, and I headed out into the city to see what I could find.

It was a bright sunny morning, but there was a cold bite in the air. I wandered wherever curiosity took me and later found out I walked right through the neighbourhood the hostel staff tell people to avoid. I didn't have any trouble. What did worry me though was, I had sharp pains in my lower legs. I wondered if I was suffering from deep vein thrombosis. Not that I did anything about it, though. I hoped it would go away by itself, and thankfully, it did.

Wow. So here I was in the almighty United States of America. I walked along the busy Market St, wide-eyed taking it all in. All the characteristics from the telly were loud and proud, front and centre. Every car seemed ginormas, large Dodges and Fords shared the city streets with the trolleybuses. There was no shortage of fast food chains. There were many chains I'd never heard of before. The American accent filled the airwaves on the sidewalk (normally I'd say footpath, but, hey, I was in the US). Someone pan-handling could be found on every corner along with newspaper vending machines. The hustle and bustle of big city life was in full view and as I reached Powell St, I could see the famous San Francisco cable car and the steep, hilly streets the city is well known for. I made the little boy inside of me happy by going for a ride on a cable car down to the bay. I had a wander around the shops and arcades of Pier 39 and took a few photos of the sea-lions living at K Dock.

That night, I ended up drinking in the pub next door to the hostel, and I met two guys from Manchester. They were both cool dudes, and I quickly noticed that one was a lot more inebriated than the other, but in a good way. After a few hours of chatting and having a laugh, the more drunk one of the two (let's call him Averal, because I can't remember his name) was well up for a party and suggested we go to a club. We went down the road and quickly found a club, called Bondage a-go-go, or something similar (after some looking around on the net, it could quite possibly have been Harlot hosting a fetish night).

Because of the no smoking indoors law in California,

there were people outside, smoking, dressed in leather, PVC, Goth outfits, and all sorts of hair colours and piercings (my kind of crowd). We went to go in and the doorman stopped us; we couldn't enter wearing what we were wearing. Basically, we were all wearing jeans (I forgot to mention it was freezing). I was wearing a denim jacket. Averal, being a smart arse, asked, "Where does it say we can't come in wearing denim?" And sure enough, the bouncer pointed to a sign on the door outlining that only fetish, leather, and Goth allowed. And in bold print, NO DENIM.

Averal was on a mission and managed to talk the bouncer into letting us in, but we had to pay a $10 cover. I was thinking it could be one of those nights that really goes off and how cool would that be, on my very first night in the country, too, or it could just fizzle into nothing. The lack of sleep had caught up with me, plus the cover charge didn't appeal to me. My savings were in $AUD, so I just thought $20AUD was too big a gamble. Averal went in, whilst the other geezer and I went back to the pub for one last pint before I went to bed.

Looking back, I kind of wish I had gone in; it would have been great if I had had an adventure my first night in the States, but you can only make decisions at the time, and at the time, I wanted to save money and go to bed. Averal and his mate left for San Diego the next day, so I never found out how Averal's night panned out in the club. He was well wasted, so I'm sure he had a good time.

The next few days in San Fran (very cold), I did the tourist things and went and saw the Golden Gate Bridge (very long), Alcatraz (very interesting), Haight-Ashbury (very cool), Chinatown (very Chinese), Golden Gate Park (very big), and I did a lot of bar hopping (very absorbing). Everything was amazing and exciting. I also moved hostels to the Green Tortoise in the North Beach neighbourhood

(Little Italy). It's a great neighbourhood with a lot of the city's attractions in close proximity, such as Lombard Street (very crooked). Lombard Street is famous for having a steep, one-block section that consists of tight hairpin turns past old Victorian houses and landscaped gardens.

The Green Tortoise was recommended to me by a friend, but as was my usual style when alone, I shunned the people and services of the hostel and spent most of my time out and about exploring the city. My thinking was, I came to the city to meet local people, not other travellers, but my motives were partly based on fear of having to converse and make friends with people in the hostel. I preferred to go to the pub, where it's common to meet new people, particularly locals, and the booze could act as a social lubricant.

I didn't really enjoy the tipping thing, and it took me a while to get used to it. I'd heard stories about bar staff not serving you if you didn't tip them. What I did was just have one drink in each bar; that way, I didn't need to be served a second time. If I wanted to stay in a bar for more than one drink, I tipped generously early and then didn't tip anything for the next few, then tipped well again, and often, the barman/maid gave me a free drink at some point.

Ever mindful of my spending, I quickly turned to buying alcohol from liquor stores and drinking discreetly in public. I was very much aware the US is not the UK and one can't walk the streets with a beer in their hand for all to see. In the US, there are heavy penalties for drinking in the street, BUT, if one were to drink in the street, you were required to have the bottle or can in a brown paper bag. Apparently, this allowed for some leniency if caught drinking by the police. In my opinion, the brown paper bag just telegraphed to everyone you had alcohol. I did away with the brown paper bag and used my trusty jacket inside pocket. That was one plus about the cool weather; it was quite natural to wear a jacket, and I took full advantage of the inside pocket that could hold a bottle or can unseen. If the drink was opened, I just had to be careful not to bend over or there would be tears.

One place I liked to have a drink and watch the world go by was Washington Square Park. One day, I met a homeless African-American guy there, who was quite friendly. Drinking in the park tends to attract your homeless types, and they love to strike up a conversation but are usually after something. This guy was different. We spent the day together chatting about life in San Francisco. He told me about the importance of having a brown paper bag, where to get blankets, and the best place to get cheap food. But the Holy Grail was when he gave me a gold token for the public toilets. There were public toilet cubicles littered around the city that required a quarter to use. Homeless people were issued gold tokens to allow them to use the toilets for free. They were easy to obtain from the cleaning crews, and this guy had a few spares. With my penchant for drinking in public and my feeble bladder, scoring a free pass for the public toilets was a welcome stroke of luck.

My last two days in town, I hung out with friends whom I knew from the '97/'98 London days. Both Colleen and Lorie are Canadian but were now living in San Francisco. They showed me around some of the cool bars on Haight and Fillmore Streets. It was great catching up with them and hanging out in the hippy neighbourhoods. Naturally, we got quite drunk, and aware of the likelihood of hangovers the next day, Lorie recommended taking milk thistle tablets. She swore by them as a great cure for hangovers. The extract from the milk thistle plant is widely used in the prevention and cure of liver damage. This was valuable information as I was to use milk thistle a lot in the future to help detox my liver before clinical trial screenings. Thanks, Lorie.

The next day, hung over, I headed for Las Vegas.

3rd May 2002

"Hey, what you are doing?"

"Oh, um, I'm just closing the window, coz I saw a kid trying to get in here. I came to stop him."

"Right ... OK. Well, thanks ... bye."

"Yeah, bye ... do you have any spare change?"

Vegas' reputation for self-indulgence, extravagance, and debauchery had aroused some hope I may get lucky and share my bed with an exotic beauty; an old black homie was not what I had in mind.

After a long trip on Amtrak and Greyhound, I arrived in Las Vegas at two in the morning. I found a cheap hostel at the end of the strip, and even though it was closing in on 20 hours since I had some sleep, I still had trouble nodding off. My room was on the ground floor and my bed next to the window. I had the window open, hoping a cool breeze might add some relief to the warm weather. About 5am, just as it was getting light outside, I started to drift off, when suddenly, this black guy walked up to the window, opened it up further, and then started to climb in.

I said "Hey, what you are doing?" He made up this lame excuse there was a younger guy trying to get in the window and that he had come to stop the boy. He asked if I had any spare change and then he left. If I hadn't stopped him, he would have jumped in through the window and landed in bed with me. That scenario certainly wasn't in the brochures. I decided then to lock the window. I'd been having weird dreams lately (from the alcohol), and when I woke up a few hours later, I thought it was all a dream. I checked the window, and it was locked shut, so I'm guessing it really happened.

It was my birthday, and I was excited. I'm quite partial to a casino and rumour had it, drinks were on the house when gambling on the machines or at the tables. Happy birthday, indeed.

Las Vegas is full-on, man: you should see the place; it's hard to believe. It's way over the top. I first ventured down the strip during the day, and it's not much chop in the light of day, but come nightfall, the place lit up. Novelty City, I called it. A lot of the casinos are themed as miniature versions of real places, e.g., New York, Paris and Venice.

I liked the casinos, and they liked me. I donated about $300 to various places over the duration of my stay. The night of my birthday, I did reasonably well, finishing the night $100 in front. Playing my favoured roulette, I placed a bet straight up on number 3 (I'm born on the 3rd and 3 is somewhat of a lucky number) and WINNER. The ball landed on red three. I took my winnings, but as with all winnings, the original chip I placed the bet with was left on the table. I was free to take it or move it, but I forgot all about it. I placed a different bet, outside this time, for the next roll, and wouldn't you know it, it came up red three again. FUCKIN' A. I still had a chip on there. The croupier lady was as surprised as I was. She knew it was an accident. Anyway, intentional or not, the house must pay. I'm guessing it was probably a $1 minimum bet table, so that meant I'd won a total of $70 in two rolls. I was happy. I'm such a high roller, hey? I lost it all, and then some, over the next two nights, though.

It wasn't all gaming and gambling; there were quite a few fun things to do for free. Quite a few of the casinos had great visual treats. Honourable mentions go to Circus Circus, which had circus acts performing to the standard of Cirque de Soleil; the Bellagio had large water fountains putting on a show to music; Treasure Island had a show in a large man-made lake depicting pirates landing at a Caribbean Island and the battle and subsequent sinking of the 'Britannia' complete with explosions and pyrotechnics; and the Venetian, which was breath taking. Out front of the building, man-made canals and bridges, complete with gondoliers that are possible to go for a ride in, and on the inside more canals and gondoliers with shops and restaurants designed as if set outdoors with the ceiling painted in a darkened, light blue as if the setting were dusk.

I did go to a few stand-up shows, which were a lot of fun, and took a day trip to the Grand Canyon. The view from the west rim was stunning, staggering, mind-blowing, breathtaking and all the other synonyms you can think of. I had to remind myself I was actually looking at the real thing, not some picture or TV show. Our tour guide took us to a few different places along the rim. He was quite entertaining as he was telling us about the area. It was a good day, well worth the visit. We also stopped for lunch at a diner on the old Route 66; been there, done that, now. I also met a guy on my tour from Hammerfest, Norway, the most northern city in the world. After the tour, we went to a bar (not the easiest thing to find in Las Vegas outside of a casino) and had a few drinks. He was a real joy to talk to. He did accents really well, including a Middlesbrough accent. I closed my eyes and I thought I was with Crazy Horse.

We also checked out Las Vegas Downtown. The Vegas strip has all the new and modern casinos, whilst Las Vegas Downtown is the Vegas you'd know from the 50's, 60's, and 70's. The main street in Las Vegas Downtown is Freemont St, which has a pedestrian mall occupying five blocks, known as the Freemont Experience, and is covered by a barrel vault canopy with some you-beaut-fandangle neon lights.

After a few days, Vegas was too much. I grew tired of the constant hard sell everywhere to try to get my money. I was angry, too, for losing around $300. I wanted Las Vegas behind me ... and fast. In my haste to leave the money sucking city, I bought a plane ticket to New Orleans. It got me a long way from Vegas quickly, but looking back, it probably wasn't the best thing I could have done regarding my bank balance. I was a bit disappointed that, during my stay, I hadn't woken up with a new bride and no memory of getting married. I say that, but it could have been a life changing moment (for the worse), which I would have been none too pleased about.

I guess I shouldn't have told you any of that, as 'what happens in Vegas stays in Vegas' but there was nothing incriminating to report. "Move along, move along. Nothing to see here. Move along."

9th–20th May 2002

New Orleans was quite the bender. I was stuck in a vicious cycle of late nights, boozing and drunkenness, and I wasn't sure how I was going to escape. Escape was made harder, too, by the fact I'd made so many friends. I met some ultra-friendly people in some of the bars, and some cool and interesting people who drank on the street, your homeless/squatter types. From impersonating an Irishman during a tarot reading, visiting haunted houses and being pushed to the ground by the police on the banks of the Mississippi River, through to meeting a Lucy Lawless lookalike, my time in New Orleans was never dull.

I got an airport shuttle van into the city that was to drop all the passengers off at their respective hotels. After a half hour drive, the van pulled into the driveway of an old, weathered, double-storied town-house. It was about 10:30 at night; the house was dimly lit and looked derelict.

"I hope this isn't my stop," I thought.

The driver looked at me and said, "This is you, isn't it?"

"I don't know."

"India House!"

"Yeah, that's me."

I'd booked this place over the phone and was embarrassed to be first drop and at a place that was none too classy. As I was collecting my bags, I felt like saying to the dapper passengers, "My other hotel is the Hyatt."

Anyway, it didn't matter. India House was a good hostel; it had a swimming pool and check-out was at 1pm, which I thought was very civilised. Not that I spent much time there, though. I spent most of my time out and about and used the hostel as a place to sleep and keep my bags.

The first day or so, I wasn't in the happiest of moods. The American people, in general, were starting to piss me off. I didn't like their arrogant, know-all, self-righteous extraversion, partly because I'm an introvert and wish I could be the extravert. I was also feeling down and lonely from travelling solo on the road. Up until then, I hadn't met many people, but the French Quarter is a small place, and my social life was soon to change.

By day three, I found a unique and interesting bar in the French Quarter. I quickly became friends with all the bar staff there and often got cheap/free drinks. It was called Marie Laveau's Voodoo Bar, named after the voodoo queen, Marie Laveau, who was prominent in New Orleans in the 1800's. The bar was only the size of a main bedroom and considerably easy to walk straight past if you didn't know it was there. It's even harder to find nowadays as, unfortunately, it's closed down.

New Orleans has a voodoo and ghost history, and Marie Laveau Voodoo Bar sold real voodoo dolls and spell books. One barmaid, Candice—tall, blonde, mid-30's—worked the day shift and gave me an education in music. She played all this 60's and 70's blues music which I loved. One song was really clever. You may have heard of it. It's called 'Shame and Scandal in the Family'. The song was about this boy growing up in a small village, and he tells his dad that he's interested in dating a certain girl. The father says, "Son, don't tell your Momma, but that girl's your sister." So, the boy must pick another girl, and it gets to the point that, no matter who he picks, his dad says "Son, don't tell your Momma, but that girl's your sister." Time passes, and the boy's mother notices he's not dating, and she asks him why. So, the boy comes clean and says Poppa told him all the girls were his sister. His mother said, "Son, don't tell your Poppa, but he ain't your Poppa." So, the boy was then able to choose whomever he wanted.

Candice was way cool and often gave me free drinks; she could make a great Long Island Ice Tea, as well. The other barmaids were friendly, too, but I always tried to go when Candice was working—for the music and the drinks. As I said, the bar was tiny and had, maybe, six stools at the bar and about eight seats at two tables. Because the bar was so small, one couldn't help but chat with other people. I met a friendly, young, American couple, and they suggested we go out exploring the French Quarter together. We roped another couple into coming out with us, and we went out drinking. I woke up the next morning with Mardi-Gras beads and a mask on (imagine my surprise) and no idea how I came to be wearing them. On some parts of Bourbon St, you can get free beads if you flash certain body parts, so I was curious to know how I got them. I met up again with the couple, later on, and they told me they had bought them for me.

Lara was another barmaid. She was an attractive, young brunette, almost Gothic in appearance. She was extremely friendly and good with people. I saw her subdue a group of rowdy men one-day, which a less assured woman would have cowered to. I couldn't go all the way to New Orleans and not have a drink of my favoured Southern Comfort. Lara was always happy to serve me the Grand Ol' Drink of the South and even had one with me when I was leaving town.

Early on in my daily pilgrimages to Marie Laveau, I went in one morning and the place was empty, except for the barmaid who was chatting away with a female friend. I hadn't met this barmaid yet; I can't remember her name, but she looked like Lucy Lawless—the New Zealand actress who played Xena, the Warrior Princess. I sat at the bar and ordered a beer. My shakes were awfully bad, and I struggled to hold the beer, which was in a flimsy plastic cup. I asked Lucy Lawless if she could give me a straw. She very kindly obliged, but I could tell I was creeping out her and her friend. So, when I finished the drink, I left so the two could feel at ease. I returned later in the afternoon after I'd had many more drinks and my shakes were a lot calmer. This time, Lara was working.

She asked me, "Were you in here earlier?"

"Yeah."

"Did you drink your beer with a straw?"

"Yeah," I said with a cheeky grin.

"I thought it was you."

Lucy Lawless had told Lara, "Some weird guy came in, shaking like a leaf, and asked for a straw to drink his beer." Another barmaid, who was always friendly and good to talk to, was Megan. She always had another beer poured for me before I even asked for it. I love that.

I met a lot of hobos, as well. Drinking on the streets in New Orleans is legal, which is why beers are served in plastic cups. You can order drinks 'to go' from the bars. I often bought booze from the liquor store and drank on the streets, which always attracted the hobo types. Some of them were really cool and fun to hang out with. I met quite a lot of people from drinking on the streets, and it was easy to bump into people you knew. There were two guys, in particular, I used to hang out with. I met them in a black out one night, unbeknownst to me, and then a few days later, they saw me again and came up and said hello. I was a bit nervous at first, having these two guys come up to me, like long lost friends, and I didn't have a clue who they were. But we bonded over a few drinks, and I drank with them often, usually on the banks of the Mississippi.

One night, six of us were drinking by the river, when all of a sudden, we all got knocked down from behind. I grazed my hands, knees, and elbows trying to brace myself as I fell onto the esplanade. I tried to get up, not knowing what was going on, but I was hit down again. It was the police. I'd heard the New Orleans Police had a bad reputation for being corrupt and above the law. They had us all sprawled on our stomachs with our arms and legs spread, shouting at us. They demanded to see ID, and as I understood it, if you didn't have ID, they could put you in jail. Well, I didn't have any on me, but I put on my thickest Australian accent,

"Struth, fair go mate, I'm just an Aussie tourist from Down Under, and I don't want to lose my passport, so I don't carry it around with me."

They let me and my two friends go, but they took the others away. I don't know what happened to them, and I still don't know what it was all about.

Through my two hobo buddies, I met this girl, called Willow, who by coincidence was staying at the same hostel as I was. They warned me she was a bit of a fruit loop, but normally, I'm attracted to people who are a bit different. She was a fruit loop, even for my standards, but that didn't stop me from hanging out with her for the next three days.

She was short and had fair hair and was somewhat depressive but had a great smile on the occasions I managed to make her laugh. She was from the US, drifting around the country from place to place. She took me to this squat she used to stay at that was supposedly haunted. We borrowed (took) a candle from a Goth bar, and we went to the squat. We'd been there for 10 seconds when, for no apparent reason, the wick fell through the bottom of the candle and landed on the floor. That was a bit freaky. Willow said that had happened to her once before in that house. Without the candle, we were reliant upon her lighter, which got extremely hot and was difficult to hold. I wasn't too comfortable hanging out there without being able to see, so after a brief guided tour, we left.

We wandered through the 9th Ward and saw the Projects (low income housing). We checked out some cemeteries, as well. Because New Orleans is below sea level, all the graves are above ground. She also took me to the 'Wall', which is where people on the streets can go and get some free food from a local charity. New Orleans is famous for its delicious cuisine, yet the only real food I sampled was soup and bread dished out from the back of a charity van. Food wasn't high on my list of priorities.

Earlier that day, we had been hanging out in a park, just talking, and Willow asked if I would have sex with her in a church. I said, "Amen Sister," but even with all the churches in New Orleans, we had trouble finding one that was open. We decided to go to the French Quarter in search of a church via the hostel to pick up some condoms. I wanted our moment to be impressive, and, so I would last longer than a few minutes, I had a quick wank at the hostel. We then left, and within minutes, we were walking past a Government office block. Willow said, "Let's use the restroom in here." My first thought was, "Fuck, I don't know if I'll be able to get it up again so soon." Security didn't let us in, anyway, and they suggested we use the restroom at McDonalds a few blocks down. No thanks. Not for what we had in mind.

We never did find a church. We became busy looking at haunted houses and touring the streets. I wasn't too upset. I thought we'd be able to find a church the next day, but come the next day, she was on another planet and kept going on about how she had renounced Jesus. We were meant to go bike riding that day, but she said she just wanted to be left alone, so I went into town to the Marie Laveau, and I never saw her again. Shame. I quite liked her.

At night in Jackson Square, there were a lot of tarot card readers, palm readers, and psychic stuff like that. Just for a laugh, I decided to have a tarot reading, except, I spoke the whole time in an Irish accent and told the guy I was from Belfast. He asked if I had any questions about my life that he might be able to answer. I asked questions about family members that don't exist. Apparently, my older sister (I don't have an older sister) will finally become pregnant and will have a healthy boy. My wife (I'm not married) will leave her current job and find another job quite quickly; there, she will find her calling in life, which will make her happy. I tried my best not to laugh through the reading. I must have been pretty convincing because, whenever I saw him again on the street after that, he always called me the crazy Irish man and I always had to put on the Irish accent again.

Noticing my funds were almost dry, I decided I had to escape the viscous cycle of waking in the afternoon, feeling like shit, drinking for a few hours to feel normal again and, by then, it's too late to organise to travel anywhere, so I stay and drink until the wee hours of the morning and the cycle starts again. I rang my friend, Monica, in DC and told her I could be on her doorstep very soon as I needed somewhere to stay, quickly. She said it wasn't a problem, and in the meantime, she organised for me to meet up with a friend of hers who lived in New Orleans.

I met up with her friend, Rebecca, in a bar, and she brought along a whole lot of friends too, all girls. I think Rebecca had enticed her friends to come out by saying she was going to meet an Australian guy. Unfortunately for them, I don't fit the Australian stereotype, but we all got along famously, anyway. One of the girls, Janie, invited me to stay at her place for a few days until her parents came to visit. Nice one.

I moved out of the hostel and into a grand house with my own room, which gave me a chance to break my daily routine and sort out my travel plans. With Janie's parents coming to visit in a few days, there was the added pressure not to procrastinate. After much searching for cheap airfares and rental cars, the decision was to catch a Greyhound bus to DC in a few days.

I hung out with Janie for a few days. Janie was a brunette in her late 20s and spoke with a comforting southern accent. We went with some of her friends to a few bars in her area that I hadn't been to before. It was great to see a new part of town. I asked Janie what ward this area was. She said the 7th, and whatever I do, don't go to the 9th; it's dangerous. Woops, too late. Willow and I had wandered through the 9th a few nights earlier.

Janie's place was right near St Charles Avenue, which is a main thoroughfare through New Orleans and is famous for the hundreds of mansions that adorn the tree-lined boulevard for much of the Uptown section. St Charles is also known as one of the main routes for the Mardi-Gras parade and is famous for the St Charles Streetcar line. Streetcars, similar to trams, are a big part of New Orleans history, since early 19th century. St Charles Avenue Streetcar is the longest line in New Orleans and is the oldest continuously operating street railway system in the world. And I had a ride on it. Well, it was quicker than walking.

We stayed up most nights just chatting about things. One night, we didn't stop until 10 in the morning. I was up again a few hours later, off to a bar, where I'd heard there was going to be some good slide guitar on show. That was definitely one good thing about Bourbon Street—the music. The bars were touristy, but you could just walk along, and from one bar to the next, there would be a band playing, and if you liked what you heard, you could go in and have a listen for a while. This is the home of Jazz, and I saw quite a lot of good music that was worthy of being on the world stage but was probably only well-known in New Orleans.

On my way to a music venue near Janie's house, I met five freight hoppers. They were after some change, but I only had a 20-dollar bill on me. I proposed we use the 20 to buy beer from the liquor store, and we find a place to sit down and drink it. They were happy with that, and we had a good time chatting and sharing a few laughs. This cheered me up, because before that, I was pissed off about not being able to find the music venue I was after. I asked for directions from a guy, and he sent me in the wrong direction. So, when I ran into the freight train riders, I abandoned the idea of the gig and thought hanging with them would be more interesting.

These dudes were young 20 something's, bumming around the country together, with nothing more than the clothes on their back. They were three guys and two girls and travelled from city to city by ensconcing free rides on freight train cars. Apparently, it's a common practice amongst hobos and transients and has been since as far back as the Civil War. They showed me their 'bible', which was a book full of maps detailing all the freight train routes in the country. At the back of the book were lyrics to dozens of train songs that they could sing to pass the time.

They told me stories of accidents and near misses and the

methodology of trying to hop a fast freight train. Carrying a bag can slow you down when you're running, so one option is to throw the bag on the train first, allowing the hopper to run faster and move more freely without the constraint of a bag. But then, say you throw your bag on the train and you don't make it on to the train? You lose your bag. So, there was some real skill and thought that had to go into freight train hopping. I thought the whole idea of bumming around, travelling with likeminded transients, with few possessions and with few worries was really romantic. Of course, the reality of it was not so fantastic. These guys had next to no money and relied on astuteness and resourcefulness to get them food and drink. I wouldn't enjoy not being able to drink like a motherfucker.

After 10 days in 'The Big Easy', I was on my way. I was absolutely grateful to Janie. If she hadn't invited me to her house, which got me away from all the drinking, I may never have left and then I would have been living in squats and on the streets, just like most of the people I was hanging out with. If I ever lived in New Orleans, I'd be dead within a few years, for sure.

The last four weeks up until this point had been interesting, but I remember at the time thinking, if I had my time over, I would do it completely different. Having escaped New Orleans, I faced my next challenge: How the fuck do I survive the next 25 days with hardly any money?

After a painfully long 29 hour Greyhound trip, I arrived in Washington DC. Monica was there, as planned, to pick me up from the bus station. I was so excited to see her on her home soil. We went and met up with Brian (who I'd met in Thailand at New Year's) in a bar for a few drinks before going back to his place for beer and pizza. I hadn't seen these guys since Thailand, and it was exciting to see them again. I was also relieved to have the New Orleans binge behind me and to be off that fuckin' bus. I didn't get to bed until 11:30 that night, for some much-needed sleep, I tell you.

May–June 2002

Monica was busy with a few things, so I stayed with Brian at his place, which he shared with three other guys in a great four storey house, affectionately known as 1103P, possibly due to the address being 1103 P Street ... you think? The residents there were no strangers to having guests stay over, so I was made welcome. I had a choice of three different sofas to sleep on. Wow, I was being spoilt. Actually, this was just what I needed. I was staying with friends in a new city, rent free. I always enjoy staying with friends and seeing their town from a local's point of view. It's a good way to get a feel of what it might be like to live in that city, rather than just experience it from the top deck of a sightseeing bus, and Brian is quite the tour guide. He's quite knowledgeable about his home city; he worked for a time as an information guy in one of the city museums and, at the time, worked as a journalist for a political magazine, which helped to keep his finger on the pulse. Our friendship grew stronger as we got to hang out with each other more. In Thailand, when we met we only spent a few days together. It was especially kind of Brian to show such hospitality.

Speaking of which, Brian invited me to go along with him and his girlfriend down to Virginia that coming weekend to visit his parents. I was up for that. His parents live in Portsmouth, (nickname P Town), close to Virginia Beach. Brian's parents, Ron and Maureen, were lovely; they were so welcoming and friendly. This was my first taste of small town America, and I was experiencing firsthand that famous American friendliness and hospitality. Their house was like a theme park, except for the lack of rides, and exorbitant prices, and long queues, and no one walking around in a Mickey Mouse outfit, but other than that, it was a theme park.

Each room was painted and decorated in a different theme. The main bedroom was the beach; bedroom 2 was the sea and ships; bedroom 3 was outer space and the night sky; the bathroom was the Washington Redskins, and the kitchen had an Irish theme. The house wasn't without a water fun park, either. Out the back of the house, inside a transparent annex, was a hot tub. "Have a nice day," indeed.

Sunday afternoon and back in DC, we went to a BBQ, and I met a load of cool people. The hostess, Natalie, was very friendly and good humoured. In her mid-20's, Natalie was tall, dark, and slim, had a little bit of a crazy streak in her, loved Johnny Cash, and I remember, one night, she let me drive her beat up blue Dodge, or whatever it was. Its nickname was the 'Scum Car' because the licence plate had the letters SCM in it, and because it was such a piece of shit. She had that thing since high school. I couldn't have been sober, plus I was driving on the other side to what I'm used to. There were no objections from any of the passengers, either. I think I managed to drive the couple of blocks to her house, OK. I may have hit the kerb once, not that Natalie cared.

She told me she was planning on visiting her sister in Dublin in August and that I should try to get over there, too, and we could hang out together. I expected to be back in London at that time. I said I'd try to visit if I could, but I didn't hold out much hope. Fuck, was I wrong. I did make it. That trip changed my life, as you'll find out.

Midweek, Brian and I caught up with Monica, and we went with Brian's friend, Graeme, to see the new *Star Wars* movie (episode II). It wasn't really Monica's thing; she claimed to have not seen the original movies, but it was good to hang out with her, anyway, whereas, for us three lads, we were *Star Wars* fanatics. The general consensus was: good action, bad acting, especially from Hayden Christensen. This was the first time I'd met Graeme, and we got along well. More of him to come, later.

Brian went out of town for some business down in New Orleans. I told him to check out Marie Laveau Voodoo Bar, and I wrote down on some scrap paper a message for each of the barmaids for him to pass on for me. He arrived there whilst Lara was on duty, and she pinned up my messages behind the bar. If I'd known they were going to be on display, I would have written better messages on a better piece of paper. Ah, well. Brian told me he was really well looked after by the girls there because of me. I felt pleased I'd been able to return the favour in some small indirect way for the hospitality that Brian had showed me.

I did very minimal sight-seeing. I saw the main things, like the White House, the United States Capitol Building, different monuments along the National Mall, and the Pentagon. I did walk around the city a lot, though, you can't really get lost in DC with the way the city is designed. Streets running north/south are numbered, and streets running east/west are named after a letter. The museums were free, but I was keeping different hours to those of the museums, so I never got around to going.

Washington DC is similar to Canberra in many respects. They were both pre-chosen capitals to be home of the Federal Government, both full of national monuments, both with geometrically designed street patterns, and both cosmopolitan. What I related to the most about DC was that, on the surface, it could be perceived as formal, boring, and quiet, but if you were to scratch below the surface and experience the community life, you'd find a vibrant, fun, and interesting metropolis. I believe Canberra is the same.

Something I managed to get off my butt and do was go to a free street concert Saturday night and see some cool bands. The main act was called G Love & the Special Sauce, but the stand out moment for me came from the support band, Laughing Colors. They performed their song "War on Drugs", which has the great chorus line, "Whatever happened to sex, drugs and rock & roll? Now we've just got AIDS, crack, and techno." You should check it out.

I also played softball in Brian and Natalie's softball team. They were short a player, or two, so I filled in. It was a lot of fun. It was a proper game in a proper league, but their team was the sort that didn't take the game too seriously. It was more of a social thing than a form of exercise, especially meeting up for a few beers afterwards.

I had a chance to look at my finances. I had about $180 to last me until I arrived in London and got paid for the job I didn't yet have. That was three weeks away. But I wanted to go to the Glastonbury Festival, too, so add another week onto that and increase my expenses by another $100 or more; so, it was quite a dilemma. What fucked me up was Las Vegas. I spent about $300 in the town and then $330 on a plane ticket to get out. I was so desperate to leave and leave fast that I decided to fly. I should have caught a train. To top it all off, my next stop was New York, not exactly known for its low cost of living.

10th–19th June 2002

New York City baby! It was just after dark as we were driving into the outskirts of New York; the excitement grew as I could see the urban jungle of Manhattan all lit up. "Wow, there's the Empire State Building. Oh, look, the Statue of Liberty." One of my main motivations for travelling to the States was to see, firsthand, the cities I'd seen so much of on

TV. Here I was, travelling through the streets of Manhattan at night, observing all the activity, people, traffic, and noise. It was just as I'd imagined. Yellow cabs, smoke rising from manholes in the street, bagel and pizza shops, the subway, skyscrapers, neon lights, American flags, they were all there. I felt so cool. If my friends could see me now.

Well, I wasn't completely without friends. Brian and I came up to New York to visit Michael (who I also met in Thailand at New Year's), who was living and working in Manhattan. Brian drove us up in his truck, and Graeme came along for the ride to catch up with mates of his own.

We parked near Michael's apartment and got straight into it. Graeme went off and met with his friends, whilst Brian and I met up with Michael, who was out at a restaurant having dinner with a friend, naturally a female. Michael's a charming guy and quite knowledgeable on many areas of life. He's right at home in 'the city that never sleeps' lifestyle. It was really good to see him again. We both expressed how it felt a bit weird seeing each other in an urban setting, when our memories of each other were of us lazing about on the beach of Koh Pha Ngan. His friend, Carol, was equally charming. She's from Hong Kong via Canada and sociable with everyone.

We checked out a few clubs and bars, and at the end of the night, we stumbled on a small bar run by monks, called the Burp Castle. It's easy to miss as it's hidden behind a fence. It's a cool little monastery-themed bar, with beer the main object of worship. They had various imported beers from Europe, which went down well, a nice change from the shit that America passes off as beer. The place was decked out like a proper abbey, with medieval-styled murals, Gregorian chants on the stereo, and the bartenders dressed in monk robes. The bar had a serene atmosphere; we felt we had to whisper when we were talking. It really had that medieval church vibe.

Michael's apartment was in the vibrant East Village, on 1st Ave, between 6th and 7th St. It was a small studio flat with one room, open-plan, and a bathroom. It would be my home for the next ten days. The best part was being four floors up and sitting out on the fire escape, watching the New Yorkers go about their business below.

First day in Manhattan, we were off for a picnic in Central Park. We met up with Joanne and Jaime, who'd just recently got married. Joanne was part of the DC circle of friends, whilst Jaime was from Barcelona. They were both very friendly; it was nice to meet them.

It was a beautiful sunny day, and the park was alive. There were buskers and roller bladders, joggers, all sorts of sporting activities. The park is super big, about 3km 2 or something, bigger than I'd expected. We set up camp at an open grassy area and got stuck into the cheese, salami, and biscuits.

That night, a whole gang of us went out bar hopping back in the East Village. We were sitting at a table in one of the bars, when I recognised one of the girls at the table next to us had an Australian accent. Cool, that was our in. She started to get out a cigarette, and Michael quickly suggested I light it for her. So, like some smooth ladies' man, I sidled up beside her, and without a word, I put a flaming lighter out in front of her. Wow, it worked. She was impressed. Well, one thing led to another, and we've been happily married for five years now. Well … no, not quite. I say, not quite; I mean more like, not even close.

One thing led to another in that I was then able to open her and her group of female friends and have them join our table. Relations were going well, but not well enough it would seem, because they announced they were off to another bar. Not to be discouraged, we asked for the address and met them there.

We were at the next bar and the roll call was: Brian,

Michael, and me; I don't think Graeme was there, but Carol was, as was her boyfriend, Steve, who had a few mates with him, and there was Miss Australia and her three friends, and quite possibly one or two more; I've forgotten. I got chatting with Steve and his mates, who were cool guys and your typical beer swilling, chauvinistic, rowdy bunch of lads. I integrated with them a bit too easily.

Steve offered to buy me a drink if I could get a woman to slap me. I didn't rate my chances, but I was willing to give it a go.

I invited a woman walking past, "Will you slap me on the arse?"

She was a real live wire and shot back, "Oooh, will *you* slap me on the arse?"

I thought, so far so good. It was time to go for gold. "Will you slap me across the face?"

"Oh now, you're going too far."

She wasn't impressed and walked away. The lads were laughing their arses off. Steve was like, "Dude, what were you thinking? She was happy for you to slap her arse."

"I was thinking of getting a free beer."

"Man, I would have aborted that mission. She was hot."

Yeah, good point. It wasn't the first time I'd failed to capitalise on the attraction of a woman towards me by putting alcohol first. Unfortunately, not the last either.

At the end of the weekend, Brian went back to DC and Michael back to work. It was great hanging with Brian again, and there were rumours he might be accompanying Natalie to Ireland in August. So, maybe I'd see him then.

Whilst Michael was busy working, I did a sightseeing bus tour and saw the famous places, like the Statue of Liberty, Times Square, Central Park, Empire State Building, ground zero, and saw where the Twin Towers used to be. I checked out some of the local cuisine and tried a bagel and a slice of pizza. Mmmm, both delicious. I thought I was so cool because I learnt a 'slice' means a slice of cheese pizza. I was slicing all over the place.

In the evenings, Michael and I hobnobbed in the New York nightlife. We caught a local live band with some work colleagues; we met up with Carol and went to the movies. We ended up watching a peculiar British film, *Secret Society*, about female factory workers who overcame taunts of being overweight by taking part in sumo wrestling—something different, I suppose.

Michael went to Buffalo, upstate New York, for the week on business, whilst I met up with Graeme, who was still in town, and we went on a bender for a few days. We hung out with lots of his friends, checking out different bars, mainly around Alphabet City. We were up all hours one night, and the only bar we could find open at five in the morning was a sports bar on 3rd Ave. At the time, the football World Cup was in progress in South Korea, and the bar was full, absolutely chockers, with Turkish fans watching football. Turkey won their match, and the bar went wild. Graeme and I looked on in wonder.

For lunch one day, Graeme suggested we eat at the deli of the fake orgasm. We had a meal at the deli, where the fake orgasm scene was shot in the film *When Harry met Sally*.

New York's a very busy place (uh … no shit). I liked it a lot. It's expensive, but there are a lot of things to do and a lot of interesting shops and pubs hidden away in little pockets of the city. I could easily live there. Being that I was staying in an apartment in the East Village and mixing it with the locals in the one and only New York, I felt really important, like I'd made it (despite being broke).

The time came to leave New York and head for London. Michael had been kind letting me stay at his apartment. It saved me a fortune. His kindness didn't stop there. He lent me some money, so I could survive the next few weeks. Thanks, mate. It was goodbye for now, but we'd meet again in just over a week's time at Glastonbury, probably both off our trolleys in a field somewhere.

Late June 2002

Glastonbury, hey. It was a great weekend that started on Tuesday staying with Simon and Jan, in Bristol, and finishing Monday with a cruisy road trip home with Tom.

I haven't properly introduced you to Tom, yet. I first met Tom back in '97 through Simon, back when I was working at the Empire. He's a football, music loving English geezer. At this time, he was in his early 40's. He can be very funny and has a natural zest about him. Tom is well-travelled and tells some funny stories about his drunken escapades around the world, including Australia. Despite only introducing him now, we mixed in the same circles quite regularly whenever I was in London.

The Glastonbury Festival of Contemporary Performing Arts, commonly known as Glastonbury or Glasto, is the largest, green-field, open-air, music and performing arts festival in the world. It's held at Worthy Farm, about 10 km east of the town of Glastonbury, Somerset, in the south-east of England, Great Britain, United Kingdom, Europe, planet Earth. There were certainly some freaks there from another planet, though.

It's organised by local farmer and site owner, Michael Eavis, with assistance from his daughter, Emily. The festival is best known for its contemporary music, but also features dance, comedy, theatre, circus, cabaret, and many other arts.

I first went to the festival in '98 with a whole gang of mates from my London circle of friends. It was an amazing weekend but it rained for the majority of the four days and the farm was a mud bath. From what I can remember, it stayed dry the whole weekend this time round. In the beginning, I missed all the mud from '98. The mud added that extra element of 'roughing it' and camaraderie with the fellow campers. This time around, there wasn't that feeling of having shared in overcoming a natural disaster, but I tell you, it sure was good to be able to sit down on the dry ground this time.

Friends attending whom I spent time with: Simon, Jan, Tom, Stuart, Jim, Leeds Dave, Laughing Chris, Michael, and Monica.

After a long trek carrying firewood up to our camp, we noticed a lot of the wood to be of similar size and length, so we had a giant game of Jenga with the wood. It quite amused our camping neighbours.

With regards to bands, the highlight was Faithless. The lights, the music, the crowd, the atmosphere, and the stage performance all contributed to make a great show. The crowd rocked as one; it was awesome. Stuart and I befriended a group of girls, as well, which added to it. I told my dad back home about it, too. He said, "You've been to London—no big deal. Seen the Eiffel Tower—so what? Stood in Red Square—whatever. BUT, seeing Faithless ... LIVE ...—now I'm jealous." As you may have guessed, he's a big fan.

The funniest thing to happen Sunday was when Simon and I were laying in front of the fire at about 7am and Tom was sleeping next to us. He unexpectedly said in his sleep, "Will you dress me in women's clothing?" Simon and I looked at each other as if to say, "Did you hear that?" Once we realised we had both heard the same thing and we weren't imagining it, we burst out laughing. Perhaps, it's one of those 'you had to be there' moments, but what happened later was a weird coincidence.

Stuart and Jim, unaware of the incident, found a one

pound stall and did a bit of shopping and, for some unknown reason, they bought Tom a present. And you know what that present was? ... A dress. Needless to say, Tom was not too happy with the gift and thought they were taking the piss, but they had no idea what he'd said in his sleep. The dress was far too small for Tom, anyway, so I took it and wore it out that night over my jeans and jumper, because it was so cold and because I hadn't shaved my legs.

Sunday night, I went out on a mission to get fucked up. I went out wearing the dress and the masquerade mask from New Orleans. I went to Stone Circle to buy some pills. I bought two off this geezer, and they looked like vitamin tablets I used to have as a kid. Naturally, they didn't work. I found the guy and told him, and he insisted they were real and would kick in soon. He told me to take a seat next to him, and if they didn't work, he'd give some that would. Whilst I was sitting there, I was watching all the freaks and then I turned back to discover the geezer had fucked off. I gave up and went back to the camp straighter than when I left.

Monday, we woke early, packed our stuff, and left at about 10am. As we were walking to the car, there were queues of cars miles long and not moving at all. I really wasn't looking forward to being stuck in a car park for hours, moving only 10 feet every half hour or so. But luck was on our side. Tom had parked in the furthest car park from the farm, which meant, when we got to the car, we just drove straight out and were on the motorway in no time. In fact, half an hour after hopping in the car, we were in a pub down the road. We phoned some friends, and they hadn't moved at all. We were back in London in a few hours, whilst four hours later, our friends were still in the car park back at the farm.

So, a cracking week-end all up.

July 2002

It was so good to be back in the UK and not have to tip for a drink. I was back in London and staying with my mate, Chris, in Shepherd's Bush. Chris and I first met through my Empire boss, Simon. I stayed up in his attic and had to climb a ladder to get up and down from the manhole. He said I could stay, for free, as long as I wanted, provided I cooked a meal once a week and always made sure there was booze in the house. His 13-year-old son, Tony, lived there, too, so there was always a bit of entertainment. I'd have been screwed if I couldn't have stayed there, as I'd nowhere else to stay (for free), and I had little to no money.

26th July

It was Friday night, and Chris, Stuart, and I met up for dinner in a restaurant on Uxbridge Rd, in Acton. It was pleasant enough, good food and good company. After the meal, Stuart was knackered after a long week and went home, whilst Chris and I went over the road to a pub/club called Shebeen. We were just enjoying a quiet drink when I needed to go to the dunny. For this visit, I had to sit down, if you know what I mean, which isn't the most exciting of prospects when you consider the state of some pub toilets. I noticed there were no locks on the cubicle doors. Why that was the case became clear later. But otherwise, the toilet was in a tolerable condition.

As I was doing the business, someone opened the door to the cubicle, and I quickly put my hand out to stop the door, so they wouldn't come in any further. I was quick to announce my presence, too, so he would be under no illusion I was there. Embarrassment was averted; I finished up, washed my hands, and went to walk back to join Chris at the table. I didn't get but a few steps out of the toilet when I was grabbed from behind by the doorman, who marched me outside.

"We don't tolerate drugs in here, mate," and with that, he threw me out of the pub.

"What the FUCK?"

Did I miss something? I hadn't done any drugs; what was he on about? That fuckwit that walked in on me doing a shit must have gone and told the doorman I was doing drugs. What an arsehole. I protested my innocence to the doorman, "I was going to the toilet, mate." But the arrogant, smarmy, puffed-up, pompous twat was on an ego trip and couldn't be reasoned with. I was furious.

Meanwhile, Chris was still sitting in the pub waiting for me to come back from the toilet. I had to ask someone to go in and tell him I was outside. He was sitting there, minding his own business, when this guy came up to him and said, "Are you Chris? You're mate's outside. He's been thrown out."

Half-intrigued and half-amused, Chris came outside and asked what happened. "I got thrown out for taking a SHIT!" I said it loudly, too, right in front of Mr Smug. This is what I don't like about doormen; a vast majority of them are unreasonable, egotistical, aggressive thugs. They won't listen to reason, and there's nothing you can do about it. Before Chris got the wrong idea, I explained to him I wasn't, actually, thrown out for taking a crap. I hadn't been disgusting and defecated on the toilet floor.

Knowing there was nothing we could do about it, Chris and I went home. Mmmm, but was there? I was still fuming and quite drunk. I decided to ring the manager of the pub to tell him off. I rang directory enquiries and asked for the number for Shebeen on Uxbridge Rd. I dialled the number, and when someone answered, I immediately let fly. I really let the guy have it. "Mate, I was just at your fuckin' place and, honestly, I was just going to the toilet when that arrogant fucker on the door threw me out for taking drugs." I didn't stop there. I kept on with the tirade until the guy interrupted me, "Hey mate, where do you think you've called?"

"Shebeen nightclub."

"Nah mate, this is Shabab, a kebab takeaway, on Uxbridge Rd."

"Woops, sorry about that mate, my mistake."

He was right, too. Shabab was at the end of my street. I'd walked past it dozens of times. The mistake I made was assuming Shebeen was on Uxbridge Road. It's a considerably long road, over 6km, but when it gets to Acton, although it's the same road, its name becomes Acton High St. So, I got the number to Shebeen and double-checked I had the right number when someone answered. I spoke to the manager and took off on my drunken, verbal attack again.

Long story short, he sincerely apologised for the mistaken eviction. He determined, if I really was doing drugs in the toilet, I wouldn't have bothered to ring and complain. He said, next time I'm there, to seek him out and he'd give me a few free drinks. He explained they'd had a big problem with people doing drugs in the toilets; that's why there weren't any locks on the cubicles and why the doorman had been so unyielding. I was happy with that explanation and accepted his apology. I never did go back and receive my free drinks. Over the next couple of days, I had fun telling people I'd been thrown out of the pub for doing a shit. Invariably, they'd ask, "Where did you do it?"

27th July 2002

It took a bit longer than I'd hoped, but I finally found a job working in a warehouse out at Greenford, picking and packing. Chris worked out at the same industrial site and had suggested I approach the onsite agency there. It was quite handy, as Chris was able to give me a lift to work each morning. I'd actually worked out there before, in early '99, for Waitrose. This time around, I was working for Harvey Nichols. My job was a typical picker/packer position. I picked orders of food and drink products and then packed them in boxes to be transported to stores throughout the country. I enjoyed the job. It was easy, and I was becoming good friends with the other workers; it was a short ride from home, and the supervisors had explained their plans to have me moved to the easier position of working in the wines section. I had settled back into London nicely and had established a routine, hoping to save money to pay off debts.

22nd August 2002 onwards

After having been at Harvey Nichols for some weeks, they produced a roster that extended past January 2003. I remember feeling weird having my future mapped out like that. Who were they to say what I'd be doing in six months? When the changeover of the two rosters occurred, it worked out in my favour, and I ended up with a week off. Michael, Natalie, and Brian were coming over from the States to visit Ireland that same week, so I organised to go over and spend the weekend with them in Dublin. And Crazy Horse, who was back living in Belfast, was also going to join us.

We all met up at our hotel in Dublin, and with introductions over, we all got on great guns. To save money for the weekend, I had stayed off the booze for three weeks beforehand, as drinking was my biggest expense. But none of us were shy when it came to drinking, and the weekend was a blur to me as my alcohol tolerance was in the toilet from the three weeks off.

It was during this weekend that Crazy Horse and I

decided to change our names. Whilst the others were at the Guinness factory, we were in a pub and Crazy Horse explained it was possible to get a deed poll on the Internet. As a laugh, Crazy bought a deed poll changing his mate Pete's name to Edgar Stuart without telling him. I wish I could have been there to see the look of confusion on Pete's face when the deed poll arrived in the mail. I do remember being in the pub, and I remember we wrote some postcards, but I was in a black out during the name change conversation. Crazy Horse says, after hearing his story, I said, "If it's that easy, why don't we change our names?" And so, it was decided we'd change our names. We wanted something cool, but nothing immediately sprung to mind, so we changed the pronunciation of our original names to make them sound more exotic and went with that for a while.

It was also in this pub, Crazy Horse and I met Brian Oliver. Well, I wouldn't say we met him as such. We were sitting with some postcards but didn't know who to write to, so we borrowed the phonebook from behind the bar and randomly chose a few people. Of the four we chose, Brian Oliver was the only one we wrote more than a few words to. The other cards we just drew noughts and crosses games. So, we started writing to Brian as if we were his best friends, and if we'd known him for years. We never made anything up. We told the truth about our travels and proceeded to send a post card from each place we travelled to. But, and here's the best bit, we never gave him any way to get back in touch with us—no return address to write to. We had no way of knowing who we were writing to, and this poor confused man was probably wondering why he couldn't remember who these friends of his were.

Months later, Crazy Horse phoned his house, pretending to be from the bank, selling insurance. Brian wasn't home, but Crazy spoke to Brian's wife. From the call, we gathered he was in his 40's, and we now knew he was married. Knowing that we weren't writing to an old senile man, was all the encouragement we needed, and we told others to write to him, as well, on their travels. We told a 14-year-old girl we met in Virginia and, within a month, she'd written Brian seven postcards and two three-page letters. From what I understood, Brian Oliver quickly racked up a collection of postcards from people he didn't know from Ireland, United Kingdom, Spain, Germany, Czech Republic, Hungary, United States, Canada, Mexico, South Africa, Hong Kong, and Australia.

Back in Dublin, some of the craziness we got up to was so funny. Crazy Horse and I went to Oxfam and bought skimpy little girly tops and then we wore them out clubbing. Mine had the words 'I just want revenge. Is that so wrong?' Generally, people thought it was funny. I also got thrown out of a pub about 30 seconds after approaching a group of girls. The bouncer said I was annoying them. I was just asking for a rubber band to play a coin game. I actually remember this happening, so I couldn't have been that drunk.

Brian picked up one night, and the next morning, we found an article about the chick in the paper, a huge full page spread about her art. She thought we were all crazy when she went to the fridge in our hotel room and saw all our passports in there. We thought it as good a place as any to keep such an important document.

I was having such a good time that, come Monday morning, I didn't want to leave. When it was time to catch my flight back to London, I didn't bother. That was partly due to the fact the flight was so early in the morning, and because I was enjoying partying with my friends. I wasn't due back at work until Thursday, so I figured I'd just catch a bus back on the Wednesday.

And here's the hole in my thinking; on Monday, we left Dublin. Natalie stayed behind to be with family, and we four lads hired a car and set out for Donegal, where Brian's family originated. How I proposed to get back to London on Wednesday when I was heading for Donegal, in the north-west, I don't know. Brian and Michael did the driving. They did a good job, too, considering it was on the other side of the road to what they're used to. Some nights, we slept in the car to save on accommodation.

We went to such places as Donegal Town, Rathmullen, 'Derry, and Letterkenny. It was Letterkenny where we decided we'd spend the night. We parked our car in an overnight car park with the intention to spend the night in the car. Brian was knackered, so he went to sleep, whilst the remaining three of us went to a nightclub. We danced the night away with no real luck of meeting other people.

When the lights came on, and we were all told to leave, the desperados that we were went to a table where some people had left their drinks, and we started to finish them off. At the table, we were approached by a group of four girls. They were quite captivated an Englishman, an American, and an Australian would be in Letterkenny. One of them kept asking me, "Where's the party?" She wanted to know where we were planning on going next and could her friends come, too. When we explained that we planned to go back to our car and go to sleep, they were quite surprised. We said any more partying would have to be done back at their place. They weren't too sure about our story, so we said we'd prove it. We all filed out and hopped in their car. It turned out they were from Moville, a wee village about a 45-minute drive north of Letterkenny. We took them to the car park, and Michael went and got Brian and the car. The girls believed us, and we all went to Moville.

It turned out one of the girl's parents owned a B & B,

and she was looking after it for a while whilst her parents were away, so we went back there. The girl was apprehensive about bringing four strange men back, but once we all got chatting and having a laugh, she said she couldn't have met nicer fellows. I was in fine form. I couldn't say anything that wasn't funny. I had everyone in stitches on numerous occasions. We drank loads of beer and wine and, needless to say, some intimate encounters ensued later in the night. The next morning, we were kicked out early, as the parents were on their way, but we were grateful to have had a proper bed for the night. Later that morning, we met a few of the girls again in the pub.

It was Thursday morning, and I was due back at work. It was this morning Crazy Horse phoned me in dead. He spoke to one guy from my employment agency, who hardly knew me, but to his credit, he acted really sympathetic. Crazy Horse said I'd been involved in a car accident on Sunday and had died Thursday morning. He explained my father was coming over from Australia to look after my estate, so if they could still pay the wages I was owed that would be most appreciative. Meanwhile, I was in the pub over the road drinking with some girls.

The girls showed us around a few of the sights of Moville and then we headed off on our travels again. Crazy Horse had business to attend to in Belfast, so he left us to it. Brian, Michael, and I spent the next few days travelling around the north-west coast visiting areas where Brian's family were from. After that, we slowly made our way to Belfast.

We made our way to Belfast and caught up with Crazy Horse and Kenny, who you might remember I met in Belfast 2001 when I did the medical trial. We had a good couple of days, drinking and partying, and it was good to be back on the old stomping ground. Brian and Michael had to leave and went back to Dublin to meet up with Natalie.

Crazy Horse and I kept partying like there was no tomorrow. After all, you never know when your time is up, hey? I could die in a car accident, for example.

After three weeks, my 'weekend' away had come to an end with a big thud back down to earth. Pretty soon, the money ran dry, and responsibility kicked in. It was all a good laugh at the time, fucking off my flight and job, but now what? I was homeless, unemployed, broke, and even worse ... I was sober and going through withdrawals. In one word, I was scared. I went and stayed at Kenny's house. This was the start of the sobering up process. I was throwing up every hour or so, and my urinary tract system wasn't the best either. When I went to bed, I had the lot: cold sweats, horror nightmares, the shakes, epileptic-type spasms, anxiety, poor sleep, nausea, and the sensation of 'electric fleas' (tingling) on my skin. The dreams scared the shit out of me, and I had to sleep with the light on. I was experiencing hallucinations of demons attacking me, and I constantly felt like I was being dragged by the feet out of bed. My screams woke me up ... and everyone else in the flat. It was a long night.

Crazy Horse was also facing a terrifying come down. Before he went to Dublin, he was about to start a new job and about to move into a new flat, where he said I could stay. But due to going on the bender, he arrived back to find he'd lost his job, and his room in the flat had been given to someone else. This was all on top of his girlfriend dumping him a few days before the weekend in Dublin.

I had somewhere to stay in London but no money to get there and no job to return to. So, that was it. I was going to call Belfast home for a while. I'd have to find a job and somewhere to stay and start my upward spiral.

My upward spiral had to begin by leaving Kenny's flat and heading back to the city. I left with nine quid to my name, with the idea of catching the bus. It was late Sunday evening, and I didn't hold out much hope for a bus. I decided to walk from Rathcoole down to Shore Rd, which had more traffic and a better chance of a bus coming along. Well, I didn't see no fuckin' buses, despite Kenny assuring me there would be. After some time, I contemplated catching a cab. I only hoped my nine quid would cover it. I stopped at a service station and phoned for a mini cab and was told £9 would be enough. Wow, so I was going to arrive in Belfast completely broke. Whilst waiting for the cab, it occurred to me to ask the people at the servo if they were going into Belfast. I asked a middle-aged man who was hopping into his car. He wasn't going to Belfast but, when he recognised I had an Australian accent, he was willing to help me out, anyway. We took off before the cab showed up, and I arrived in Belfast with my £9. Woohoo.

We had been staying at Arnie's Backpackers, in Fitzwilliam St, a stone's throw from Queen's University. It was an old Victorian Town House converted into a small independent hostel of about 22 beds. The place had a real family atmosphere with a coal fire and piano in the lounge room (no TV), a small courtyard out back, and Arnie's two dogs were often there during the day. Arnie dropped by from time to time, as well. He seemed like a good guy: Northern Irish, in his 40's. The staff there were really friendly: a young married couple, David and Megan, from South Africa, a Danish lass, Birgitte, an Aussie chick, Kylie, and Arnie worked there some weekends, too.

Having arrived back in town, thanks to the free ride, I knocked on the door of the hostel, and Megan answered. I explained I had £9, and I would be getting a job, and when I got on my feet, I'd pay what I owed. Megan said, "Alright." Wow, thank goodness. I had chatted to Megan a few times by that stage, and it had been friendly, but we weren't best mates. I was so grateful, and somewhat blown away she would let me stay for free. I think it helped I was a mate of Crazy Horse, who had been staying there before our get-together in Dublin. I asked Megan, months later, why she allowed me free rent when she hardly knew me. She gave a playful smile, "I knew you were telling the truth."

Megan and I ended up becoming good friends. She was in her 20's, alternative, with different coloured hair each week, a great sense of humour, a kind heart, and the two of us had a love affair. Not with each other. We both loved The Doors and Winona Ryder. We joked the reason we got along so well together was because we both had the same taste in women.

I managed to get a job working in a chicken factory, in Ballymena, which was, how can I put it? Um…really shit. It was cold and miserable; the people weren't the friendliest I've ever encountered, and the pay was crap: £4.10/hour. My first day on the job, I was full of regret as I lamented my circumstances. I enjoyed my job in London; this, by contrast, was the ice-cold version of hell. Most days, I worked in the 'crumbed chicken' room (2°C) arranging chicken on plastic trays to be covered in cling film ready for the supermarket shelves. Other days, I was in the 'freezer room' (-5°C) putting strips of bacon onto whole chickens. Fuck, it was cold. My toes and fingers suffered the most. The uniform was a laugh. We wore white lab coats over our own clothes with rubber shoes and hairnets. I actually kept those shoes, and I painted them to look like cool bowling shoes.

I stuck with the job for three weeks until I caught a cold. Because I needed the money, I returned to work before I was fully recovered. I then caught a bad chest infection, which ruined any chance I had of being accepted in the clinical trial I was hoping for later that week. I then had to put my name down for another trial at a later date. On a funny side note, I went to the hospital when my chest infection was quite bad and I was having trouble breathing. The woman at reception asked what I did for a living. I told her I castrate chickens. Discouraged, she asked, "What am I meant to write on the form?"

"Chicken castrator." Wasn't it obvious?

Crazy Horse was working in a call centre at a half decent rate, and we helped each other out with money whenever necessary. Our mission statement was: 'We're in this together'. Crazy had better luck getting onto a trial, but two days out from check-in, a few of us enticed him to join our drinking session, and he ended up not being used in the study because his liver enzymes were too high.

Drinking always brought us undone.

Getting a well-paid trial was my golden ticket out of Belfast and back to London, but in the meantime, life was lively at the hostel. We had party after party at the hostel whenever possible, and we often went around and partied with the ex-pats living at 16 University St, next to the Ark Hostel. We indulged in all sorts of substances and spent whole weekends up without sleep. Crazy Horse and I found a local, The Royal Bar, on Sandy Row, which was a loyalist pub, and the people in there were very sociable. We quickly set up a tab there, and people bought us drinks and were happy to share a laugh. There were some real characters in there, I tell you. It became our second home.

About mid-October, sitting around the table in the reception area of the hostel, Crazy Horse and I were deliberating over different names for ourselves. He came up with the suggestion I change my name to the bracelet I'd bought in South Africa that read: S. AFRICA. He suggested I could be Saleem or Siegfried Africa or something like that. I said, "Fuck that. I'll be Spaceman Africa." Spaceman, of course, was my nickname from the Shepherd's Bush Empire days. And so, on 25th October, I went to the netcafé, Revelations, in Shaftsbury Square, with a few friends and invested £28 in a deed poll on the internet. A few days later, my deed poll arrived by mail.

Crazy Horse came up with his name weeks later. I don't know the reasoning behind it. I do remember he was quite keen on the word 'horse'. If anything he drank tasted bad, he'd often say, "This tastes like horse urine." I remember the day he told me of his choice. We were lying next to each other in bed (I'll explain later), and he told me, "I'm going to change my name to Crazy Horse."

I said, "You are aware it's the name of a chain of strip clubs?"

"No."

"Do you know it's the name of Neil Young's backing band?"

"No."

"You are aware it's the name of a well-known Native American Indian, don't you?"

"Yeah, I know that."

"Cool. Nice to meet you, Crazy Horse."

One day, Crazy was watching a football match on telly in which the players had their surnames on the back of their jumpers. One player grabbed the attention of Crazy Horse. It was Danny Invincibile, playing for Kilmarnock in the Scottish Premier League. He had Invincibile emblazoned on the back of his footy jumper, and Crazy Horse thought this was a magnificent name and so, now, he is Crazy Horse Invincible. The name suits him so well; it's just so natural to call him Crazy Horse now. Danny Invincibile is, actually, an Australian lad with Italian heritage, born in Brisbane. G'day mate.

With more people enjoying the atmosphere of the hostel and staying long-term, we had a good little family of globetrotters: 25-year-old Dave, from Vancouver. He became a good friend, and with Crazy Horse, we became the three amigos. Other than being enticed to stay by the frivolity of the hostel, Dave met a local woman, Toni, who also motivated him to hang around; 18-year-old Atira, from Seattle. She was a cool semi-gothic chick, who was her own person and wasn't afraid to join in on the mischief we got up to; Emily, 22, from Melbourne was quite the adventurer. A seasoned skydiver, she was in Belfast on break from her nanny job in England. We had a brief fling for a while; she really was a lot of fun to be around; Teresa, 18, was from Ottawa, yet half Italian. She had a gentle personality and seemed to be constantly filled with amazement or shock at our antics; Bo, a 40's something guy from the Isle of Man, travelled Europe as a human statue. Chris, 20 odd, from France, loved a drink and dancing on tables. I saw him almost lose his head one night when he failed to notice a ceiling fan above the table he wanted to dance on; Uzi, from Canada/Israel, was a serial guinea pig, earning money by continuously doing clinical trials.

I still had no luck getting on a trial. I failed one screening due to my liver being slightly out of whack. Due to the binges I went on, I'd do my best to stop drinking a week prior to the screening. The alcohol left my body, but often, my liver enzymes were elevated, and my blood thinned, producing abnormal test results.

There were also times when we were completely broke. One night, Crazy Horse and I had no money between us, and it was a few days' until pay day. We didn't have any booze, and we were climbing the walls going insane for a drink, not enjoying this sobriety lark, at all. I was moping around the kitchen, chatting to others, when I put my hands in my fleece pockets. There was something in the right pocket. I pulled it out and had a look. I couldn't fuckin' believe it. I looked up at Crazy Horse; he was standing next to me and had seen it too. I cheered, "You fuckin' beauty!" It was thirty quid. We didn't go to bed sober that night.

There were many nights we did go to bed sober, suffering from the horrors. They usually lasted two nights, and the dreams were always intense. There was always someone or something trying to kill us, and the dreams seemed so real, always starting from the bed we were sleeping in. Crazy Horse and I used to have a great laugh sharing with each other our weird night's sleep. He had a dream where I was lying on my back in the stairwell of the hostel with my head at the bottom and feet at the top. Crazy Horse was up on the landing, looking down at me as I had brown sauce coming out of my nose. He was a bit freaked out by it, and I stopped what I was doing, looked up at him, and said, "Do you think this is real?" And with that, he woke up.

I found work at a place called Irish Bonding Co. out on the Castlereigh Rd. Irish Bonding is a bottling/can factory for Guinness. If you think of the opening credits to the sitcom, 'Laverne and Shirley', except with alcohol, you'll have a good idea of what the plant was like. I worked night shift from 8pm until 8am. My job was to stand next to the conveyor belt and place any fallen bottles back upright. Some places I got wet from the sprays of water cooling the bottles, which wasn't fun, so I used to take along a spare pair of shoes and socks. There was an added incentive for everyone to keep the production level high, because if a certain amount of product was produced during a shift, each staff member received a case of Harp cans for free. This occurred during my first week there, but I sold the case because I needed the money more.

Working with me were two local guys, an uncle and nephew combination. They were friendly, at times, but generally, I found them to be controlling bullies. The one good thing was they were agency staff, like me, and so weren't concerned about toeing the company line. They encouraged drinking on the job and often smuggled a few bottles home with them after each shift. I certainly welcomed drinking on the job; most nights, I drank about 20 bottles. I was more into it than they were, and they often kept watch for me. But a lot of the time, they loved to tease me and gang up on me. Drinking made it somewhat bearable. The plant bottled Guinness, Budweiser, Harp, Bulmers, and Carlsberg. On any given night, only one brand would be produced, so that would be the only beer on the menu. There was the odd occasion when I showed up to work and contemplated slitting my wrists as I saw the beer for production that night was Kaliber. Kaliber is alcohol free.

During this time, Crazy Horse had been in negotiations with a real estate company to move into a rental house, and he invited me to move in, too. It was going to work out to be a lot cheaper than the hostel. It was a no brainer and I accepted the invitation. I put off returning to London until the New Year. Crazy Horse signed the tenancy agreement, so we were free to move into the house the following week. Nice one. We couldn't wait until we were living in the new house. And on the 5th of December, Crazy Horse took ownership of the keys to 37 Olympia St in the area of town known as The Village. It's a Protestant area right next to Windsor Park football stadium, and most of the housing is of the 'two up, two down' red-bricked terraced variety.

We moved in and settled in very quickly. The rent was something ridiculous, like £200/month between us, whilst at the hostel, we were paying *£200/month* each. Crazy Horse found out early on, through applying for rent assistance, that the landlord owned many of the houses in the street and had bought them cheaply under the proviso he wasn't going to rent them out. So, under those circumstances, after the first payment, we didn't pay any rent at all. Brilliant.

I don't know about Crazy Horse, but I certainly thought our social life would suffer now that we were out of the hostel, but it wasn't the case. Our friends started coming around to the house and hanging out there. We didn't have a TV, so we all sat around drinking and chatting whilst watching the next best thing—the fire. There was a coal fireplace and Crazy Horse took prime position next to it, forever poking and topping it up. The fire really was extremely captivating, and we sat there for hours watching the flames dancing.

About two weeks into our occupancy, Crazy and I were sitting around the house when there was a knock on the door. I opened the door, and there was Teresa with two suitcases. Teresa was our 18-year-old Canadian friend from the hostel. "I'm moving in," she said. After a second or two of shock, Crazy and I said, "Right. You better come in then." We didn't mind. Once again, we enjoyed being hospitable. Canadian Dave returned from his adventures around Europe and moved in around the same time, as well. Sleeping space wasn't abundant, but it worked out well. Crazy Horse had the main bedroom, whilst Dave had a small storage room about 2m x 2m, and Teresa and I shared the second bedroom. She had the room at night when I was working, and I had it during the day when she was working.

Christmas day was fantastic. The four of us, as well as a neighbour who came around with a TV, spent the day at the house, so we got to watch the Queen's Christmas Message. Days earlier, Dave and I had gone on a Christmas tree hunt, and we managed to find a nice tall Christmas-styled tree in someone's front garden, which we cut down and took back to the house. We also found a miniature tree in the garden of a bank, so we made a withdrawal and took that, too.

The tree stood proudly decorated in the corner of the lounge room, and when we woke Christmas morning, we were surprised that Santa had left us some presents. It was, actually, Dave, not Santa, but he'd managed to give us all something individually that we really appreciated, mainly because we already owned the fuckin' things. It was a great idea. Secretly, Dave had commandeered something that belonged to each of us and then had wrapped it and then gave it back to us for Christmas. Brilliant. I received a guitar. I couldn't have been happier. Crazy Horse received the tongs to the fireplace, and Teresa received something she owned; I can't remember what. Crazy Horse cooked us a roast chicken with all the trappings, including gravy, and it was delicious. We had a really relaxing, informal day. I loved it.

New Year's Barcelona

After all the fun we had in Thailand, we decided to get together again for the next New Year's. In September, Michael explained he wouldn't be able to make the party as he'd just moved to Barcelona and couldn't afford a trip away. So, it was decided; Barcelona would be the venue for our 2002 New Year's. Come December, Crazy Horse and I had booked our flights leaving late afternoon from London on the 27th, but we hadn't made any arrangements to get to London. Not wanting to spend a fortune, we were running out of time and options. In the end, we decided to catch the train.

On Boxing Day, we packed our bags; we said our farewells to Teresa and Dave, and we caught the last ferry to Stranraer, Scotland. I planned on living in London again after Barcelona so I packed everything I had into two bags, except my guitar and sleeping bag; I'd have to pick them up later. We arrived at Stranraer and settled in for the night at the ferry terminal departure lounge. The plan was to catch the first train the next day and get ourselves to London. It's a long journey by train, and we knew any delays with our connections and we'd be in danger of arriving at Heathrow late for our flight.

I didn't sleep too well. If we didn't make our flight to Barcelona, not only would I be disappointed not being there, but we'd be letting a lot of people down. Some people were only going to Barcelona because Crazy Horse and I would be there, and I didn't want to be a no-show after having talked the party up for the last few months. All we really had to worry about was getting on the train in the morning and hope there were no delays. Oh, yeah ... and hope we didn't get arrested for fraud.

Crazy Horse and I planned to ride to London ... on the train ... with a ... travel warrant. A travel warrant is like a blank cheque. Companies give these warrants to employees to pay for their travel on business trips. You just hand over the travel warrant with all your intended travel details at the bus, train, taxi, etc., office in exchange for a ticket and the company picks up the tab. A few weeks earlier, a mate of Crazy's had sent us this travel warrant from a security company as a gift. This mate had also partly filled in the details, so we had to try to match the ink colour and handwriting when filling it in, so it didn't look too suspicious. I was really worried of getting caught. Neither Crazy Horse nor I worked for this security company, and I wasn't too confident of thinking on my feet if anyone asked questions. Crazy Horse was pretty confident we wouldn't have a problem.

Days earlier, we'd attempted to exchange the travel warrant for tickets. I was hoping Crazy Horse would just go alone to the ticket office, but he insisted I go with him. As we walked to Europa Station, I wondered if we'd be returning to The Village any time soon or be detained by police. We arrived too late, and the ticket office was closed. Our only option now was to give the travel warrant to the ticket collector when we were on the train. Great (sarcasm). We had to wait another few, anxious days before knowing our fate.

We woke on time and boarded the train. We were hoping the conductor still had some Christmas spirit and would give us the tickets, no questions asked. We handed him the travel warrant and held our breath. He looked at it and started pushing buttons on his ticket machine. So far so good. More time passed, which seemed like ages. Oh, shit, he's going to say something, "London, Euston?"

"Yes please, mate."

Cool, nothing to worry about. The machine is making the right noises. I can see two tickets. He's handing them to us. Must act nonchalant. I have a ticket in my hand, and he's walking away. Just stare out the window until he's gone …YOU FUCKIN' BEAUTY!

What a relief. I felt a lot more relaxed after that. The tickets were return and had a price tag of £107.

It wasn't too much later before we were drinking and enjoying the ride. Halfway through our trip, we missed a connection by a few minutes. We had a half hour wait for the next train, which gave us time to stock up on more beers. It also meant we were going to be pushed for time when we arrived at Euston Station. After a packed train ride and some banter with the other passengers (the beer was starting to have an effect), we arrived at Euston and made a dash for the Underground. We caught the tube through to Heathrow, and during the mad rush to find our check-in desk, Teresa phoned us for a chat. Needless to say, we didn't give the conversation our full attention. We quickly checked-in and then had to go immediately to the departure gate for boarding. We'd made it. Bloody hell, that was tight.

Crazy and I were both on a high. Despite all that could have gone wrong, we were on our flight to Barcelona and would be there to fulfil our obligations, so to speak. Not only that, but we were quite drunk and on a British Airways flight with free booze, which both Crazy and I took full advantage of. One of the air stewards was definitely on our side. Her name was Karen, and when we asked for a drink, she gave us a few at a time. Usually, she gave us miniature bottles of vodka. Crazy Horse and I both had aisle seats, but I was a few rows ahead of him. Each time Karen served us with drinks, I'd turn back and look down the aisle and raise my glass to Crazy Horse. He raised his glass, and we smiled to each other with the biggest grins on our faces. By this stage, we were flying in more ways than one.

When we arrived in Barcelona, we were in quite a state. It was about 10pm, and we'd been drinking since early morning. I don't really remember much of what happened after we left the plane. I know we both still had some vodka, and we downed them in quick succession. I don't remember immigration at all. It would seem Spain just let anyone in. I have a vague memory of us looking for our luggage. After a hopeless search around the terminal, we found out that all luggage from our flight was delivered to a different terminal. What's all that about? After that, I don't remember anything.

I opened my eyes. It was early the next morning, and I was still at the airport. I was slouched on the floor against a column in the middle of a main walkway. I was still too drunk to function. I couldn't move to save my life. I literally could not get up, and I couldn't fight the urge to go back to sleep. I was lucky the airport was rather empty, and I was out of view a bit. I woke again later and found out I was in front of the customs gate at arrivals. Had anyone come up to me and tried to harm me, I would have been helpless.

Sometime later, but still relatively early, I got up to have a look around and search for Crazy Horse. I ventured to the lower level and found Crazy Horse lying on some cardboard, on the floor, asleep. I thought it odd that he was sleeping at a weird angle in the middle of a walkway, especially when he was only a metre or two away from a perfectly good bench.

I found a store selling cheap cans of beer (Oh, how I love Spain), and I sat on the bench waiting for Crazy to wake up. He later woke up and then, to his horror, he noticed something missing. "Where are the bags?"

"We couldn't find them, remember?"

"No, I found them, and I put them under the bench, here."

During the night, after we'd lost each other, Crazy had managed to find our bags and had put them under the bench against a wall. He then lay on the floor in front of the bags thinking, if someone tried to take the bags, they'd have to move him to do it, and he'd wake up.

Someone did move Crazy Horse.

Someone did take our bags.

Crazy Horse didn't wake up.

I roared with laughter. I thought it was hilarious. Every moment seemed to be an amusing adventure. Could we not do anything without having some crazy anecdote to tell afterwards? Not that I cared, mind you. I was having a great time. I also laughed it off in the hope Crazy Horse wouldn't feel bad about losing our bags. He told me much later he was worried I blamed him. Nah, I didn't care. I was impressed Crazy Horse had managed even to find the bags in the first place. I wasn't even capable of that.

Neither Crazy Horse nor I owned very much, so we had lost nearly every bit of clothing we owned. There was nothing of any value to anyone else in there, so we checked around the terminal to see if our bags had been dumped, but, no, we couldn't find them. Luckily, we both had our wallets and passports on us. I also had my toothbrush on me, so not all was lost. We went into the city and contacted

Michael. Unbeknownst to us, he had gone out to the airport the night before to meet us. He didn't find us and thought we hadn't arrived, so he was happy to hear we'd made it. We arranged to meet up with him later and, in the meantime, we went wild, bouncing off the walls.

We went from bar to bar, had a drink each time, and then did a runner. We almost brought ourselves undone by walking back into a bar and not realising we'd been there before. We quickly made our escape. We found that cigarettes were cheap, so we bought a packet and started smoking. Neither Crazy nor I smoked, but we thought we'd take it up as a New Year's resolution. We had a lot of fun with the people on *Las Ramblas*, which is a long street in the city centre, lined with trees and full of stalls, tourists, and street performers. Crazy Horse started saying hello to everyone in French. It became his catch phrase for years, maybe even still today—"Bonjour." Thank God he didn't, but Crazy Horse was considering buying me a live chicken from one of the shop stalls. What the fuck would I have done with that? In the silly mood we were in, I wouldn't want to guess. We found a sex shop, and despite not being able to afford it, Crazy Horse bought himself a gimp mask, as a joke, as always.

Fast forward to the next morning; Crazy Horse woke, and for about five seconds, he had a blank mind. He had a sore head and felt rough from the super long session we'd had the day before. He could also feel some pain in his right arm and then it hit him. His memory of yesterday returned to the forefront of his mind. "Oh no, I didn't, did I?" He leaned over to survey his arm and cringed with horror at the confirmation that he had, indeed, gotten a tattoo. Not just any tattoo, mind you. No. As a self-practical joke, Crazy Horse walked into the tattoo parlour and asked for the most offensive word in the English language he could think of. And so, half an hour later, Crazy Horse was the amused bearer of the word 'cunt' tattooed on his arm. Not only that, but he chose a Celtic font, suggesting partiality to the Irish culture, which is the exact opposite of where Crazy Horse's loyalties lie—another self-practical joke.

Over the days leading up to New Year, our team started to arrive: Brian, of course; Atira and her love interest, Gordon; and my love interest, Emily, who I'd met at Arnie's in Belfast. We were staying in the hostel, Barcelona Mar, on *Carrer de Sant Paul* in *El Raval* and enticed some of the other guests to join our party. We met Illeises and Matoula, brother and sister from Greece, and Sage from the States. Unfortunately, Natalie, from DC, couldn't make it. We rang her one day, and she told me how disappointed she was she couldn't be there to catch up with Crazy Horse and me. I jokingly said Crazy and I would just have to go and visit her in the States, instead. Brian, Michael, and I were the only three from the Thailand chapter. Also, joining us, or perhaps we were joining them, were Joanne and Jaime, friends from New York, as Jaime is from Barcelona and his family lives there.

We all had a great time exploring the city, sampling the culinary delights, and touring the many bars. The next ten days involved drinking, drugs, doing runners from bars (and getting caught), running around the hostel naked, self-practical jokes, a trip to the hospital to get stitches in my wrist, peep shows, being asked to accompany the police down to the station, and we may have fitted in some sight-seeing. The story of the stolen bags was recounted many a time, second only to the story of the tattoo self-practical joke.

During the day on New Year's Eve, Emily, forever the adventurer, talked Crazy Horse and I into going for a ride on the cable-car that travels over the harbour and up to a mountain lookout. Crazy Horse and I aren't the biggest fans of heights. First, to get on, we had to take an elevator ride up to the top of a tower. Crazy Horse nicknamed it 'The Tower of Death'. That was scary enough, but along came the cable-car, and it was bouncing around everywhere in the wind, which didn't instil any confidence in us. We hopped on, with our legs shaking, and making jokes to try to hide our fear. It was an enclosed car, and we had about ten people on board plus a guard to make sure nobody opened the door and jumped out. He needn't have worried about that. I was standing in the middle, holding on tight to one of the poles. The trip took maybe four or five minutes, and we were glad to make it to the mountain. We quickly got off and, finally, we were able to enjoy the view with our feet firmly on the ground.

After a look around, we queued up for the return trip. I think I was even more scared this time because I knew what lay ahead. We hopped on, and this time, I sat down and just looked at the floor of the car, commenting on people's shoes. The return trip was one of the longest five minutes I've had to endure. As we were nearing the end, there was a loud crack noise, and the car slowed down to a snail's pace. I thought the fuckin' thing was going to stop. I had lifted my head, at this point, to see we still had a good ten metres to go. It took fuckin' ages; I wasn't sure we were going to make it. To top it all off, as we were pulling up to the tower, the car was bouncing around so much it slammed right into the side of the tower instead of pulling up beside it. When the doors opened, Crazy and I were off like a shot. Emily enjoyed the ride and was in hysterics at our behaviour. Going back down in the lift, we noticed parts of the tower deteriorating. I was glad I didn't notice it on the way up. Once back on the ground, it was straight to a bar for a relaxing drink to calm the nerves.

In the evening, the group assembled, including Joanne

and Jaime and some of their family members, and we saw the New Year in on Las Ramblas. At midnight, it is the tradition to eat a grape for each twelve chimes of the clock. We didn't hear any clock, so we just munched on some grapes, anyway. As you might imagine, the street was heaving with people, and the atmosphere was charged. I don't think I've experienced a more clamorous and electrifying crowd. We wandered down the street, taking in the vibe; people were cheering, blowing horns, and hugging and kissing. Brian took advantage of this and orchestrated celebratory kisses with as many women as he could. By the time we reached the end of the street, he'd kissed 33 women.

Also out in force were pickpockets. Gangs of Indian youths would run, cheering and shouting at individuals, and give them a group hug on the pretence of celebrating the New Year. At the same time, they'd rummage through the person's pockets, and because the target had so many people touching them, they wouldn't notice someone stealing from their pocket. This happened to Crazy Horse. I saw it happen and watched for anyone making a quick getaway from the group. One little guy broke from the group-hug early and came walking straight towards me. I didn't know if he had anything, but I grabbed him, and without any resistance at all, he handed over Crazy Horse's mobile. I gave it back to Crazy, who wasn't even aware it had been taken. Later, Crazy spent some of the night, as a vigilante, barging these gangs as they went in for the group hug. From Las Ramblas, we went to a few bars, including a club at Plaça Reial. I remember not being allowed in. I can't remember why, but, somehow, I managed to talk my way in to join the others. That's possibly the only time I've ever talked my way into a club.

During my time in Barcelona, I got quite caught up in all the tom-foolery and debauchery, so much so that Emily became rather disgusted in my behaviour and downgraded our relationship status to 'just friends'. I felt bad for having upset her and sorry the relationship was over; she was a very friendly, outgoing person. Plus, she was a Melbourne chick. There's something about the women of Melbourne that I find very attractive. I think they're so diverse and alternative, artistic, creative, and just simply cool.

2003

4th—9th January 2003

Slowly, our group diminished as people had to move on or head back home. It was time for Emily to leave us. She had an evening flight back to England, and we saw her off in a taxi from outside the hostel. We learned the next day, the cab driver had ripped her off by demanding more money before he allowed her to get her luggage from the boot. Hearing this added to my already high level of guilt. It probably would have been a good idea for me to have gone with her to the airport.

We assembled at the pub in Rambla Del Raval for Gordon and Atira's farewell. The Spanish group were in the area, as well, and joined us, making us a group of 10. Michael had ordered octopus, and there weren't many takers. The bodies of these octopuses were the size of a large marble. Crazy Horse managed to eat three. I tried one, just so I could be justified in saying I didn't want to have any more.

Gordon and Atira said their good-byes, and being Christmas Eve in Spain (5th Jan), the Spanish headed off to be with their family. The rest of us—Michael, Brian, Crazy Horse, and I—headed off to the football at Camp Nou Stadium, which has the largest capacity of all stadiums in Europe. Michael and Brian had bought tickets, but Crazy and I were going to have to blag our way in. Seeing as it was Crazy's birthday, we were going to play on that fact to see if anyone would take sympathy on our cause. We asked the security guards if they'd be kind enough to let us in. Crazy Horse showed his passport to prove it was his birthday, and, blow me down, they let us in. It was a pretty exciting experience. Crazy Horse, being a football fan, was over the moon to be at the famous Camp Nou (I bet you never heard at school the nursery rhyme about the crazy horse over the moon). We were watching from high up in the stands, and it was really fuckin' steep up there. It was a national league match, as opposed to a first class international, so the stands weren't very full. We settled in to watch the game with a few cans of Sin Beer. Sin is Spanish for 'without' and, you guessed it, Sin Beer is without alcohol. We saw one goal scored, but otherwise, the game was rather boring. The most entertaining part was making paper planes out of the numerous flyers that were being handed out and throwing them out over the terraces below. Everyone was doing it; there were planes flying everywhere.

Afterwards, the four of us saw a Christmas parade as they celebrate the giving of Christmas gifts on the 6th of January in Spain. The 6th January is known as *Día de los Reyes Magos*, the day of the Three Wise Men. This is the day children wake to find the Wise Men have left gifts for them. There were loads of cool floats with people in highly elaborate costumes, travelling through the streets of the city. On a lot of the floats, people were throwing candy into the crowd, which caused big push and shove matches between the revellers trying to get hold of some sweets. A lot of the kids were sitting on their daddy's shoulders, so they could see the parade better. Being Crazy Horse's birthday, I didn't want him to miss out, so I let him sit up on my shoulders, too, so he could see the parade. He had the best view of everyone.

Crazy Horse and I managed to catch our flights back to London, a surprise to everyone, I'm sure. Check-in was quick as we had no luggage. We arrived at Gatwick and thus ended a rollercoaster of a four-month bender, that originally just started as a weekend away in Dublin. Crazy Horse went to stay with his parents up north and then onto Belfast, whilst I made my way to Shepherd's Bush to stay with my mate, Chris. Chris was expecting me but surprised when I showed up with nothing but the clothes on my back.

It wasn't long after Paddy's Day, in March, that I managed to be accepted for a clinical trial at The Charter House, Stamford Hospital, just up the road from Shepherd's Bush. The beauty of this research unit was, passing the screening usually guaranteed you a place on the study; there was no 'competition line'. The study was spread over two months and finished around the middle of May. It was five days/nights in hospital then four days of outpatient visits then about ten days break then repeat the same sequence, three times in total. I can't even remember what was being tested. The pay cheque was a handy £2020.

My time doing the trial was pleasant enough. It was a mixed study of guys and gals and, as expected, full of Aussies, Kiwis, and South Africans. As often is the case on these studies, watching *The Simpsons* is a staple diet. Coincidently, whilst on this study, the episode where Homer is a human guinea pig and does a clinical trial was on the telly, much to our amusement.

Crazy Horse was doing a trial at the same time in Belfast, and our plan was to travel to the States from the middle of June for 89 days. We didn't really have a plan for once we were there, but we wanted to travel around and catch up with friends along the way. Of course, we wouldn't be able to catch up with Michael, because he was making a life for himself in Barcelona. So, to compensate, we took advantage of some super cheap flights and booked us an eleven-day sojourn to Spain scheduled for early June.

June 2003

Our time in Spain was a real stereotypical holiday in that we did very little but laze on the beach during the day and dine and drink at night. We had a great time, but spent a fortune; the majority of my trial money was gone, and this was just the entrée. We still had three months in 'the land of the free, home of the brave' ahead of us. This was going to be interesting. Spaceman and Crazy Horse travel for three months around America with fuck all money. I'd like to see that. Our master plan to survive whilst in the States was to earn some extra dollar bills by doing a few drug trials.

Well, what a surprise. Could Crazy Horse and I really go travelling without there being some kind of drama? We woke up at silly o'clock to catch the train to Stansted. We made it OK and caught our flight to Dublin for our US connection. When checking in for our US Airways flight, security took one look at us and decided to give us a right going over. First, they took ages checking the authenticity of our passports, and then they searched through our bags. They took out everything and looked over it all. They read documents, found Crazy Horse's gimp mask, and put silly things, like my electronic chessboard, through the x-ray machine. I was lucky I'd decided not to take the list of drug clinics with me, because Crazy and I weren't legally allowed to be earning money in the US. It was our intention to enter the country on the 90-day tourist visa, which meant no working. Whilst they went through my bag, I was shaking like a leaf from a few too many drinks the night before. I was worried they would think I was nervous and trying to hide something. They asked us all sorts of questions, like how the two of us met and how much money we had for the trip. Regarding the money, we both lied. We said we had a few grand between us. We passed the search and had to check-in quickly, because after all that rigmarole, the plane was ready for boarding.

We then had to go through immigration, and the American officer didn't want to let me on the plane, because I had been in the States the year before. He was thinking I'd made some contacts last time around, and I was going back to work there. Crazy Horse was having similar troubles with a different officer. Crazy had his wallet searched, and the officer found his US tax card. We both had applied for US tax cards, because we had to have a US tax number to participate in drug trials. Our applications had been successful, so naturally, we had the cards on us. The Officer asked Crazy about the card, but Crazy is quite smart and said he had the tax number on the off-chance he might want to open a bank account in the US, making it easier to access his spending money, rather than keeping it in his UK account. The officer bought it.

I could see and hear this from where I was and started to panic. I wasn't confident I'd be able to think on my feet fast enough if the officer started questioning me about my tax card. Whilst he was busy staring at the computer screen, with my hands under the desk where he couldn't see them, I got my wallet out, took my tax card, and put it in a small pocket in my bag. And sure enough, the officer asked to see my wallet, but he didn't find anything incriminating.

By this time, Crazy had been cleared and told to board the plane. Worried that the officer might want to search my bag, as Crazy walked past, I asked him to take my bag for me. The officer sternly said, "No. Leave it here." Shit! Nice try, though, I thought. Crazy Horse waited for me outside immigration but was ushered onto the plane as it was ready for take-off. He explained that he was waiting for me, but security insisted he get on the plane. Crazy went to his seat, afraid he'd be going without me.

I jumped through all the officer's hoops, and he said, "OK, you can go." I thought, "Finally." I went to board the plane and, fuck me, the same two security guys who searched Crazy and me before check-in were there again to search my bag and, this time, me. I saw some rubber gloves on the table, and my shaking was then fear related, not drink related. Luckily, for me and all involved, there was no cavity or strip search, but I was sure that, with my tax card now in the bag, they would find it. But he didn't look in the small pocket of my bag, and I was through, at long last, on to the fuckin' plane. I boarded the plane, and they closed the door behind me. I was finally able to sit down and relax ... just in time for take-off, which scares the shit out of me, especially when suffering from alcohol withdrawals. Crazy could relax now, too. It had been a tense wait for him not knowing if I was going to make it onto the plane.

During the flight, there was some time for reflection. Crazy Horse leant over and asked how this whole trip to the States came about. The answer was Natalie. Back at New Year's, I told Natalie over the phone that, because she couldn't make it to Barcelona, Crazy Horse and I would just have to visit her, instead. It was just a throw away comment I'd made to be funny and to add some cheer. But once Crazy Horse and I got on a trial each, the idea gained momentum and actually eventuated. I obviously had forgotten to tell Crazy the reason for going, and up until now, Crazy hadn't asked. He obviously didn't need a reason to go on a three-month bender.

We touched down in Philadelphia for a transit stop before going on to New York. Even from just hanging out in Philadelphia airport, the American culture hit us in the face. American accents, loud people, everything up-sized. We weren't in Spain, anymore. We kept reminding each other where we were.

"Hey mate."
"Yeah?"
"We're in fuckin' America."
"I know. Can you believe it?"

I'd been to the States before; of course, it was almost a year to the day since I last flew out of New York. Crazy Horse had been before: a trip to New York when he was 18. Even though he was under 21, he still managed to have some fun in a few of the clubs.

We finally arrived in New York, and the relief and joy to be there after travelling all day was quite high. And then what should happen? Crazy Horse's luggage didn't show up. The airline had lost it, so he was stuck wearing just the clothes on his back, which wasn't the first time. Welcome to America. We had insurance, and the airline provided Crazy Horse with a daily allowance to pay for some replacement clothes and toiletries, whilst they tried to locate his luggage. Crazy was happy to go shopping and buy new clothes, but really, he just wanted his bags returned as they had irreplaceable stuff in them, like the camera with all our Spain photos.

On our second day in the ol' US of A, in New York—not the cheapest city in the country—we had but a few hundred dollars between us. We wasted no time in ringing around to find us a drug trial so we could get by. We didn't have much luck to begin with. We made the calls from some public phones at the city transit authority—the busiest train, bus, and coach station in the country—and I remember feeling tiny in this biggest of big smokes and feeling really worried about what we were going to do if we couldn't get a trial soon. We did do some sight-seeing, all on foot, but our main focus was organising a screening. And success, we had a screening appointment in ... Trenton. Never heard of it? Neither had we. It's actually the capital city of the state of New Jersey.

We couldn't find any cheap, budget accommodation in Trenton, so we made Philadelphia our base for the time being and stayed at the hostel on Bank St. And so began our detoxification and diet of milk thistle and cranberry juice. And this almost goes without saying; we were back to our regular routine of Crazy cooking delicious meals of spaghetti bolognaise, whilst I took care of the washing up. For late breakfast, we became regulars at a hot dog stand on the corner of Chestnut and South 3rd St. Man, these mobile hot dog stands in the US are more like mini kiosks. They sell everything from candy, drinks, and crisps to ... well, other stuff. This guy had a cheap offer for $2: bacon and egg roll and drink. Sensational.

As luck would have it, US Airways contacted Crazy Horse; they'd found his bags, and they were at Philadelphia airport. Hip, Hip, HOORAY. That was handy, considering we were already in the area. So, Crazy Horse was reunited with his backpack; I think it was about day four by this stage.

Amongst other things, we went and saw the Philadelphia Museum of Art, best known for its appearance in the film *Rocky*, where Sylvester Stallone runs up the 72 steps to the entrance of the museum to the inspiring song 'Gonna fly now'. At one point in the early 80's, there was a bronze statue of Rocky erected at the top of the steps, which is featured in *Rocky III*, but was later moved to the Spectrum Arena. When we went there, we walked the steps (we were never going to run up them) and at the top, instead of the statue, there were a set of footprints with the word 'Rocky' above them.

The day came of our screening, and we caught a train to Trenton where we, and about ten others, were picked up in a van and taken to the research clinic, which on this occasion, was the Bristol-Myers Squibb Company, Pharmaceutical

Research Institute, in nearby Hamilton. The screening was the usual fare—blood draw, urine sample, ECG test, blood pressure—the only difference here was, we got paid for doing the screening. That's not the case in the UK. $20, I think it was; it wasn't much, but we weren't complaining. After the screening, we were driven to the bank to cash our cheques and then returned to the Trenton station.

The study was to be 11 days straight for a handy cheque of $3030. The study was trialling new medication for anaemia—a deficiency in the quality of red blood cells. Actually, I've just remembered something. At the screening, we were given a sample kit that we had to take away, and when we could produce a sample, we were to post it back to the clinic. What kind of sample? Stool sample, of course.

If you don't want to know the specifics, skip this next paragraph. The idea was, after a stool producing visit to the toilet, you take the miniature, wooden, spoon-like thingy provided, and take a sample from the toilet paper you used to do the business. You then wipe that sample from the spoon onto a small piece of cardboard, also provided, which then has a cardboard flap to cover it, and the card is put into a clip-lock bag and into an envelope, all provided, and then posted, postage paid. It was a really moving experience, I tell you. I think we may have had to keep it refrigerated before sending it, too. The only fridge we had access to was the one at the hostel. Can you imagine little Johnny Backpacker coming along, and in the process of trying to find some spare space in the fridge, finds a stool sample kit?

On the train back to Philadelphia, I started to read through the trial information more thoroughly, "Fuc - king hell." I had to read the possible side-effects for a second time. During the trial, you weren't allowed to shave, because if you cut yourself, they couldn't guarantee you wouldn't 'suffer from a life-threatening bleeding episode'. They had tested the medication intravenously on dogs, and the dogs had died. It's well-known the standard of ethics in the States is lower than the UK when it comes to clinical trials, and here was our first introduction, USA style.

I showed Crazy Horse. He was somewhat shocked, as well. This posed a difficult question; if accepted on to the trial, would we do it? At the end of the day, we needed the money, and despite feeling some trepidation, we were both going to go ahead with it. We called for our results a day or two later, and the nurse said our liver enzyme levels were too high. We'd failed the screening. Our livers hadn't fully recovered from our drinking sessions in New York. Well, that solved that problem. We weren't going to have to face the dog killing poison. With that news, we joined a few people from the hostel for a drink out on the town.

Last week of June:

With nothing keeping us in Philadelphia anymore, we headed to Washington DC to visit Brian and, of course, Natalie. We rang Brian and told him we were in town. He was expecting us at some point, and it was great to see him again. He kindly let us stay at 1103P for which we were truly grateful; you can't beat free accommodation.

We settled in quickly. Once again, there were various couches for us to sleep on. Crazy Horse was introduced to Brian's housemates. There was: John, 40's, the elder statesman of the house, worked from home, was friendly, enjoyed a laugh, as well as his vodka, which he'd drink at any time of the day, and he drove a gold Monte Carlo, which looked so cool; Richard, 39ish, worked as a barman at a pool hall, originally from Boston and a big Red Sox fan. Crazy Horse and I had some really engaging conversations with him late at night when he'd come home from work; Valente, 30's,

Mexican, was bass player in a band; he was a lot of fun and explosive at times, as, too, was his girlfriend, Beth. Crazy Horse and Valente really bonded over Crazy's snuff tobacco.

Earlier in the year, Crazy Horse developed a liking for snuff—ground tobacco sniffed through the nose. It often causes a sneeze, which can be funny when watching people take it for the first time; it often causes the eyes to water, too. The European snuff is usually scented or flavoured; the typical flavour we snuffed was menthol. We bought some American snuff whilst in DC, and it was like snorting dust; it wasn't good quality. I certainly enjoyed taking a 'pinch' from time to time, but Crazy Horse was the main advocate. When we were in Spain, he learnt the Spanish for, "My snuff is your snuff." He offered it to anyone and everyone, and most Americans had no clue as to what it was. Fair play though, most people were willing to give it a go, and then seeing the look of disturbance on their face as their nose and eyes were triggered off was priceless.

One day early on, Crazy Horse and I spent the afternoon in the pool hall where Brian's housemate, Richard, worked. Brian joined us later with two lovely ladies in tow and introduced us to Kristen, his girlfriend of the last six months, and Annette, a friend of Kristen's from Denmark. Kristen was a long-haired, red-head with a sweet accent and bright smile. Annette was fair-haired, a bit reserved, and over on holiday from Copenhagen. They were both opera singers.

We became quite the socialites. Brian invited us to several work functions and took us to a keg party. I can now say I've been to an American keg party. We arrived fashionably late to Brian's work farewell and made an appearance at his softball game on the Mall. We were well-received wherever we went, especially with our names. Although, I lost count of the number of times people thought I said, "Spiceman." Something else we did frequently was write to our good mate, Brian Oliver. We wrote to him more than we kept in touch with our friends.

One cool friend we met through Brian was Tom. He came around to 1103P one day, and we got along really well. In his 40's, Tom had long, fair hair, had an awesome sense of humour, was knowledgeable and intelligent. His music tastes were quite varied, and he was no stranger to the Australian acts Nick Cave and Rose Tattoo. Tom also liked to pace back and forth as he talked. Ah, he's a very interesting guy.

You know what? The stereotype I'd heard of Americans being fat, dumb, and ignorant, well, that just wasn't my experience. All my friends, and the friends I met through them, were so smart and knowledgeable. I'd say the majority of people we met were plugged in. That stereotype may be in abundance out in the rural areas, and often, stereotypes exist for a reason. I've certainly met my fair share of dumb Americans travelling through Europe, but in the States, it wasn't my experience at all.

At 1103P, there were some issues with the rental agreement coming up for renewal. I believe the guys wanted to stay, but for some reason or another, it looked like they'd have to move out. Crazy and I had been there for two or three weeks by this stage, and to make matters easier during the rental discussions, we were told politely that we needed to get out.

As luck would have it, we were able to stay with Tom. He'd just recently bought a house up in Colombia Heights and was in the process of renovating it. We could stay with him on the proviso we helped with work around the house, we didn't keep him up drinking on work nights, and we didn't cook our famous spaghetti bolognaise every night. Deal. We were grateful for the free roof over our head and were happy to be able to help any way we could.

It was a pretty interesting neighbourhood. Tom's house

was on 14th St, near Quincy. There were quite a few shops over the road to service our spaghetti bolognaise and alcohol addictions. We'd been there for a while when we met a black guy on the street, who told us of a bordello only a few doors up from where Tom lived. How we missed that, I don't know. I'm not entirely sure it was true; it was guised as a hair salon. Whilst Washington DC is known as 'Chocolate City' for its large African American population, there was also a strong population of Hispanics in Columbia Heights and very few whites.

After a week or so at Tom's, we finally caught up with Natalie. She came around to visit Tom and see his new house. She was in fine form, and it was great to see her again. She was very busy, having just bought some property. She'd bought a church with her sister, which they were going to convert into a café.

July 2003

Crazy Horse and I had a screening lined up for a drug trial on Monday 28th, and to make sure we were in good health, we stopped drinking a week before. If we were to be accepted, we'd start on the 4th August and finish on the 11th, so that would be 23 days sober, all up. Our medical trial screening was in Neptune, New Jersey. Long story short, it was a no go to the Neptune show for me; the doctor had failed me for my shaking. As for Crazy, we have a winner; he had passed the screening and was on the study. He left the next day. We were unsure when or where we'd see each other again. Meanwhile, I stayed at Tom's.

Tom and I had an extremely fun weekend. On Saturday, we went and saw the band, A Perfect Circle, play at the 9:30 Club. Tom was old mates with the guitarist from the support band, so we were able to get free tickets. Man, it was a write-off. I don't remember any of it. I'd been drinking all day, and by the evening, I was blacked out. Tom said, before the show, outside the venue, a big black woman came up to me and offered me $200 for my ticket. Apparently, I declined the offer. I'd been looking forward all day to seeing A Perfect Circle, as I'm a fan of the singer from his other band, Tool, so I wasn't surprised when Tom told me I'd passed on the offer. The woman wasn't about to give up. She offered $200 plus a fondle of her breasts. Still I declined; she mustn't have been my type. Fuck, I burst out laughing when Tom told me the next day. What was I thinking? I really could have done with an extra $200.

When we got inside, Tom said I bought a round of drinks, and then I wandered off. He didn't see me for the rest of the night. Who knows if I even saw the show? The night wasn't a complete black out; I remember 'making friends' with a black guy as I was walking back to Colombia Heights from the gig. This man was nice enough to threaten me physically, and being the thoughtful man that he is, decided that I shouldn't be burdened carrying my wallet anymore and that a big strong lad, like him, should carry it. Feeling guilty of him carrying the entire load, I managed to lighten the load a bit by grabbing some of my plastic from the wallet before handing it over to the model citizen. I was late for bed, so I then proceeded to … run as fast as my flip flops would allow. I made it back home to realise, out of the four random cards I grabbed from my wallet, three of them were well-important—my credit card, my driver's licence, and my Spaceman Africa bank card. One other bank account that I had money in, I no longer had access to. Some internet banking quickly fixed that up.

Sunday, we went kayaking on the Potomac River. Tom was good mates with Chris, the owner of The Velvet Lounge, who was a keen kayaker and took us out for a paddle (or whatever the term is). It was really good fun. The guy showed us proper techniques on how to paddle, how to read the water for obstacles, and what to do if we ended up, upside down. The spot we went to was quite good; it had areas for kayakers of all levels of proficiency. By the end of the day, Tom and I were up at the rapids, with the big boys, giving it a go. I didn't do too badly but usually capsized and had to bail; I didn't quite master the knack of pushing myself upright again.

Tom and I were discussing what I would do next. It was coming up to the two thirds mark of my holiday; perhaps, it would be an idea to see more of the country. I only had $600 to my name, and I didn't want to wander too far from New York as that's where I was to fly back to the UK from. Travelling solo would be difficult, too; as when together, Crazy Horse and I supported each other financially. Tom said, "The problem is, now that Crazy Horse is in New Jersey, the Fellowship of the Ring has been broken," likening our travel partnership to that of Hobbits on a quest to save Middle-Earth. I thought that was pretty clever and took the expression and applied it to the core group of faithfuls who attended the New Year's parties: Brian, Michael, Crazy Horse and myself. The title stuck, too. As a result of the discussion with Tom, I rang MDS in Montréal. They had a screening appointment available in two days if I wanted it. The next morning, I was on a bus to Canada.

Montréal was a breath of fresh air for me. It was exciting to hear French spoken everywhere, yet not be in France. The city was amazingly colourful and lively. Old Montréal was a favourite of mine, with its historic buildings and cobbled streets. I didn't go inside, but from what I saw on a postcard, the interior of the Notre-Dame de Montréal Basilica was magnificent. Montréal is also host to the F1 Canadian Grand Prix. I'm a big F1 fan so I enjoyed window shopping as many shops contained Formula 1 merchandise. The rumours I heard about there being lots of eye candy in Montréal were true.

What also had me intrigued was Montréal's underground city or indoor city. In and around Downtown Montréal is a set of interconnected complexes and tunnels, both above and below ground, connecting areas such as shopping malls, apartment buildings, hotels, museums, and metro stations. During Montréal's harsh winters, people are able to travel about Downtown without having to go outdoors. There's 32km of tunnels spread over more than 12km^2, making it the largest underground complex in the world. Can you imagine how pale the Montréalers are in winter? They must look like ghosts.

I found the people to be friendly; unfortunately, I didn't get to sample the city's bustling nightlife. The Montréal subway is clean and efficient, and there's some beautiful parks and gardens around the city. Man, just do yourself a favour and go see it for yourself. Tell them I sent you. And let me know the reaction.

I went to MDS for my screening. I thought the screening went rather well, and no one seemed to notice my tremor disorder. I rang MDS two days later for my results, and they said I passed the screening, but they didn't need me for the trial; they had everyone they needed. Shit! I could have really done with that trial.

Meanwhile, I'd received an email from Brian. He told me he was heading to Chicago for a few days on business and then heading to Milwaukee to visit Graeme, and he invited me to meet up with him in Chicago. "Well, why not?" I thought. There was no light at the end of the tunnel in Montréal, so I thought I'd try my luck for a trial in the big smoke of Chicago. As well as that, I was excited about seeing Graeme again. You might remember him from such benders as DC and NYC '02. He'd since moved from DC and was now a permanent resident in Milwaukee.

Milwaukee. Episode 1: The bender begins August 2003

Milwaukee was a bender I wasn't sure would ever end. I would never have predicted seeing Kid Rock, having to escape the affections of a self-confessed killer or going dress shopping. I headed to Chicago by train from Toronto to meet up with Brian. But, as usual, everything's a story.

I was on the train in the food car talking to the waiter guy, and we were talking about Chicago, and he asked me where I was staying. I told him the Marriot, which was true. Brian's work place had booked a room for him, and he was going to let me stay, too. So, the waiter guy, a chubby man in his 40's, pulled out a map of Chicago with all the major hotels listed. We looked under M, but there was no Marriot listed. I told the guy, I'd go back to my seat and check in my bag the exact name of the hotel as I had it written down. I found out the hotel was called Downtown Marriot and then I headed back to the food car. The waiter guy met me halfway, and we came together at that area between two carriages where the doors are. We checked the map and we found the Downtown Marriot.

At this point, for no other reason than 'just because', I adjusted myself, if you know what I mean. There was no one else around and the waiter guy saw me and took this as an invitation to help himself. At lightning speed, he grabbed my package and started to explore. Before I had time to consider what was going on, my reflexes took over, and I jumped back within seconds. The guy acted as if nothing had happened, which made me doubt whether anything had happened. But his quick exit back to his post in the food car made me think otherwise. I offered the map back to him, but he said, "No you keep it." He couldn't leave quick enough. I went back to my seat and just burst out laughing. The first thing that popped into my head was, "I have to tell Brian Oliver about this."

The plan was Brian and I would hang out in Chicago for a day or two then go to Milwaukee for a few days to meet up with our mate, Graeme. It was then my intention to head back to Montréal to try for another drug trial. Well, that was the intention.

After arriving in Chicago, I found a great dive bar in the form of Rossi's, a city secret, the locals told me. The people I met there were super friendly. Shame we only had 24 hours scheduled for Chicago. There I had my first drink in over a week and, my God, I just didn't stop. Brian met me in the bar, and to my surprise, he had brought with him my drinking partner in crime, Crazy Horse.

We made it to our mate Graeme's house and partied with him for a few days. We met some of his friends, who were really fun, and we all had a big barbecue out the back of Graeme's place. Brian, walking down the street, managed to buy a cooker for $1.

Naturally, we visited the Miller Brewery and went on a tour of the establishment, for free, finishing at a makeshift bar and given free beers. Not only that, but they had Miller postcards that were free for everyone to use, and they paid the postage. Crazy Horse and I were in heaven. Free beer and free postcard postage. Brian Oliver definitely received a few, as did anyone else whose address I could remember.

In the gift shop, Crazy Horse and Brian bought Milwaukee's Best shirts in recognition of the previous few months of drinking nothing but Milwaukee's Best. 'The Beast', as it's affectionately called, is cheap and does the job. Upon seeing the shirt, Tommy, one of Graeme's friends, gave Crazy Horse a Miller Brewery jumpsuit his father used to own. Crazy Horse then pretty much spent the next three weeks walking round in a fuckin' jumpsuit, much to the amusement of everybody.

Brian headed back to DC whilst Crazy Horse and I went on a bender. A few days into our stay, Crazy Horse and I stumbled upon gold. We found a bar, near where we were staying, called the Roman Coin. It opened at 7am, and beers were only $2. We had no idea how much this bar would affect us over the coming fortnight when we first walked through the door. Over the next two weeks, a typical day for Crazy Horse, his holiday romance, Liz, and I would be to get up somewhere about 9 or 10am and go straight to the Roman Coin, top up from the night before, meet some of the regulars, get along famously, and then often we'd be invited back to someone's place for a party. In fact, we became regulars ourselves, and everyone was asking how long we'd be in town. We quite genuinely said we were leaving in a day or two, but such was the vicious cycle we were caught up in; we never had the motivation to leave. It became a common question whenever someone we knew saw us, "Are you still here?"

One morning, we walked into the Roman Coin and met a guy, called Patrick. He worked night shift and was having a few quiet ones after work. We invited him to join our drinking session, which he accepted, and we proceeded to get exceedingly drunk. By about 12pm, it was getting past Patrick's bedtime as he had to be back at work for a 4pm start, and he hadn't slept in about 24 hours. So, we decided, the bad influence that we are, it was best if Patrick skipped work and came drinking with us. Maybe we stunk or just looked like we needed a good wash, but we weren't complaining when Patrick invited us back to his apartment to do some washing and to clean ourselves up.

At this stage, we weren't staying at Graeme's anymore, but just relying on invites to crash at someone's house or, if not, we'd sometimes sleep in a shed out back of Graeme's. Graeme wasn't a fan of Crazy Horse, so staying with him wasn't an option. Sometimes, I'd just spend the night on a patch of grass or wherever in my drunken state seemed comfortable. It was exciting not knowing where I was going to wake up the next morning, and often upon waking up, I had no memory of how I got there. And this is where the friendliness of the people of Milwaukee really impressed me. I already knew the people in the bars were friendly, but how's this?

One time out on the town with a group of friends, I was so wasted, I excused myself from the group before I could embarrass myself. I walked down a quiet street and found a house with a hedge in the front garden. I thought I'd lie down behind the hedge, so no one walking past would see me or bother me. Not long after I laid down, the resident of the house came out. I was expecting him to come over and say something like, "Hey, what the fuck do you think you're doing lying in my front yard? Fuck off, before I call the police."

But instead, he came over and asked, "Hey man, are you all right?"

"Yeah, I'm just really drunk and need to pass out for a while."

He said, "Oh man, I've been there. I'll leave you to it."

How friendly is that?

Milwaukee. Episode 2: Tartan, terror & a tattoo.

So yeah, before I went on the tangent, our heroes, Crazy Horse, Liz, and I, were on our way to our newly found friend's apartment. Patrick went beyond the call of duty. If I had to guess, I'd say Patrick was in his late 30's. He was a stocky guy, about 5'6"; he had fair hair, wore dark rimmed glasses, and had a cool 'clit tickler' goatee. He was from Wisconsin but had spent some time living in Texas. His philosophy was "*mi casa, tu casa.*" For someone who had just met us, he was showing kindness of someone we'd been friends with for years. I can't even explain how grateful we felt to be able to wash our clothes and have a shower.

The best thing, though, was Patrick's apartment block. On the 7th floor was the roof. Up there was a fridge and a balcony that looked over Lake Michigan in one direction and the city in the other. Never have I seen a lake where I couldn't see the other side. Lake Michigan is huge, and as far as the eye could see, out to the horizon, one couldn't see land. Anyway, without rambling on, Patrick made us feel at home.

On the Friday, Patrick drove upstate to pick up his daughter, Amanda, and her friends, Heather and Duncan, who were staying for the weekend. On his way, Patrick drove us to Liz's house, where we stayed the night. The best way to describe Liz would be to say Courtney Love. Liz's apartment block had a swimming pool, so we had fun going for a swim. The next morning, Patrick gave us a call and invited us back to his place again for some more drinking and revelry.

Now, I was living in the clothes I was wearing. At this point, they'd been washed the day before, but now, my shorts were wet from the swim, so I had nothing to wear. I asked

Liz if I could borrow something of hers to wear. She had a long, black and red skirt that was available, so I wore that. Patrick picked us up and took us back to his apartment, and there I was, meeting his 15-year-old daughter and her friends, wearing a skirt. But they didn't care. Actually, the next day, Liz, Amanda, Heather, and I went skirt shopping (for me) around some of the cheap clothing stores. We managed to find a nice tartan-esque type skirt that came to just below my knees. I wore that for the next day or so and had to learn a whole new way of sitting down.

After many parties on the roof with other residents and friends, the weekend finished. Patrick had to take the posse back to their home upstate and go back to work. We parted ways, and I'm guessing we went to the Roman Coin and had a few drinks.

A few days later, Crazy Horse and I walked into the Roman Coin to start off another fine day the only way we knew how. Drinking at the bar, I met this guy, and we started chatting. It was about 10 or 11am, and this guy was already wasted. Like a lot of other people, he found it refreshing to chat to us. He wanted to buy us a drink, but by this stage, the barmaid refused him service for having had enough already. Well, that was easily fixed. This guy invited us to another bar. After all, we were on East Brady St, which was full of bars.

So off we went to discover the world, with yet another new friend showing us some warm hospitality. We were down the road drinking in another bar, Jo Cat's Pub, and the guy and I were rather rambunctious and upset Crazy Horse so he left us to it. So, it was just me and our new friend; we were talking about Europe and different things. I can't remember the exact details as I was starting to notice the effects of the booze, as well, but he had been in some kind of armed forces and was talking about different times he'd killed people, which was a bit full on for a morning drinking session, I thought. He then started to drop all these compliments, saying I was an intelligent and handsome man. Then he suggested we buy a few bottles and go back to his place, get drunk, and take some drugs. I said, "Sure." This kind of invitation wasn't new to me in Milwaukee, but I was starting to have suspicions about this guy's intentions. Soon, my suspicions were realised and, yes, this guy was trying to seduce me.

By now, he was seriously drunk and started to knock over his drink a lot. He kept repeating the invitation and added we should get some whores (his word). He stressed, "They can be women or men." I thought I'd be subtle and give him a hint, "Well yeah, women would be good." And then he said, "But you told me you were gay." And then the penny dropped. No, that's an understatement. The whole fuckin' Royal Mint dropped.

This whole situation was of my own making. I'd completely forgotten about it, because it was just a throwaway line I thought I was telling a heterosexual. When I first met the guy in the Roman Coin, he was sitting two bar stools away, and when he was talking, I had trouble hearing him. So, I asked him, would he mind if I moved closer and sit at the stool next to him. He said, "Sure. I'm not going to bite you." I guess he didn't know I was joking when I said, "Yeah, but I'm gay." And little did I know, he thought I was serious.

Well, my travel guide book mentioned nothing about being raped by an aggressive, drunk, self-confessed killer in the 'Things to Do' section. I wanted him to be sure where he stood, so I was pretty blunt and said, "Mate, I'm not going to fuck you!" He seemed to be alright with that for a while, but being so drunk, I think he forgot what I said, so I had to repeat it. I told him I was up for going back for a few drinks and having a laugh, but that was it. I told him what the story was twice, now, so I gave him the benefit of the doubt that his intensions were genuine; after all, the Milwaukee people had shown themselves to be quite hospitable.

But, on the way to his place, he was very aggressive and almost ended up in a fight with this huge black guy, who would have kicked his arse. Luckily, the black guy wasn't interested. The signs were on the wall that this guy was a loose cannon and I shouldn't be anywhere near the fucker. I was thinking, "How do I get out of this?"

We got to his apartment block, and we walked up the stairs. You know those movies, where you just know someone's about to 'get it', and they're walking down to the cellar, or through the door of the haunted house or whatever, and you're screaming at the screen, "Don't do it. What are you? Fuckin' stupid? You're going to die." I'm sure that's what people would have been screaming if this were a scene from a movie.

We got to the top of the stairs, and he said, "I just want to fuck you!" I was like, "WHAT?" He brushed it off, saying he just wanted me to be 'fucked up' as in wasted on booze and drugs. I let him walk a bit ahead of me, and then I ... ran ... really fuckin' fast. I didn't care where, just as long as it was in the other direction to him. He called out to me, "Spaceman, come back."

As I was his guest, I thought it was rude to run off like that, so I did as he asked and went back to see what he had to say. DID I FUCK! I kept on running, and I didn't look back. When I was on the street, I changed direction continually to lose him. He probably didn't even chase after me, but I wasn't taking any chances. I slowed to a walk and saw a shop I could go in and lay low for a while. I thought, whilst I was there, I may as well buy something. I was in a tattoo parlour and became the proud owner of the word 'Spaceman' tattooed on my left arm.

A bit vain, I know, but it looked cool. It was intriguing that I was able to get the tattoo. I'm sure it would have been a little obvious I'd been drinking. And despite filling out a form saying I wasn't drunk and I *was* pregnant, they allowed the tattoo.

Although I had the deed poll from the internet confirming my name change, I still hadn't changed my name over in all domains of my life—including my passport. So, when I told people my name, many people dismissed it, saying, "It's not your real name. It's not the name on your passport." This pissed me off, so when I was deciding on a tattoo, I chose Spaceman as some sort of affirmation, "My name is Spaceman, God damn it." The following year, I changed my name via mail with the Births, Deaths, and Marriages registry in Australia. My passport was Spaceman Africa then, but some people still dismissed it. "You weren't born with that name." Whatever. It doesn't piss me off anymore. I kept the tattoo for a couple of years. I have a bass guitar covering it now.

Milwaukee is known for the TV show, Happy Days, breweries, and the home of Harley Davidson. Now, I'm sure a festival commemorating Happy Days would have been cool, seeing all these Fonzie impersonators saying, "Heeeeeeeeeeeeeeyyy" or "Sit on it." A beer festival is always popular, but it's also common. But a Harley Davidson festival ... celebrating its 100th birthday ... well, that's once in a life time. we couldn't leave Milwaukee now.

Milwaukee. Episode 3: Harley Fest.

Harley Fest was officially from August 28th to 30th, but Harley riders were showing up from around the world, with their bikes, up to a week earlier. It was Harley Davidson's 100th anniversary, and a big party was organised with parades, music, block parties, and fireworks. The bars were filling up more each day, and the noise of bikers revving their steel horses became more deafening the closer we got to the weekend. All of a sudden, the staff in the bars were women in bikinis, and some bars provided a bike washing service by bikini clad beauties. Crazy Horse and I were continuing our daily pilgrimage to the Roman Coin but fast running out of coins. We so wanted to stay the weekend for one of the biggest parties in the world, but we needed some way to fund it. We tried the usual avenue of ringing around for medical trials, but we weren't able to find one suitable. It occurred to us to try the local sperm bank. This is where the Miller line came in handy (no pun intended). Man, let me tell you about the Miller line.

Miller products in the States have a free phone number on the can or bottle for comments or enquiries. The alcohol companies in the US aren't legally bound to print the alcohol content on their products, so we first used the number to ask for the alcohol content of different beers. I'm sure those sorts of run of the mill questions were what the lovely people at Miller were used to, but Crazy Horse and I thought 'enquires' was a broad description. So, we tested it.

I rang and asked a beer related question like, "Why is Milwaukee's Best nicknamed the Beast?" You know, just to use the consumer line in the manner in which it was intended. Then I asked, I think it was Blaine, if he could tell me the weekend's results of the Formula One Grand Prix in Germany. Blaine checked the Internet and told me the podium winners and gave me a race report. Nice one. From then on, we used the line for anything. Crazy Horse rang up and asked if they could check if he was listed in the Belfast phone book. One day, we rang up for directions, and once we even rang and asked what time of day it was, as we weren't confident the clocks we had were telling the truth.

That happens when you keep all sorts of weird hours and wake up dazed and confused late in the afternoon.

In the Roman Coin one morning, a man saw the advertising strip of Michelin on my F1 shirt and asked me if I knew in which country Michelin originated. I said I didn't know, but I told him I could find out. I rang the Miller line, and Carl, this time, checked the internet and was having trouble finding out the information, but the absolute winner that he was, said he'd call me back once he had found it.

I gave him the Roman Coin's number and told the barmaid, Alison, who didn't know me too well, at this stage, if there was a phone call for a Spaceman, it would be for me. She just looked at me funny and humoured me, thinking I was being silly, but sure enough, 15 minutes later, Carl rang back; Alison, in disbelief, gave me the phone. Crazy Horse and I were just so impressed with the effort the Miller staff made to find out info for us unrelated to Miller that we spread the word and told everyone they should use it. Michelin tyres first originated in France, by the way, in 1889, by brothers Ándre and Édouard Michelin and five years later, the Michelin Man was first introduced at an exhibition in Lyon. The Michelin tyre company is also responsible for the travel guides and road maps of the same name, as well as the Michelin stars awarded to restaurants.

So, quite naturally, I rang the Miller line and asked if they could give me a phone number for a sperm bank in Milwaukee. Jane, this time, came up with the goods. I have a vague recollection that we may have even rung the sperm bank, but I know we never got around to making a deposit.

It was the worst timing in the world to go on the wagon but that's what Crazy Horse did in the hope he would find a medical trial early in the next week. Giving up the booze would give his liver a chance to pass the medical if he found a trial. Me? I managed to do a bit of phone banking and scored myself about $200. So, while Crazy Horse was being dry, I looked up my mate Graeme, and he almost fell off his chair when I walked into his house. He wasn't expecting me and hadn't seen or heard of me in over a week and a half. I told him of all the adventures, and he laughed hard. It was Thursday night, the night before the fest officially began, so we went out with a few of his friends to see the shenanigans. The streets were closed to cars, and there were people everywhere. The usual burn outs, bare breasts, and booze were order of the night.

The next morning, I woke at Graeme's, having enjoyed my first sleep under a roof in days. I'd slept quite well, and it was late in the morning, by this stage. Graeme and I went and had breakfast, of the food variety, at a deli and ran into some of Graeme's friends. Graeme had to go, and he left me with his friends, who later left me by myself. As I was walking out of the deli, who should I run into, but Patrick and Crazy Horse. So, I hooked up with them again. There were bikes and bikers everywhere, all showing off their wheels and wanking over how good they looked. Lots of police were there too, but there was never any trouble.

We were on another session with Patrick. It was so cool hanging out with him. We went out, and everyone in the bars and on the streets were in good spirits. We'd invite girls back to the flat and impress them with the view from the roof of Patrick's apartment block and then let our charm do the rest.

Friday night of Harley Fest, we went to the local bars in Patrick's area. All the bars were full, and there were stages set up in the streets with loud, really loud, bands performing. We went into this Irish bar and saw something I've never seen before. The toilets for the men and women were one cubicle each, and get this: the queue for the men's was longer than the women's. The women's moved quicker, too.

No bullshit. We'd found ourselves a booth to sit, right where the queue for the ladies was. So, we got to talk to all the women in the bar. We had a good laugh with some cool people.

But it was time to hit the streets and soak up some of the action. We drank on the streets for a while and then did a bit of a nightclub crawl. A lot of the clubs were playing 80's rock to get the bikers in, but we managed to find us a place playing some dance music. Patrick and I met a girl each, separately, and by coincidence, they turned out to be sisters. They came back to the roof, and we stayed up all night. It was someone's crazy idea that the older sister and I get married. I was up for it there and then, but there was nowhere possible to do it in that place or time. Patrick's girl was up for some bedroom action, but my girl was playing big sister and chaperon and stopped any chance Patrick had. I got her number but I never saw her again after that night.

Saturday of Harley Fest, we went down to Brady St, and the crowds were huge. We found ourselves a place to sit, and we just drank cheap booze from the bottle shop and soaked up the atmosphere. Once again, booze, bare breasts, and bikes were the order of the day. I can't describe the buzz one got from the revelry going on. I went to the supermarket and joined the long queue of people buying disposable cameras. I ended up using the whole film in a few hours. Not only was it a Saturday night, but it was Harley Fest. Combined, those make for a great reason to celebrate. But not only that, it was the 29th of August, which meant it was the one year anniversary of my fake death. So, with all those excuses to have a big drink, Patrick and I, along with our friends, proceeded to get shitfaced. Poor Crazy Horse was still on the wagon.

The whole festival was going to culminate in a large concert down by the lakefront on Sunday evening. The organisers had kept secret who would be performing. All week leading up to Sunday, people were speculating who might be headlining the show. The big favourites were The Rolling Stones. Tickets for the gig were about $70, but some people paid double that from scalpers, thinking The Stones would be playing. Others rumoured were U2, George Thorogood, and even Page & Plant. But most expected The Stones. There were even rumours they'd been seen checking into a hotel.

We had no plans Sunday evening, so we decided we'd go down to the lake and just stand around outside the barriers and listen to the show from there. We walked down to the lake and arrived just as the main act had come on. We walked as close to the concert as possible, expecting to come across some fences or gates. As well as a lack of barriers, we noticed we were walking against the flow of traffic. Shitloads of people were leaving the gig, which made us think maybe the show had finished, but as we got to the concert site, for free, we realised what was going on.

All week people spoke of their hopes that The Rolling Stones would be playing, and some payed a lot of money to see them. Either the organiser had a warped sense of humour or was just completely ignorant to the Harley Davidson demographic, but who should be headlining at this great, US, bike institution, "sex, drugs & rock 'n' roll"—esque, type concert? None other than the British, gay, pop star, Elton John. Classic.

We got really close to the stage and enjoyed a really good, inappropriate maybe, but really good, Elton John show. The most awesome part was when Elton played 'Saturday's alright for fighting' and Kid Rock came on stage and sang. I couldn't believe what I saw. Elton was rocking hard at his piano whilst Kid Rock was standing on top of Elton's grand piano screaming out the words.

Fuckin' excellent. Patrick quite weirdly predicted Elton John as the main act before the show. Fuck knows how he guessed that. After the show, there was one of the best fireworks displays I've seen. The colours weren't too special, but the bangs and colours were choreographed to music, and there were all sorts of different formations and shapes going on that were really inventive.

The weekend was over. The bikers were on their way back home and my bank balance bare. The 20-day drinking session had finished and the come down well and truly in full swing. Once again, I'm talking night sweats, nightmares, the shakes, chills, and being totally wired. With no money and nowhere to stay, I was forced to ask the family back home to bail me out. It was never my favourite thing in the world to do. Patrick, once again, stepped in and let Crazy Horse and me stay until we organised some transport back to the east coast. I had a break from the booze for a few days whilst Crazy was off the wagon in a big way. He'd set up camp in Rascal's Bar and enjoyed the cheap drinks and friendly people. Crazy often earned free drinks from winning drinking games with the bar staff.

A few days later, the three of us did a farewell pub crawl, saying good bye to all the friends we'd made. Of course, none of them believed us when we said we were actually leaving. I managed to catch up with Graeme, too, before I left. I originally went for five days and ended up staying for 21. Patrick's kindness showed no boundaries, and he drove Crazy and me an hour and 45 mins down the road to Chicago's Midway Airport.

We caught our flight to Washington DC and thus ended one of the craziest, random, never a dull moment, three week benders. Although, we didn't really stop there. The next few days in DC were booze fuelled, farewell gatherings with mates. It was Tom's birthday, and we celebrated at the

Velvet Lounge. Natalie was there too, and she and I had a good one-on-one chat with each other.

15th September 2003

The flight home was surprisingly uneventful. My only worry was going through immigration when we arrived in Dublin. About two months earlier, Crazy Horse and I were playing scrabble and had nowhere to write the score, so we used page 22 of my passport. Writing in the passport I think is illegal, being government property and all. To make matters worse, during one game, I put down the word 'cunt', which was an automatic win as it matches Crazy Horse's tattoo. This was written in the passport, as well. But, thankfully, I had no worries at all getting through immigration nor the next day at Gatwick. I ended up losing that passport two months later, so it wasn't an issue again after that. I didn't have to worry anymore about page 22 being discovered. Crazy Horse and I parted company at Dublin airport and ended 3½ months together on the sauce. Crazy Horse went home to Belfast, and I stayed in Dublin for a night out on the town with some friends.

We'd managed to survive the three months, largely due to our friends' hospitality, the kindness of some strangers, and in the end, a loan from family back home. We'd met some great people and formed some strong friendships. Our trip hadn't exactly gone to plan, but then again, we didn't have a plan other than to catch up with Natalie. So, it was mission accomplished, really. An interesting piece of information you might be like to know: In the 12 weeks we spent in America, Crazy Horse and I only paid for 15 night's accommodation between us. Crazy Horse—six, and me—nine. Now that's travelling on a shoe-string.

New Year's 2003

I was lucky to land a place on a medical trial with HMR at Middlesex Hospital, West London, leading up to Christmas. This study was 17 nights straight for £2000, testing medication for gout. This was perfect timing as I had a New Year's party to attend on the other side of the world. As far back as March, the location for the Fellowship of the Ring New Year's party had been decided. And the location? Playa Del Carmen, on Mexico's Caribbean Coast. Caribbean beaches, tequila, Mexican food, warm weather, hammocks, we made a good choice, yeah? I didn't even know Mexico had tropical beaches. My perception of Mexico was desert.

Christmas day came, and I was on a flight to Mexico—awesome. I mean, MEXICO. Wow. It didn't bother me at all to be spending my Christmas day on a plane. I was happy to be avoiding all the obligations that come with Christmas. Passing through Cancún airport was a bit confusing. They have a unique traffic lights system of determining if you need to have your luggage checked by customs or not. Christmas Night, I stayed in Cuidad de Cancún. It's full of locals and a lot less touristy than the resorts on Isla Cancún. I did a bit of a bar hop and was able to practise speaking Spanish, as there wasn't much English spoken.

Next day, my first full day in paradise and … it rained. I went for a wander around the town to absorb the vibe. I found a place to get my hair cut and due to a language barrier problem, instead of getting the haircut I thought I'd asked for, I ended up with braids and beads in my hair. It didn't take me long to realise the woman was giving me braids, but I thought, "What the hey. Maybe I'll look good with braids."

Wrong. I looked like a complete dick. Worst of all, I looked like a tourist. Nearly every second person had them, and with my red and yellow beads, I looked like a fuckin' Christmas tree. I was near the central markets, and I went there in search of a hat to see if I could hide my hair. But I couldn't find one big enough. I wanted to keep the braids to show my friends when they arrived on the 30th, so we all could have a good laugh, but I just felt so silly. About three hours later, I found a quiet spot in the markets and took all the beads out and then unravelled the braids. Not before getting a photo of my bad hair moment, though. A few days later, I found a hairdresser that spoke English, and I got the haircut I wanted.

I left Cancún and made my way to Isla Mujeres, which is a short ferry ride north. The island has a relaxing vibe and has a good beach at the north end. In the small town, there was a small strip of restaurants and bars, and because of this, it was easy to run into people you'd met the night before or during that day on the beach. I stayed at Poc na Hostel not far from the strip and the beach.

The first few nights, I didn't drink much, knowing that when I met up with The Fellowship of the Ring, I'd be drinking very heavily. But (there's always a but, isn't there), one night I met a guy from San Diego; we went to a tequila bar, and I don't remember much after that.

I woke the next morning and knew something had happened to me. I wasn't in my own bed. I had a hazy recollection of going to a medical centre. I was so sore. Any and every movement of my body was painful. I went to the bathroom and saw myself in the mirror.

"FUCKIN' HELL."

I had dry blood trails on my face, and I had a big, swollen, purple black-eye. Thoughts that I'd been involved in a fight ran through my mind. The last thing I remember was getting along famously with Mr San Diego. A man walked out of his room and greeted me, "Here he is. How are you?"

"Not the best. Tell me ... what happened to me?"

"You fell out of bed."

"*Really?*" I was astonished.

From different people, I was able to piece together what happened. I'd been out drinking heavily and passed out fast asleep in bed. In the hostel, I had a bed on the top bunk that was well over six-foot-high (no shit). The room was full, eight of us, passed out asleep. All of a sudden, there was a loud THUD that woke everybody up, except me, because I was dead to the world from the booze. What was the thud? I'd just gone and fallen out of bed, hadn't I. Six feet I fell onto a tiled floor. I hit my eye on the corner of the bed next to me, and blood was pissing out everywhere. I'd hit my ribs on the side of the bed and bruised them heavily. They still hurt more than four weeks later. I banged both knees badly on the ground and had some nice purple bruises on them, too, and I landed right on my hip.

I don't know if I was out through alcohol or if I was knocked out from the fall. The people in the room shat themselves. There I was, motionless on the floor, with blood everywhere. I was told it took about five minutes to wake me. I'm sure it was the longest five minutes the others have ever experienced. I was taken to a medical centre, where a nurse patched me up. I remember a few vague seconds of the medical centre, and that's the only thing I remember of the night.

Apparently, I was taken back to the hostel, and the night manager took me to a new room. He opened the door and said, "Here you go," and just left me standing in the doorway. This woke up two girls in the room, and they said I was just standing there in a daze, looking down at my cupped hand, which was catching dripping blood from my eye. One of them helped me to sit down, and the other made me a bed (lower one this time), and they put me to bed after that.

Other than being heavily bruised, I was alright, nothing broken.

I was a bit freaked out when sitting on the beach, hiding my huge black eye with sunglasses, and complete strangers, well, so I thought, were coming up to me and asking if I was OK. It turned out these people in some way had helped me the night before by either helping me to the medical centre or cleaning me up or putting me to bed, but I remembered none of it. Apparently, when coming back from the medical centre, I was continually thanking everyone for their help and explained, "I won't remember this in the morning."

The accident improved my social life immensely. I was known as the guy who fell out of bed, and people were always coming up to me asking how I felt. Lots of girls were mothering me, which was great. People struck up conversations with me all the time, my black eye being the perfect ice breaker. And this sort of attention happened the whole trip. I loved it.

On the 30th, I headed to Playa Del Carmen, about an hour down the road from Cancún, to meet up with The Fellowship of the Ring. The usual suspects were there, plus some special guests: Michael, Brian and Kris, Atira and boyfriend Peter, and friend Ursula, Crazy Horse and his new girlfriend, Nadine, and me. We had booked two cabins at the basic Campamiento La Ruina close to the beach. There wasn't room for everyone, so Michael and I slept outside in hammocks.

Playa, as it's known, was originally a small fishing village, but as tourism grew in neighbouring Cancún and Isla Cozumel, people started to escape to Playa Del Carmen and discovered its beautiful beach with crystal clear water. The place is a big tourist spot, now days, with scores of hotels and bars on the beach. Off the beach, the main action is a few hundred metres away on Fifth Avenue, lined with countless shops, bars, and restaurants.

I adjusted to being in Mexico quite smoothly. With my extended travel experience and basic Spanish skills, I was able to successfully manage all the necessary situations a traveller comes across, such as catching public transport, asking for directions, and ordering food and drink. I was in great spirits. I had my friends around me, the sun was shining, beer and food was cheap and the place was a hive activity. It was a lot of fun.

We soon became well-known in a few places, especially Crazy Horse and me with our unusual names, and me with all my bruises and black eye. No one ever forgot meeting me. I had people come up to me and call me by name, and I had no idea who they were. Just for my own amusement, I made up different stories on how I ended up with the black eye. Sometimes, I'd run into people I'd met before, and I'd have to try to remember what bullshit story I'd told them, so I could keep up the facade.

I told these two guys we met, I'd been chatting up a girl, when her boyfriend came up to me and told me to fuck off and leave her alone. I then said, "Why don't you put a toilet on your head and keep it there while I shit in it." And then the boyfriend punched me in the eye. Anyway, I made that up, but the two guys bought it.

We spent the next few days in Playa, eating, drinking, laying in the sun and swimming. Paradise. For New Year's, we were in a bar, by the beach, getting drunk and enjoying each other's company. New Year's Eve doesn't stand out so much as we partied with great enthusiasm every night. I do remember drinking vodka mixed with a cheap substitute for Red Bull. And there was some dancing on the bar. I remember that.

We also did a few day excursions. I went with Brian and Kris to this great Mexican-themed eco-archaeological park, called *Xcaret*. There, you can see all these cool animals from birds to bats to dolphins to pumas. We went swimming in an underground river that meandered through caves. That was way cool, right out of an Indiana Jones movie. We also went snorkelling in a small inlet, and I saw the funniest thing. I was looking at all the fish swimming around when I saw a handrail down at the bottom of the sea bed, and people with diving helmets on were walking along holding onto the hand rail. It surprised me; I just didn't expect to see that.

The next day, it was off to *Chichén Itzá*, one of the largest Mayan ruins sites in Mexico. The site is a few hours drive inland from Playa del Carmen. The main structure is a huge pyramid about 24 metres high plus six metres for the temple on top; it felt higher than that. The sides and the steps were astonishingly steep. Most people sat on their bums as they made their way down the steps.

On the way back, we stopped off at a cenote and went for a swim. A cenote is an underground pool of water in a cave. There was a hole in the ceiling of the cave, and tree roots from a tree right above were stretching about 30 metres all the way down to the water. We had fun jumping in from a platform about 10 metres above the water. The pool was quite deep in some parts.

That night back at Playa, we were drinking at our local bar near the cabins. I ended up drinking with some of the local mafia types. One of them, an American wanna-be gangster, saw how beat up I was and demanded to know who had hurt me. Eddie, his name was, offered to take care of whoever had done it to me. It took a bit of convincing before he believed it was an accident and not the result of a fight.

He invited me to sit down at the table with his Mexican mates. They looked like the real deal. The head honcho was a man of few words and just sat there observing, whilst his flunkies bought him drinks. He was wearing your stereotypical mobster Panama hat.

One person in our group was after some coke, so I became the unwilling middle man to do the deal. It was all a bit scary, really. Eddie was very forceful about everything. I complied, though. I didn't know if his tough persona was genuine or just his inflated ego. We went for a walk, and he gave me a pill. I put it away for later, but he insisted I take it straight away. I necked it and he took one, too. A few things were running through my head at that point. One: it's going to be a messy night; two: I hope this guy doesn't want to join our party after the deal is done; three; I hope I get through this deal OK.

We walked a few blocks and stood on a street corner. A car pulled up and Eddie said, "Get in."

"I'm not going anywhere in a car, mate."

"OK, wait for me in there."

He pointed to a bar. Phew, I was glad, to say the least, he was willing for me to sit out the car journey. I waited for about ten minutes in the bar when he returned and insisted I buy him a drink. He gave me a cigarette packet with what I wanted; we finished our drinks, left the bar and went our separate ways. It all felt a bit tense, and I don't know if it was warranted—whether I was dealing with the big boys of a major cartel—or whether the melodramatic routine was just a bit exaggerated.

The person didn't want the coke in the end, so I got to have it and share it with some friends. I tell you, it's a great paradisiacal moment, swaying on a swing at a bar on a Caribbean beach with a cold beer, coked up, with bikini clad women all around—some even topless.

After a few days in Playa, we all decided to move to Tulum, a smaller, less touristy, part of the coast about an hour down the road. Tulum was great. The locals there were friendly, and the place was less populated, with a rustic and laidback charm to it. On our way, we met an Australian guy, James, who was travelling alone, and he joined our group. I got chatting to him later in the day; it turned out he used to work at the Empire in Shepherd's Bush less than 12 months ago and knew some of the same people I did.

We booked ourselves into cabañas, right near the beach, built in the traditional Maya style with thatched palm roofs and no electricity. There was a cool little outdoor bar on the beach, where we spent most of the afternoon and night. The seats at the bar were swings—it looked and felt authentically Caribbean. We were on the Caribbean Coast, after all. There was a group of bongo drummers playing there too, to add to the atmosphere. The lack of sleep caught up with me, and I fell asleep on one of the deck chairs near the bar. My friends said they were playing with my limbs and putting me in different positions, but I didn't wake up. Nadine woke early the next morning to go for a walk along the beach and found me still asleep at the bar.

Whilst in Tulum, we went and saw some more ruins. This time, they were on a cliff face overlooking the ocean. Wow, it's a real prime piece of real estate. I wonder what the Mayans paid for this beachfront property with ocean views. A few of us also went snorkelling far out to the coral reef. The coral reef there stretches all the way down the coastline, making it the second longest in the world. It made a great defence against attacking ships back in the day.

Otherwise, we just enjoyed ourselves doing nothing. On the 5th of January, it was Crazy's birthday. We celebrated the same as every other day. We became good friends with the staff at the bar and hotel. There was a local fisherman, who cooked us his catch at night for dinner over an open fire. He had such a cool name. It was Amador, which means lover.

As happens every year, the group slowly went their separate ways. We lost two members one day, and two days later, three more were on their way home. That left five of us: Crazy Horse, Nadine, Atira, Ursula, and me. My flight was in two days, on the 9th, whilst the other four didn't fly out until the 27th. After a few drinks, I was talked into putting my flight back and going with the others to Palenque. It didn't take much persuasion, let me tell you. I managed to push my flight back to the 20th.

The ruins of the ancient Mayan city of Palenque are surrounded by jungle. We spent the first two nights at a campsite near the ruins. We all shared one large cabin. It had its own bathroom and shower, and for the first time in the 2½ weeks that I'd been in Mexico, I had a shower with hot water—oh what luxury. At night, all the jungle animals came alive, and we heard all sorts of noises. We weren't always sure who or what was making what noise.

The ruins were just up the road, and naturally, we went to have a look. This time, we all went there tripping on mushrooms. I liked these ruins the best of all the ones we saw. They were just as big as Chichén Itzá, and there were more pyramids, but it was the surroundings that really made it special. The place was surrounded by the jungle, and it started to rain. The fog crept in, and in my eyes, it was just how I imagined a jungle to be. I loved it. I'm sure the mushrooms played a part in my euphoria. I had 'Welcome to the Jungle' by Guns 'N' Roses stuck in my head, which was fine. I only wish I knew the words better.

The five of us moved from our cabin into, Palenque, the city a few miles away and found a nice little family run hotel, where the family was so sweet. They let us use their kitchen and eat in their lounge room. As usual, we made friends wherever we went, and being the small town that it was, we could hardly venture out without running into someone we knew. We thought Playa was cheap, until we went to Tulum. We thought Tulum was cheap, until we arrived in Palenque. We paid about $5 each for a room with five beds. A 1litre bottle of beer was just under $2.40. One thing that stood out was the large military presence throughout the town, left over from rebellions in years gone by.

Atira and Ursula decided to go to San Cristóbal de las Casas, a town even further inland, whilst I was going to go south to Guatemala with Nadine and Crazy Horse. Although, come time to go, I realised, it was only five days until my flight, so I decided to head back slowly to Cancún alone.

I took a bus back to Tulum. The bus arrived in the morning, and I made my way to the beach. Still being very early, the place was deserted. I made myself comfortable on a sand dune with a bottle of rum and soaked up the serenity of the crashing waves and gentle breeze. If you've ever pictured paradise as a beach scene, then this place would have to come close to representing that picture: white sand, the blue water of the ocean, the palm trees and the hammocks spread between the trees, all alluding to utopia.

Time was getting on, and I was out of booze, so I went to see if there was any activity at the bar at *Zazil-Kin*. As I got closer, I could see the place was open—happy days. I got a beer and sat outside to watch two older guys playing chess. I don't mind the odd game of chess, and I was in good form as I'd had some good battles with Michael when we were staying in Playa del Carmen. I asked if I could play next, and they were cool with that. The winner, Taso, suggested to the loser, Rico, he play me next. Taso thought it would be a more evenly matched contest as he didn't rate my playing abilities. I don't know why they judged my chess playing based on how I looked. I did look a mess though; I was unshaven and had the shakes, plus I still had some bruising visible.

We started the game and, long story short, I beat Rico quite easily. Upon seeing this, Taso wanted to play me immediately. Long story short, Taso beat me but said it was the closest fought game he'd had in a long time. I didn't win, but I had earned their respect.

I'll just go on a tangent here for a moment; Taso, from Austria, and Rico, from the States, were both long-term residents of Tulum. I remember Taso was an artist and sold his paintings to support his life on the beach. Meanwhile, in Guatemala, Crazy Horse and Nadine had gone their separate ways. Nadine returned to catch her flight back to the UK, whilst Crazy Horse pushed his flight back indefinitely. He ended up staying in Guatemala for weeks and then made his way back through Mexico and back to Tulum. His is quite the story, which is best told by him, but from being penniless in Guatemala City to being held up by armed bandits in Palenque to a non-legally binding marriage in Tulum, it never was a dull moment.

So anyway, Crazy Horse made Tulum his home for quite a while and became part of a brotherhood of drinkers, who became known as the Breakfast Club. During this time, Crazy Horse was sitting around a table with some friends, and the topic of his name came up in conversation. Someone prophesised, "Isn't Crazy Horse Invincible the most unusual name you've ever heard?"

One guy piped up, "I met a guy a few months ago whose name was Spaceman Africa."

Crazy Horse nearly fell off his chair. The guy was Rico, with whom I'd played chess. Crazy Horse explained we were mates, and Rico explained what he was thinking when he first met me. That's how I know they didn't hold much regard for me when I asked to play chess. Rico gave Crazy Horse an amulet to pass on to me as a gift of goodwill. That was nice of him.

So, tangent over, and back to mid-January, and for some reason, many places on the beach were closed that night, so I didn't see some of the friends I'd hoped.

That night, my friend's bar was open. Antonio had looked after me the first night I was in Tulum, passed out on the deck chair. It was good to see him again. At the bar, as always, I met some other people. This time, I met four crazy Mexican guys in their mid-twenties. They all spoke English well, and they invited me to join their party. We drank and drank, and when the bar closed, they invited me back to their house in town where we drank loads more whilst listening to the Beatles.

I ended up staying with them for the next two days and nights. They had a one bedroom house with a lounge room, kitchen, and bathroom. Guess how many people were staying there? Six. There was enough bed space for five, so they took turns sleeping on the cold cement floor. They were so hospitable; they made sure I always got one of the beds. We partied and drank like there was no tomorrow. They were happy to have me around to speak English to and to have some willing ears listening to their stories and explanations of Mexican life.

The moment I had dreaded had arrived. It was the day to go home. I managed to wake early and get to the airport in plenty of time. I walked inside to find a queue a mile long. As usual, I hoped it wasn't the line I had to queue up in, but it usually is. But today was my day. I found my queue, and there was only about three people lining up. Not only that, but when I rang to put my flight back, I was told I'd be charged £100 at check-in, but instead, they charged me US$100. Nice one. At the time, that was about half.

My eye, at this stage, was looking a lot better. The external bruising was gone, but the internal bruising was still quite visible. Blood in my eye was still evident. Add that to the fact I'd had little sleep and had been drinking, my eyes were very bloodshot. The woman at the check-in handed me my new ticket and then asked me a question I was to hear numerous times over the next 18 hours. "Are you alright?" Paranoid that I might not be allowed on the plane if they knew I'd been drinking, I made up the excuses that I'd travelled all night without sleep on the bus to get to the airport, and my eyes were tired from having to see without my glasses. I was to use these excuses many times to come.

I was well-impressed with the amount of help people gave me when they saw what my condition was and learnt I didn't have my glasses. Other passengers, air stewards, and immigration officials helped me all the way to London, with finding my seat through to filling out my immigration landing card. It made me realise that there are some really nice people in this world and that the rude people in London are shit.

In Houston, after boarding my connecting flight, I asked a steward if it was OK to use the bathroom before take-off. She said it was no problem and then she asked, "Are you alright?" After the bathroom, I was back at my aisle seat looking at a magazine, when three people came up and stood in the aisle surrounding me. I saw one was a steward. I thought "Fuck, I've done nothing wrong; leave me alone." I thought maybe the previous steward had told her superiors I was drunk and maybe I should be taken off the plane. One of them, a woman in plain clothes, knelt to my level and said, "Are you alright?" She introduced herself as a doctor for Continental. I gave my excuses, and she decided I should have three seats to myself so I could stretch out and get some sleep once we had taken off. Winner.

Of course, once in the air, I started drinking the cans of beer I'd bought cheaply in Mexico. On the long-haul flights, Continental has a screen for every seat so I was able to watch whatever I wanted from their selection, and I had a great time, too much fun to find time for sleeping.

Immigration at London Gatwick went well. It was about midday, and I didn't have any house keys, so I had to wait until Chris finished work before I could go home. I caught a train to Olympia and went to the nearest pub—The Beaconsfield. One barmaid was speaking Spanish, so I thought I'd practise what I'd learnt in Mexico. Turned out she was from Barcelona. After a few minutes of talking to her, she looked a bit concerned and asked, "Are you alright?" After a few pints, the next stop was to order some new glasses. The woman in the opticians examined my eyes and guess what she said?

"You should go to hospital."

Which I did, a few times, over the next couple of days, including a CT scan. But all was well, no permanent damage done. The horrors were particularly bad, though. The shakes were awful and the electric fleas, extreme. Chris commented he'd never seen me so bad. I took a break from drinking for a few weeks after that, whilst my body slowly recovered. I had a new pair of glasses, too.

Mexico had been awesome. A few suggestions were already made for the following year: Iceland, Sri Lanka, Philippines, and South Africa. Atira and Ursula were pretty keen on Sri Lanka. When they said good bye to me in Palenque, they said, "See you in Sri Lanka." Ultimately, the final decision would come down to wherever was easiest for everyone. At the time, though, I was well up for Sri Lanka.

2004

Mid-April, I received a call on my mobile; it was a UK number, but I didn't recognise it. I answered it and ... fuck a duck, it was Crazy Horse. After four months in Mexico and Guatemala, he'd finally returned to the UK from the New Year's party. That weekend, he dropped around to Chris's flat and we spent the night catching up and playing drinking chess. Just after Crazy Horse arrived back from Mexico, he rang Brian Oliver, pretending to be someone else: Andrew Pye. He told Brian he was looking for Crazy Horse and did he know how to get in touch with him. Brian said, "The last I heard, he was still in Mexico." How funny is that? That meant Brian actually read our postcards. Not only read them, but it seemed like he didn't mind receiving them.

Mid-June 2004 onwards

Around mid-July, I ended up scoring a job as a distributor in the glossy magazine trade. That's what I would have put on my résumé, anyway. In reality, I worked in a newspaper/magazine warehouse, Dawson News, sorting out papers/mags to be recycled. Many of the magazines were soft porn, but the professional that I was, I was too busy to distinguish a porn mag from a glossy celeb mag. So naturally, I couldn't tell you there was *Razzle, Penthouse, Men only, Club, Only black, Teens, Over 40's, Housewives,* or *Big and beautiful.*

The majority of the other workers at Dawson News were from Nigeria or Ghana. There were a few exceptions, including a young, gorgeous lass from Lithuania. I didn't give her much thought to begin with. My experience working with young, eastern European women in their early 20's was that they generally just mixed with their own kind and certainly didn't waste their time befriending me, a man in his 30's. And so, I didn't make any effort to talk to her; most days, I was hungover and didn't feel like talking to anyone, anyway. One day though, we ended up working on opposite sides of the conveyor belt, so it was only natural that I said hello.

Alé was 21 and from Vilnius in Lithuania. She was quite short, probably only about five-foot-tall, shoulder length brown hair, and a smile from here to next Monday. Much to my surprise, we hit it off. The more I got to know her, the more I realised, she was very much like a young female version of me. We had the same sense of humour; she loved to roam free and had hitch-hiked all around Europe; music is her life, in particular, Bon Jovi (that explained the superman tattoo on her arm, then), and she loved drinking beer, which you may have guessed, I'm quite partial to, as well.

Whilst she may have been reserved, she had a great inner strength and was unusually perceptive. Her intuition was first-class; there wasn't much I could hide from her. Work became fun and something to look forward to, as Alé and I talked and laughed all day. One of my favourite memories of Alé was meeting up before work one morning, sitting by the canal, drinking beer, and eating crisps. I haven't met too many women who would be up for getting together for a drink before work. She brought the crisps and a newspaper to sit on, which I thought was a nice touch.

More often than not, I'd show up to work stinking of booze, and there were some people there who were not afraid to tell me, either. I used to just sit around the flat and drink about ten pints a night. It helped that I had a special deal at my local off-licence. At most offies, there are various deals on offer, such as six cans for £5, or eight cans for £6. Not just any cans but whatever brand they were featuring that week, usually the medium to shite range beer. My local offie on Uxbridge Rd had a deal of eight cans for a fiver, and it was usually good imported beer from Germany.

One day, I went in, and they didn't have the deal anymore; the price had gone up. So, the next time I wanted some booze, I went to a different offie across the road and found they had an eight cans for a fiver deal. I went there a few times over the next few days, before going back to my local offie to see if they had brought back the eight cans for a fiver deal. They hadn't, but the owner surprised me by saying, no matter what the advertised price, I could always have eight cans for £5. Woohoo! He must have seen me one time going to the offie across the road and didn't want to lose my custom, which I thought was hilarious. I thought it was fantastic that I could always have the cheap deal, but I thought it was very funny that I was such a valued customer that the owner didn't want to lose me. I was in there every day, sometimes buying 16 cans, and even more on weekends. Was I providing such a good turnover for him that he couldn't afford to lose me? Was I keeping his shop afloat? Was I included as part of his guaranteed income when he was doing the books every month? Probably, yes, no, and no.

At Dawson News, we were being paid £5/hour. I told Alé about my deal at the off-licence, and from then on, we always referred to our pay rate as, eight-beers/hour. Another hour would pass by, and we'd get excited, "That's another eight beers."

It was the end of August by this stage; the end of summer was drawing near, and I was suffering from withdrawals of a different kind. I was suffering badly from travel withdrawals. This was my first summer (northern hemisphere) in four years that I hadn't been travelling (poor me), and I wasn't in my most cheerful of flavours. The plan was to find a medical trial worth at least £2000. With that, I'd buy a ticket back home to Australia and, with the change, do a tour around Europe visiting all my friends I'd made over the years. I was fast running out of time, though; it was only four months until December. I just needed a fat cheque with my name on it.

As a self-practical joke, I thought it would be funny if I made a decision by rolling the dice, like Luke Reinhardt does in the book *The Dice Man*. I decided, if I roll an even number, I'll cut ties with Alé. Fuck, who invented the number four? I rolled a four and told her I wouldn't be seeing her anymore. She took it better than I did. Fuck that dice.

My summer depression was partly due to girl troubles. I'd fallen for Alé, but she was doing my head in by wanting to take things slowly or, in some cases, not wanting to move forward at all. In an attempt to alleviate the torment, I thought cutting ties would help, which is why I tried the dice stunt. However, as much as I tried to follow the dice, two days later, I was ringing Alé again, and we met up. Alé was aware I had plans to go home to Australia and so didn't want to get serious, unless, of course, I decided to stay. Well, I wasn't going to stay unless the relationship was serious. I'd had enough of the UK and longed to go home. I felt, as far as Europe was concerned, I'd been there, done that. It was time I shifted my base to Australia and started travelling to new places in south-east Asia and the Pacific, for example, and ultimately work towards another trip to Latin America. So, the situation with Alé was at a stalemate. Even so, we still continued to spend a lot of time together and had some great craic: drinking in Holland Park and down by the river, going to the movies, dancing in the pub to Bon Jovi songs on the juke box, sitting at the bus stop for hours after work, drinking beer and discussing life, love, and the universe.

November 2004

One Saturday afternoon, I needed Chris to accompany me down to Soho for a significant purchase. No, not from one of the sex shops; it wasn't toys I was buying but travel—that other love affair. We went to a travel shop to pay for a flight I'd booked over the phone. I needed Chris, because it was easier to pay using his credit card. Where was I going? I was going home, *BABY!* That's right; January 18th I'd be taking a flight bound for Sydney. Yeeha. But the best bit was a five-night stopover in Hong Kong on the way. I was fuckin' wrapped, to say the least. January would mark 33 months away from home, three months shy of three years. Chris said it had been a long time since he'd seen me so happy.

After a miserable and boring last six months, the next two months promised to be very exciting. The plan for the rest of the year was coming together nicely. The Fellowship of the Ring had decided the location for the New Year's party was going to be, "Envelope please … and the winner is … (drum roll) … Bratislava." Never heard of it? It's the capital city of the Slovak Republic. In the end, Sri Lanka was deemed too expensive, whereas Eastern Europe was much easier on the bank balance. As well as Bratislava, we were going to travel to some of the neighbouring cities such as Prague and Budapest.

You may have seen the 2004 film *Eurotrip*, which quite humorously exaggerates the cost of living in Bratislava: It features four American high-school graduates touring around Europe. They ultimately end up in Bratislava, and due to an exaggerated exchange rate, they get the executive suite at a lavish Slovak hotel with only $1.83. There's a scene after that where the American tourists are in the hotel restaurant and one of them tips the waiter:

Waiter: Ah! A nickel! (waiter shows his demanding

manager) You see this? [waiter slaps the manager] I quit. I open my own hotel.

December 2004

It wasn't long now before I started my travels. My first jaunt was going to be a weekend away in Belfast from the 10th. I was excited and getting into the spirit of party mode. I let Emma, Chris's daughter, who was a trainee hairdresser, practise on me, and she did a great job of dying the top of my head, pillar-box red. The back and sides remained my natural dark colour. I must say, it looked really cool.

Before my departure to Prague on the 20th, I had a lot to organise for my trip back to Australia. Moving countries is a lot of work. Expenses I never counted on kept cropping up. I was organising a new passport in the name of Spaceman Africa. I was told the new passport would be free, but it turned out to be £80. I had to pay £130 to ship some things home, including my guitars, as I couldn't take everything with me in my backpack.

And then this:

Crazy Horse and I made the news worldwide.

Saturday 4th December 2004

Google search: *ABC Crazy Horse Spaceman*

Here you can read one of the many articles that went viral on the internet. To find other version, google: *Jeremy turns crazy* and/or *He's plane crazy: Crazy Horse Invincible*

I was checking my email on the morning of the 7th and noticed a message from my mate, Dan, back in Canberra. The subject line read: Crazy Horse is famous. Dan had been made aware of the ABC article and passed it on to me. I was blown away. Picture Michael J. Fox at the beginning of the first *Back to the Future* movie, when he strums his electric guitar that's plugged into a super charged amplifier, and he gets thrown back off his feet about ten metres. That's how blown away I was.

I rang Crazy Horse and said, "Hey mate, are you aware of this?"

Crazy told me, a few weeks earlier, he was at home snoozing after a night shift at the bakery, when he received a phone call from a woman regarding a flight he'd booked online with Jet2.com. The woman was with the bookings department and wanted some answers regarding Crazy's name. She was aggressive and pushy, demanding to know what his real name was. Having been woken up and then being rudely interrogated, Crazy Horse was not in the most magnanimous of moods. He snapped back, declaring that it is his real name. The woman became irate and said, if he didn't give his real name, the ticket would be cancelled.

What the fuck was her problem? Obviously, the airline is worried about fraud but they had his money; what did they care if the name was real? If it's not real, then he misses out on catching the flight, doesn't he? It's no skin off their nose; the ticket had been paid for. And anyway, what kind of person, just for a prank, wastes money on a flight they have no intention of catching?

Crazy Horse retaliated, "Listen, it *is* my real name. It's the name on my passport." And with that, he was asked to go to the airport to prove it.

He also received a phone call from a guy, called Adrian, who was part of Jet2's PR department. He wanted to do a write-up about Crazy Horse and his name for the in-flight magazine. Crazy Horse told him the story behind the name change and of other benders he and I had been on, and Adrian found it all hilarious. As a result, Adrian offered us both free flights. When Crazy Horse went to the airport to prove his ID, they took photos of him in front of a plane with his passport and toothbrush, for the in-flight magazine. Crazy Horse was hoping that they'd let him on board and give him a free ride somewhere, but no.

It turned out, Adrian was from the Middlesbrough area, and he and Crazy Horse both support the Boro football team. That's where the football reference comes from. I was flying to Prague from London with easyjet, and as the article reports, I had no trouble securing my seat.

The news article went viral. It appeared in newspapers and magazines and on web pages all around the world. We had friends from all over, telling us in which obscure publication they had seen the article. At the time, if you were to put 'Crazy Horse and Spaceman' into a search engine, hundreds of results would come up of pages and pages of discussion forums with people posting comments about our names and the article. You can still find a few if you google: *FARK Crazy Horse Invincible*

I flew into Belfast early on the morning of Friday 10th. The plan was to stay with Crazy Horse over the weekend and catch up with as many friends and acquaintances as possible. Crazy Horse wasn't around because he'd gone on a little adventure. About a week earlier, on the spur of the moment, he got up out of bed and decided to go to the airport to catch a flight to Barcelona to visit Michael. He phoned me from the airport, completely drunk, telling me what he was up to. It was very funny and outrageous, I thought. Nadine, who you might remember was part of our crew in Mexico for New Year's, now lived next door to Crazy Horse. She let me in, and I stayed there until Crazy Horse arrived back in Belfast that evening.

The weekend consisted of mainly drinking at the house, whilst friends like David and Megan dropped by. I had a return flight early Monday morning ... I mean, really, why did I even bother? I had no chance. I remember sitting upright in the foetal position, on the lounge, half-asleep, and Nadine telling me I had a plane to catch. I grumbled back that I didn't want to get up. And sure enough, I didn't catch my flight. What was I saying earlier about people who waste money on flights?

Well, not to worry, because by staying on, I got to dress up and wear a suit whilst Crazy Horse wore his Miller jumpsuit. Naturally, whilst in Belfast, I made a few appearances at The Royal. When Cooper, the owner, realised I was going to be in town for the Christmas party, he said Crazy and I must attend. It was amazing. The pub put on a Christmas lunch, the full works, for their senior customers as a thank you. It was invitation only, and Crazy Horse and I were special guests. Cooper made up a special table for us, and it was A1 service. The turkey was delicious and covered in gravy—heavenly—and the drinks just kept flowing. As I said before, Crazy and I dressed up. Crazy lent me a suit, which I wore with trainers. It was such a magic occasion, and everyone was so well looked after. Thanks for that, Cooper; it was awesome. The party continued into the night with the younger set. Crazy Horse had a lie down for an hour or so on one of the lounges, whilst everyone turned into the paparazzi, taking snapshots of him passed out in his jumpsuit and wearing a Santa's hat.

I didn't bother going back to London before flying to Prague. I'd managed to get a seat on the same flight as Crazy Horse's Jet2 flight. So, my easyjet flight from London to Prague was another flight I failed to catch. We were due to fly out on the 20th, and the night before, we had a big session. We had to be up at something like 6am in time to catch our flight. We still hadn't gone to bed by 4am. It was suggested we not bother going to bed at all, but we did. I didn't hold out much hope of us waking up, but BANG, we just woke up. I checked the time; it was 5am. We thought we may as well get one more hour of sleep, and we woke up again ... at 10. Shit. Another missed flight.

Crazy Horse called Jet2, requesting we be able to use our free flights. We were lucky to have that up our sleeve. We had a new booking on the same flight, two days later, on the 22nd. Crazy was pretty confident we'd catch the flight this time, but I didn't want to take any chances and declared I was going to spend the night at the airport, no matter what Crazy decided to do. He decided to spend the night at the airport, too. I had some heartfelt farewells with David, Megan, and Nadine before I left. I gave them all a big hug good-bye before I went to the airport. I didn't see myself being in Belfast again anytime soon.

Well, we'd made it. Out of the five flights I was meant to be on in the last two weeks, I'd managed to catch just two of them. We rocked up to our hostel, The Clown & Bard, in the afternoon ... two days late. It wasn't a problem though; the staff at the hostel were remarkably friendly. Crazy Horse had stayed at the Clown & Bard before, in 2002. Crazy Horse raved about the place and, I must say, it truly was a most excellent hostel—a bit dingy, but with character. The staff were wonderful and extremely helpful. The place was booked out, so there were loads of interesting people to meet in the downstairs bar. Although the building needed renovations in places, it was fun we were looking for, and we'd come to the right place.

The first night was wild. We partied in the hostel bar with our fellow guests for a couple of hours and made friends easily with our names and with Crazy Horse offering snuff to everyone. Afterwards, Crazy Horse and I went out on the town. We went to a restaurant, and in our state, we kept unintentionally testing the staff's patience. We kept asking for more things and knocking things over. I had a really dodgy chair and ended up snapping the leg off. I didn't dare tell the staff and just propped the chair upright as we made our escape. I made it back to bed at the hostel at about 5am and stayed there for the next 24 hours. I'd taken a few pills, plus on top of all the booze the day before, I was one sick puppy. My shakes were full on. Crazy said he'd never seen me so bad. I didn't have the stomach to leave the room until the next day, which, by that time, was Christmas Eve.

I was still a bit fragile and decided not to drink for a while. We went out for dinner with a group from the hostel. It was really nice to be out and about during Christmas time and to be able to enjoy it without the commercialism of it being rammed down your throat. Sure, there were decorations around the place, but we didn't have any exposure to the media. That meant no annoying Christmas songs on the radio, no annoying ads on TV, no Christmas rush at the shops, and no Christmas carols played repeatedly over and over again. Christmas day, I was up early and went for a walk. "Where's the snow?" It was a cold, sunny day, and not a cloud in the sky. There'd be no white Christmas this year, kiddies.

Seeing as I was sober and had been cooped up in my hostel room for the most part of the last three days, I wanted to move on. There had been a lot of talk amongst the guests that Český Krumlov was a beautiful place to visit. I heard from Crazy Horse a gang of them had gone down there for Christmas. I was keen to go and see somewhere different. We'd be back in Prague for seven days or more again in January, anyway. Crazy Horse was happy to stay and continue the party in Prague. So, Boxing Day morning, I went alone to Český Krumlov.

26th December

Český Krumlov is a small town in the south of the Czech Republic of about 14,000 people, with a large castle and a fairy tale styled old-town, which is a UNESCO World Heritage Site. Do yourself a favour and check out Český Krumlov on YouTube; it's stunning.

On the way there, the bus I was on broke down. We waited about an hour for a replacement bus to come and pick us up. We got going again, but I had no idea when I had to get off. I'd managed to tee up with the driver to tell me when I had to get off, but with the new bus, we had a new driver. Now that we were out of Prague, no one spoke English. At each stop, I asked people getting off "Český Krumlov?" They just looked at me blankly. It was getting late, around 9pm, and I had told the hostel in Český Krumlov I'd be there at 8pm. The bus started to empty, and I was really getting worried I'd missed my stop. At the next stop, I went to the driver and showed him the flyer to the hostel with its address. I didn't understand a word he was saying, but it didn't sound good. He called out to a young lad, who had just hopped off the bus, and then motioned for me to go with him. "OK, I guess this is where I get off."

I hopped off and placed my total trust in the driver that he'd organised something with this lad to get me to where I had to go. The bus drove off, and I looked around. I was in the middle of nowhere. It was exceptionally dark and quiet, with only a handful of houses around. I tried to communicate to the young lad; he would have been about 20, I reckon. I found out he didn't speak English—what a pity; that really would have helped matters. I tried another avenue. Nope, he didn't speak German, either. He made a phone call and motioned for me to wait. So, there we were, in the middle of the night, standing by the side of the road, the surrounds were so peaceful and quiet, my breath was the only noise I could hear; I could see my breath in the cold night air; we were total strangers, and all we could do was stand there in silence and politely smile at each other.

A car showed up a few minutes later, and it was the lad's mother. He spoke to her, and her reaction seemed positive. The car was full, including a young child in the back. They started making room in the back and moving things to the boot. I thought this is where I'd be sitting, but no, the young lad got in the back, and I was in the front. In a breakthrough for the success of this journey, it turned out the mother could speak German, so we were able to converse and get to Český Krumlov without any trouble. It was only a short fifteen-minute drive, but I was so grateful for their generosity. *Děkuji*, very much.

I found Hostel 99 easily enough. It's located just within the medieval walls of the old-town and is part hostel, part restaurant and pub. First thing was to check-in, and I found the manager in the pub. His name was Sam, about 30 years old, and from Sydney. When I'd made the booking that morning, Sam asked for my name. When I told him, he didn't question it, and he carried on routinely with the booking. When I checked in, he asked for my passport, and once again, he showed no reaction. I thought that was great; it was a nice change not having to explain my name. He quickly showed me around, and we went back to the pub.

The pub was about the size of a large lounge room and decorated in medieval style, yet at the same time, it was bright and cosy, and warm, which I was happy about after a cold bus ride. The place was quite full, with both locals and travellers. I was feeling a lot healthier, at this stage, from my time off the booze. I was ready again to have a few drinks. I bought a pint, found a spare seat, sat down … "and relax." It had been a long day.

The time came for me to go to the toilet. The toilet was past the entrance, through the restaurant, and up the stairs. There was a group of about eight people sitting in the restaurant, being terribly rambunctious, playing drinking games. I walked past and was about to climb the stairs when a girl at the table called out with great excitement, "Spaceman!" I turned to see who it was. I couldn't imagine who might know me in this small corner of the world. Everyone at the table was now looking at me, and a few others were cheering my name as well. I didn't recognise any of them. I was in good spirits, though, and showed great excitement to see them and, at the same time, asked them,

"How do you know me?"

"We drank with you at the Clown & Bard. Where's Crazy Horse? C'mon, sit down; we're playing a drinking game."

I joined the drinking game. I didn't remember having drunk with any of them, but whilst I'd been stuck in bed, Crazy Horse periodically came up from the bar to check on me, and he told me about the various people he'd met. As the drinking game went on, I started to recognise people from Crazy Horse's descriptions. They were all super jovial and friendly, and it was a fun time.

I may have been sober when I arrived at Hostel 99, but I was quickly addressing that issue. The drinks were going down well, and I was back in the groove. I went to the bar and obviously looked like I was enjoying myself. Sam looked over at me with a big smile, happy to see that I had settled in nicely. Playing over the stereo was Powderfinger's, "Odyssey Number Five." The festivities kicked on past closing time, and we migrated to the hostel kitchen until the wee hours of the morning. Welcome to Český Krumlov.

The next morning (27th), I was at reception speaking with Sam. He was surfing the net and browsing the news headlines.

"Over 200,000 people dead now, they reckon."

"What's that, in Iraq?" I asked.

"No, in the tsunami yesterday. You don't know about this?"

"No," I shrugged, as if to say, "I had nothing to do with it."

"Where have you been, man? It's big news."

Well, I had been recuperating in bed and then busy voyaging to Český Krumlov, so I knew nothing about it. But, up until about two months earlier, my plans were to be in Sri Lanka at this time. After Indonesia, Sri Lanka was the hardest country hit, with over 35,000 dead and 21,000 injured, prompting a state of emergency to be declared.

It's a pretty safe bet to say, had I gone to Sri Lanka, I would have spent some time enjoying the beautiful beaches. I remember reading in guide books, leading up to New Year, how paradisiacal the beaches were there. Who's to know in what way I would have been affected had I been there? It was usually only two, maybe three, at most, of the greater Fellowship of the Ring group that ever arrived before Boxing Day, so most of us would not have been at risk, just our party disrupted, which we would have willingly tolerated under the circumstances. The fact we weren't caught up in it was very fortunate. It felt like we'd dodged a bullet.

The next two days and nights were relaxing. I spent my days wandering around the town with others from the hostel. I used this time to write to Brian Oliver and other friends using beer coasters instead of postcards. In the evenings, people gathered at the hostel pub, and after a few drinks to get us started, we'd venture to another hostel bar that had live music. On the morning of the 29th, it was goodbye Český Krumlov. I had plans to arrive in Bratislava on the 30th, so leaving now gave me plenty of opportunity to take my time. I caught the short bus ride north to

České Budějovice, often referred to in English as Budweis, the home of the original, tasty, Budweiser Beer, not to be mistaken for the cheap American imitation. Here, I had to change buses to take me east to Brno and then catch a train south to Bratislava.

I remember I arrived quite late at night to Brno, around 10 or something. I had a bit of a walk around the city before finding a Herna bar near the train station and made myself comfortable for the night. A Herna bar is a gaming bar full of slot machines that's open 24 hours, usually frequented by your seedy types. It served its purpose, though. It was a place I could hang out and drink until my train the next morning.

To get to Bratislava from Brno, I had to change trains on the way. Once on the train, I fell asleep having been up all night drinking. I was woken later by the train conductor wanting to see my ticket. I showed him, and he wanted more money. I argued the point; I was sure I'd bought the correct ticket, and why was he speaking to me in German? I'll tell you why. Because I'd missed my stop, and I was now in Austria. It was no great problem, other than having to pay extra money. I took the train all the way to Vienna and then caught a direct train to Bratislava from there. Vienna and Bratislava are only 60km apart—the closest two capital cities in the world.

It was a beautiful, sunny morning when I arrived in Bratislava. I felt excited and rejuvenated, having had some sleep on the train. This marked the beginning of the main event. More friends would be arriving today and then the games would really begin. I wandered the streets, heading loosely in the direction of our hostel, stopping off at bars along the way. I didn't really know which way to go, so I kept asking people for directions. Rather than try to pronounce the address of the hostel, I swallowed my pride and asked for directions to the US Embassy. Our hostel was in the same square as the embassy, so if I could find the embassy, I'd find the hostel. I decided finding the hostel easily was more important than people thinking I was an American tourist. Here, make up your own mind: 'American Embassy' or '*Hviezdoslavovo námestie.*'

I found the square and found our hostel, not to be mistaken for the four-star Radisson SAS Carlton Hotel, also at Hviezdoslavovo námestie. There wasn't much in the way of backpacker accommodation in Bratislava at the time. That's not the case now, of course, as more people are aware of the cheaper, quieter alternative Bratislava offers over Prague. Our hostel was called something like, George's Hostel, a privately-run hostel converted from a residential flat, run by George, a middle-aged Slovakian man. There were signs in the stairwell of residents upset with the constant presence of lost tourists ringing the wrong buzzer or knocking on the wrong door. I didn't make such a mistake and met your man, George, who confirmed everything was sorted for our stay over the next few nights. He said the rooms weren't ready yet and suggested I pop back in an hour or two. When I popped back, I found Crazy Horse there. Let the games begin.

We went exploring around the area and left a message at the hostel for the others arriving that we'd be in the large bar across the square. Drinking away to our hearts' content, we were tapped on the shoulder, and we turned around to see our good friends, Brian and Kris. Hooray. Also with them was their mate, Carl. Carl was from DC, as well, and in the marines. I hadn't met him before, but I liked him immediately. He had a great sense of humour and was of the same temperament as Crazy Horse and I when it came to drinking.

We met up with Michael, later; he came with his own entourage from Barcelona. He was with his girlfriend,

Maria José, and a few of her family and friends. They were staying in a different place than the rest of us. And that was us, all present and accounted for. Atira and Ursula had booked trips to Vietnam before we had decided on coming to Eastern Europe. So, unfortunately, we wouldn't be honoured by their presence this year.

New Year was fantastic. There were lots of stages with live music set up in the streets and lots of stalls selling hot wine. All the dazzling architecture was lit up with different coloured lights, and there was a stunning fireworks display. We gathered in the square at Hviezdoslavovo námestie; it was pretty cold, down to the bones cold, and we took full advantage of the hot wine for sale. We partied on through the night at different bars and hung out with other tourists we met. I remember we were at a bar on a large river boat at one stage, too. I don't know if that was New Year's or on January 1st, but anyway, we could now say we'd been drinking on the river Danube. Good fun was had by all, and it was 5am before we made it to bed.

For me, the night did involve some memory loss, so I was surprised to wake up and find Crazy Horse and me in the same single bed together. Haha, up to our old tricks again. Carl told us, the Polish guys in our dorm were all talking about us, partly puzzled, but mostly displeased with our sleeping arrangement. Ah, that was funny. That's the kind of response we were trying to provoke. Brian and Kris had their own room up in the roof. I remember wishing them a happy New Year as they poked their heads out through the manhole. The rest of our time was wandering the city and partying in the evening. I don't remember a great deal of it, to be honest. I remember Bratislava was quite pretty, architecturally, and the Danube River added to the city's charm. I don't think I ate that much, but I remember the others complaining how tasteless the food was.

2005

Thank you, Bratislava; you were great. Meanwhile, we hit the road again, and the plan was to go to Budapest via Prague. I know Prague is in the complete opposite direction to Budapest from Bratislava, but certain people in our group were only hanging around for another few days, so Prague was the preferred option.

These two days or so were marred by me throwing up a lot and being constantly freezing cold due to having a fever. I was drinking very little and stayed in bed whenever possible. Normally, I might have battled on through the illness and kept drinking heavily, but I wanted to get well again, so I was in good shape when the second wave of revellers arrived. On the 7th, a group of my London friends were coming to Prague to party for a few days as a farewell of sorts in celebration of my departure back to Australia. Not that we wouldn't have a farewell bash in London, as well, but this was going to be an extra delight, and I wanted to be healthy–ish upon their arrival.

Speaking of bed, I did manage some sport during this time. One night, I went to a nice family restaurant and enjoyed a quiet drink at the bar. I then relocated to the club downstairs where there were some women dancing to the backdrop of a great big fish tank. I got chatting to one of the women that worked there. She showed me around; there were more rooms downstairs, all themed, that were highly decorative.

She was quite friendly and didn't seem to mind when I touched her body affectionately. I was very mindful of touching her though, as there were cameras everywhere. We spent about two hours together, getting to know each other, until she had to get back to work. There was a connection between us, but I could tell that she thought of me as just another typical man who was only after one thing. I hung around a bit longer at the bar, watching the dancing and the aquatic movement in the fish tank, before calling it a night at about 5am.

That's one way to look at it.

The above description doesn't tell the whole story. Another way to look at it would be, when I said, 'family restaurant', I meant brothel; and when I said, 'there were some women dancing', I meant strippers, pole dancing; and when I said, 'one of the women that worked there', I meant prostitute; and when I said, 'we spent about two hours together, getting to know each other', I meant having sex. But that's still only half the story. The sex was free. That's right, free. This was no ordinary brothel. This was *Big Sister*.

The curious part about it was that, when you first walk into the club, you actually are in a family restaurant. There was a bar, dining tables and chairs, and booths for dining, all lavishly furbished in black and red. The only hint of it being a brothel was numerous TV monitors behind the bar, screening the pole-dancing shenanigans going on downstairs. Downstairs, in the brothel proper, was a smaller bar where you could sit on a stool or you could relax in one of the many booths around the room. At the booths, you could pull out a computer screen from under the table, access all the particulars of the women available and then choose one.

There were a few women pole dancing to keep the men entertained as they waited for an available room. As well as that, at one end of the room the whole wall was taken up with a fish tank. When I say fish tank, I mean more of a swimming pool and, instead of fish, there were naked women swimming around.

So, once a woman was chosen, she led the man to one of

a number of themed rooms available. Themes ranged from the Rocky Mountains to the Arctic, through to heaven and hell. Then, free of charge, the man could enjoy the company of a beautiful, young lady and share a private moment together. And what's the catch? Why was it free? Well, when I said, '*The man can enjoy the company of a beautiful, young lady and share a private moment together*', what I meant was, that the man could enjoy the company of a beautiful, young lady whilst being streamed *live* on the internet.

The name Big Sister is a reference to the cameras in every room, similar to that of *Big Brother*. The brothel made its money from DVD sales and from subscribers paying to watch the action on the internet, thus allowing the brothel to offer the women's services for free. I speak in the past tense because the brothel has since closed.

Because of the filming, before I could even go downstairs, I had to show ID and sign a contract giving the screening and distribution rights of the recorded footage to Big Sister. The manager gave me the lowdown on how the process worked and, just as he was about to walk me downstairs, he stopped, turned, and said, "Oh, yes, I must apologise. There is a restriction on the amount of time that you can spend with the women."

I thought, "Here we go. What's it going to be, another ten minute power shag?"

"You can only have two hours," he declared.

I tried to keep a straight face. I was pretty sure I'd be able to cope with two hours. There's plenty of ten minutes in two hours.

Down in the club, I sat at one of the booths and, as I said, there were women pole dancing and naked women swimming in the pool. Big Sister had not long started offering the free service, but there were still about 20 or so guys in the club. I sipped on a drink as I browsed the menu. All the ladies were young, gorgeous, fit women from either the Czech Republic or Slovakia.

I still wasn't feeling 100% but, not surprisingly, I found the strength to soldier on. I chose a blonde from the menu but, unfortunately, she was busy. I chose another and she was unavailable too. So, I ended up choosing a woman that was sitting at the bar and she came and sat with me. Denny was blonde, Czech and about 25; she didn't speak English but she did speak German which was handy. It would have been awkward sitting there together in silence. Seeing as we were about to star in a porn film, I thought it only fitting that we speak in German anyway.

We sat there for a while waiting for a room to be available. I was somewhat curious as to how I'd perform knowing that potentially thousands of people could be watching. I really would have preferred to have been a lot drunker than I was but I didn't feel up to drinking much. Denny was friendly enough and we shared a few jokes. After about half an hour, a woman handed Denny some keys. Right. This was it: lights, camera, action. We arrived at our room and Denny opened the door.

"What... the... fuck?"

Denny was just as surprised as I was. She'd never been in the room before either. Fuck, I wasn't expecting this. We were in the Arctic.

The walls were painted to look like a snowscape, with icebergs and water. The lights in the room were very bright and the bed was on a raised landing about three steps higher than ground level, just like being on stage in the theatre. The bed was amazing; it was a roofless igloo. But standing next to the igloo, overlooking the bed, was the real mind fuck. Complete with a camera sticking out of its belly was a huge, fuck-off, polar bear mannequin over two metres tall. There was also a bathroom with a shower and spa... and camera.

I was conscious of the cameras to begin with—you could hear them when they were panning from left to right—but it wasn't long before I paid them no attention. Denny wasn't the most obliging woman I've met when it came to positions, I must say. So anyway, one thing led to another and I had my 23½ minutes of fame. We then fooled around in the spa after that until the two hours was up. Somehow, I don't think my performance made the cut on to the DVD.

Afterwards, I sat in the club watching the strippers and swimmers. Time passed and I was ready to go again but, with only an hour remaining till closing time, there wasn't going to be any rooms available in time. Not to worry. I'd already come away with a story to tell the grandkids.

I heard that once word had spread and the popularity of the club really took off, the club made a few changes. The guys had to wear dressing gowns when in the club and they only got one-hour sessions with the ladies. But like I said, the place is no more, so you can abandon any ideas of searching for the Spaceman and Denny DVD. Haha. However, if you google *Big Sister brothel*, there is a Wikipedia page which you can read, if you're interested.

The night of the 4th, we were Hungary bound. The group had slimmed down to just Carl, Brian, Crazy Horse, and me, whilst Michael was going to meet us in Budapest. Kris had returned home, as did the Barcelona brigade. We caught the overnight train to save on a night's accommodation and froze our bollocks off. Getting very little sleep didn't help my health issues any, and I stopped drinking booze altogether.

An interesting fact I learnt about Budapest was that the city is made up of two parts, divided by the river Danube: Buda on the west bank and Pest on the east bank. We stayed in a hostel in Pest, the livelier of the two sides, supposedly. I can't remember the name of the hostel, but one of the female receptionists was a bit of a dragon. It was a comfortable place, with big rooms and an upstairs bar. The lift was a bit dodgy, though. It was rather small, and we were never sure if it was going to be able to carry our weight.

One thing I'd been looking forward to the whole trip was going to the thermal baths in Budapest. The city sits on a skinny layer of earth above thermal springs, generating the source for its many baths, and in the 1930's, was awarded the title of 'City of Spas'.

Crazy Horse had a lie-in, whilst the remaining four of us went to the Gellért Baths, located in a fancy hotel. The baths there are said to be one of the most beautiful bath complexes in Budapest, attracting both locals and tourists. I certainly felt like I was in an ancient Roman setting. There were many baths in different rooms, and each room was elaborately decorated with mosaics, sculptures, and stained-glass windows with large pillar-type columns. The main bath was in a spacious, large hall with columns either side, and the roof was a few storeys above and made of glass. Awesome. We'd gone back in time.

Only Brian came prepared, the rest of us had to hire swimwear. Michael quickly grabbed the black pair on offer, whilst Carl and I were left with immensely 'attractive', fluoro, cyan coloured ... Speedos. This was one moment I wasn't thinking, "If my friends could see me now." Unfortunately, my body isn't as chiselled as those of the statues that were displayed around the baths, and I felt very self-conscious walking around in swim briefs. Fortunately, though, once in the water, my bottom half was submerged out of view. I felt more comfortable naked at Big Sister than wearing Speedos.

In the main hall, the large bath, like an Olympic pool, wasn't being used, but there was a smaller, semi-circle shaped bath behind it that was in use. This bath was open to both genders and was a comfortable 26°C. It had streams of water flowing into the pool and marble seats around the sides, so you could sit, relax, and enjoy the soothing qualities of the water.

We then moved to another bath in another room that was men only. Any awkwardness I may have felt about what I was wearing quickly disappeared as I saw what seemed to be the local fashion statement. A large percentage of the men were wearing short, beige coloured aprons that started at the waist and extended to the knees at the front, whilst at the back, the arse hung out for all to see. I think I would have preferred to wear the apron.

This bath was a purifying 38°C. It was so relaxing; I almost fell asleep. This room was just as ornate as the rest of the complex, whilst just outside the room was a large water hole at an invigorating 18°C and a door to a sauna, too. We spent some time in the 38ºC bath and then jumped into the 18ºC and went into shock as we froze our balls off. We only ever stayed in there for a few seconds. It was good fun, though; we did that a few times. The complex also offered some medicinal services, and Carl had a Thai massage whilst we were there. It was a really good experience. It's not something I get to do every day; I'm really glad to have done it.

Something we lads liked to do was dare each other to do things. Anything from take a pinch of snuff, to dance on the bar, to talk with a stranger. If you were dared, you had to do it, but you couldn't dare someone to do something you wouldn't do, yourself. We weren't disgusting pigs about it; we didn't do anything revolting involving bodily fluids or anything. Just simple funny things that were out of our normal comfort zones.

Whilst in the hostel bar one evening, we spied a Japanese girl sitting on her own. Carl is fluent in Japanese, so we dared him to go and talk to her. He did and she came and drank with us. The following night, we bumped into her on our way out of the hostel and told her we were going to Prague, and if she was quick and got her bags straight away, she could come with us. She didn't hesitate, and subsequently, she became part of our travelling circus for the next week. She and Carl hit it off and started a holiday romance. Her name was Mai; we called her Mai Thai. She was in her early 20's and had a beautiful, classic, Japanese face. She could be a little reserved sometimes and, at other times, the life of the party. Man, could she drink—well, sort of. She'd drink us under the table for the first four rounds, and then after that, she'd be unable to walk. I lost count of the number of times we had to carry her or the number of times she just sat at the table with her head rested on the table in her arms, too ill to move. All the same, she was good fun and enjoyed taking part in our shenanigans with us.

One nightclub we went to, in Budapest, Carl dared Crazy Horse to dance with a large blonde woman on the dance floor. We were all sitting at a table, whilst the woman was already on the dance floor with a female friend. The only other people on the dance floor were three guys. Neither the two women or three guys were dancing. They were just standing near the wall, using the counter to rest their drinks on.

Carl said to Crazy Horse, "I dare you to go over there and dance seductively in front of that big blonde woman." Crazy Horse looked over in the direction of the dance floor, and a look of acceptance came over his face as he psyched himself up for the challenge. He looked at Carl and said, "You better come and help me if anything kicks off." He then looked at me and said, "You too," as he stood up and walked towards the dance floor. I didn't know what he was on about. Why would anything kick off? Carl and I looked at each other puzzled and shrugged our shoulders. We turned back to see him march right up to the dance floor and give it his all. He danced like a motherfucker, doing his best John Travolta impersonation, inviting his target to join him.

Carl and I were in hysterics; it was so funny. Hysterics is actually an understatement. We were laughing so, so hard, partly because Crazy's dance style was off the wall, but mainly because he must have misheard his directive. Crazy Horse was swinging and moving to the beat, in front of one of the guys. Even as I write this, I still find it hilarious. The guy just looked confused; he didn't know what to make of Crazy Horse. He didn't become aggressive, so there was no call for Carl or me to intervene. To be honest, I don't think we could have. It was just so damn funny. Michael, Brian, and Mai were deep in conversation and missed the whole thing.

The morning of the 7th, we were on the move again, back to Prague. We'd arrive in Prague mid-afternoon in time to meet the London crew, who were arriving in the evening. Sadly, we farewelled Michael, who got off the train in Bratislava to catch his connecting flight home to Barcelona.

We went back to the Clown & Bard, which was a lot quieter now with Christmas and New Year over. It was also a lot cheaper. The manager did us a deal giving the five of us our own room together. Whilst the others crashed and caught up on some sleep, I went out into the night to meet the London larrikins. I went to Wenceslas Square and thought I'd have a drink whilst I waited for my friends. A great feature of the city centre was the food stands that also sold beer in plastic cups. I was feeling a lot better and had started drinking again, just easing myself into it. I stood there trying to keep warm, when out of the darkness came Tessa and Tom. Fifteen minutes later, Chris arrived, and not long after that, Stuart was with us, too. Woohoo. Welcome to round two.

We had a good night drinking at different bars in and around Wenceslas Square and watching the street hookers. The bars were a bit touristy and pricey, but I was enjoying the company and feeling fit enough to join in on the drinking. There are some great photos of us playing around in the bar, including a few pics with some strangers, who I've got no memory of meeting.

The next day, the whole lot of us met in the Old Town Square. We split into two groups: those that wanted to do some sightseeing and those who were just happy to relax and enjoy a few samples of that good, tasty, Czech beer. Tom, Brian, Tess, and I were the sightseeing group, and we headed off on a walking tour. I was pretty keen to see some of the city, as I hadn't managed it in any of the earlier visits. I had seen a lot of the place back in '97 when I was there on Eurobus, but that was a while ago. The best part was, we had our own tour guide. Brian had been on a walking tour a week earlier when we were there, so he took us around the Old Town, relaying what he'd learnt from his tour. It was brilliant. What he couldn't remember, he made up. It was the usual freezing cold day, but Tom, the character that he is, wore a Hawaiian shirt, as you do.

Today was also absinthe day. As a tribute to the movie *Eurotrip* and for no other reason than it was fun, Carl initiated absinthe day, where we had to have a drink of absinthe at every bar we went to, as well as our regular drink of choice.

Absinthe is a highly alcoholic spirit of aniseed flavour. It's sometimes colourless, but usually, it's green and is commonly known as The Green Fairy. It has a reputation of having hallucinogenic qualities and, in large quantities, making the drinker go crazy. Because of this, it's banned in many countries. I think it's more folklore than fact, but still, it was a fun novelty for the day.

There are a few different methods in which to drink it.

The most common and exciting is with fire: you put a sugar cube pre-soaked in alcohol on a spoon over the shot of absinthe and set it alight. You then drop the burning sugar cube into the glass and let it burn itself out. This is said to make for a stronger drink; some say it releases herbal aromas or, depending on how you do it, it's said to remove a lot of the alcohol.

There's a funny scene in *Eurotrip*, where the young American tourists are drinking absinthe, hoping to experience its supposed hallucinogenic qualities:

Jamie: I gotta say, I'm not feeling anything.
Cooper: Me neither.
Scott: Sober as a judge. How about you?
Green Fairy: I'm not feelin' a goddamn thing. This Absinthe is BULLSHIT!

Us sightseers certainly kept to the mission. Every so often on our tour, we stopped at a bar to have a drink and an absinthe. No green fairies for us, unfortunately. The next evening, we all had a great time out drinking together as a group. There's a great photo of Tom standing next to a car that had a sign on top of it that read, 'Drink S.O.S'. It must have been some sort of medical car. There were two guys sitting in the front, looking utterly bored. I'm guessing we weren't the first tourists to take a photo.

Monday the 10th, we farewelled Brian and Carl, who returned home. Thanks lads, it was a pleasure. Despite not feeling so well some of the time, it had really been another good New Year's with the Fellowship of the Ring. It was felt, this time around would be our last New Year together, and with me returning to Australia, I had no idea if or when I'd see these guys again. I tried not to think about it. It's a small world, though. I was sure we'd meet up again in Hollywood, when we all became movie/rock stars. Stuart was gone too, but I'd see him in London. Mai left also, back home to Japan. The next day, the London gang departed for home. Tessa flew back, having been up all night without any sleep, and that left just Crazy Horse and me.

Crazy Horse and I went out for something to eat. We found a restaurant near the hostel; we just wanted something light, and we both ordered a cabbage dish. It was basically a small plate with cabbage and onion. Naturally, we had a beer each with our meal. With me flying back to London the next day, this was our last supper. We sat talking about the good times we'd had and what we thought the future held. Mainly, we talked about how I was going to deal with returning to Australia after nearly three years away. It was a real head-spin for me, contemplating life back in Australia. I just couldn't imagine what it would be like, other than weird.

As we spoke, we continued to drink. Rather than pay for each round as we went along, the waitress drew a line on our beer mats for each beer we had, and we'd pay for them at the end. We were both in fine form, and it became a bit of fun seeing line after line drawn on our beer mat. We were wondering if it was going to get to the point where the waitress stopped serving us, citing that we'd had too much to drink. But she let us go, and we had 15 pints each. That's 7.5 litres, plus we'd had a few before we got there. The night was still young, and we then went out on the town and drank some more.

It was late in the morning, light outside, and well after check-out time by the time we went back to the hostel. I was flying home that evening, but Crazy Horse was staying. The hostel wasn't busy anyway, so it didn't matter that I hadn't checked-out yet. We walked in, and we didn't have to say a word. The receptionist took one look at us and knew exactly what we wanted. She handed us the keys to our room, and we both crashed out for some much-needed sleep.

In the evening, we sat in the hostel bar with some of the other guests. I'd managed my ATM withdrawals perfectly.

My remaining Czech kroners would be just enough to get me to the airport. After a few drinks, it was time to go. I gave Crazy Horse a hug, and after 4½ weeks on tour together, not to mention all the adventures over the last few years, it was "Adios amigo."

Crazy Horse hadn't booked a return flight home. I had visions of him staying in Prague for weeks, or months, like he did in Mexico. A few days earlier, an ATM had swallowed his card, so money, or access to it, rather, was an issue for him. He transferred his money into the account of one of the other guests at the hostel, and he returned to Belfast about a week later.

I arrived back at Tunis Rd, Shepherd's Bush, to find Chris waiting at home with a bottle of *Becherovka* he'd bought in Prague. He invited me to sit down for a drink. It was a great welcome home.

It was another five days before I would be leaving on a jet plane. I used this time to catch up with as many people as possible. I also had to organise things, like shipping a carton and a bass guitar home. It would have been sensible if I had used this time constructively to pack my backpack, but I left that until just hours before I left for the airport.

I caught up with Alé. It was really good to see her again, despite it being the last time in the foreseeable future. She'd been at home in Vilnius for Christmas and brought me back a bottle of Lithuanian beer and an awesome beer mug with an insignia of Vilnius Castle on it. We had dinner at the dodgy kebab shop, of all places, before we said our farewells, and Alé caught the bus to Acton. I added her to the long list of people I was going to miss when I left.

Saturday night was my farewell bash. Chris and I discovered a few days earlier, the Askew Arms, on Uxbridge Rd, was open until 1am on weekends, instead of 11pm, like most pubs. It was a no brainer; we'd have the farewell bash there.

It was pretty conveniently located for everyone, and as well as being open late, it had a DJ playing some funky beats. All the usual suspects were there, as well as some acquaintances celebrating a birthday, so we had quite a sizeable group. Liza, from the flat below Chris, was the stand out funster. She didn't often get out, and the excitement and drink went straight to her head. It was a good vibe, and we all had a smashing time. Other than a vodka and coke for Julia, I didn't buy a single drink the whole night. Afterwards, about half a dozen of us kicked on back at Chris's flat.

18th January 2005

Here is a group email I sent on the morning of my departure from London:

> What a ride, both emotionally and geographically.
>
> Back in early December, I went to Belfast for the weekend and, as usual, got drunk and missed my flight. So, I stayed in Belfast for a week and then went to Prague and celebrated Christmas there, and New Year in Bratislava with my good friends. Fuckin' excellent.
>
> As fun as it has been, it's been a series of goodbyes. I don't like goodbyes. I said goodbye to my mates in Belfast, mates at New Year, and I returned to London and said goodbye to close friends here I've known for over 7 years.
>
> Today is my last day. In a few hours, I'll be on a jet plane to Hong Kong. Who am I to complain? I'm going to fuckin' Hong Kong for five nights. Woohoo. As soon as I check into my hotel, I'm straight down to the races to lose my shirt over some horse.

I'll write to you all individually when life slows down a bit.

Can you believe it? I'm going to Hong Kong ... and, oh yeah ... Australia, for the first time in 3 years. I'm mentally a mess.

It's 9:30 in the morning, and I'm on my 2nd beer.

Time to go pack my bags, I think.

Cheers London.

Tessa and Julia kindly came and saw me off at the airport. It was great to have them there—two of my closest friends to keep me company. I felt down about leaving my friends, yet excited about my trip to Hong Kong. There was no mention in any of the travel brochures I'd seen of having to go through difficult, touching farewells upon departure. I want my money back. Thanks London, I won't forget you. See you next time.

For once, I didn't miss my flight. In Hong Kong, I caught a bus from the airport to Kowloon. Shit, Hong Kong looked big, with huge blocks of apartments everywhere in the middle of trees and mountains. Then in Kowloon, it was exactly like I'd seen on TV—traffic everywhere, billboards and signs everywhere, people everywhere, modern and old rundown buildings everywhere.

My time in Hong Kong was amazing. It's semi-different to the western world. It has the Chinese culture but with British influences, which makes it easy for an English speaker to get around. A lot of things were cheap, like food, clothes, and electronics, I spent a lot of time shopping at markets. Eating was always an adventure. There were lots of places cooking food and selling it to people on the street. I didn't always know what I was eating, but I didn't get sick, thankfully. I could have stayed another week in HK. There were many other things I would have loved to have done but didn't get the time. But shit, I still saw a lot and had a great time.

However, one of the highlights of my trip to Hong Kong was my trip to China. I thought I'd take a day trip to the border town of Shenzhen in China and take advantage of the cheap shopping there. My hostel in HK organised a Chinese visa for me, and the HK metro had a train to the border. Very stupidly, I went clueless. I arrived at the border with just a few $HK and no idea what the Chinese currency was, no idea what the exchange rate was compared to any other currency, and no idea that no one spoke English, unlike in HK.

After having passed through HK and then Chinese immigration no problem, on the way out of the station, I saw an ATM. Nice one. I went to the ATM and realised I had no idea how much to withdraw. I mean, fuck. I didn't know if 100 RMB was a lot of money. There was a travel office nearby, and I thought they should be able to tell me the exchange rate. After a lot of language barrier problems, I realised they were explaining there was an exchange place outside the station. I abandon the ATM idea for the time being, thinking I'll go to the exchange place, where there should be a board up with all the foreign exchange rates, and I'll then know how much to withdraw from an ATM.

I exited the station past security. There looked to be no entry back that way into the station, but hey, this is a developed country, I should have no trouble finding another ATM. I left the station and, fuck me, what a contrast in just 100 metres. 100 metres behind was HK, and China was a whole different world. Upon leaving the station, the first thing that hit me was the extreme number of people. Being a Westerner and with my bright red hair, I stood out a mile and attracted all the touts. I had fuckin' all sorts coming up to me. With the Lo Wu Commercial City (a large five storey mall with any consumer good you could want) right outside the station, there were touts everywhere trying to get people into their shop.

No, I didn't want a taxi. No, I didn't want to buy some golf clubs. No, I didn't want some new curtains. No, I didn't want accessories for my pet squid. OK, yes, I wouldn't mind some new shoes, but the heavy-handed sales tactics put me right off. Plus, first things first, I didn't have any local *dinero*. I couldn't find this Bureau de Change I'd heard so much about. I walked around the station and the mall. I was approached every 30 seconds and, with a smile, I politely declined whatever shit they had on offer, but I couldn't find an ATM anywhere.

I found an information desk in the mall and asked for a bank. I thought the woman didn't understand what I'd said, but she pointed me in the direction of another counter. I went there and figured it must have been an exchange place, even though there were no signs to suggest this. I asked if I could change some $HK, and after some conferring amongst the women behind the counter, one woman grabbed her handbag and pulled out from her own purse some Chinese RMB. Fuck knows what service that counter was really providing, but I'm pretty sure it wasn't for changing money.

So now, I had some local money, but I'd only handed over about £30 in $HK. I only hoped I'd been given about the same back in RMB. I had no idea how far that much money would go. First thing was to get some food and booze into me. Still with no clue as to where I might find an ATM and needing money for a ticket back to Hong Kong, the plan to go shopping was quickly shelved. Assuming I wasn't ripped off with the exchange, I concluded 100 RMB was equal to

£6.50, which later turned out to be close to the mark.

Without much money to play with and this whole fuckin' circus putting me off the whole day, I was tempted to have a bit of a look round, then fuck off back to Hong Kong. I thought I'd try my luck and try to get past security to go back to the original ATM I'd found in the station. Security posed no resistance, and with my guesstimation of the exchange rate, I withdrew 600 RMB. High roller.

Just around the corner were loads of small little newspaper stands that also sold drinks. I was straight in there and bought a few cans of beer. When I walked in, the penny dropped. These stands were the money exchange places I'd been first directed to by the travel office. I thought they were primarily selling drinks, but inside, I quickly noticed there was a lot of money exchanging hands. They even had machines they fed money into and the machine counted the money for them.

With some money in my pocket, I thought, after a few beers, I might be able to deal with the craziness of the mall and do some shopping. I went and sat down in the main square, outside the station and mall. I wasn't sure what the local laws were on drinking in public, so I chilled for a few minutes before opening a can. I was shaking like a motherfucker. Combined with my tremor disorder and having been on the lash for the previous six weeks, my hands weren't in any shape to perform heart surgery.

Being a westerner, the locals saw me as a walking ATM and within moments, I had a few beggars and touts surrounding me. I politely said, "No thanks," but they persisted and wouldn't leave me alone. Just when I thought I'd drawn enough attention to myself, this other guy joined the fray. I looked at him, confused. He was a westerner; he was well-dressed in a suit and had a cigarette in one hand and a beer in the other. What the fuck did he want?

He didn't look too friendly, so I was quite wary. I said "Awright," the English form of hello.

He replied, "How you doing?"

His accent suggested he was North American. Then he started telling the beggars and touts to fuck off in Chinese in no uncertain terms. He really tore strips off them. They were probably just as surprised as I was to hear Chinese coming from his mouth. They quickly left. He asked where I was from, and I asked him the same. The crazy fucker was Canadian.

Vance was from Vancouver; he'd been living in this part of the world for a year or two and was married to a Chinese woman. We shared a bit of small talk, when suddenly this young guy, from out of nowhere, ran up and sat beside me. He had a great big smile on his face and acted as if I was some kind of long lost friend. I'm no stranger to people knowing me and me not having a clue who they are, so I wondered if, perhaps, he did know me. But it soon became clear this geezer was trying to sell watches and DVD's. Vance told the guy to fuck off. The conversation turned ugly and turned to English. Vance lit up a cigarette, and the Chinese lad said, "No smoking." What the fuck? We were outdoors in the middle of a square. Although, it was China, I don't know anything about their laws.

Vance wasn't in any mood for this guy's shit and told the local that he'll do whatever he wants. After trading a few more insults, the Chinese lad told us not to move, and he got up and walked away whilst making a few calls on his mobile. Shit. Obviously, he was calling for some reinforcements. Vance motioned me to follow him, and cautiously, I followed him into a nearby shop, where we hid for a while.

Just like in Milwaukee, when I was hiding in a store from a guy keen to have sex with me and I ended up with a tattoo, the same was the case here. I felt obligated to buy something, so I was the proud owner of some new black lace lingerie. Like fuck. It was some sort of food shop. Not only did we not buy anything, but we drank our beers, and Vance lit up a cigarette. It was scary at how quickly I settled into the role of arrogant western tourist. "It's like the wild west here," Vance said proudly.

Shenzen, being a border town, is full of people that aren't from Shenzen. Vance told me all about the theft, gangs, and pickpockets to be aware of around the station. When I'd been at 'Information' in the mall, I wasn't met by flyers selling the great tourist attractions of Shenzen. There were no flyers telling me of hop on - hop off bus tours or guided walking tours. Instead, I found a flyer from Shenzhen Police that warned:

– Resist the temptation of unfamiliar women, who are often used as bait by criminals. Keep away from strangers and do not follow them into unfamiliar surroundings.

– Beware of pickpockets and shout loudly for help. In the event of an attack, the police will come to your assistance.

– Do not pick up items from the ground that do not belong to you. Criminals are known to extort members of the public after accusing them of stealing.

– In general, it is safe to visit Shenzhen during the day or night.

Yeah, well, I didn't feel safe at all. I had people from all directions wanting my money. I had a knight in shining armour that had pissed off a local street gang member, and I had no idea if this knight could be trusted, either. Either way, neither of us wanted any trouble. With my red hair, I thought we were bound to stand out, so I told Vance I'd meet him later at Henry J. Beans, the bar in the Shangra-La Hotel, which I'd heard was the best in all Shenzen. Ha, that's so typical of me. I arrived with no knowledge of the local currency, or where I could change money, nor the local transport system, or the level of English spoken. But I certainly knew of a good bar to go to. I found the Shangra-La, but the bar was closed—not open until 5pm.

Vance was waiting for his wife, who was arriving from a job interview in Hong Kong. He had offered to show me around town. I accepted with caution, but with the bar being closed, I went back to the station, thinking I wouldn't ever see Vance again. But Vance found my bright red crop of hair in the big sea of people.

Vance was now with his wife, Tammy, who was just beautiful. They both made me feel at ease, and Vance, no stranger to a drink, knew the best remedy for me was some food. We went to a restaurant, and Tammy looked after Vance and me. She ordered us vegies, dumplings, and beer. They both taught me how to use chopsticks and taught me some Chinese words. Vance, being a big drinker, knew the importance of eating. I was considerably sick over Christmas/ New Year because I drank so much without eating. I didn't want a repeat of that, so I did as I was told and ate half the plate.

We then headed off into the shopping jungle of Shenzen. My newfound friends took me shopping and how lucky was I to have them with me. Tammy and Vance made sure I didn't get ripped off. It was so handy having someone who could speak the language, and Vance explained to me the art of haggling. Thanks to my friends, I bought some shoes and some jeans for about five quid each. I was drunk and feeling really euphoric. Hours earlier, I had been so intimidated by the hustle and bustle that surrounded the train station. I was grateful I had Vance and Tammy to show me around, and they were happy to be able to mix with another westerner.

After some bargain shopping, we went to a Sushi restaurant for lunch. Tammy wasn't drinking, but if there was any doubt that Vance and I were drunk, then the *sake* put all doubts to rest. That stuff is lethal. Vance and I had been drinking all day and then *sake*. I think we both did well to function after that.

After a bit more sightseeing and shopping, we headed to Henry J Beans in Shangra-La. Naturally, we ordered double whiskies and a pint of beer each. The day's drinking had caught up with us, and Vance and Tammy went home. I thanked them so much. What a shit, depressing day I would have had without them. I stayed for a few more beers but was also fading. I made my way to the border and, after a lot of formalities, caught a train back to Kowloon.

Travel is way cool.

25th January–8th February 2005

I arrived in Sydney, 25th of January at 7:30 am, I touched down in Sydney and stayed with my dad and the family for two weeks. The plan was to stay with him for a while and live and work in Sydney. They were expecting me, but when I showed up, sporting bright red hair, they had to do a double take.

Welcome home.

I looked for work and even registered for the dole. I went to Centrelink, and they wanted original copies of all sorts of papers that I didn't have on me but had in Canberra. So, I thought, fuck it; I might as well go home, where life will be a lot easier.

I decided to stay another week, though, before going to Canberra. One morning, a few of us were sitting around the lounge room table. My sister, Joanne, had just arrived, and it was the first time I'd seen her since I got back. It didn't take long before she asked me if I ever made it to a football match when I was in the UK. I didn't think anything of it and said no. She said her boyfriend, Dave, found an article in the men's magazine, *People*, about two football fans that changed their names. Jo suspected it was me because of my Spaceman Africa email address, and she'd often seen Crazy's name in some of my group e-mails. I admitted it was us and told the family the story behind the story and about the free flights. They took it well. I hadn't told them of my name change before this.

I got bored of the usual sitting on my butt all day, so Friday night, I went into the city for a drink. I walked into a random pub in Kings Cross, and this woman was staring at me. I was used to getting looks over the last two months because of my bright red hair, but this woman kept looking. I wondered, what did she want, and she called me over. She asked what my name was; I said, "Spaceman."

"I thought so; it's me, Tania."

I took a closer look, and blow me down; it *was* Tania. Tania was a Kiwi chick that was part of the Ark Hostel crew in Belfast. I had a look around the table and recognised other people I knew from Belfast. I didn't recognise Tania, at first, because I sure wasn't expecting to see her in a pub in Sydney. Tania went running to another table of guys and said, "You remember those guys in the paper who changed their names and are friends of mine?"

"Yeah."

"Well, here's Spaceman."

I was treated like a celebrity for a while. It was a very exciting surprise. We then went ahead and got absolutely shitfaced in celebration of seeing each other again and I spent a fortune. There was a $10 haircut place outside, and one of my mates dared me to get my head shaved. I'd managed to escape any dares during Christmas/New Year, but here was a challenge. It was my intention to grow my hair long again, but he even gave me the $10. Half an hour later: done. I was a skinhead ... and no more red hair.

February–March 2005

After making my way back to Canberra, the plan was to work in another fantastic, dead-end job and go about paying off debts owed to my family. Canberra is the porn capital of Australia; after my Big Sister experience, I jokingly considered looking for work in that field. Once my debts were paid off, I'd have a clean slate, *baby*, and the world would be my oyster.

Returning to Canberra wasn't the big piss up I thought it would be. I moved in with my aunt and grandmother. I hadn't seen my family or friends since April 2002, and I met my nephew, James, for the first time, who was born in April 2003. But, I had returned to Canberra broke and was confined to keeping a low profile. The same issues I had adjusting to life in Canberra in '99, after two years away, I experienced again. Nothing had changed, yet everything had changed.

In the first few weeks, I caught up with some friends but hadn't yet been out on the town to introduce Canberra to Spaceman Africa. Canberrans can be quite conservative, so I wasn't sure how they'd take to my new name. I thought they'd probably think I was a weirdo or stupid. The first dealings I had with the community was going to various government departments to alert them of my name change. The name evoked many different responses, from laughter to disbelief and denial ("I'm not calling you that") to total acceptance. Because of the name Africa, when I showed up to appointments, many people were expecting a black man with dread locks and were surprised when a shaved-headed, white man showed up.

My name got questioned a lot over the phone. "Africa? As in the country?" If they were polite and friendly, I'd say yes. But if they were being rude and unaccepting of my name, then I'd put them in their place and correct them. "No. Africa as in the continent."

Some people thought it was my name since birth and asked about its origin. I answered that it was a Northern Irish name. Others asked, "Your parents must have been hippies when you were born; were they?" I replied with, "I don't know; I can't remember. I was quite young when I was born."

Whilst I'd been away, friends of mine had built up the legend of Spaceman Africa and relayed stories to their friends and work colleagues of the numerous adventures I'd experienced. When I met them, many of them expressed their surprise and disappointment to discover I was a nerd. My attitude was, "Well, fuck you." It put me off meeting friends of friends. If someone said, "My friend wants to meet you. I've told them all about you," I invariably knew I wasn't going to live up to expectations.

7th May 2005

Tuesday, the 3rd, was my birthday. It was a pretty quiet affair on this occasion, but I had a good weekend away down the coast the weekend before. The weekend afterwards ... well, that was pretty special, too. It's not every day you get to dress up and see Tori Amos live in concert ... at The Sydney Opera House. My mate, Pauly, and I were keen to see her, and the fact that she was playing at the famous Sydney Opera House just added to the excitement.

We arrived in Sydney at our hotel around 6pm. Seeing as we were having a night out at the 'opera', we chose to get all dressed up for the event. Pauly had two velvet suits, which we wore. The one he lent me was black, whilst he wore a burgundy one similar to that which Austin Powers would wear.

Neither of us had been to the Opera House before.

When we arrived, we saw that it was just as magnificent as one would expect. You might know, The Sydney Opera House is a multi-venue performing arts centre situated in Sydney Harbour. It's now a UNESCO World Heritage Site and one of the most famous performing arts centres in the world. From the street up to the venue are scores of steps nearly 100 metres wide, used for ceremonies and the occasional benefit concert. The two main halls are arranged side by side with white-tiled roof shells. I've always thought they look like sails on a yacht.

Tonight's show was in the Opera Theatre, as opposed to the Concert Hall. The theatre is what's known as a proscenium arch theatre, with an orchestra pit and the seats configured in an arch shape. The room looked so grand with its high ceiling, 1500 seats, and boxes lining both sides of the theatre. The lighting was down low, giving a more intimate atmosphere. The furnishings were made of an elegant timber and the seats with a posh red upholstery. I felt like I should be on my best behaviour.

It was a sell-out crowd, and it was my kind of crowd. The majority of people were young, attractive women dressed in classy, alternative wear, bordering on medieval. The evening was both a feast for the ears and the eyes. We bought drinks from the foyer bar when we first arrived and had to drink them quickly, as we weren't allowed to take them into the theatre. I also made sure I went to the toilet beforehand, as I didn't want to have to get up during the show and have to squeeze past the other people seated in our row. We had good seats about three quarters of the way back, stage left, and had a good view of everything. In keeping with the formal tone of the venue, Tori Amos played her more downbeat, reflective songs from her repertoire. Unfortunately, she only played two songs that I recognised, and one of those was a cover, but it was a great experience, none the less.

Pauly is a long-time mate of mine. We first met on the first day of school in Year 6 when we were both eleven years old. It was my first day at a new school and we sat next to each other in class. We got along ok but we weren't best buddies. That was how it continued until Year 10. Things changed when we teamed up in woodwork class and helped each other with our respective wood building projects. Additionally, our respective school house's were paired together on the Year 10 spiritual retreat. Here we got to have some down time and, along with our other school mates, have an amusing couple of days together which was quite a bonding experience for all involved.

Pauly's Canberra born and bred. He's blond, usually with long shoulder length hair, perfect for head banging. We bonded over our love for music, mainly hard rock. Pauly is the biggest AC/DC fan I know. Once we'd left school, at the end of Year 12, we hung out a lot together, jamming on the guitar, listening to our favourite bands and going to live gigs together. We're still good mates today.

June–October 2005

In the first week of June, I went with Pauly to the ANU bar to see Australian rockers, Magic Dirt. They have some great catchy, fast-paced songs with a distinct fuzzy guitar sound, and on vocals, one of the coolest rock-chics around, Adalita. After the show, we hung around to talk with the guys from the band (and to drink some of their beer). They were all extremely lovely, and we had a really good chat about playing music and what it's like for them to be on tour. As the conversation was coming to an end, Pauly thought he'd formally introduce me to the band. They were like, "What do you mean, Spaceman Africa?" I explained it was my name, and they flipped out. I showed them my driver's licence, and they started calling over all their mates to come and have a look. The bass player, Dean, rushed away for a minute and came back with a video camera to film me as part of their tour video diary. They were so excited; I thought they were going to ask *me* for *my* autograph. I told them I had many more funny stories, and the guitarist, Raul, was particularly interested, so he gave me his email address, and we kept in touch. It was an unexpectedly fun night out.

A few months earlier, I dusted off my bass guitar and started jamming with Pauly and our mate, Kyle. It just sort of came about, naturally. I was hanging out at Kyle's house whilst he was playing the drums and Pauly played the guitar. I went and collected my bass from my brother's place and joined the guys to add that extra element. Pauly had quite a few originals he'd written, which we jammed on, and one thing led to another; we became a band. We used to practise in the lounge room of Kyle's place and received a few complaints from the neighbours about the noise. Someone who didn't complain was Kyle's girlfriend, Brooke. Whilst we were rocking out with our amps set at 11, Brooke sat in the lounge room, enjoying the audio onslaught and sang along. She was great, always very supportive. Kyle and Brooke were considerably much younger than Pauly and I, around ten years. Kyle was good to play with. He was one of those talented drummers that could play and sing at the same time.

In June and July, through one of Pauly's work colleagues, we were able to record some songs. Our new best friend, Bob, had a home studio and was studying music production, so it worked out well for both parties. We got to record a CD in a professionally equipped studio with someone who knew what they were doing, whilst Bob was able to get study credits and gain more experience.

It was a good experience for us, as well, to see the recording process in action and marvel at what the technology could accomplish. We recorded all the instruments separately, starting with the drums. Pauly did his guitar tracks next, and then I did the bass parts. At some point, Pauly laid down the vocals, and we were done. It took about six weeks, from memory, of meeting a few hours once or twice a week. I certainly came away with a more meticulous ear and a larger vocabulary of adjectives from trying to describe different sounds. When I say we were done, I'm referring to our part in the recording process. Bob still had the post-production to do, mixing and mastering, which can sometimes take a while. before the album would be completely finished. We used to refer to Bob as Bob Rock, after Bob Rock, the Canadian musician, sound engineer, and record producer, who has produced such bands as Aerosmith, The Cult, Bon Jovi, and Metallica.

As a bit of fun, I recorded a song of my own. I played the guitar and bass on the track, as well as doing the vocals, whilst Bob mixed a drum track from his computer to it. It was a short, simple song about a brothel in Prague that went a little something like this:

Big Sister, where the sex is free.
Big Sister, now you're on DVD.
There's naked women swimming in the fish tank;
They're free to fuck, so there's no need to wank.

I'd like to kiss her on her luscious lips.
I'd like to kiss her on her clit and her tits.
Fuck her in a bed that's like an igloo,
Or in the hot tub that's in the bathroom.

I'd like to fist her; that can't be missed.
I'd like to fist her up past my wrist.

Fist her with a smile 'cause you're on camera;
Give us a big wave as you ram her.

Big Sister.

Around this time, it came to my attention, others were using my name. Dozens of people were using my name as their username on internet gaming sites and profile pages. That didn't bother me so much, but there were a few cases of my name being used as a band name, Crazy Horse's too. There were bands called Spaceman Africa in Young, NSW; Weston-Super-Mare, UK; and in Michigan, USA. There was a band called Crazy Horse Invincible in Sydney and, in the States, a combination of the two: Spaceman Africa & The Invincibles. This did piss me off. I didn't go to all that trouble to come up with an original name just for other people to use it. I was also worried about what might happen if they were to become successful. People might think I got my name from the band. I paid the mandatory $260 to apply to the Australian Government to register the name as a trademark with the intention of applying internationally after that. The government rejected my application and I lost the $260 in the process. Ah, well. Life happens.

My favourite story regarding the use of my name comes from Massachusetts, USA. A woman sent me an email, telling me my name was legend in her office at work. Her work colleague's unborn child was nicknamed Spaceman Africa. They had seen my story in a baby book. When the boy was born, and christened Drew, they still called him by his nickname.

I didn't understand, at first, what she was referring to when she said, 'baby book'. I found out years later there's a book of 10,000 baby names. As well as lists of suggested names, it has funny and cool stories in the margins, and the story of Crazy Horse and me is one of them.

In June, I returned to work at Toll Logistics. I had worked there as a picker/packer on and off from '98 through to 2002. These employment agencies have a habit of pigeonholing you and sending you to the same few places all the time. It had been over three years since I last worked there; the place had changed a lot. There were still quite a few people there, though, from three years earlier—some of them, from six years earlier. I couldn't believe it. Why would someone stay there so long? Who knows, maybe they enjoyed it? That's not the impression I got, though.

Still sporting a short hair-do, I looked different than what I did three years earlier; plus, I had a new name, so I stayed rather quiet when I first arrived. I wasn't sure if anyone would remember me; they must have had scores of casuals go through there in the last three years. I didn't want to act all chummy with someone and then realise they didn't know who I was. I noticed there were a few women working there this time around that I didn't know. I thought having some women around would make a delightful change from the usually male dominated warehouses. After I had a few more opportunities to look at the ladies, I realised I had met one of them before. It was the hair that gave it away. I'd met her back in 2001. Here's what I wrote about her then:

There were a few new casuals ... including a quiet chick, called MJ. She was a few years younger than me and had big hair. She wasn't so quiet to those she knew, though, and I heard her talk in the lunch room of her gigs as a bass player in a covers band. I thought she'd be a cool chick to get to know, but she was always rather distant whenever I tried to have a conversation with her, which is a shame. I thought we'd get along well. I guess we'll never know.

I never expected to see her again. I wondered if she was a bit more approachable, three years on. Morning tea break came, and I pondered where to have my morning snack. It appeared everyone was going outside, where they could smoke and get some fresh air. I thought maybe I should go out there, too; if I wanted to make friends, I was going to have to mix with the others. But I didn't want to go outside and sit amongst smokers in the cold. Plus, I was anxious going out there on my own, being the 'new kid', whilst they all congregated in their little cliques. I went and sat in the lunch room on my own. I'm glad I did.

MJ came into the room and went to her locker to get some things. I sat there silently, nervous about what I should say if she was to sit down in the room. I needn't have worried. She looked at me from her locker and said, "Jason rang me last night and told me to be welcoming to you."

The night before, I'd rung my old mate, Jason, who now lived in Adelaide, and used to work at Toll, to tell him of the news I'd be returning to work at our old haunt. I didn't know he was going to do this, but he then rang MJ. That was nice of him. It certainly helped to break the ice, and we chatted for the whole break.

MJ (full name: Miss J Love) and I slowly got to know each other over the next few months. We had similar personalities, shared a love for music and the bass guitar, the same witty sense of humour, and an appreciation for dad jokes.

We formed our own non-existent band, called Jungle Mother & the Big Hands, based on a postcard Crazy and I sent to Brian Oliver from Spain. We gave my bass guitar a personality. Her name was Macy, and she was band leader of the group Macy & the Formula Ones. Due to MJ's tendency to stay up late, I coaxed her into watching F1 races on the telly and, subsequently, she's now a fan. Watching the races is our version of watching a soap opera. We talk about the latest gossip going around about the drivers. So, needless to say, we got along well, despite our fierce battles at work, when we fired rubber-bands at each other.

October–November 2005

In January 2005, I left the UK with no intention of going back there anytime soon. I felt there were other parts of the world to explore, and as far as Europe was concerned, I'd pretty much, been there, done that. Only eight months later, I was on a plane headed for Heathrow.

My friends, Simon and Jan, were getting married, and I was flying over for the wedding. I was really happy for the two of them. Of course, I knew both of them separately before they had met each other—Simon my boss at the Empire, and Jan my upstairs neighbour when I was living with Jim. I joked that they could have saved me a lot of money by getting married when I was still living in London, but in reality, I was excited to have the opportunity to travel to Europe once more and see all my friends again. Who knew this trip would send my life on an emotional roller-coaster for the next nine months?

The trip was cool shit. I was in London for a week before the wedding. I caught up with everyone there, including my Lithuanian love, Alé, who took me to The Redback, a popular Australasian tavern and music venue in Acton. It's her favourite place, and she had never invited me before. How funny that it was my first time there, considering I'm Australian and lived so many years in Shepherd's Bush. I had a good night and loved seeing Alé again.

The wedding was in Portugal, but I flew a few days earlier into Spain, to have a look around. Days later, I was on a bus from Seville, Spain, to Lagos in Portugal. I really had no idea where I was going. Tessa had texted me in Seville, saying I should get off the bus at Lagos and then catch a taxi from there to the village Almedena. But, once I crossed the border into Portugal, my phone didn't have any service. It was late when I arrived in Lagos; the place looked dead, and I was lucky to find a cab straight away. I went to Almedena, and with no idea where to go from there, I went to a bar. A bottle of beer there was less than a euro; I could certainly get used to this place. The barman spoke English and one thing lead to another, and he gave me directions to the hotel complex I was looking for. It was about midnight, by this stage, and as I walked through the gardens, I could hear a party. So, at midnight, out I walked from the darkness with my backpack on, and all my friends cheered when they saw me. They had all arrived at different times during the day and were somewhat surprised to see me at that hour. Talk about being fashionable late.

This was Thursday night. The wedding was Saturday and was being held in the gardens of the hotel, so we just had to walk out of our apartment door and we'd be at the wedding. The wedding was the best. Anyone who was anyone in that circle of friends was there. I saw friends I hadn't seen in years. People travelled from all over to be there—Canada, the States and, of course, the UK. It was such a good atmosphere, celebrating in the gardens, and everyone had a great time. Most people stayed for a week, so it was one big, week-long party with a wedding thrown in the middle.

As a result of the wedding two romances developed. And wouldn't you know it? I was involved in one of them. I hooked up with Mary, whom I'd met briefly a few times, years ago, such as Glastonbury '98, when she was married to Simon's brother, Laughing Chris (a different to Chris to who I lived with in Shepherd's Bush). Because she was married and I had a girlfriend (Manny), I had never really looked at her in the past. She'd heard in advance that she'd be sharing an apartment with a guy called Spaceman Africa and, to some extent, dreaded meeting this weirdo. She had no memory of me from years earlier, and we hooked up that first night when I arrived out of the darkness.

Mary was slim, blonde, a wee bit taller than me, and a few years older. We had a lot in common, e.g., we both liked to have a drink or two. The morning after we hooked up, we woke up on the sofa next to each other, and neither one of us had any memory of how we ended up there together. We spent most of our time that week by each other's side.

I got a sneak peek into what it might be like to be a celebrity on the red carpet dealing with the paparazzi. The whole wedding entourage, about 50 people, went out to dinner together in Lagos. In the main square by the town hall, we came across a statue affectionately known as 'The Spaceman'. It's actually a sculpture of Dom Sebastiao, the 16th king of Portugal and the Algarve, but it looks like an astronaut. I stood in front of the statue as 50 people stood in front of me, taking photos and calling my name. There were flashes going off in my face, and I could hardly see a thing. For a brief minute, I knew what it was like to be a celebrity.

After the wedding, I went and stayed with Mary for a week in Modbury, near Plymouth, Devon. It's a great little village, pop. 1500, and the countryside was just beautiful. I got to drive Mary's car along the small, narrow roads. It was a whole new ballgame to what I was used to driving in Canberra. There were hedges six feet high on either side of the road and only room for one car, but it was a two-way road. Plus, the speed limit was 60mph. Unbelievable. Mary was a local volunteer fire-fighter and drove the fire truck for the local fire brigade, so I felt quite confident when she was driving, at speed, on the twisting, winding country roads.

I liked the small village atmosphere there and it wasn't long before I was known in the pubs. I met quite a few characters, including the famous Alexis, Modbury's local

TV personality, who was just blown away by the medical trial stories I told. She offered to show me around some of the moors in the area, but I didn't take her up on the offer. I think Mary would have cut my balls off if I had. Mary said the small village atmosphere did have a downside, as people tended to gossip a bit too much.

From nearby Exeter, I flew to Belfast and spent about six days with Crazy Horse. He'd just come back from Canada, so it was good to catch up and hear all his stories. No trip to Belfast would be complete without going to The Royal. We went there one busy afternoon, and when I walked in, everyone was like, "SPACEMAN." I had my own *Cheers* moment. Most of our time was spent drinking around the house or at The Royal. I made a few new friends at the pub, too, so that was cool. I was also reacquainted with snuff. Oh, how I had missed it. Snuff isn't available in Australia.

I caught a bus down to Dublin and spent two nights there. I flew back to London Saturday night and flew to Australia Monday afternoon. I was away for six weeks, and rather than run out of money, like I thought I would, I ran out of time and, unfortunately, didn't get around to seeing everyone I wanted. Anyway, not to worry; it had been an awesome time, and because of the wedding, I'd managed to catch up with loads of people. I arrived back in Canberra safely, having had a good time and happy to be in warmer climes. I came back with many stories to tell, but none better than this:

Brian Oliver story

You may or may not remember, Brian Oliver is the guy Crazy Horse and I chose randomly out of the Dublin phone book. We were both in Dublin for the weekend and were enjoying a pint in the pub. We'd bought some postcards, and with no idea who to write to, we borrowed the phone book from behind the bar. We opened the book up, randomly pointed at the page, and came up with Brian Oliver.

From then on, we wrote to him as if we were mates and had been for years. Wherever our travels took us, we sent him a postcard and told him everything we'd been up to. But we never revealed our last names or gave a return address and definitely didn't mention he was chosen randomly. On our travels, we told others about Brian and encouraged them to write to him, too. Brian received postcards from all over Europe, North America, South Africa, and Australia. We started in August 2002, and over three years later, we were still doing it.

Whilst in Europe for the wedding, I knew I'd be going over to Dublin at some stage to visit a friend from Canberra. I was contemplating the idea of finally meeting up with Brian. I didn't expect to be in that part of the world again anytime soon, so this was maybe my only chance to meet him. Meeting up would answer so many questions we'd pondered for years: What's he like? What's his family like, if any? What's his life story? Does he read the cards? What does he think about it all? Does he keep them? Does he share them with his mates down at the pub?

Then there was the downside to meeting up. If we were to meet, the joke would be over. No doubt, I'd tell him about being chosen randomly to get the answers to our questions, but what fun would it be writing another boring old postcard to someone you know?

Over the last three years, I'd become so used to experiencing something and thinking, "I must tell Brian about this," e.g., It was my first thought after a male train attendant made a move on me and grabbed my crotch whilst on a train to Chicago. It's so easy to write to a stranger. You just write as if it's your diary and then make a joke that hints at the fact you've never met. For example: "I had my head shaved today. You wouldn't recognise me," or "I went out drinking with my mate, Kenny. I don't think you've met Kenny."

After much thought and with a lot of encouragement from friends, I decided to give Brian a call and see what would happen. I rang on the only night I was free to see him and his wife answered the phone. I asked for Brian and was told he was at work and asked if I wanted to leave a message. I asked her could she please let Brian know that his mate, Spaceman, called. After saying that, I was expecting the Spanish Inquisition. "Spaceman? You're that fucker that keeps sending postcards and we don't even know who the fuck you are!" But there was none of that. She took my number and then the call was over.

I later realised I couldn't receive incoming calls on my mobile so I'd have to phone back. I spoke to Mrs Oliver again and found out that Brian would be home at 7pm. After a few more pints in the pub, I phoned at 7:30 and this time Brian answered. "This will be interesting," I thought. Crazy Horse had rung a few times in the past as Abdul Al Halleel, pretending to sell insurance, to try and get some idea of what kind of person Brian was. But here I was ringing, revealing my true identity.

"Hi, is that Brian?"

"Yes."

"Oh, hi. It's Spaceman."

Now, surely, I would get the third degree, but no. Brian asked, "How are you?" as if I was some long-time friend. I explained that I was in town for the night and asked if he wanted to catch up for a pint. We arranged to meet up and he gave me the bus number to Coolock—his part of town—and we arranged to meet at the bus stop where I was to get off. I'd know to get off because the stop was in front of a church.

I was a bit lazy and didn't feel like catching a bus so I caught a cab and asked the driver to take me to Coolock. On the way, he asked me where in Coolock I wanted. "Oh, just in front of the church, please mate."

"But there's a church on every second corner in Dublin."

Not to worry, we worked out which was the correct church and, because I caught a cab, I'd arrived early. I sat at the bus stop waiting for Brian. Unbeknownst to me, he had arrived and was standing behind me, thinking I was someone waiting for the bus. After a while, I noticed a guy standing behind the bus stop. Was this Brian? God, he's older than I thought. Well, let's find out.

I went over and asked, "Are you Brian?"

"Yes."

"Hi, I'm Spaceman."

I put my hand out to shake his. The moment of truth. Face to face with Brian Oliver. A man I knew only by address. The man who, for the last three years and three months, had been bombarded with postcards from all over the world, from people he didn't know, and I had been a major player. Was Brian going to shake my hand or punch me in the face? We shook hands.

"Let's get in out of the cold," he said.

We walked together to the pub a few hundred metres down the road. We made small talk as we went, once again as if we were old friends catching up. Did Brian think that we were, indeed, friends but couldn't remember from where and was too embarrassed to say? But only minutes earlier, I had to ask him if he was Brian Oliver. Surely, he realised we were meeting for the first time.

We arrived at the pub and Brian got the first round in. We sat at the bar, said cheers and took a sip from our beer. And then it came, the first acknowledgement from Brian of the last three years.

"So," then a brief pause, "what's the story with all the postcards?"

I couldn't help but laugh. After that we both told each other our sides of the story. Brian was a nice guy and appreciated the humour behind the cards. Brian, I'm guessing, was in his fifties, about 5'7", had short dark grey hair, wore glasses and had a grey moustache. He is a Dubliner born and bred. He is married with four grownup sons and works as a computer technician.

Brian explained that, when the first cards started coming, he threw them out thinking we had the wrong person. But when they kept coming, he suspected something was going on and started to keep them all. It was a big thing in the Oliver household when a new card arrived. It was Brian and his youngest son Dave who tried to get to the bottom of it all. They looked for any clues as to how they might track us down.

The closest they came was when our friend, Jane, in Virginia, US, left an address on a card of a riding school she went to. But after tracking down the school phone number, the Oliver lads thought it was a bit absurd to ring up asking for someone called Jane who knows a Spaceman and Crazy Horse. Brian didn't believe we used our real names. Otherwise, if he'd put our names in a Google search he would have found us. We also once let slip that we drank in The Royal Bar, in Belfast, but he never called the pub.

After a few rounds, Brian's son Dave came and joined us. He was a good guy as well and introduced me to Fat Frogs (Blue Wicked, Orange Cruiser and Bacardi Breezer; all mixed together to create a green lemonade tasting drink that goes down so smoothly). Another son, Keith, also dropped in on his way to the theatre and brought with him a pile of postcards. Brian and I counted 120 postcards in just this one pile. Brian said he had more at home and then there were the ones he'd thrown out. I sat there looking through them.

I could have sat there for hours reading them but it would have been a bit anti-social. I just glanced through them and saw postcards from people who I had no idea who they were. Crazy Horse and I never made copies of the cards we sent, so it was a good trip down memory lane reading some of them again. We spent the night chatting and getting very drunk. I was on such a high when we called it a night.

All in all, Brian took the whole experience in the good humour in which it was intended. None of the postcards were ever rude or vindictive in any way. So, the joke was over now but I had made a new friend. Well, actually, we'd been friends for years, but now we knew who each other was.

8th December

(This paragraph sounds best when you say it in a deep, dramatic voice, as if you're Don LaFontaine, the famous American voiceover artist of more than 5,000 movie trailers). The evening's festivities were the moment we'd all been waiting for. The last seven months of practise came down to this moment. This was not a drill. Our first gig was at the loud, hard-rock friendly Pot Belly Bar in Belconnen. Our name … was Mirrored Chaos.

Since arriving back from Europe, I went to band practise a few times, and we worked hard to be ready for our first gig. Bob Rock still hadn't finished the mastering of the CD. I was expecting it to be finished by the time I got back, but we had our fingers crossed it would be finished by Christmas.

On the day of the gig, we met up at Pauly's in the afternoon. We were all full of nervous excitement, including Brooke, the honorary non-playing member of the band. She was all dressed up in her cool gothic rock look. I'd gone to a lot of trouble to look like I hadn't gone to any trouble at all, when choosing my wardrobe for the night. We also put some gel in my hair and spiked it up to look like Cameron Diaz from *There's Something About Mary*.

It was a good turnout at the Pot Belly. Many of Pauly's supporters from work showed up to cheer us on. We'd all played live on stage before, but this was the first time we'd played live together as a band. The stage was rather small, but the three of us managed to fit our gear and ourselves on there. We plugged in and then rocked out, loud and proud. Pauly put on a good show, moving about the crowd and getting them involved. We fucked up a few times, but the audience didn't notice; they all seemed to enjoy the show.

For the last three songs, we mixed it up a bit. I hopped off the bass and took over the guitar duties. As a treat for a friend of mine, Jenny, who was in the audience, I played and sang one of her favourite songs, "Rainbow Connection", originally performed by Kermit the Frog. She had no idea I was going to perform it and couldn't believe it when I led off with the first few lines. Anyway, that was enough easy-listening for one show. After "Rainbow Connection", with a big drum roll from Kyle, I stormed straight into "Big Sister". The song was a big hit amongst some sections of the crowd. Then, to finish the show on a high, we went out with "Rockin' in the Free World" by Neil Young. With me on guitar, that left Pauly free to focus on singing and cavorting amongst the crowd, emulating his rock heroes and putting into practise all those years in front of the mirror. The show was a big success and, needless to say, we were all on a high after the show.

As predicted, the Fellowship of the Ring New Year's rendezvous didn't take place this year. I wasn't upset about it, though. My friends Brian and Kris of Washington DC fame had invited me to their upcoming wedding in April. So, I'd catch up with them and many other friends then. For New Year's, I rocked out at a Magic Dirt gig at the

Esplanade Hotel in St Kilda, Melbourne. Unfortunately, Bob Rock still hadn't finished mastering the CD. You can, however, listen to a few tracks online. Google: *Mirrored Chaos Triple J Unearthed.*

2006

After my trip to Europe, Mary and I kept in touch with phone calls and emails. One thing lead to another, and I was bound for Modbury again. We had our future all mapped out. I was going to move to Modbury and live with Mary. In April, I was going to go to the wedding in DC and Mary was going to come and meet me in New York after the wedding, and we'd celebrate my birthday there together. We were going to have a ball spending the summer in the English countryside, with weekends away and a busy social life. Then, later in the year, as winter started to surface, we were going to get away and travel to Central and South America for six months. I was excited. I was looking forward to living the village life, in the Devon countryside. Whilst I'd lived in the UK before, Devon was no London. This was going to be different altogether.

Preparations for moving to the UK were in full swing. I found it weird having a girlfriend again. All the women I'd been with in the previous five years had just been casual flings, with no future plans together. I had to remember I was spoken for when I was out drinking. Mary was good craic, though. She liked a drink and liked to travel. She was a bit weird and different, like me, so we got along well. I didn't know if moving in with her was the right decision. My attitude was: whatever happens, happens. I was just going to enjoy myself. Mary said she'd like kids one day, which I wasn't too keen on. But, once again, that was the future's problem. I was just looking forward to spending a summer in Europe, with sex on tap and catching up with my mates at the wedding in DC. The outlook was pretty good, I thought.

March 2nd was the departure date. I was going to need to find work pretty quickly once I arrived in the UK. I didn't have a lot of money, and I had the trip to the States to finance. After four months of talk and planning, constant phone calls with Mary, packing my life up, and preparing for a giant leap into the unknown, the moment had come. I was leaving Australia, bound for Devon, south west England, to live with ... a woman. This was going to be interesting.

After four months in Australia, talking, texting, and emailing, Mary and I were jumping out of our skin to see each other again. I sold off what little possessions I had that I could live without for the time being, and I packed my life into a suitcase and arrived at Heathrow, where Mary picked me up, and we went straight back to Modbury. But no rest for the wicked, as we had an early flight the next morning to Malaga, Spain. Mary had booked a week's holiday for us in the sun. One, because she needed a break from her job, and two, because we had only ever been together whilst on holiday.

And what a great week it was, too. We stayed at a great resort, saw some of the neighbouring towns, practised speaking Spanish, and met some cool people. We met some English lads on a jolly boy's holiday, and we went with them to a strip club. Then it was back to Modbury to start our new life together.

TWO WEEKS! Two fuckin' weeks it lasted: one of the biggest anticlimaxes in history. Mary had been talking up my arrival to everyone for months, and her friends were keen to meet me. But when Mary told me she needed her space, and not a spaceman, I went to stay in Belfast with my partner in crime, Crazy Horse. So, my time in Modbury went relatively unnoticed.

March 2006

Let's go back a bit to when we returned to Modbury after our trip to Spain. We returned Wednesday evening, and for the rest of the week, I set about getting my new life set up. I went into Plymouth to establish myself at the bank, Inland Revenue, and a number of employment agencies, as well as register with the local GP in Modbury and the clinical trials unit in Plymouth.

My presence in Modbury that first week consisted of just a walk to the shops and back. When I spent a week there the November before, I got out and about. I drank in the pubs, met some locals, and saw some of the surrounding countryside. This time round, I went into hibernation to save money. After Spain, I stayed off the booze, and when I wasn't in Plymouth or Kingsbridge looking for work, I was at the house on the internet, desperately looking for any jobs available. I only had about £200 to my name and still needed to save for a two-week trip to the US. I wasn't having much luck, though. I tried the warehouse angle as usual, but without a car, I was reliant on public transport, which made life difficult. I wondered if my name was scaring the country folk off, too.

At the two-week mark, we went to a wedding in the countryside, north of London, and Mary's demeanour changed. Mary's friends, Ruth and Duncan, were getting married and we drove ... somewhere. I don't remember where the wedding was, but we drove there Friday afternoon and hit the M25 peak hour traffic. Mary was stressed. Peak hour traffic and struggling to find our hotel in the dark, didn't help matters. The mood was tense when we arrived at the hotel. This was the first sign of trouble.

Then, at the wedding reception, I decided not to drink, so I could drive us back to the hotel and save on an expensive taxi fare. But without alcohol, I was a killjoy. Rather than cheerfully mingle with the other guests, I kept to myself, which was ruining it for Mary. She couldn't fully enjoy herself with me moping in the corner. Without booze acting as a social lubricant, I just wasn't in the mood to make conversation with anyone. This didn't help matters between us and, in the end, Mary said, "Look, you may as well have a drink. We'll catch a taxi." I did as I was told and perked right up. I got pretty drunk and spoke to anyone and everyone. It showed how reliant on alcohol I was. It spelled the end of the relationship right there.

We drove back to Modbury on Sunday, and I went to the pub. I'd been sober until the wedding, and now, I'd tasted the blood, and I was keen to continue. I returned to the house a bit later to find Mary in the bath. She raised some concerns she had about her feelings towards me, such as, why we hadn't had sex for over a week, why she wasn't able to introduce me to her friends as her boyfriend. I told her it was nothing to worry about. I put it down to being sober and focusing on settling in. I was wrong.

The next few days, I noticed Mary was distant and stopped showing affection towards me. I was off the booze again and busy job hunting, but Mary had dispensed with her alcohol fast and had a few drinks after work to wind down. She came home from work on Thursday and said she "couldn't keep this up anymore" and just basically said the relationship was over. Although I had suspected it, and half expected it, hearing it made me angry. I didn't lose my cool; instead, I became withdrawn.

By the way, over six months later, Bob Rock still hadn't finished mastering the CD. Just thought you'd like to know. Haha

Mary said I'd lost my spark; I wasn't the guy she had met in Portugal. That hurt. Of course, I was different; so was she.

In Portugal, I was on holiday. Here, I was in responsibility mode trying to get on my feet financially. Mary felt rather guilty and was really nice to me for a few days, but I stayed guarded. It was a shame. Things were just starting to come together for me, too. A few job offers came through, and Mary's friend, Tina, had offered me her car so I could get around and drive to any job I might have.

With no need to be on my best behaviour anymore, I hit the bottle ... and hard. I drank vodka around the clock and was often passed out when Mary came home from work. And then I'd stay up for most of the night, drinking, and avoiding going to bed whilst Mary was in it. If she had any doubts about breaking off the relationship before, they were dispelled now. I thought the whole situation was fucked. I didn't know how we were going to live together for the next three weeks until I flew to the States. Mary and I still planned to meet up in New York; everything had already been booked. I was resentful and decided to fuck off to Belfast and stay with someone who was happy to have me around. I had hoped me leaving would upset Mary. She said I didn't have to go, but deep down, I'm sure she was quietly thanking me for that one. I grabbed just a few of my things, and Tina kindly drove me to the airport. I haven't been back to Modbury since.

I met Crazy Horse in The Royal Bar, and we caught up over a few pints and a pinch or two of snuff. We continued back at Olympia St, just like old times. Then the next day, DOWN. I had no money, and I was sobering up. Whilst Crazy Horse was at work, I spent my days sitting at the house watching TV and coming to terms with a broken heart and shattered dreams. Nights were just as fun, lying in bed with only my thoughts to keep me company and alcohol withdrawals in full swing. I had fear, paranoia, and the complete negative vibe that comes from a detox, as well as a scattered head space that just wouldn't quit. I was so grateful to Crazy Horse for taking me in and supporting me the way he did. I was fortunate to have such an understanding and like-minded soul to turn to. He's a great friend.

It took forever, but two weeks passed. It had been great to see Crazy Horse and other Belfast friends again. The circumstances weren't ideal, but nonetheless, we'd still had some good times. We, naturally, had a few farewell drinks in The Royal before I flew to Bristol and then on to Newark, USA, for the wedding in DC. Unfortunately, Crazy wouldn't be able to make it.

I'd booked my flight through Expedia and, coincidentally, Crazy Horse worked for Expedia at the time. For a laugh, he accessed my file on-line and ordered me a Hindu meal. He also thought about ordering me a wheelchair upon arrival, but as the alcohol on Continental Airways isn't complimentary, I didn't think I'd need one. Another idea was that Crazy Horse register me with the code 'P', which means prisoner, which we were sure would have raised a few eyebrows considering I was travelling alone. Anyway, during the flight, I received my Hindu meal before anyone else. Even before the vegetarians. It was awesome. I'd finished my meal before others had even received theirs. The Hindu meal looked much like the vegetarian but with a Hindu sticker on it. That was fun receiving the Hindu meal and being a complete Caucasian westerner.

I arrived at Newark airport and went through immigration. I had the Space shakes quite badly, and when it was my turn to see the immigration officer, he said, "Do you know you're shaking?"

I said, "Yeah," and explained I had a tremor disorder. He said that was the first time anyone had answered yes to that question. He said, normally, people say, "No, man, I'm not shaking."

I caught a bus to Washington DC, to meet up with Brian who I'd be staying with for two weeks. When I arrived, there was no sign of him. I'd arrived about 45mins after we'd arranged to meet, so I thought maybe he'd come and gone. I thought I'd go to the bank and then catch a cab. After I finished at the ATM, I heard someone calling my name. It was Brian. Excellent. I love it when a plan comes together.

Two days later, and it was the weekend. It was Brian's bachelor party, and we were going to Atlantic City. Rock on. There was a gang of about 12 of us, and we'd booked a room in one of the hotel/casino complexes. Brian was given challenges, and on each challenge, someone accompanied him on his quest whilst the rest of us stayed in the room partying. He had to get kisses, and get women to draw on his armour-plated chest, and then ... he had to get slapped. He had 15 minutes to get a woman to slap him, without mentioning it was his bachelor party. And guess who was to go with him? Yep, I was his wingman. I'd got the idea from Stephen when in New York in '02. I mean, it was a raging success back then, wasn't it? Yeah, right.

So, we walked out of the room, down the corridor, turned right to the elevator, and standing there was a young woman. Wasting no time, I went straight up to her and gently slapped her across the face. She looked more confused than offended. I said something like, "You should take it out on him," whilst pointing at Brian. "He likes that sort of thing." She gave him a slap, and we thanked her and went back to the room, ignoring her repeated questions, "Why? Why?" We walked back into the hotel room less than five minutes after we'd left much to the surprise of everyone.

Later, we ventured out of town to a karaoke bar, where Brian's brother Lucian stole the show. He sang like a champion and gave a really entertaining performance. He sang when it was his turn, when it was someone else's turn, and danced whenever given the chance. I looked over at Brian, and he had a smile from ear to ear.

From there, we hit the tables in the casino. We had a lot of fun. Brian and I gambled together on roulette, and after an up and down evening, we walked away with a $30 profit, which we blew straight away at the bar. Michael, Brian, and I called it a night at 10:30 the next morning. We'd been drinking the whole time and hardly felt drunk. That's casino drinks for you.

We returned to our room with bodies strewn everywhere. We found a piece of floor and slept for an hour before it was time to check out. Driving back to DC, one of our vans broke down, so we had a party by the side of the road whilst waiting for a tow truck. All in all, Atlantic City was very entertaining. It was great having a road trip and seeing friends I hadn't seen for years, such as Carl, Graeme, and Michael.

The bachelor party weekend was over, and Brian and I spent Monday recovering, trying to get our heads around final wedding preparations. Tuesday was April 25th, also known as Anzac Day. Anzac (Australia New Zealand Army Corps) Day is observed annually throughout Australia and New Zealand to honour members of the Allied Forces with particular reference to those that fell at Gallipoli, Turkey, April 25, 1915.

I went down to the Australian Embassy in DC to see if there were any Anzac Day functions on. The Embassy directed me to the hotel across the road, where they'd organised some celebrations. I arrived to find it was free food and drink, including Australian wine and beer. Nice One. Free booze. Oh, how I was proud to be an Australian. There was quite a big crowd of mainly Defence Force personnel and their families and the odd American or two. After being away from Australia for seven weeks, it sounded weird hearing Australian accents again.

But anyway, let's be honest. The real reason I was there was to play two-up. Two-up is a game where you gamble on the outcome of the toss of three or sometimes two coins. Two of either heads or tails wins. The game is illegal to play, except on Anzac Day. It's a law dating back to the Depression, which has never been changed.

Normally, you bet against other people in the crowd, but at this ring, it was a bit different. There was still someone in the ring tossing the coins from a small bat, but to gamble, you had to put pre-paid tickets on one of two place mats in front of you, marked heads or tails. Each ticket was $1 in value, so if you won and had put down 5 tickets, you'd win another 5.

I played, and I couldn't lose. I wasn't betting much, but I kept winning and winning. I was having great fun. Eventually, I lost two in a row, so I decided to call it a day. I'd invested $19 and finished with $44—a nice little $25 profit, which is enough for two cases of Milwaukee's Best with a bit left over. So, a good day, I thought.

I went to cash in my tickets at the desk where I'd bought them, only to find out they were tickets for a freakin' auction. With the two-up now finished, the tickets were useful only for the auction of various hampers and boxes of wine, with all proceeds going to the Defence Forces. Little did I know that betting at two-up was really just to build up a collection of tickets to be able to bid in the auction. Fuck, that wasn't my motivation for playing.

I only had $44, but people were bidding well above $200, so I didn't have a chance. There was one guy who was regularly bidding, and I thought maybe he'd be able to use my $44 better than I could. The bid for a box of 12 bottles of wine was about $200. I offered the tickets to this guy, and he just grabbed them and shouted, "$240." I wasn't expecting anything in return, but I did expect at least a thank you. Ah well, I hoped he'd be the highest bidder and that my money would have been useful. And SOLD, to the Gentleman up the back with my $44 donation.

The auction was over, and people were mingling. I'd just come back from the bar and was standing at a table, when a woman came over and gave me a bottle of wine, compliments of auction man winner. Bonus. I went over and thanked him and ended up leaving after that, having had an enjoyable and unexpected Anzac Day. In the end, I'd spent $19 and had loads of beer and food and came away with a bottle of West Australian wine. Not a bad outing at all. I gave the bottle to Brian and Kris.

29th April 2006

The main event, the wedding, was a big success. The church service was held at St Matthew's Cathedral, and I'm told it's one of the most beautiful and impressive in the United States. I wouldn't argue with that. The interior art work and sculptures were breathtaking. Both the bride and groom said, "I do." We were treated to some opera singing by the bridesmaids, and we all got to shake each other's hands and say, "Fish be with you." The bridal party were whisked away in a limo for photographs, whilst the rest of us headed to the reception.

The reception was on the top floor of the Hyatt Regency Hotel overlooking the US Capitol. It was a great location; there was good food and drinks, fantastic company (friends I hadn't seen in years—Natalie and Rebecca), the speeches were entertaining, and a good time was had by all. My only responsibility for the whole day was to help set and pack up the DJ equipment. When I arrived early in the morning, the DJ told me he was fine, and he didn't need my help. But he stressed he definitely needed my help when it came time to pack up.

Unfortunately, during the reception, the wine had gone straight to my head, so I went outside to get some fresh air and sober up. I ended up missing the end of the reception, so the DJ was left to pack up on his own. I only had one job, and I didn't even manage to do that. After the reception, the party continued well into the night in various hotel rooms. No rest for the bride and groom, though. They had to leave at 4:30 in the morning to catch their honeymoon flight to Antigua.

Monday, I was on a bus to New York City. After a failed attempt to meet at the clock at Grand Central Station (apparently, it's *the* meeting place), Mary and I finally met up at our hotel room. We'd organised a few days together in New York to celebrate my birthday. We'd organised the trip long before our break-up, but we were both still keen to share the time together. It was New York, after all. It was well dark by the time we met up, so we didn't do much that first night but grab something to eat and drink.

I can't remember any of the pubs or clubs we went to. I do remember giving Mary a hard time. It was the first time I'd seen her since Modbury, and as much as I wanted to keep the peace and have a laugh, I just couldn't hold back how hurt I was, and many times, I ripped into her. It wasn't something I was pleased about, but I found it hard to control my words. Thankfully, when I asked Mary a few days later if she'd enjoyed her time in New York, she said yes. I'd hate to have thought I'd ruined her holiday.

Oh, but how I remember the next evening. We went drinking in Greenwich Village. we went bar hopping around Manhattan. During our adventures, we met this guy, and it turned out he was a stand-up comic. He was blown away by meeting a Brit and an Aussie. Then, when he learnt my name, he was like, "You've got to come to my show tonight." I love stand-up, and it was my birthday week, so it was my call. We went and he introduced us to the whole crowd. He, and every comic after him, talked to us, and the whole venue knew who we were. I was drunk as a motherfucker, and during one set, I just randomly got up and walked onstage and took over the show. I thought I was really funny, but in reality, I probably came across as a rambling drunk. Mary was hilarious, though. We both heckled the shit out of each comic, and Mary was on fire. Afterwards, we partied with the comics and had a great night. The next day, my birthday, both Mary and I felt rough. We decided to pretend the day before had been my birthday and this day would be a quiet one.

We caught our flight back to Bristol, and like before, I got my Hindu meal before anyone else got their meal. I'd finished my meal before Mary even got hers. When I left Modbury for Belfast early April, I left a lot of belongings behind with the plan to pick them up after the US trip. Not so. Mary had packed my bags and had them in her car at Bristol airport. I guess she wasn't taking any chances of me overstaying my welcome at her house. After we landed, she gave me my stuff from her car and then drove off. And that was that. Good bye. I stood all alone in the carpark in shock. Mmmm, now what? I caught a bus to the city centre and then a bus to London.

In case you were wondering, Bob Rock still hadn't finished mastering the CD.

For Christmas last, my brother, Neville, bought me a suitcase. I don't think I've seen a bigger one. It was about 80cm tall standing up and about 60cm wide. This was the suitcase I was presented with when Mary unloaded my belongings from her car at Bristol airport. When full, the suitcase weighed over 30kg, and I had to carry it, a backpack, and a guitar on board the Megabus to London. Megabus is a budget coach line with a fleet consisting of converted suburban double-decker buses to accommodate long distance travel. This means they don't have luggage compartments. I had to carry my entire luggage on board. What fun that was. By the time I arrived in London, I'd had all the fun I was prepared to take and decided to catch a cab to Shepherd's Bush.

My plan was to stay a few days and catch up with mates over a few pints, then fly back home to Australia. No more chasing girls halfway around the world. I could have stayed in the UK; I had a freshly stamped four-year visa. But I'd been there, done that. With a few projects on the go in Canberra, I decided it would just be easier to conduct my affairs back in Oz.

My long-time mate, Chris, from Shepherd's Bush was kind enough to drive me out to the airport for my flight. Pulling up to Heathrow brought back memories of three months earlier, when I arrived from Australia, full of excitement and hope for the future. Today, I just felt sadness. I was quite emotional and had been crying at times during the day. Of course, drinking beer always assists in being emotional. The positive aspect of the last three months was getting to spend time with friends, such as Crazy Horse, the DC crowd, Julia, Chris, Tessa, and others.

Just for a change, instead of the coach, I took the train from Sydney to Canberra. I stayed at my aunt's again and almost cried when I started unpacking in my old bedroom. I wasn't meant to be back so soon. The plan was to start again, get a job, pay off the debts I'd accumulated over the last three months, save some money, and then travel to Central America. I didn't feel it at the time, but looking back, Mary did us both a favour. I was way too immature to be in that relationship. I believe it would have broken down, sooner or later, and sooner was as good a time as any, I suppose. The upside to all of this was, it now appeared I'd be able to make it to my sister's wedding later in the year.

July 2006 marked one year since Pauly, Kyle and I had recorded our album and, yet, Bob Rock still hadn't finished mastering the CD. What was all that about? I don't pretend to understand what mastering involves, but it's a process of some sort that enhances the music and shapes it into a more equalised and compressed state. Why it was taking so long, I don't know. I dropped around to his studio and managed to get a mastered copy of 'Big Sister' from him. With the help of my brother, Neville the Devil, we made about 30 copies with a CD cover, which I passed around to a number of friends. On the front was a picture of the Big Sister igloo and polar bear, and on the inside cover was a picture of two women swimming naked. 'Big Sister' had become the most requested song at Mirrored Chaos gigs; surprisingly, it was mainly women who requested the song.

30th September, Mirrored Chaos played a gig at the Holy Grail in Canberra's city centre, a stage once graced by Magic Dirt. It was an awful show on our part. We had feedback problems throughout the set; my bass was a major offender. Coincidently, that was the last time I played in the band. Such a shame it ended on a bad note.

Living on the edge at the Cliffs of Moher, Ireland, 2001. A 120 - 200 metre drop off the side of the cliff.

Grand Canyon. I did a day trip there from Las Vegas in 2002.

The core group of The Fellowship of the Ring. L—R: Brain from DC who I met in Thailand; myself; Natalie from DC; Michael from DC but lived in New York and Barcelona who I met in Thailand; Crazy Horse Invincible from Redcar, England, who I met in Belfast. Here we are in a pub in Dublin, Ireland, 2002. It was this trip that involved a name change, choosing Brian Oliver from the phone book and calling in dead to work.

Posing for a photo on a Harley Davidson during Harley Fest on East Brady St, Milwaukee, 2003.

Sporting a black eye on the beach in Isla Mujeres, Mexico, the day after I fell from a top bunk bed in my sleep.

Maroubra Beach, Sydney, 2005. This was a few days after I arrived back in Australia after nearly three years away. You can see my shaved head which was the result of a dare.

A shot of many of my close UK friends, taken at Simon and Jan's wedding in Portugal, 2005. L—R: Mary, who I hooked up with at the wedding and with whom I had a long-term relationship that lasted only two weeks; Monica (standing on the wall), from DC, worked at the Empire and we did a three week trip around Europe together in '98; myself holding a postcard ready to mail to Brian Oliver; Chris, my mate from Shepherd's Bush; Tessa, my good friend overs the years and we had a relationship for a while, too; Stuart, who was a co-worker at the Empire. We had a lot of memorable moments together such as rocking out during a cracking Faithless set, Glastonbury, 2002; Laughing Chris, Simon's brother; Tina, from Modbury who kindly gave me a lift to the airport when I made my exit after the relationship with Mary went sour; Tom from Shepherd's Bush. We've shared some fun times at Glastonbury, parties down by the Thames and he's visited me a couple of times in Canberra; Mike, another brother of Simon. My good friend, Julia, took the photo.

Mirrored Chaos. A shot from one of our live performances. Myself on the left, Pauly upfront on vocals and Kyle, obscured at the back, on drums.

This shot was taken on the side of a freeway when one of our vans broke down coming back from Brian's buck's party in Atlantic City. We had a bit of fun and games whilst waiting for a tow truck. L—R: Lucian, Brian's brother and karaoke king; Tom, who let Crazy Horse and me crash at his house in DC; Carl, who was part of the group who went to Bratislava for New Year's 2004; and myself.

With Miss J Love, my travel companion in Mexico and Cuba, 2006. This shot is taken in the Sierra Maestra, the mountain range where Fidel Castro and a band of rebels, including Che Guevara, hid before the Revolution of the 1950's. It's also the location where we drank some dodgy orange juice and had to stay near a toilet at all times for the next 24 hours.

November 2006

After three years in the making, I was finally heading to Central America for my next adventure. I'd bought a return ticket to LAX, departing November and returning six months later in May. It was twice as long as I'd first planned, but with working extra shifts and cutting back on my drinking over the last few weeks, I'd managed to save some additional money. If I took the budget option and was thrifty whenever possible, I hoped to make it through. Oh, who was I kidding? I knew there was every likelihood I'd be broke within six weeks.

My plan was to travel overland from LA down to Mexico and south along the Baja Peninsula. I had four weeks to arrive in Mexico City and, from there, fly over to Cancún on the 28th November. There, I'd be met by my sidekick, Miss J Love, who would join me for six weeks. She'd never been out of the country, so it was an exciting prospect. We planned to spend two weeks exploring the Mayan Riviera. Then we were going to dangle in Cuba for four weeks. The idea of going to Cuba just blew my mind. We just hoped Castro didn't cark it in the meantime. He had spent a lot of time in hospital in the recent months. After Cuba, we would have reached mid-January. MJ would head home, and I'd cruise south from Cancún to Guatemala and beyond. I was curious to see if the reality would match the plan. It usually didn't.

It was no surprise, once I passed through US Immigration at LAX, Customs Officials held me back. I was shaking quite badly, and I guess I just had that dishevelled look of unrespectability about me. Thankfully, they let me enter their country. I went directly to the Greyhound station and bought a ticket to San Diego. I've never had any real desire to visit Los Angeles, except maybe Venice Beach, a hang-out back in the day for The Doors. Whilst waiting for the bus, I sat in the station going through all my paperwork, double checking (probably for the umpteenth time) the directions for when I arrived in San Diego. Later, when I was queuing to hop on the bus, a man came up to me and handed me my passport. I had dropped it under my seat when I was going through my things, and the kind man found it and returned it to me.

I was so grateful that: 1. the guy was honest enough not to keep the passport, and 2. he was able to return it to me before I'd left on the bus. What a tragic anticlimax that would have been, losing my passport within hours of starting my much-anticipated adventure. Thankfully, through the generosity of a stranger, it hadn't happened. I felt like I'd dodged a bullet and luck was on my side. I wondered what I would have done had I lost my passport. I didn't have to wonder for long. A week later, my passport was stolen.

I caught the San Diego Trolley to the Mexican border. It only took like half an hour. I hopped off the trolley and just walked towards the border, across an overpass to the other side of the highway, through a turnstile, and I was in. I couldn't believe there was no border control. Security is a lot stricter coming back the other way, obviously. I found a taxi and asked the driver to take me to a cheap hotel. He took me to a suitable hotel in the nearby *Zona Norte* (north zone). I don't know why he took me there; maybe that's where all the cheap hotels are. I don't remember our conversation; maybe I asked to be close to nightlife, but whatever it was, staying in Zona Norte set me up for an extreme rollercoaster ride of indulgence and intense struggle.

Zona Norte was both heaven and hell, in that order. I'd liken it to the spaceport town of Mos Eisley on the planet Tatooine—a wretched hive of scum and villainy. Zona Norte is the red-light district of Tijuana. It's known for its brothels, street prostitution, and illicit drug sales, and attracts a lot of Americans from over the border, as well as locals. It was here in Zona Norte, my travel plans ... how can I put it ... suffered a few hiccups, shall we say. The difficulties I faced whilst there were completely down to my own stupidity; perhaps, through telling my story of misfortune, you can garner some satisfaction or pleasure out of the fact it was me and not you. Having said that, my time in Zona Norte wasn't all bad. I did manage to experience ... how can I put it ... one or two sensuous pleasures.

Wednesday 8th November

My second night in town, I met a young Mexican guy, called Damien. He spoke very good English, which was rare in these parts. He was friendly and had a sense of humour. He didn't look like your typical Mexican, looking more like a Jamaican with his dreadlocks. When he suggested I move and stay in the same hotel as he was, I jumped at the chance. I thought it would be a great advantage to have a local connection, who could speak both Spanish and English.

So, I moved into a small hotel on *Calle Coahuila* a few doors up from the *La Tropa* bar. Damien made me feel welcome and told me, if I needed anything, I could call through to his room on the hotel's internal telephone system. My room was one of the more pricier rooms in the joint, yet it was still cheap. It had its own ensuite, double bed and television, complete with porn channel.

To begin with, though, I hung out in Damien's room. I guess he saw me as a way to make money—get me whatever I want, charge me a bit extra for it, and make a small profit. Within an hour of meeting him, I was sitting in his room with one or two others, drinking beer and smoking crack. Damien could organise women, as well, and it wasn't long before I had one up in my room. Whenever I needed more beer or another woman, which was quite regularly, I was on the phone to Damien to get me some more. I was in heaven. This was the sex, drugs, and rock & roll lifestyle I'd always dreamt of. For 24 hours, I hardly slept: drunk, high, and shagging like a rabbit.

Thursday 9th November

In the early evening of day three, Damien sent another woman to my room ... a lesbian. He had told me about Heather but failed to mention the lesbian part. He'd told me she was looking for an activities partner. I didn't realise sex wouldn't be one of those activities. I tried it on with her, but she politely explained she wanted someone to go out bar hopping with. Of course, she did. She didn't have much money and saw me as a possible sugar daddy. But I didn't mind so much. It has always been in my nature, when having a good time, to provide for others so they can join in on the fun. We got dressed up and headed out. Heather explained the rules, "We can party together, but you can't fall in love with me."

Heather was a good laugh. Originally from West Virginia, she spoke Spanish fluently and was in her late 20's. She certainly wasn't a butch lesbian. The best way I could describe her would be to say she was a short version of Laura Prepon (the redhead in *That 70's Show*), with one of the best racks I've ever seen. She had a wild side to her and was particularly good with people. I couldn't bat my eyelashes like she could, but I learnt a lot from her on how to deal with the riffraff we invariably came across.

We went to La Tropa, which was a strip club/brothel. I quickly discovered how awesome it can be to go out partying with a good-looking woman who's into chicks just as much as I am. The bar was relatively empty, except for the women working there. Heather and I basically had them all to ourselves as we ran around like two kids in a candy store, drinking and dancing with the ladies. I even tried my hand at pole dancing (that's not a euphemism, by the way). Let's just say, no one slipped any dollar bills into my underwear. We left La Tropa and Heather crossed the road saying she'd be back later, whilst I went back to my hotel.

I walked down the corridor to my room, and there was a woman outside my door. My memory of events is somewhat hazy, but I remember her being friendly and the two of us having a shower together in my room. I got the impression she was a bit down on her luck, and I was helping her out by letting her clean herself up. I don't remember anything else until waking up a few hours later. I'm guessing the lack of sleep over the last 36 hours caught up with me, and I mistakenly fell asleep.

When I woke, she was gone and I knew, I just fuckin' knew, immediately, I'd been robbed. I would have put money on it, except I didn´t have any; the fuckin' bitch had taken it all. I got up and checked my belongings, and my fears were confirmed. My wallet, my passport, and my money were all gone. I was surprised she even found the Euros hidden in my bag. I don't know why she just didn't take everything, but I'm glad she didn't. Her choice of 'souvenirs' was weird. She took my steel caps boots, my towel, and all my paperwork outlining my itinerary over the next two months. Did she plan to follow me? Or, perhaps do the trip for me? After all, she now had my passport. She took some of my clothing and left some of it behind. She took my Walkman and all my CD's, except for one—a copy of my song, 'Big Sister'. Wow, she was a music critic, as well.

Upon realising my predicament, I think the word 'fuck' was used many times. I'd been screwed and not in quite the same way as the other encounters I'd had since arriving in TJ. I didn't have any ID or money or any access to money. This was going to take some intelligence to get out of this fix, something that had been lacking when inviting women into my room.

I went to Damien. He helped me out big time. We managed to get some change to phone home, which wasn't cheap, to organise getting some money sent to me. I also cancelled my bank cards. Having money wired to me was going to require a leap of faith on my part, but I didn't have any choice. As I didn't have any ID, I had to have the money sent to me in another name. Damien gave me the name of a guy he knew and that was the name I told my aunt. I just had to wait for my aunt to send the money through Western Union and get back to me with the ten-digit, code transaction number.

Zona Norte is a small place, and I told some people on the street I'd been robbed. One guy told me where I could find the woman who robbed me, and I went back to tell Damien. When I got to his room, he said, "Is this yours?" He had my passport. He said he knew someone who was able to get it back for me. Well, that was some relief. If I could have picked one thing out of all that was stolen to get back, I would have chosen my passport.

Damien sorted out my accommodation until I was able to get some money wired to me. Of course, I knew I'd be paying for it later when I got some money again. You don't get anything for nothing in Zona Norte. I moved rooms to a cheaper one that consisted of a bed and no windows, just like a cell. It was a case of playing the waiting game. I couldn't do anything until tomorrow when, hopefully, I'd be able to get hold of some money and go about sorting out some replacement bank cards. I slept as best I could to pass the time, but the mess I was in played on my mind. What little memory I had of this woman played over and over in my head. It smelt somewhat of a set-up. What was she doing at my room door? I started to sober up, as well, which didn't help matters. I was fearful and paranoid enough as it was, without adding withdrawals to the mix.

I did what I could on the internet to improve my situation. I emailed my financial institutions back home. Getting replacement cards was going to be difficult: 1. because they wanted me to go into the branch to activate the cards, and 2. where was I going to have the cards sent?

Email: Friday 10th November

> I've had fun, Dad, especially in San Diego, but now, I'm in Mexico, and I was robbed. So now, I'm up shit creek. Don't have access to any of my money. I'm completely penniless and gonna have to do a runner from this internet café. Wish me luck.

As well as being helpful, Damien was being controlling. He wouldn't give my passport back until he'd gotten paid from the money he'd spent on me. He insisted I stay behind when he went with his friend to get my money. He was concerned that, if I went with them, the Western Union officials might think they were stealing money from me. It all made sense, but I felt trapped and powerless. I was at the mercy of whatever he wanted me to do. Damien was just protecting himself, I guess. That's what comes from spending a lot of time in Zona Norte; you don't trust anyone.

My aunt had already sent the money, so we had to go with using the other name. This is when I had to hope I could trust Damien. He could easily pick up the money and then come back, saying there'd been a problem, and he wasn't able to get the money. I never even saw this supposed guy whose name we were using. Having been robbed once, I was paranoid about being robbed again, and I wasn't sure if Damien had anything to do with me being robbed in the first place.

It was a nervous wait as I sat in Damien's room with his girl whilst he went to collect the money—and, hopefully, come back with it. His girlfriend didn't speak any English, and my Spanish was good for ordering things in a store, not having a conversation. The two of us sitting in the room together in silence made every passing second feel like an eternity. Damien finally came back ... and success. He had the money. It wasn't much, about $500 I think, but would tide me over until I could get some of my own money sent to me. Damien took his cut, naturally, and I was able to buy some beer.

Whilst we sat in the room, the hotel cleaner showed Damien some cards he'd found in one of the rooms. Damien got all excited. They were my bank cards and drivers licence. "You can get your money again."

"Nah, the cards are cancelled."

Well, I had my cards and ID back; my only dilemma now was staying afloat financially until I got replacement cards. My stress levels had dropped, for the time being, anyway. That night, I ran into Heather again. I told her I'd been robbed, and she lectured me about not listening to her about looking after my things. She told me I should move my things and move in with her. We went back to my room, and as I was debating about whether to move, I checked my money. I couldn't be certain that some wasn't missing. Damien was the only person who knew where I'd hidden it. WTF? Was he a thief with a conscience, or was I just imagining it? That made up my mind; I was checking-out. Heather went to Damien and got my passport back (I was glad I didn't have to do it and that it happened without a fuss), and then we were out of there. I was going to put as much distance as I could between me and this nightmare. So, I went and shared a room with Heather in the hotel … all away across the road.

Heather took me under her wing and organised a room for us. This hotel wasn't as much as a dive as the last one. I felt a lot safer here. Heather went out to play whilst I stayed in the room and slept over 12 hours. Man, what a rollercoaster ride the last five days had been. I ran into Damien a few times after that on the street, and everything was cool. Without his help, I would have really been in trouble. His efforts to help me compelled me to think he was one of the good guys of Zona Norte.

12th–20th November 2006

I woke in the afternoon, and Heather went and got us something to eat and brought it back to the room. With her Spanish being better than mine, she organised most things. Only problem was, she had less money than I did. Still, we were going to have some fun.

We went to the club, Playboy, on *Avenida Constitución*. The ground floor was a drinking bar with live music, but upstairs was more our style. It was only a small area with a bar at one end of the room with one or two couches, and a stage at the other end of the room surrounded with poles for girls, and seats for those watching. A bucket of ten beers cost $10; that would do for starters.

We were early; there weren't any dancers performing yet, but we were happy to wait. There was some Rammstein playing, and we rocked out on the stage whilst on our way to getting pissed. Heather was a great mover of her body. She pushed me down onto one of the lounges and gave me a lap dance. She was good at it, too. It got us both worked up for when the strippers came on to perform.

One stripper worked the stage, whilst there were other women dancing at each of the poles around the room. As the woman on stage finished her routine and went backstage, all the women moved round one spot to the next pole or onto the stage if they were the next in line. It was great; there was something to look at in every direction. It was possible to get American dollar bills at the bar to tip the women with. Heather and I had front row seats with our bucket beside us. Heather was cheering and whistling as much as any guy and kept calling the women over to give us lap dances.

"HEY CHICA."

We always made sure to tip them, and they made sure to give us a great show. I tell you, if ever there was a Kodak moment, it was then. The club, the price of beer, the women and music was enough to get a guy in a frenzy as it was, but sharing the experience with an erotic lesbian was ... well, stuff that one only dreams of. At that time, you could say, I was high on the peak of the TJ rollercoaster.

On Monday, I managed to score some more dinero, wired from my aunt. This time, it was my money I'd transferred to my aunt, and she had sent it through Western Union. This meant it was a much greater sum, and I'd be ok for a while. I felt some relief as I didn't have to stress about money for the time being. I decided it was worthy of a celebration and gave Heather and me a budget of $50 each for the night. That was enough for ten beers and two women off the street. But before we hit the town, we needed to do something about the wad of cash I had. I was paranoid about leaving it in the room, especially where Heather could get at it. So, she suggested we give it to reception to look after. The staff at this place were truly friendly and were happy to hold onto the money for us. All the notes were rolled up into an empty cigarette packet and wrapped in a piece of paper with a note letting all staff know that the money was to be given only to me. Sorted. Let's play.

We went to Playboy and got stuck into another bucket of beer. The women were putting on a great show, and Heather and I were really getting into it. After a few beers, Heather disappeared. I was pissed off for being left behind. I wanted to go out and play, as well, but there were still quite a few beers left in the bucket. It was going to take me a while to get through them, but I felt like I'd been dumped with them (Oh my God, what was wrong with me? I was upset about having a lot of beer whilst in a strip club? That doesn't make sense). I wanted to get out and hit the street, and I was also suspicious of Heather going back to the hotel to try to steal the money.

I asked the matradee if I could leave the beers and come back for them later, which she said was fine. I took one with me and raced back to the hotel. I asked the lady at reception whether Heather had been to collect the money, and she said no. I reminded her to give the money only to me. I went up to the room and walked in on Heather having sex with a woman who I thought was one of Heather's many hot friends. I asked if I could join in and Heather said, "If you hurry."

"OK. I'll just go to the toilet first."

I wanted to enjoy my first ever threesome without the sensation of needing to take a piss. As I was in the toilet, I was quite excited, telling myself what a great moment it would be, a dream come true. I'd had quite a bit to drink, and the piss took a bit too long. When I got out of the dunny, the girls had finished. "You fuckin' what? Finished?" I couldn't believe it. I tried to talk them into having round two, but they'd had enough.

Speaking of finishing, Bob Rock still hadn't finished mastering the CD.

Tuesday marked one week in Tijuana, and now that I had enough money to get by for a while, I figured it was time to escape the hellhole. My original plans had been to travel south along the Baja Peninsula. I had expected to be somewhere near Cabo San Lucas by now and thought it was about time I got going. Heather wanted to come along, and I said, "Fine."

I felt so high-and-mighty that we were leaving Tijuana. We caught a taxi from the street on Calle Coahuila, where everyone could see us leaving. I felt like we were the chosen ones; we had been clever enough to get our shit together and leave this nasty neighbourhood. For me, it was a middle-finger salute to the people of Zona Norte, always stopping me, pretending to be friendly, but, really, just wanting something from me. I was pleased to see all eyes in the street were on us as we got into the taxi. We hopped in, and we were away. We got as far as the next block. We had an argument with the driver, so we bailed and got another taxi. This time, we were away.

Even still, we didn't travel far; we went 40 minutes down the road to Rosarito Beach. We found quite a classy hotel near the beach and booked a room for two nights. We were quite excited about our swanky room and all its flash mod-cons. Compared to where we'd come from, this was luxury. Again, I left a cigarette packet full of money at reception.

We went for a wander down the main drag of town, browsing antique stores and stocking up on toiletries and beer. Just before dusk, we took a stroll along the beach. It was a long and tranquil beach, and Heather had fun taking a lot of photos. Shame the weather was so gloomy.

After a quiet night in Rosarito, Heather was bored and decided to return to Tijuana the next day. I stayed because the room was already paid for, and I weighed up my options and came to the conclusion I, too, would head back to

Tijuana. Being a larger city meant it would be easier to sort out replacement bank cards and easier to organise travel to Mexico City. I gave up on the idea of traveling the Baja Peninsula and was quite in favour of going back to TJ for one last hurrah.

Heather and I were back sharing a room in Zona Norte across from La Tropa. We settled back into the Zona Norte lifestyle: drinking, smoking crack, strip clubs, and prostitutes. A stone's throw from our hotel was *Avenida Constitución*, and a small alleyway ran off that, called *Callejon Coahuila*. Prostitution is legal in this area and is there for everyone to see. It was around here that the street hookers, known as *paraditas*, Spanish for the standing girls, could be found at any time of the day. It cost as little as $20 to acquire the services of one of the women, and it was up to the man to pay for the hotel room. When walking past, these girls would try to get the man's attention by chirping, "Tssst, tssst," or sometimes reaching out to grab the guy. Callejon *Coahuila* had many of the popular strip clubs and brothels. I went to the Hong Kong Bar a few times, but otherwise, as far as strip clubs went, Playboy and sometimes La Tropa were my clubs of choice.

Heather and I were often out partying together and became well-known around the place. I learnt from my mistake and didn't take any women back to my hotel room. I also made it a habit to leave my valuables at reception. When out partying, I paid for an el cheapo room in another hotel and took women back there, five or six a night, much to the amusement of the guy working at reception.

One night, after a bit of sport, if you know what I mean, I relaxed in my hotel room, drinking and watching TV. Heather walked in with a woman she'd met on the street. I recognised her face; I'd been with her a few nights earlier. Heather turned off the lights for some privacy, and they had sex in the bed next to me whilst I left them to it and drank my beer. This girl wasn't a prostitute as such. She didn't work at any brothel or occupy a certain street corner. She was homeless and sold her body when she could, just to get by. She had all her belongings in one bag. With nowhere else to go, when she and Heather finished, she hung around. I later learnt her name was Emma. She was Mexican, spoke no English at all; she had dark, short, spiky hair and a long slim body, similar to Posh Spice, except it was obvious from her face she'd lived a much harder life. Because of that, I could only guess her age. She could have been in her 20's, but she looked older. She was a bit loopy, as well, too many drugs, perhaps. The three of us stayed up all night drinking and smoking in the room. Heather was quite affectionate towards her. I can remember us leaving the hotel at dawn and going for a walk in the quiet deserted streets.

When we got back to the room, Emma pulled out a book and started drawing. Completely unprovoked, she got up and took off all her clothes and went back to her drawing as if it was too hot to be wearing anything. I started to give her a massage, and she was quite receptive to it. One thing led to another, and we spent the best part of the next two days in bed, drinking and shagging each other. Our sex sessions were stopped only to get more booze or to check my email. Getting money sent from my dad was turning out to be problematic (of course, it was; nothing happened smoothly or quickly). After transferring him money from my account, he claimed he hadn't received it. Struth. I tried again.

My money supplies had severely dwindled and I hadn't paid the hotel for the current night. They had my valuables, so they weren't too concerned, but still, I was facing the possibility of spending a night or two outdoors if I couldn't get my money soon. The weather at night had been comfortable. I usually walked around in shorts and a t-shirt, so sleeping rough didn't concern me; it was not having money for food or water that worried me. I'm sure I would have survived, but I just didn't fancy the prospect.

When I wasn't at the internet shop, I was in my room with Emma. We just hung out in bed doing our thing, and periodically, Heather came by. She dropped by one time and asked for money or if I planned on going out. I'd just got back from spending literally my last pesos on a six pack. I was quite happy where I was. Dejected, Heather left, and we didn't see her again that night.

Wednesday 22nd November 2006

I woke early and went by myself to the internet shop to see if there had been any development overnight regarding the money transfer. On the way there, one of the neighbourhood residents, a guy I'd spoken to briefly once or twice, stopped me on the street. He was asking something. I didn't know or care. I just wanted to go check out my email. He then asked if I wanted any drugs. I said no, and then kept going. One block later and two cops had me up against a car with arms and legs spread, going through my pockets. They saw me talking to the drug dealer and were asking questions about him. I didn't have anything incriminating on me, and they let me go.

I logged into my email. "Please, please, let the money be in there." There was a message from my dad. Would this be the news I was waiting for or another step backwards? Would I be back on my feet or was the TJ rollercoaster about to come completely off the rails? I opened the email ... and ...WE HAVE A WINNER!

That was good news, but only the first step in getting back on my feet. Picking up the money at the Western Union had always been a hit or miss affair. Not all of the Western

Union outlets were willing to do the transfer, and because of the language barrier, I could never understand why. I also needed to explain to the manager at the hotel that I knew I owed him money but just needed some time, and I'd have it to him by the afternoon. Hopefully, he'd be happy with that. How I was going to explain that in Spanish, I didn't know.

On top of that, when leaving the internet place, I realised my hotel key was missing from my pocket. The police had stolen it. How do I explain that to the manager? Heather usually helped me with such matters, but she was nowhere to be seen. Also, I felt really rough. The excessive alcohol abuse had caught up with me. My guts felt crook, and I was moving in slow motion.

Walking back to the hotel, I passed a Mexican guy I'd never seen before. He told me in perfect English I looked like Gene Simmons, of KISS fame, without make-up. At a stretch, you could say my hair looked the same, but really, this guy was just using any opener he could think of to get to talk to me. It worked. I knew he probably saw me as an opportunity to make some money and, had I had any, I may have kept walking, but with nothing to lose, materially or figuratively, I stopped to talk to him.

His name was Johnny; he was a middle-aged guy, who had spent a lot of time in the States, which explained why his English was so good. One usually assumed that anyone who had been in the States for a while and was now in the dog-eat-dog Zona Norte didn't leave the US by choice. It was likely they'd been deported for some reason.

Johnny came across as quite friendly, but that was no reason to trust him. He asked me a few questions, trying to gauge what he could get from me. Normally, I'd play it cool and not give anything away, but I thought I'd tell him my predicament and then he'd realise he was wasting his time with me.

However, my tale of woe had the opposite effect than I expected—and I'm glad it did. Johnny saw this as an opportunity to help me. He offered to be my translator and go with me to explain the situation to the hotel manager. He was also prepared to come and translate for me at Western Union. No doubt, he'd want some money at the end of it for his trouble, but I was happy to do that. I took him up on his offer.

The hotel where I was staying was small and family run. Most, if not all, of the guests were long-stay visitors. The staff had been friendly towards me during my stay, but I didn't expect what came next. Johnny told the manager-guy about the stolen key and my plans to get money. The manager looked at me and nodded his head in sympathy. He said he was willing to wait until later in the day for me to pay my bill and that, when I got back, he'd move me to another room; that way, the cops, or whoever, couldn't come and steal from my room. Wow, some genuine kindness and compassion. I didn't think those qualities existed in Zona Norte. I was very pleasantly surprised. I didn't think I'd done anything to warrant the manager's generosity; he was obviously one of the good guys. I grabbed the stuff I needed from my room, including two cans of beer, and headed off to Western Union with Johnny. Emma came along, too.

What a fuckin' mission that was. We went from place to place without any luck. In each one, we joined the mile-long queue, only to get to the front and be told they didn't do international transfers or they were experiencing a computer system failure. After about four or five places, we went to a large, big-name bank. Johnny said it was best if I went to the counter by myself, this time, so no one thought he was stealing from me. A cheerful woman served me, and everything went smoothly. We even shared a light-hearted moment about my name. I signed the papers, and after 2½ long days of organisation, I had the money. Happy-happy, joy-joy.

I gave Johnny some money for his assistance, and we went our separate ways. He'd been a godsend. Just when I needed help, it appeared, totally unexpectedly, in the form of Johnny. The guardian angel of 'stupid, naive, drug tourists' definitely looked after me on this one. My fortune was looking up. I had more than enough money to last until I met up with MJ in Cancún. I just had to not do anything stupid in the meantime. Yeah, good luck with that one.

Emma and I went back to the hotel. I was so pleased to be able to pay the manager and show him his trust hadn't been misplaced. He had a young woman, Anita, with him, this time, translating for him. She explained I needed to be careful in the neighbourhood, and if I needed any help, just to ask. We then set about changing rooms. Not that I had much worth stealing in my backpack anymore, but I thought a change of scene would complement my change in fortune. When we went up to the old room, we found Heather in there sleeping.

I didn't know how, where, who or what, but Heather was getting money from somewhere. Some days, she'd show up in new, fresh clothes or high as a kite. She had plenty of friends in Zona Norte to get money from, and she knew how to use her body. I'd seen her a couple of times give lap dances for money. One night, for a $100, she offered to let me fuck her. I could have had five women for that price, but after perving at her body for over a week, the desire to have sex with her was high. Unfortunately, with all the drink and drugs in my system, it was taking me an age to come, and Heather called an end to it before I'd finished, saying I must be gay if she can't make me come.

So, she had money but hadn't shared any of it with me or contributed to any of the activities we got up to. Right or wrong, I cut her loose. I wasn't going to have her staying in the new room. She didn't take the news too well. She was yelling at me, reminding me how much she helped me. Realising that I wasn't going to change my mind, she gave me a big push in the back. Then, unexpectedly, Anita stepped in and told Heather off. Geez, it was never a dull moment. Heather then squared up to Anita, and they had a very heated exchange of words that looked like it was going to get physical there for a second. It didn't, but Heather was told to leave, and then she was gone. It did feel like a fresh start in the new room as Emma and I moved the furniture around to suit ourselves.

22nd–28th November 2006

Over the next few days and nights, I spent the majority of my time relaxing in the hotel room. I sat in bed drinking beer whilst watching TV. When I wasn't doing that, I was having sex with Emma and/or smoking drugs with her. What need was there to leave the room? Emma was happy to have a roof over her head. She was quite the fruitcake. She was on a completely different wavelength to most people. She used to scream with laughter one minute, at God knows what, and then, sometimes, she wouldn't say a word. It was really interesting sharing a room with someone, living in each other's pockets, yet not sharing the same language. I could communicate basic things to her, but understanding what she was talking about was another matter. Because we couldn't communicate in any depth, there were times when both of us just went about our business in the room as if the other person wasn't there. Unlike Heather, Emma wasn't all take; she did little things for me, such as go to the shop to get me beer or buy me food with her own money. She came in the room, one day, with a bag full of used clothes. I don't know where they came from, but she pulled them out and threw me the items she thought would suit me. I was able to bolster my clothing supplies again after having had a lot of them stolen. Some nights, she'd pack up all her things and say goodbye, only to return late at night, asking to stay again.

Although we got along well, I didn't trust Emma. I never left her alone in the room with my valuables. I didn't have any reason not to trust her, other than we were in Zona Norte. I had a shoulder bag, where I kept my passport and cigarette packet full of money, which I left at reception whenever I went out. The staff continued to be super helpful.

I still poked my nose in at Playboy some nights. I went there with Emma, and we bumped into Heather; she was flying on something. She started to give me grief, and I bought her a beer to shut her up. Emma had gone back to the hotel, so I wanted to get back there to make sure she wasn't stealing anything. On the way, I got into a wee bit of trouble.

Walking back to the hotel, two cops stopped me and discovered I had a beer in my pocket. They wanted to do me for drinking in public. After all the bullshit I'd had to deal with recently, I was in no mood for their crap and started arguing with them. One of them was an American and asked if I had anything else "on my person." I've never been a fan of that expression, and I snapped, "What the fuck are you talking about? Speak fuckin' English." He didn't take to that too kindly and threatened to take me to jail. I wanted to make his life difficult and was tempted to take him up on his offer, knowing what a pain in the arse it would be for him to process me.

Actually, what the fuck did I know? Apparently, Tijuana Police are well-known for extorting bribes from tourists with threats of going to jail. I read somewhere they have to take you before a judge before they can throw you in jail, so their threats were just bluffs. But I didn't know any of that. For all I knew, they could have locked me away for days, and I'd miss my rendezvous with MJ. It wasn't uncommon to see guys walking around without shoelaces because, so I believed, they'd been confiscated whilst spending a night in the cells. Because I wanted to check on Emma and because I didn't want to leave MJ stranded, I apologised to Mr Policeman. He said, if I give him $20, all would be forgotten. I gave him the money and then got back to the hotel room to find Emma wasn't up to anything.

The 28th was drawing ever closer. I toyed with the idea of catching a bus to Mexico City, but I was warned that was a 30+ hour journey. So, I settled on the idea of flying to Mexico City on the 27th, in time for my flight that I had already booked for the 28th to Cancún.

On the night of the 26th, Emma had moved out of the hotel room. I was at a bar around the corner on *Avenida Revolución*. A male friend of Heather's, whom I used to run into a lot, was at the bar. He hassled me to buy him a drink but I didn't. Then I was at the juke box, and the machine swallowed my coin without giving me any credits. A young punk nearby showed me how to get my coin back. I knew how to get the coin back, but this guy acted like he'd saved my life. He insisted I let him choose a song. I told him no, and he suddenly wanted to get all physical with me. That was it. I'd had enough. I stormed back to my hotel and told reception to call me a cab. I packed up all my shit, including some high-heel boots Emma had left behind, and I went to the airport.

I was angry—angry at all the bullshit. I was sick of all the leeches wanting money from me. I didn't like what Zona Norte was turning me into, either. To get by, I adopted the same uncaring, greedy attitude that pissed me off about Zona Norte. I'd never left a town before full of despise and hatred for the place. As a joke, I had considered buying a t-shirt that read: I ♥ TJ, but I never found them on sale anywhere. I often wonder if Emma or Heather went back to the hotel looking for me, only to be shocked with the news I'd gone.

I managed to escape the TJ rollercoaster after 19 days. I learnt my lesson. I didn't get mixed up in any of that kind of shit for the rest of the trip, with the exception, maybe, of Palenque. I spent the night at Tijuana airport and managed to get a flight to Mexico City the next day. I then spent the night in Mexico City airport and caught my flight to Cancún the next day as planned.

This next leg of my six-month fiesta was the start of a new chapter. It required a shift in thinking and planning. MJ had never been out of Australia, so I felt a certain responsibility for her care and wellbeing. There'd be no more putting myself in dangerous situations, like I had in Tijuana. MJ was only going to be with me for six weeks, two in Mexico and four in Cuba. That meant managing our time and planning our trip in advance, which was the opposite of how I usually travelled. But I must say, I was looking forward to the different approach and excited to be travelling with my friend. I was even more excited we'd be travelling together at one of my favourite locations—the Mayan Riviera. Sun, surf, and sangria—here we come.

MJ—Mexican Journey
28th November—12th December 2006

My flight arrived in Cancún mid-afternoon, a few hours before MJ was due to arrive. MJ was flying in from Australia via a brief stop in Los Angeles. When her plane had landed, I waited anxiously, hoping she'd managed to negotiate her way around LAX and catch her connecting flight. Of course,

MJ was just as anxious. She wondered what she would do if I wasn't there to meet her. She was relieved, to say the least, to see me when she came out of the airport. As for me, after all the shit in TJ, I don't think I've ever been so over the moon to see a familiar face.

We headed straight to Puerto Juárez and caught the ferry to Isla Mujeres. Being MJ's first time on foreign soil, I was excited for her. I kept asking her questions about her flight and time at LAX. We got to the island and made our way to the hostel, where I'd booked a room online. The hostel had no record of our booking, nor a room for us. They weren't even aware of the website I'd made the booking through. Well, that was a great start. Here I was, Mr Seasoned Traveller, supposed to be taking care of things and what should happen? My planning fell at the first hurdle.

It was getting on in the evening; we'd just arrived on the island, and we didn't have a room booked for the night. It wasn't the end of the world. I'd been in trickier situations than that, only three weeks earlier, for example. The hostel management, to their credit, found us a room in a hotel only a stone's throw away. Problem solved ... now, time for a margarita.

Miss J Love was certainly in love with Isla Mujeres. We had a good-sized room, not poky, with an ensuite and, the best bit, a balcony overlooking the street below. MJ came armed with her camera and took some great shots from the balcony. The beautiful white sand, the palm trees, and warm water of the beach had us both excited.

The island proved to be the perfect first destination for us, being that it's so relaxed and slow-paced. It allowed MJ to settle into holiday mode and me to let go of the anger that had built up in Tijuana. We spent a few days on the island, taking part in various activities, including the most strenuous of activities—lying on the beach. After all, we were in the Caribbean. We spent a day on a snorkelling tour with a very filling barbeque lunch. There were quite a lot of fish to look at and some coral. The real trick when snorkelling was staying on course; the current was surprisingly strong.

The island is about 7km long and 650metres wide, making it easy to do a lap of the island and take in all the sights. Both of us being Formula 1 fans, we hired the fastest mode of transport available to hoon around the island. Well, not quite. We hired a golf buggy and had a good time exploring the areas further south on the island, such as the small neighbourhoods, where the locals live, the Sculpture Garden and lighthouse at the South Point, which was a popular spot for the iguanas to hang out, too.

Our evenings were spent sampling the many restaurants and bars along the lively tourist strip and, sometimes, indulge in a bit of shopping at the jewellery and clothing stores. Prices at the shops were negotiable, and MJ sure tested the shopkeepers' patience, spending ten or fifteen minutes deciding whether to buy something at a reduced price, only to decline the offer. She did buy a few things, though.

There were a few stalls along the main drag promoting 'time share' accommodation, with agents outside the shopfront approaching passers-by to drum up interest. And so, began a two-week barrage of being accosted wherever we went to join these fuckin' time shares. Always being asked, "Are you two a couple?" As soon as we heard that question, we knew where the conversation was headed. We usually stopped and had a chat with the agents, anyway, and got to know a few of them quite well, as we usually saw them at the same place every day. As part of the agents' approach, they try to guess where you're from. Coming in at number one, as the most guessed nationality of where I was from, was ... Italian. It wasn't just the time share agents; the majority of people, based on my appearance, thought I was Italian. I could certainly see the resemblance, particularly when I hadn't shaved and my hair was wet. My hair was long, dark, and straight when it was wet as opposed to medium, brown, and curly when dry.

MJ kindly brought my replacement bank cards with her from Canberra. She'd been a great help. I would have struggled to find a place to have them sent, otherwise. So, now I had them, they still needed to be activated. I spent quite a bit of time in and out of the internet shops, sending emails and faxes to my banks to authorise the activation of the cards. I jumped through all the hoops and then it was just a matter of waiting for them to get back to me and give the go ahead.

2nd December 2006

You might remember; last time I was on the island, I had an accident where I fell out of bed and suffered a lot of bruising, including a nice black eye. Well, once again, I found myself at the island's medical centre requiring treatment for a bed/sleep related injury—or so I thought.

I went to bed one night feeling fine but woke the next morning with an extremely sore big toe. I thought I must have bumped it against the bed frame in my sleep. As the day wore on, the pain got worse and spread to the ball joint of the foot. It really fuckin' hurt, and I could hardly walk. MJ was down at the beach whilst I'd been attending to some emails. I hobbled down the street, and one of the shopkeepers asked if I was OK. His name was Ulysses; MJ and I had spoken to him a few times. I told him my foot was killing me. He insisted on driving me to the medical centre in his golf buggy. I didn't argue. It was so kind of him. He closed his shop and stayed with me at the centre until I was seen by a doctor. Ulysses was a funny guy. We bonded over our mutual fanaticism of Star Wars.

I saw the doctor and tried my best to explain in Spanish what the problem was. He gave me a shot in the bum for the pain and a prescription for pain killers. When I left the centre, I couldn't feel any pain and could have easily competed in a hop, skip, and jump competition. The prescription proved to be invaluable, as it seemed to be unlimited. I had it filled many times during the two weeks in Mexico whenever the pain flared up again. It was about two years later that I realised the injury wasn't as a result from a knock to the toe in my sleep but, in fact, gout.

Our next location was Playa Del Carmen. Playa is much bigger, touristy, and faster paced than Isla Mujeres. We stayed in quite a comfortable hotel, off Fifth Avenue, the main tourist thoroughfare. This was our base camp for the next few days as we ventured out on many day trips. We went on a tour to Chichén Itzá, the largest of the Mayan archaeological sites in the Yucatan. The focal point of the site is *El Castillo* (The Castle), a 24-metre-high pyramid with a six-metre-high, two-storey temple on top. I remembered last time, in 2003, climbing the pyramid steps to the top and having to come back down, extremely carefully, slowly, one step at a time, sitting down; the steps were that steep. This time around, climbing the pyramid wasn't allowed. Our tour guide said there had been a death from someone falling down the steps.

Something else we did that I didn't do last time was go to the island of Cozumel. It lies about 20km off-shore from Playa Del Carmen and was made famous for its scuba diving through the documentaries of Jacques Cousteau. The island is quite sizable, 48km long and 16km wide, and is a popular destination for cruise ships touring the Caribbean. The cruise ships were huge, skyscrapers on water. There was at least half a dozen docked at the piers, and at night, when they were lit up, they looked awesome.

Our motivation for going was to do some snorkelling. We booked places on an organised tour that served beer in-between snorkelling sessions. Unfortunately, the weather was really rough when we arrived, and the tour had to be cancelled due to safety. Ah well, that gave us an opportunity to check out the shopping and dining available in the main town, San Miguel.

In the evening, we caught the ferry back to the mainland. The customary passenger ferry taken by most people was a large, enclosed, super jet, catamaran that was able to do the crossing in about 45 minutes. We took the lesser known, slower, and cheaper ferry, which was a small, two-level boat, with the seats open to the elements. The weather was still rough, at this point, and it was a wild ride. The boat got tossed from side to side, and it was a real challenge to walk straight on the deck. At no point did it look like the boat would tip, but it certainly lent a long way to the side a few times. It was good to get back on solid ground.

On the 7th, my bank had finally come to the party and activated all my cards, exactly one calendar month from when I had the old ones cancelled.

In Tulum, we ended up staying at the hostel, El Crucero, a place I knew from last time, situated just out of town near the Mayan ruins. It wasn't anything flash but had a good bar/restaurant, and the staff were very friendly. One of the long-term residents ran a diving business and took us snorkelling through some caves, which was pretty awesome. We went and checked out the ruins—they were still there—and went for a walk along the beach as it was starting to get dark. Unfortunately, the weather wasn't on our side whilst we were there, and it rained a lot of the time. The beach was much the same as I remembered it from '03, except a few of the resorts had expanded.

One evening, we went into Tulum Town to visit *la feria* (the fair). There were the customary bright lights, market stalls, food stands, and fun rides. I bought a cheap wallet to replace the one I had stolen in Tijuana, except I set it up as a decoy should I ever get mugged. I put my cancelled credit cards in there and one or two dollars, and it was good to go. Anyone who wanted to steal my wallet was welcome to it. While I had the decoy wallet, I continued to use the cigarette packet to store my cash, and I did so up until I arrived back in Australia.

At la feria, I saw a brutal fight break out between two males, a real cock fight, each one trying to show who ruled the roost. I mean it; it was a real cock fight. One thing I can cross off the list of having done, and something I don't need to do again, is see two cocks going at it. There was an enclosed area at the fair that cost extra to enter, where one could witness the blood sport of two roosters fighting. It was much like a boxing match; it had a ring and the crowd gathered around, placing bets and cheering. There was one other white guy there, and we were the only two gringos at the fight. MJ chose not to see the fight.

The fighting was a lot like a boxing match. The two roosters met in the middle of the cockpit with their trainers. Both cocks were circumcised—comb and wattle cut off in order to meet show standards—and stood erect in readiness for the thrusting that was to come. The trainers aroused the cocks with their hands to get them in the mood; they didn't want the roosters going into the fight half-cocked. A bell rang to indicate the beginning of the fight, and then the two cocks went at each other without any protection. I expected the encounter to be fast and furious but any hope of a quickie wasn't forthcoming, as the cocks eyed each other. One of the roosters acted altogether vain and cocky, teasing the other cock as if to say, "Come and have a go if you think you're hard enough."

The cocks started kicking each other and rubbing each other up the wrong way. Their wings were flapping wildly and looked rather vicious. The fight got more intense as it went on as the cocks got angrier and the blood rushed to their heads. The fight went on for ages. One of the roosters finally started to dominate and to beat the red feathered cock. The fight was coming to a climax. The losing cock became flaccid, lost all drive, and struggled to get it up. It drooped over and hit the ground. There was no premature emancipation; the fight wasn't stopped, despite there being a clear winner. The fight eventually finished with the winning rooster proving he was no soft cock. As for the loser, I don't know if he was dead, but he was certainly impotent.

12th–31st December 2006

Viva la Revolución.

Mexicana Airlines kindly gave us a lift to Havana. We landed at José Martí International Airport to a warm, cloudy day. MJ and I were both excited and anxious about what lay ahead. I'd read as much information as I could about Cuba on the Lonely Planet forum and was eager to arrive and see things for myself. Other than a day spent in China, I'd never been to a Communist country, and I had no idea what to expect. It was good neither of us had been there before. It meant we were experiencing everything for the first time together; unlike in Mexico, where I had to be careful not to always talk about my visit three years before.

As Australians, we needed a visa to enter the country. I have a vague memory of passing through immigration at the airport and being on my best behaviour, minding my p's and q's. Fortunately, once we walked outside the airport, we had directions on what to do and where to go. The cheapest and most culturally enriching form of accommodation in Cuba is the *Casa Particular*. A casa particular is a bed and breakfast style lodging in a private home. Citizens are allowed to rent out rooms to tourists, provided they follow certain regulations and pay the required tax. As well as offering a room, meals were available for a few additional pesos. It was a great opportunity for us to meet with locals, learn about life in Cuba, and for us to practise speaking Spanish. The casa owners could also give us the inside info on where to go and what to avoid. A room, on average, was about $25 - $30, so it was handy we were travelling together to half the cost.

We'd booked a room online with the welcoming couple of Nelson and Aurora. They provided us with directions of the type of taxi to catch, how much to expect to pay for the ride, and their address. They had a large apartment in the vibrant neighbourhood, Vedado, close to the city's heart, Old Havana. We arrived with no problems and met our new hosts. Nelson spoke English and over a *Cuba Libre* (rum and coke) gave us the low-down on everything he thought we needed to know. The information was extremely helpful, and we felt confident we'd survive. He helped us to devise an itinerary for the next four weeks that was time-effective with as little time spent travelling long distances as possible. The best part was, Nelson had a network of friends around the country, all with casa particular that he could organise for us in advance. We didn't have to worry about organising a thing, and someone would be there to meet us when we arrived in each town.

We weren't the only guests staying with Nelson that night. Two young English siblings, Vicky and Eddie, had arrived that day, too. After a long day, they decided to call it a night and retired to their room. Minutes later, they came back out. They had the wrong luggage. They'd taken someone else's luggage from the airport carousel by mistake. It was difficult not to laugh.

Our room was small and comfortable with a double bed, ensuite, and an air-conditioning unit. We woke after a good night's sleep and sat down at the dining table for a filling breakfast. Next on the agenda was to do some sight-seeing around Havana. Just one small problem; we'd accidently locked ourselves out of our room. We shut the door, not realising it would lock, and unfortunately, the key was still in the room, along with all the things we needed for the day. There was no spare key, either. Nelson, forever the problem solver, was on the case. He lent us money and a camera and sent us out to do the tourist thing whilst he organised a locksmith. Luckily, we'd already showered and changed out of our pyjamas.

We headed straight for Old Havana and spent the day absorbed by its endearing charms at every turn. The old 50's American Chevys weren't just a myth featured in tourist brochures; they were everywhere and looked awesome. Many of them are taxis, so we went for a ride in one when we returned to Vedado. The stunning architecture of the city's buildings ranged from neo-classical, baroque, and Spanish colonial to rundown and dilapidated. There were some cool little pockets of the city with narrow streets and overhanging balconies from the buildings either side.

There were plenty of interesting landmarks, including, *El Capitolio*, home to the Cuban Academy of Sciences, based on the design and name of the United States Capitol in Washington, D.C. There was plenty of graffiti and signs around, advocating Castro and the revolution, and loads of images of Che Guevara. MJ snapped over 140 photos on our first day.

The main hang out for locals and visitors, especially during sunset and at night, was the *Malecón*, a sea wall that ran along the Havana coastline. We had a bit of chit chat with some of the locals, and they all seemed genuinely cheerful and friendly. The only time we ever encountered unpleasant Cubans was when we pushed in line at the bank. I don't know why; don't they know who we are?

Cuba has two currencies, the Convertible Peso (CUP) and the Cuban Peso (CUC). The Convertible Peso was created in the late 90's to replace the extensive use of American dollars by tourists. When we were there, it was about 24 Cuban pesos to the Convertible. The cheap bank notes and coins depicting Che Guevara made great souvenirs, and kids often sold them to tourists for a higher value than the face value.

The two currencies are available to locals and tourists to use, but Havana is a surprisingly expensive city, and most purchases and costs are in Convertible pesos. The one awesome exception was ice cream and pizza. With Cuban pesos, you could get ice cream for only 1 peso ($0.04) from small street booths scattered around the city. You could also get a filling *bocadito* (small ham sandwiches) or a small pizza for 7-10 pesos ($0.40).

The main national beer was Bucanero, which I quite liked. A can cost 1 Convertible ($1.05), whilst there was a less common beer found in some places, called Cristal, which tasted weak and awful. Another lesser known beer, Mayabe, which tasted OK, usually sold at local bars, cost only 18 Cuban pesos ($0.67). From what I gathered, drinking in public was tolerated. I certainly didn't get in trouble for it, anyway.

We did alright getting money. There were ATMs at banks and change houses, CADECA (*Casa de cambio*), in most places. We were always wary, though, when leaving these places with large amounts of money on us. We usually went straight back to our house and left our money there, where it was safe. We never had any trouble.

We stayed in Havana for three nights and then headed east to explore the rest of the country. There's two different ways a visitor can experience Cuba. One is to stay at one of many luxury resorts that line the coastline and experience a relaxing Caribbean beach holiday, and two is to travel independently visiting the characterful colonial towns, getting a taste of what life is like for the locals. Partly due to cost, but mainly due to our taste for some Cuban culture, we were taking the independent route. The mode of transport we chose to take was the national coach service, Viazul. It was a pretty good, comfortable service that went to all the major places. Everywhere we were going, anyway. A lot of the coaches sold beer, but the one downside was at night, when the air con was ridiculously cold, and we all froze to death.

First stop was the small town of Cienfuegos, on the southern coast, about 250km from Havana. Nelson had helped to organise our accommodation in advance, and it was quite funny to arrive at the bus station to a crowd of people and see a tall guy in the middle of the pack, holding up a sign with our names on it.

We stayed with a nice, elderly woman. Apparently, Nelson's usual contact didn't have any vacancies, due to a party of Australians staying there. We were invited to join them for dinner, but we didn't want to mix with other Australians. We heard they had a similar itinerary to us, but we managed to avoid them the whole four weeks.

Our house overlooked the bay and had a wonderful veranda, surrounded by a tidy garden, where we sat, taking in the scenery and listening to music. The town's history included French immigrants, which was noticeable in the town's architecture, with buildings displaying the same vibrant colour schemes I've seen in French cities and Louisiana in the States, too. The fact that the town square contained the *Arco de Triunfo* also added to the Frenchness.

Eating at the Casa Particular was optional, and we always chose to have breakfast and, sometimes, dinner there, but generally, we ate out. The problem with that was all the restaurants are owned by the government, and the food was consistently bland. Finding restaurants wasn't always an easy proposition, either. Often, their shopfront showed no indication on the outside of being a restaurant. Generally, we found small snack places that were cheap. One option for eating out was eating in. One form of restaurant in Cuba are the *paladares*—non-government owned restaurants in private homes. We tried one in Cienfuegos, and although the experience was pleasant enough—we had chicken and veg—the price and the atmosphere wasn't so good. We only tried that one paladare.

We ran into the English siblings, Vicky and Eddie, down by the bay. They still hadn't been reunited with their luggage. Some local lads who befriended us invited the four of us to a restaurant/bar, where I got particularly drunk. My memory of the evening is somewhat hazy; MJ tells me I had a puff on a cigar that one of the lads was smoking, except apparently, I couldn't do it properly. That was the only time I attempted to smoke a 'Cuban' during the whole trip.

From Cienfuegos, we travelled an hour down the road to the beautiful Trinidad. It was like going back in time 500 years, as the town's Spanish colonial architecture is still very well-preserved. Although it's only the size of a few square blocks, Trinidad is a popular destination amongst visitors for its cobblestone streets, pastel coloured houses, and awesome palaces and plazas. All of that was cool, but being right on the coast and having the Caribbean Sea on its doorstop was what got us excited.

At the bus station, we were able to recognise our host by the card with our names on it. We stayed with a sweet woman and her mother in a cosy house. The mother took quite a liking to me. Despite the language barrier, we had some good conversations whilst relaxing in the house's courtyard. We chose to have dinner at the house on the first night, and it was very tasty ... and large. This was becoming a recurring pattern. Any sort of formal evening meal we had, the servings were just way too much. We felt like ungrateful Westerners when our hostess came to take our plates, still with plenty of food left on them. Because of the expensiveness and wastage, we tried to steer away from having dinner at our Casa's.

Naturally, we spent a day down at the beach. The weather was lovely, and the water was so inviting. We jumped in, splashing about, excited to be swimming in the Caribbean. I know that the Mayan Riviera is the Caribbean, too, but that's on the Caribbean rim connected to mainland. This was an island in the middle of the Caribbean, so it felt more Caribbean. Whilst enjoying the sunset over the water, we sat at the beach bar, enjoying some cocktails. Life was good.

Trinidad was our first taste of live music. At one of the bars in town, we sat watching in awe as the locals moved their hips to the beat. The music was always lively in Cuba, and one usually didn't have to look too far to find some live music being played somewhere. The popular music amongst the kids was reggaetón, labelled Latin urban music; it's a mix of calypso and reggae with an electronic hip-hop character to it. I couldn't fuckin' stand it. If there's two genres of music I don't like, it's reggae and hip-hop. How thoughtful of reggaetón to consolidate my musical dislikes into one manageable genre. Whilst the live music was your more traditional, Latin, salsa music, any other music that emanated from stereos or juke boxes was reggaetón. And that was the case in Tijuana and the Yucatan and now in Cuba, and was the case for the rest of my travels over the next months, not to mention the cheesy, fuckin', mariachi music in Palenque.

To escape it, I often hijacked juke boxes in bars and put loads of credits in, choosing any decent music available, just for some sanity.

We stopped in central Cuba in the city of Camagüey for two or three nights. No name placard this time, our contact at the bus station must have been given a good matching description of us, because he picked us out of the crowd and called us by name. I was called Africa a lot, as my surname comes first in my passport and was sometimes mistaken as my Christian name. Our contact, Rudolpho, was the taxi driver who would be taking us to our host's house. The taxi, on this occasion, was a bicytaxi: a bicycle with a seat for two on the back behind the driver, much like a *tuk tuk,* except pedal power.

On the ride into town, Rudolpho was giving us a running commentary on the different landmarks we passed. Of course, we only understood about a quarter of what he was saying, but MJ feigned curiosity and said in an exaggerated intrigued voice, "*Caramba,*" which means, wow. It was so unexpected and sounded so funny that Rudolpho lost it. He stopped what he was saying and laughed uncontrollably, bowing his head to hide his amusement. Just thinking about it now cracks me up. MJ came out with some great lines from time to time, and that was one of the best. Not much to report about Camagüey, other than our host family being very friendly.

We headed deep into the south of Cuba to a place called Bayamo. We arrived in the evening and, once again, were transported to our house by bicytaxi. As we cruised through the streets, I sang a heartfelt rendition of '*Ti Amo*', the Laura Branigan version, substituting the words Ti Amo for Bayamo.

Our hosts, on this occasion, were an attractive couple that had a teenage daughter and the grandmother lived with them, as well. Like a scene from Cinderella, I was finally able to find a perfect fit for the high heel boots I'd been carrying around since Tijuana. For the daughter, that is, not the man of the house, in case you were wondering. We had a pokey little room with our own bathroom, and there was a picture of F1 driver, Juan Pablo Montoya, on the fridge, which didn't escape our attention.

Our main goal whilst in Bayamo was to get out of Bayamo and visit the *Sierra Maestra* mountain range that runs westward across the southeast province of Granma. Our hosts kindly made us packed lunches and organised an outing to the National Park, home to Cuba's largest mountain range.

A particularly common make of car in Cuba is the Russian Lada. They exist everywhere from privately owned vehicles to taxis. Our driver for the day to the Sierra Maestra, a young Latin, raver guy, picked us up in his own hotted up, pimped out, Lada. It was a tough looking metallic green with various bells and whistles adorning the exterior. Inside was like a nightclub, with black light fluorescent tubes, a serious sound system, and a DVD player. It felt like such a contradiction to the day's theme of 'experiencing nature'. It was a stimulating novelty, nonetheless.

Our driver took us to a small settlement at the foot of the mountains, where we met our guide, who would be leading us through the forest trails. The Sierra Maestra has a long history of rebellion and guerrilla warfare, from the wars of the late 19th Century to the Cuban Revolution of the 1950's. Fidel Castro and a band of rebels, including Che Guevara, hid out in the Sierra Maestra, building an encampment in the lush, dense greenery as a base to mount their assault on the government of the time. Many of the buildings and structures of the camp are still in place and in good condition.

Our guide took us deep into the forest and showed us the

site that is a symbolic point of reference for the Revolution. The structures were less primitive than I'd expected, with proper thatched roof huts and living quarters, as well as designated huts for weapons and medical operations. They were surrounded by trees and easily hidden from planes flying overhead. The walk there was rugged but not too strenuous. The real challenge was avoiding the puddles of mud from recent rainfalls. As well as the camp, there were some great views and plenty of bird life. I really enjoyed it. It was an interesting firsthand look at the rebel base and an invigorating walk through the forest.

After our hike, our guide took us to one of the houses at the small settlement, where we had a few refreshments before our driver returned to take us back to Bayamo. When we got back into town, we did have plans to meet someone we'd met on the tour at a certain bar, but we couldn't find it and then we became very sick. We were in a park, and both of us required the use of the public toilets there. I don't know about MJ, but the release of my stomach's contents was a concern for me at both ends. If I didn't think I was going to throw up before I entered the toilets, I certainly did when I got in there. Oh, man, the place was disgusting. I'm sure I don't need to describe it; I'm sure we've all got our own public toilet horror stories. We were a good half hour walk from our casa, and once we felt our stomachs were up to the task, we set out on what was the most important trek we were to make that day. We kept our fingers crossed we wouldn't need a toilet in the meantime. Safely back at the house and with access to a clean toilet, we could at least rest a bit easier. And rest, we did. Neither of us felt good, so we tried to sleep it off. We didn't resurface out of our room until over 18 hours later. We felt tired, groggy, and dazed, with no concept of time, as our room didn't have any windows. It was 2pm in the afternoon ... Christmas Day.

For a long time, Christmas wasn't celebrated under Castro's regime, but in the last decade or so, Christmas was reintroduced, but not everyone observes it. Our host family didn't have any celebrations, which suited us fine. We were quite happy to have a quiet Christmas, without all the usual commercialism that comes with it.

We ventured outside to get some fresh air. We put our sickness down to the refreshments we had at the bottom of the mountain in the small settlement at the Sierra Maestra. We had some orange juice or something, and we're sure that set us off. I don't believe we fully got over it until we left Cuba; it was always lingering in the background, often diminishing our appetite. My guts weren't coping too well from all the white rum I was drinking, either. Before coming to Cuba, our biggest concern was Dengue fever. There had been reports of a breakout, but from the moment we arrived until we left, there was never any mention or sign of it.

When we were at the station, waiting for our bus to leave Bayamo, I needed to use the toilet and went to use the station's facilities, which are always a disaster area. Unfortunately, my visit was going to involve sitting down. There´s no toilet paper in the toilets in Cuba; you have to ask the attendant at the door for some. So, I asked the attendant if I could have some paper.

He said, "Newspaper or toilet paper?"
"Toilet paper."
"Sorry, I only have newspaper."
That was so typical of Cuba; all you could do was laugh.

Our next destination was Santiago de Cuba, Cuba's second largest city located in the far southeast of the island. For us, Santiago was just an overnight stop on our way to Baracoa. We had set aside more time in the city on our way back through. It was rather late when we arrived at the bus station, and there was a large crowd of people there to meet the passengers. Casa owners often go to the bus station to try to find guests for their house, and on this occasion, there were a lot. About thirty or forty people.

We didn't need to worry, because we had already organised a room, so we casually made our way out of the station. We looked for our contact, but there was no one with a sign or anyone approaching us telling us they were friends of Nelson. In the meantime, the large group of Casa owners had descended upon us. They were like a media scrum, all shouting and grabbing at us, trying to get our attention. It was like being besieged in a mosh pit, and they were all shouting in Spanish, and it was really intense.

It didn't look like our contact was going to show, so we were compelled to choose one of the mob, but which one? Some of the crowd had pictures of their rooms, but it wasn't easy to browse through them all, not whilst being bombarded from all sides. It was rather stressful. I didn't go on holiday to deal with that shit. MJ lightened the mood by shouting back at them.

"Look, I'm not going to sign any autographs unless you all get in an orderly line."

Classic. And that's what it was like. It was like being rock stars mobbed by crazy fans. We chose to go with a sweet, young woman, the selling point being she lived close by. She lived with her husband in a small house with basic furnishings. We felt happy that our money was going to such nice people who really needed it. My first suggestion with what to do with the money would be to buy a new mattress. The double bed MJ and I shared must be one of the most uncomfortable mattresses I've ever had the displeasure to lie on. There were springs poking me, no matter what position I lay in. Despite the mattress, our stay was delightful; the hostess was lovely and gave us a salsa lesson. She cooked us breakfast and offered to organise our accommodation in

Baracoa. We thanked her but politely explained we already had a place sorted.

We arrived at Baracoa station to find we were two very popular individuals. There wasn't one person, but two, holding a sign with our names. Our friend in Santiago had gone ahead and organised a room with one of her friends, despite us declining her offer. It was going to make for an awkward moment. We needed to find the correct contact and reject the other one at the same time. I've always wondered if the two people waiting were aware they both had the same names on their placards. Anyway, we walked up to the correct person straight off; I didn't even look at the other person, and we were then whisked away in our awaiting bicytaxis.

It was about lunch time when we arrived and a clear, sunny day. We were in good spirits as we'd had an awesome bus trip from Santiago. We travelled through the mountains, surrounded by lush, tropical vegetation, and stunning views out along the ranges. I bought a few beers off the driver, too, which helped with the enjoyment factor.

I'd have to say, Baracoa was probably the highlight of the trip for me. It's a really isolated town, located on the coast near the eastern tip of the island in Guantánamo Province, surrounded by tropical rainforest with a malecón and beaches, and in the distance amongst the ranges, a table-topped mountain, called *El Yunque* (the anvil).

Nelson's contact in Baracoa was a woman by the name of Ikira. She picked us up from the station with a bicytaxi each and took us to our home for the next three nights—a luxurious, beautiful room on a second-floor terrace situated in Baracoa Heights (I made that name up), with great views of the forest and the sea. It was heaven. Our residence wouldn't have been out of place at a Fiji resort. Our hosts were Marzo and his adult son, Nine, who looked after us exceedingly well. We spent an evening drinking with Nine, who taught us some very bad-mannered words.

Our time in Baracoa provided us with some calm, peaceful walks, exploring all the little hideaways of the tiny village. There was a lively street concert whilst we were there with some great music and dancing. Being tourists and with me always drinking, we attracted a lot of attention from some of the local lads. They were all good guys, and we became friends with two, in particular. But in the evenings, I had a queue of locals a mile long wanting me to buy them a bottle of rum. I bought a few bottles but grew a bit tired of all the hounding, so MJ and I removed ourselves from the main square and drank in peace by the sea wall.

One of our young friends, Pico, offered to take us on a hike through the forest to a waterfall site. We accepted and met him the next day, excited but somewhat unsure of what to expect. We caught a taxi for a few miles and then walked on a rocky trail beside a wide and fast flowing river. We had an adventure trying to cross the river. It was difficult enough as it was to get through the water; the current was strong and the water came up to my chest, but we had to keep MJ's camera from getting wet. Pico was the lucky volunteer to carry MJ's bag above his head, whilst navigating the rocks and the rapids. Then it wasn't far to a beautiful pool with a ten-metre waterfall flowing into it. We stopped here for about an hour, swimming, chilling out, and enjoying being one with nature. Pico pointed out a large rock that looked a lot like someone's butt. I jumped onto the rock and exposed my butt, and MJ was able to overcome the trauma long enough to take a photo of the two asses.

Pico was a fit young lad. He didn't say much; he was more your strong, silent type. He surprised me by saying he was a fan of the Australian bands, Midnight Oil and Yothu Yindi. He knew them from the Sydney Olympics opening ceremony. He wasn't impressed to learn Peter Garret had moved away from music and into politics. When I got back to Australia months later, I posted him some CD's; I hope he got them.

Baracoa is a large producer of cocoa and, subsequently, chocolate. Pico and his mate saw us off at the bus station and gave us some chocolate for our journey. Nice one. Goodbye friends, goodbye Baracoa, awesome place. Check out www.baracoa.org

We returned to our adoring fans in Santiago (the bus station crowd), although, this time, we were met by a contact of Nelson. We ended up staying with an elderly woman in her apartment in a high-rise building about 17 storeys up. We often sat out on the balcony, watching the world go by at the busy intersection below and an ice cream parlour across the road. There were usually long queues waiting for ice cream so, naturally, we just had to go try it for ourselves. Delicious.

Santiago had a few captivating pockets of activity and character. A few times, we stumbled upon live music playing in the street. There was also a small area, where all the restaurants and bars were located, where we often hung out. There didn't seem to be anywhere else. We met a few locals, who were quite friendly and interested to talk to us and to learn about Australia.

On a whole, we weren't that impressed with Santiago. I was expecting a place with a bit more life in it than what we found. Perhaps, we weren't looking in the right places. It wasn't for lack of trying. We found it particularly difficult to find any shops or restaurants. We walked through many neighbourhoods, and whilst we did enjoy the atmosphere of the crowds congregating in and around the town square, there wasn't a great deal else on offer. Maybe I was just expecting too much.

We spent New Year's there, mainly because we thought

there would be some big celebrations, being a large city, but it was rather tame. We had a good night, though, in the Town Square. We ran into two Norwegians that we'd met at Nelson's house in Havana and celebrated with them. The night mainly consisted of drinking and dancing. *Feliz Año Nuevo.*

2007

1st–9th January 2007

There's nothing like a sleepless, ten-hour, overnight bus journey to make you grumpy the next morning, but to have to endure the trip in arctic conditions is enough to make anyone frosty, in every sense of the word.

Due to the schedule of Viazul's timetables, we travelled from Havana all the way to Santiago in little hops but, now, going back, we did the trip in two large hops. We caught the bus from Santiago at 10pm, and the air conditioning was so freakin' cold. It didn't help that we were dressed for temperatures in the 30's, which we'd been experiencing over the previous few days. Over 10 hours later, we arrived in the city of Santa Clara in the heart of Cuba; I don't know that I slept at all during the night. We arrived to a wonderfully bright, sunny day, which was most welcome as we defrosted in the sunshine's rays.

I wasn't in the most chipper of moods when we got off the bus, and when our contact failed to show, I became very unresponsive. I just didn't give a fuck anymore. MJ was no barrel of laughs, either. Thankfully, there was no repeat of the media scrum type crowds of Santiago. Everything in Cuba seemed to be a mission to find or organise, and I was over it. Rather than jump into action and try to sort out our next move, I just casually enjoyed standing in the morning sun, watching the people around me. Even when I decided to do something about our situation, it was a real task to try to find change for the phone. Anyway, finally our host came and picked us up, and we left the station in a horse and carriage.

For us, Santa Clara was just a stopover on our way to Havana, but it proved to have some points of interest. The ones that grabbed our attention were the museums and monuments devoted to Che Guevara and the Battle of Santa Clara. Santa Clara was the site for the decisive moment of the revolution, when Che Guevara and rebel troops derailed and captured a train carrying weapons and troops of the Cuban army. Today, there is a monument at the site with information and photo exhibits inside old train carriages.

The city also features the Che Guevara Mausoleum, a memorial that contains the remains of the revolution's main figurehead and a museum dedicated to his life. The focal point of the site is a bronze 22-foot statue of Guevara. Although he was killed in Bolivia in 1967, in 1997, his remains were found and returned to Cuba and laid to rest in Santa Clara in remembrance of Che Guevara's role in the victory at the Battle of Santa Clara.

Group email:

Greetings all from Santa Clara, Cuba.

Nothing to see here, except a big, Che Guevara, statue. I've stopped here to break up my trip from Santiago to Havana.

Sorry haven't been in touch. Internet is scarce and expensive, $8.40 an hour. It cost me $7 per minute to ring home at Christmas.

Cuba has been good, but I can't wait to get back to a bit of normality in Mexico.

Never thought I'd say that Mexico was normal.

Happy New Year.

Our last few days in the country were spent in Havana. Having done a lot of sightseeing when we were there earlier, this time around, we looked at indulging in many of Havana's night time entertainment options. We certainly were entertained, from a thrilling coco taxi ride and restaurant staff wearing pyjamas, to simulated kangaroo sex and a strenuous salsa lesson.

Nelson's place was occupied, so he organised for us to stay with a lovely woman and her family a few blocks down the road. Celia and her family lived in a large house and only occupied the back half, whilst MJ and I had the whole front part of the house to ourselves. It was quite grand. Celia served us some tasty guava fruit juice for breakfast each morning. It was most welcome in the Cuban heat and to soothe a sore head from a heavy night of drinking the night before.

Across the road from Celia's house was John Lennon Park. On one of the park benches, there was a sculpture of John Lennon—of Beatles fame, just in case you've never heard of him—seated on one half of the bench. Apparently, the sculpture originally featured John Lennon's signature round-lens glasses, but they kept getting stolen or vandalised. When we were having a look at the statue, an old man sitting nearby came over and put some glasses on the statue for us to take a picture. Apparently, that's the guy's job, to guard the statue and place glasses on Mr Lennon when required.

Opposite the park was a fantastic, four-storeyed French restaurant, each floor providing a different dining experience. Something I'd never experienced before was not being able to leave the restaurant grounds without showing our receipt. We paid for our meal and just left the receipt on the table. Then we walked downstairs, outside and down the path, when the restaurant attendant at the gate wouldn't let us leave without producing our receipt. We didn't understand what he wanted. Thankfully, our waiter had seen our mistake and came down with the proof of payment, and we were free to leave. I imagine they must have had a lot of people doing runners in the past.

That wasn't as confusing as the experience we had at another restaurant. A waitress sat us at a table and gave us each a menu. The menu was extensive and varied: beef, pork, fish, lamb, rice, pasta. When it came time to order, the waitress surprised us with, "Oh, sorry, we only have chicken." What the fuck? How can you only have chicken? And why go through the whole process of seating us and giving us menus? Why not tell us in advance? We weren't really in the mood for chicken and went somewhere else.

Havana has an interesting array of public transport choices: the old American 50's Chevys, the regular Lada taxis, and camel buses—half truck, half bus, with two humps in the shape of a camel. If the crammed buses aren't your style, then it's possible to stand at an intersection and when the cars stop at the lights to ask any of the drivers there for a ride. We saw people hanging around busy traffic lights, looking like they wanted to cross the road, but they were, actually, looking for a lift. There are also coco taxis—a three wheeled motorcycle under a big yellow shell with a driver and a seat at the rear for two passengers. We enjoyed some fun nights out, dancing in Vedado and hanging out in the barmy Havana night by the sea at the Malecón, but we had quite an eventful night that started with a ride in a coco taxi.

We left our house and walked to a nearby busy street in the hope we could wave down a taxi. The first one to come along was a coco taxi. Cool. We'd never been in one before.

The driver pulled up, and I said, "Hola, Señor."

"No, Señorita."

I stood corrected; the driver was a woman. She turned

out to be one groovy, wild chick. She was in her late 20's and drove like a speed demon through the city. It was great chatting to her and enjoying the ride with the wind blowing through our hair. We asked if she could recommend a good restaurant, and she took us to Old Havana to a Viennese place. She said she'd be back in an hour to pick us up, on the off-chance we'd be finished at the restaurant by then, but we didn't end up seeing her again.

Inspired by the encounter, we composed a verse about the experience over dinner.

I'll take you for a ride in my coco taxi;
There's room for you and a friend in the back seat.
I'm no Señor. I'm a Señorita;
I'll drop you off here, and I'll be back to meetch ya.

There was another verse composed a few weeks later:

I'll take you for a ride in my bicytaxi,
A custom built bike that's powered by two feet.
I'll pick you up from the Viazul station;
Strap your bags on and we're off and racin'.

Our dining venture was yet another experience to write home about. First, I thought we were at a bizarre slumber party. The staff were young, beautiful guys and gals wearing thin, almost see-through white clothing that looked like sleepwear. I thought the women were wearing nighties. I wasn't complaining though; they looked gorgeous. Second, was the food. MJ ordered the chicken and veg, and due to my constant diet of alcohol, I didn't have much of an appetite, so I only ordered soup. I'm glad I did, too. When our meals arrived, the servings were just ridiculous. My soup was over-the-top large but probably manageable had I had the appetite to go with it, but the amount of chicken they put on MJ's plate could have easily fed four people. Just the sight of a meal that big was enough to make my stomach shrink in fear. It looked so overwhelming. Not being much of an eater, I really resented it when I was served with a whole buffet on my plate.

The restaurant was a few floors up in a high-rise office building. We never would have found it on our own. As we were leaving, we found a night club, of sorts, on the upper level. It was more like a hall. People were seated at tables, and there were waiting staff bringing people their drinks. We found seats at one end of the room near a two-foot-high stage and sipped on some mojitos. We got chatting with one of the guys sharing our table, who could speak English, and when the MC asked for volunteers to get up onstage, our newfound friend volunteered MJ.

MJ was one of five volunteers. I can't remember if she performed any tasks at the beginning, but it wasn't long before each volunteer was told to pick a partner from out of the crowd. Naturally, she chose me. She thought, if she was going to make a fool of herself, then she wanted me to do so, as well. So, we were both now partners in a competition, and the guys at our table were our cheer squad.

Round one saw all contestants having to dance in the most entertaining way possible to different styles of music. One couple was voted off, and we made it to the second round. We also got through that round and made it to round three.

Our next task was to choose an animal. The MC and the whole 200 strong audience knew we were from Australia, so we went with the obvious choice and chose kangaroos. The MC started outlining what we had to do, and our friend offstage tried to translate it for us. From what I understood, we had to jump around like kangaroos, court one another, and then simulate having sex. I remember thinking, "How did we end up here?"

Not wanting to embarrass ourselves, when it came around to our turn, I wanted to ask the MC directly what we had to do. I didn't understand his answer but judging by the reaction of the crowd, I could make a pretty good guess.

MC: OK, now, are you two ready to show us your sex scene?

Me: What do we have to do?

MC: Well, mate, if you have to ask ...

Audience: Roars of laughter.

Without further ado, the music was playing, and everyone's eyes in the room were on us. I looked at MJ and asked, "How do kangaroos have sex?" I missed the episode where Skippy got laid. I thought that, with their long tails, surely kangaroos wouldn't be doing it doggy-style. But there was no time for a committee; we hopped around the stage for about 10-15 seconds until I got behind MJ and pretended to mount her. I knocked her off balance, and we both fell to the ground. It wasn't pretty; I landed on her leg and injured her.

The crowd was shouting and cheering. Thankfully, they weren't after a true depiction of the kangaroo mating ritual. Our exhibitionist days were over, though, as we were voted out of the competition that round. Our friend kindly organised us some free drinks. We both sat down, glad to be off stage and coming to terms with what just happened. What a totally unexpected turn of events. The joys of travelling, hey.

Despite getting through the two dancing rounds of the competition, we were humble enough to seek some help, and we had Nelson organise us a Salsa lesson. We went around to the teacher's house, a bubbly woman who showed us some moves for two hours. We did well to begin with, but towards the end, I became tired and felt ill. My body wasn't used to such physical activity.

We had an early flight back to Cancún, so we spent our last evening taking it easy at Nelson and Aurora's place. There was another couple there, Australian, and we chatted about our travels and thanked Nelson with a big bottle of rum. Travelling around the country and staying with Nelson's network of friends was certainly extremely helpful and took out a lot of the legwork for us in organisation. It helped with our peace of mind, too, knowing that we were going to be well looked after. We were very grateful.

As we caught our flight the next morning, I was more than ready to leave. We were certainly leaving with some fond memories but after travelling around the country a while, one colonial town seemed just like the next. Struggling with the language barrier all the time and nothing coming easily, everything was a real process. I couldn't wait to get back to the Mayan Riviera, where I understood how things worked, and I could just get pissed and lay on the beach. I guess what I'm saying is, after four weeks in Cuba, I needed a holiday.

I booked a room in Cancún, where we dumped our bags and went to the markets to do some souvenir shopping. I knew these markets well from three years earlier. The hair salon where I hopped out of the chair with braids and beads in my hair was just across the road. Ah, the memories.

MJ quite wisely had left her souvenir shopping to the last day, so she didn't have to lug the stuff around with her. Amongst other things, she bought a good quality hammock, which I've since seen her put to good use in Canberra. After our time at the markets, it was time for MJ to depart. Her flight back to Australia flew out that afternoon. With her departure, I felt relief more than anything. I was pleased everything had gone well and that we survived unharmed. MJ had had a ball and was sorry to be going. It had been a thrill sharing the last six weeks with my good friend. Caramba, indeed.

8th–11th February 2007
Day 1 in Guatemala:

Day 1 in Guatemala started in Palenque, Mexico. I went to bed, around a quarter past midnight, as I hoped to catch an early minibus to the border. An hour and a half later, I was wide awake again and couldn't sleep. A shower and a shave and a few beers later, I went and caught the 5am minibus to Frontera Corozal on the Mexican side of the Mexico/Guatemala border.

The trip went fine. I had a few beers to help pass the time, and we arrived about three hours later. The driver charged me 10 pesos more than he earlier quoted (naturally), but sometimes, I just couldn't be arsed arguing over $1.20.

As I was alone, the small boat owners charged me twice the price to make it worth their while taking me up the river to Bethel, the Guatemala side of the border. To their credit, they suggested I take the cheaper boat ride across the river to a small town that was there, and I could catch a bus the rest of the way to Bethel. We crossed the beautiful Usumacinta River and arrived at this town that was basically one short street with a restaurant, a shop, and a few houses nearby.

Welcome to Guatemala.

I'm Australian, and I get asked numerous questions and my belongings fully searched whenever I arrive in Australia. I crossed the border from Mexico to Guatemala and not a suggestion of any border control anywhere on either side. It was a beautiful sunny day and still rather early in the morning. Arriving in a new country at the beginning of a new day, gave an air of excitement and opportunity about the unknown. Anything could happen today and the day had only just started. I was already happy with the opportunities available. For $2, I bought a 1 litre bottle of beer called *Gallo*, which translates to cock; you know, as in male chicken.

Let me tell you about fuckin' chickens. Every man and his dog has a few chickens in his backyard in this neck of the woods. And they crow all fuckin' day and night. I had one outside my hotel window in Palenque that was lucky I'm not a fox, because I would have fuckin' killed that fucker. So, after all that, I arrived in Guatemala to find the national beer is named after a fuckin' chicken and has a chicken's head as the logo. You may have guessed; I wasn't happy about the chicken situation.

After a few beers in God knows where, the shop-keeper pointed out there was a taxi available to Bethel. I took the opportunity, as I couldn't imagine one coming by too often. The driver was hilarious. He was one of those big guys, who laughs a lot, and his whole body shook in joy as he was laughing. He gave me a discount as I was going his way, anyway. We started chatting, and the guy had me in stitches on a couple of occasions.

I asked, "Is there a cantina in Bethel?"

He said "No, but there's a church."

It was probably too much for me to hope it was like the church in Kings Cross, London. But anyway, we were driving in his sedan family car, and he was driving at super speed down a dirt, rocky road. It's funny how some people drive around the city in a 4WD. He was chatting away but looking at me, not the road, and from out of nowhere came a car in the other direction. I shouted out, and he managed to miss it …just. God knows how. Neither car slowed down. We laughed it off and then it happened again. I thought, "I'm going to die out here in a car crash, and my family and friends won't know where I am. I don't know where I am."

We made it to Bethel and still no sign of immigration. I was tired and decided to put off my trip to Flores until the next day. I booked a room—a small shoebox with a single bed and side table. I slept a few hours and then woke to look for some food and drink, which I thought might be difficult, as Bethel is rather small. I found what I was looking for at a kiosk by the local playing fields. I sat and relaxed whilst watching the local lads play football. I survived day 1.

Day 2:

Next day, my main concern was money. I had very little on me and no access to any, not out in the middle of nowhere. I checked if I still had my ten $US hidden in my bag and ended up finding another $30. Get in there! It was now time to catch the bus to Flores. As I was expecting, it was a chicken bus.

MY ... GAWD. What a trip!

Bethel was the starting point for the bus. As there weren't many people at that stage, I sat in the back seat in front of the small storage area. I settled in, excited about being on a chicken bus, and I made myself comfortable for the four hours ahead.

Chicken buses are old school buses from the US, once yellow but now painted in various colours. They're the cheapest form of bus travel and are called chicken buses, because they're usually crammed with cargo and chickens.

We drove for five minutes and finally some immigration. I was legal now, and we headed off. The road was a dirt, rocky track and, of course, the driver wasn't taking it slowly. Sitting at the back of the bus over the back wheels meant I was being shaken around everywhere. Some passengers decided to use this time to catch up on some sleep in what can only be described as an earthquake simulator. I've no idea how they managed some sleep.

Things were fun until I realised another reason the back seat was a bad choice. The bus started filling up, and after a while, I was surrounded by cargo and people. I was jam packed against the window. The bus often tilted to one side as the driver drove to different sides of the road. I really was concerned that the bus was going to tip and I'd be crushed.

Then we got to a major town, and the woman sitting in front of me got off the bus to buy some food and drink, and she left her bag on the seat. Suddenly, a fuckin' live chicken poked its head out of the bag. It didn't look happy, and I was definitely not happy to have it near me. It then tried to get out of the bag, and it flew straight for me. I nearly made a Mayan sacrifice in my pants, I tell you. I quickly held up my small daypack as a barrier between the two of us. Luckily, the woman returned at that point and put the chicken away.

Finally, we arrived in Santa Elena, and I caught a taxi the short ride from there to Flores. I checked into a hotel and was overjoyed to be able to relax and explore the beautiful little island.

Day 3:

Day 3 and I moved hotels. I asked the receptionist if I could pay later, as I needed to go to the bank in Santa Elena, first. He was cool with that, but the banks weren't so accommodating. It was Saturday, which didn't help.

First, none of the ATMs had any money. I met some Kiwis on the street, and they said, on Saturdays, there's never any money in the ATMs. I went into the bank for a credit card, money advance, and they didn't accept Visa. Shit. I went to another bank, same story, and another and another. A few people pointed me in the direction of the Industrial Bank. I went there and, YES, they accept Visa. But I'd have to wait until Monday. Firetruck. I only had $2.50 on me. How was I going to make that last until Monday? I still hadn't paid for my room, either.

I walked around town in the soaring heat, wondering what

to do. Morale was quite low at this point. I had no money; I was new in town; I didn't know anyone, and I hardly spoke the local lingo. I went to the markets, which were a madhouse. You can buy anything you want there: clothing, food, jewellery, furniture, a house in the Bahamas. Maybe not that last one.

I decided to give the Industrial another try and found they had an ATM I hadn't noticed before. It didn't work, but I got talking to the security guard and told him I had no money whatsoever. He pointed me in the direction of a commercial centre. I thought he was crazy and couldn't see how that would help. I walked off, feeling the situation was hopeless. I just so happened to walk past the commercial centre the guard mentioned and *really* thought he was crazy. The place was like a gift shop and had Valentine's Day decorations everywhere. But anyway, I went inside and asked the lady behind the counter for a cash advance. And fuck me, she gave it to me, even though my shaky hands couldn't produce a matching signature to my passport.

Life was good again, and a smile returned to my face. What a relief. The rest of the day was pretty good—hanging out with other travellers, and I met some locals, too, which was cool.

Day 4:

Today was Sunday, a day of rest. Thank God. The next day would mark ten years since I started travelling. In 1997, I hopped on a plane from Sydney to London without any vaccinations, and I caught the travel bug big time. But all was well ... for now.

Guatemala continued:

Flores was slow-paced, and on a typical day, I'd drag myself out of bed, and after a shower and getting changed, I'd head out for some breakfast. Beer in this part of the world was the same price in a bar/restaurant as it was in a shop. So, I always had breakfast in style and drank in a bar. Sometimes, I even had something to eat. After a few more bars and many more drinks, I'd go shopping at the nearby open-air markets in Santa Elena or catch up on some emailing in one of the net cafés.

On the hot days, which was most days, I bought a few cans and went swimming in the afternoon to cool off. As the sun started to disappear, I went up the hill to the church and watched the sunset over the lake. It was an awesome sight. Then, at 7pm, I would head to the hostel, Los Amigos, where it was happy hour, and I got drunk with fellow travellers. Quite an enjoyable existence, I must say. Do yourself a favour and check out photos of this island of bliss online.

Saturday night in Flores, the night life came alive. The bars and clubs were full of beautiful twenty-somethings, and I wondered where these people were during the week? My newfound friends I'd met from the hostel went to bed early, but I stayed out and found a club overlooking the lake with free entrance. Nice one. Some clubs were charging $3.30 cover charge. Where do they get off charging so much? Haha

In the club, there were a few different levels with different rooms. I walked into a small room that looked out over the dance floor on the floor below. I don't quite know how it happened, but before I knew it, I was dancing salsa with one of the local girls. Her name was Andrea, and I'm guessing she was originally from Belize or had spent some considerable time there, because her English was perfect. English is the official language of the neighbouring country, Belize. She said she absolutely loved Salsa. Shit! In Cuba, I had a grand total of three hours salsa tuition, and here I was dancing with a self-proclaimed fanatic. Not only that, but being male meant I had to lead. I looked at the other guys dancing and copied them step for step. I only hope I was good enough for Andrea to enjoy herself. We danced a few times, so I think so.

After Andrea and her friends left, I met some guys and one of them, Jorge, also spoke perfect English. We drank and chatted until the club closed. Then Jorge and his mates offered to walk me to my hotel, saying Flores streets weren't safe at night. I found it hard to believe them. I had found Flores to be safe and the people to be incredibly friendly. Who knows? Maybe they wanted to walk me home and rob me when we were out of sight of anyone else. Either way, I agreed to the escort home.

On the way, we stopped at a 24-hour pharmacy that sold soup. One of the guys, Melvin, wanted to have some soup, so his breath didn't stink of alcohol when he got home to his mum. As we were waiting for the soup, a local girl came up and asked if we could escort her home as she'd just been attacked by two guys but had fought them off by kicking them in the balls. There was a lot of talking going on in Spanish, so I didn't understand everything. Jorge ran off, no idea where or why, and then returned 10 minutes later on a motorbike with a guy on the back. Turns out this guy on the back and his girlfriend had been attacked as well. Shit! What's going on? During the attack, he and his girlfriend got separated, and he didn't know where she was. Turned out, perhaps, my escort to my hotel was warranted. I never would have thought it.

A few days later, I met a Belizean couple, and we went over to the other side of the lake to a zoo. The only way there was by boat. We travelled there in a narrow motor boat, called a *lancha*. Once there, I couldn't really be arsed walking around looking at animals. Most of them roamed free, anyway. They can come to me, I thought. I went swimming and later passed out in a hammock. I woke up later, face to face with a wart hog on one side and a giant parrot on the other. It was quite a shock, I tell you. It took a few seconds for me to remember where I was.

I walked back to the boat, but it had gone. Shit! Back to front as usual. Here I was, stranded on the mainland, unable to get back to the island. I walked through the zoo and onto the small village of San Miguel. I wandered through the bush and came across a restaurant hiding amongst the trees. The staff looked horrified when I told them I'd been left behind and needed a ride to Flores. They made a few phone calls and organised a boat for me. Yay, I'd been rescued. Goodbye mainland; hello small island.

I arranged with my rescuer, Miguel, to pick me up again the next morning to take me across the lake to a small village of 3000 people, called San José. I'd heard San José had a Spanish school. Miguel was already waiting for me when I arrived at the dock the next morning. Off we went in his lancha. I'd brought a few beers for the 45-minute trip, which Miguel really appreciated.

Upon arrival in San José, Miguel wasn't able to give me any change, so I suggested we go to a bar and get some there. We went to a bar that was one large circular room, about 20 metres in diameter, with a large thatched roof, called *El Bungalow*. This was to become my second home over the next two weeks.

Miguel and I ended up having a session. Miguel was in his late 30's and quite a character. At $1.25 a bottle, we stayed at El Bungalow for hours, drinking beer after beer, putting songs on the juke box, and chatting to the female bar staff. One of them, Maylin, was quite nice, and Miguel was trying to set me up with her. It's difficult to be charming to a girl when you speak fuck all of her language.

By the time I rocked up to the office of the Spanish school, I was flying. Emilio, the director, asked my name. I told him, and he said nothing about it. Later, though, I found out he had dismissed my answer as the ramblings of a drunk man, and he didn't believe me until he saw my passport on the first day of classes.

Language schools like this exist all through Central America. Guatemala has some of the cheapest schools and are quite popular, especially in Antigua. But, in the bigger towns, there's a lot more travellers, and English is more widely spoken, so any Spanish learnt can be slow progress, as it's possible, and easier, to speak English outside of the classroom.

I wanted to immerse myself in the language as much as possible, and I felt a small village, like San José, would provide that. $200/week covered 20 hours of one-on-one Spanish tuition, afternoon school excursions, accommodation with a local family, with three meals a day. The opportunity was there to be surrounded by Spanish all the time. In San José, it was extremely rare to find anyone that spoke English. That suited me fine.

My registration was all sorted. It was Friday, and classes started on Monday. I said farewell to Miguel, and Emilio took me to the home of the family I'd be staying with. I met my new family: Maritza and her two children, Mario 18 and Jeffrey 13. On first impressions, they appeared to be kind and friendly. But I rudely didn't hang around to find out. 15 minutes later, I was back down to El Bungalow for some more drinks and to chat to Maylin.

Come nightfall, I was in a black-out state. There's a lot I don't remember, but I learnt over the following few days from various people what I got up to. Maritza was visiting her mother in town near El Bungalow. Her mother said to her, "Check out that drunk gringo. He looks lost." Maritza looked outside the house and saw a drunk man sitting in the park. "Ahhh, that's my gringo," she said and came and grabbed me by the hand and led me back to her house. I actually remember the walk home. Everyone was asking Maritza what was going on. I heard the word, *borracho*, a lot, which means drunk.

Maritza was widowed and lived with her two sons in a five-room house: the kitchen, the living room, and three bedrooms. One bedroom for the live-in student (on this occasion me), one for storage, and the last one was shared by the three family members. The laundry, toilet, and shower were outside. There was a fireplace outside, as well, sometimes used for cooking. Maritza was privileged to have an electric cooker in the kitchen. Most households cooked using a fireplace, which involved going to the surrounding forest and collecting wood every second or third day. Maritza also sold maize, used to make tortillas, from the back of her house.

To make the maize, corn beans were poured into a blender-esque type machine to produce a fine powder. This machine was powered by a loud, fuck off, motor. Have you ever been woken early on a Sunday morning by the neighbour mowing their lawn? 6am every morning, as people came to buy the maize for breakfast, I was woken to the dulcet tones (joking) of what sounded like a propelled plane starting up right in my fuckin' bedroom. It would last for a few minutes and then start up again not long later, when another customer arrived. After a few days, I got used to it and eventually even slept through it. Can you imagine, though, the first morning this happened? I was startled, to say the least—"*¿Qué diablos?*"

The family was exceptionally kind and hospitable and always joking around and laughing, which was quite infectious. Sometimes, I didn't know what I was laughing at, and sometimes, I think the joke was at my expense, but what the hey. San José, at 3000 people, is naturally quite a small place. I met a lot of the local people, especially in El Bungalow, and I'd later be talking to Maritza and tell her, I met so-and-so. She'd usually reply with, "That's my brother," or "That's my cousin," or nephew or sister in-law or whatever. And there was always people coming in and out of the house. Maritza worked as a chef at the local school, and the boys obviously went to school there, too, so there were always kids around.

On Sunday, I wasn't well, so I just took it easy. I went to a store and bought a beer and sat outside. The guy in the Pizza store next door called out my name. I said hello, but I had no idea who he was. It turned out I'd met him Friday night in one of the bars. Federico was from Salvador but had lived in the States for 15 years, so his English was perfect. He'd been living in San José for 3 years with his wife and children and just loved it. He was kind and friendly, and during my stay in San José, whenever I felt my head was going to explode with Spanish overload, I'd go and have an English chat with Fred. He was the only person I spoke English with in all of San José.

We chatted about a lot of things, and one day, we got onto the subject of when I travelled to Ireland. I told him about the weekend trip that lasted four months. Fred thought it was very funny and told me of a story. I don't know if it's true, but it's good, anyway.

A guy was travelling through India and wanted to experience one of the opium dens he'd heard about. So, he went to one and had a go at smoking opium. After a while, he asked the den owner, "What time is it?"

The owner said, "4:30."

"Oh, I gotta go."

"Why?"

"I've got to meet some friends at 5:00."

The owner laughed and said, "Shit man, you've been here for 3 years."

Monday morning was my first day of classes. Emilio picked me up from the house, and we walked to the school. The school was in a garden, and the classrooms were small, open-aired, thatch-roofed huts. The teaching was one on one, so Emilio introduced me to my own personal teacher, Joanna. Joanna was 26, married, with a four-year-old boy, Jonathon, with another on the way. Originally from Guatemala City, Joanna had been living and teaching in San José for five years. And like everyone else in San José, with the exception of Federico, Joanna didn't speak a word of English.

We hit it off immediately. A smile or laugh was never far from Joanna's face, and the way she taught was fun. It wasn't just copying grammar from the board for four hours. We talked about each other's families, other people in San José, my travels, Guatemala, and Australia. Joanna couldn't pronounce 'Spaceman' in English and felt silly calling me the equivalent in Spanish, so she called me Chico, which means boy.

A typical school day was the life of Riley: Up at 7:30am for breakfast, which Maritza always had there, ready and waiting. 8:00am - 12:00pm were classes with a drink break in the middle. Then I went home for a cooked lunch with the family. I'd then study or do whatever until 2:00pm, and then join Emilio for an afternoon activity.

As I was the school's only student at the time, it was just Emilio and me doing the activities: anything from caving, Eco-garden tours, Mayan school visits, cycling to nearby ruins, shopping trips into Santa Elena, walks into the jungle (that was really so Emilio could collect firewood), to canoeing and swimming. Then after activities, it was back home to chill out before dinner, and then after a delicious home cooked meal, I was straight down to El Bungalow to mix with the locals. Shit. Why'd I ever leave?

Joanna taught me about the many festivals that happen in San José. One of them is called *La Cabeza de Coche* (The pig's head). It's an annual celebration, on May 3rd, in honour to receive rains, an omen for a good harvest. The day before, upon a hilltop overlooking Lake Petén, the head of the pig is placed in a furnace in the ground and buried. The town folk let off rockets and pyrotechnics. Some people play the national instrument, the marimba, whilst the rest dance with elaborately decorated hoops, whilst getting drunk on rum. This goes until 5am.

The next day, the pig's head, now cooked, is placed on a tray and is decorated. In the evening, a volunteer carries the tray upon their head and parades through the main streets of the town, whilst people drink and dance to the marimba. Joanna said the men get unbelievably drunk and pass out in the street. The slang for this was *sucio de coche*, which roughly means, dirty as a pig. May 3 just so happens to be my birthday and about the time Joanna's baby was due.

One night, I was notably drunk and became sucio de coche in the town park. A neighbour informed Maritza, and this time, the whole family came to get their 'gringo' and take me home. San José is a small, safe community, and passing out in the park posed no danger. Having said that, a week and a half after arriving in town, I went to a small bar for a few drinks before going to El Bungalow. I got to El Bungalow to find it closed with police hanging around. The only night I didn't head straight to El Bungalow after dinner and some guy inside had been shot dead.

After two weeks, I thought if I didn't leave San José then, I was never going to leave. I managed to get my act together and leave town, but I only got as far as Flores. This time around, I lost my glasses. I was in my hotel, and I took them off before I jumped in the shower in a shared bathroom, and later, when I went back for them, I couldn't find them. I still had my prescription sunnies for during the day, but at night, I was struggling.

I don't always divulge my luck with the ladies, or lack of it, but this is unique. It was late one afternoon, and I was quite drunk and feeling in a playful mood. I found a bar I hadn't been in before, so I went inside, and there was a Guatemalan chick sitting at the bar by herself. I ordered a drink, and then I went up to her, and my first words were, "Would you like to have sex with me?"

She said, "Yes."

We finished our drinks and then went back to my hotel. That approach probably only works once in a life time, and now I think about it, that's the first time I can remember using it. So, I'm 1 for 1. I should probably quit while I'm ahead. The funny thing is, she said she's never done anything like that before.

Something on my 'must do' list was to visit the National Park of Tikal, about an hour and a half drive north of Flores. I booked a day trip to Tikal, the largest Mayan archaeological site there is, to see the pyramids. The site is situated in the rainforest, and some of the permanent residents include howler monkeys, which I was lucky to see. I also saw a toucan. Man, that bird has a fuckin' big nose.

The whole place was truly impressive, and some of the pyramids were tall and steep. I came down the steps on my bum. One could easily spend all day walking around, taking in the energy from the jungle and the history of the site. The ruins are best seen at sunrise and/or sunset from on top of one of the pyramids. This is when the jungle comes alive with all the animals. But without my glasses, I wasn't going to hang around in the dark.

That night, back in Flores, I went to my local Los Amigos

and settled into happy hour. I ended up meeting an English couple, who lived in Scotland on the Isle of Mull (there's no actual mull there, Australians). Her name was Kate, and his, Ben Harper. If I had any Ben Harper CD's, I would have got him to sign them. Anyway, I had a good night chatting with them and others at the table. They were really friendly and had a good sense of humour. They were both around my age and had travelled extensively and told some great stories.

They told me of their plans to go to a place called Lanquin and that I was more than welcome to join them. I'd never heard of Lanquin, but what did I care? It would be an adventure. Ben and Kate said, "If we see you at the bus in the morning, we see you. If we don't, we don't." I was at the bus in the morning.

We took the bus to Cobán, including a river ferry crossing that was powered by an outboard motor, and then rode in the back of a pick-up the following two hours to Lanquin. It was a great ride. We were chatting, drinking beers, and the scenery was amazing.

Ben and Kate had been given a recommendation of a place to stay, called *El Retiro*. We arrived there to find a picturesque lodge with cabin accommodations on a hillside set by a river. Paradise. Each room was named after an animal, and all food and drinks, internet and phone use were billed to your room, and you paid at the end of your stay. On the hill was reception with internet access and a mega music library available for anyone to download what they liked. Down by the river was the bar/restaurant with cold beer. I was happy.

El Retiro's run and owned by a couple of college mates from Fort Worth, Texas, with a few other cool travellers thrown in. It's a bit of a gringo haven, but the environment and atmosphere made it fun. The cheap rooms were full, so the three of us shared the 'bat' room. We dumped our bags in the room, and so it began: days filled with good weather, good company, good food, swimming, laying in the sun, and drinking. Nights included more eating, drinking, and dancing, for those who had consumed many a Cuba Libre. That first day and night, we participated in all the above.

On the second night, one girl I danced with, let's call her ... um ... Carmyn, and let's say she was ... um ... Swiss German. I'm not far from the truth, but I can't remember exactly. Anyway, we became friends. I remember she had blue nail polish, and she gave me the bottle, so I ended up wearing it, too. A dorm bed had become free in the 'spider' room, so I took it whilst Ben and Kate moved to a twin. But I never actually went to the room. I just dumped my bags at reception and hung out by the river and bar. Late that night, as the party was winding down, I was ready for bed. As the path up the hill to the rooms was in the dark, I couldn't see and needed someone to walk me to my room.

This became a nightly occurrence. Guests and staff took turns walking me to my room at night, so I wouldn't hurt myself walking in the dark. Some nights, I was carried by two people, because I was so drunk. But as I found in Mexico, three years earlier, when I lost my glasses, people can be so kind. I never had any problem finding a volunteer to guide me. Often, other people in the spider room, before going to bed, would come down to the bar to see if I wanted to be taken to the room. I certainly played up to it a bit and tried, when possible, to receive help from the girls.

On this particular night, my first night in the spider room, Carmyn walked me up to the room. I was way drunk and don't remember any of this, but Carmyn told me we stumbled up the hill to reception, where she collected my bags. She then carried my bags, what an angel, and took me to the room. It turned out, I had a top bunk, not the safest of places for me to be sleeping, especially with my history in Mexico. You might remember years earlier, I fell out of a six-foot-high bunk, banging myself up pretty badly and having to go to hospital. Carmyn helped me climb the ladder up to the bed. I got to the top and BANG. I fell from the bed and hit another bed on my way down to the floor. I appeared all right, so Carmyn helped me up, and I managed to climb up successfully the next time and went to sleep. Carmyn must have thought "Thank God."

In the middle of the night, I woke up needing to go to the toilet. Being my first night in the room and not remembering having ever been in the room before or how I got there, I had no idea where I was. The room was pitch black but I managed to make my way safely out of bed, but I was unable to find a light switch or a door. My fumbling around the room woke up someone else, and I could hear them laughing. By this stage, I was ready to wet myself: I needed the toilet so badly. I said into the darkness, "There's someone there. I can hear you laughing. Can you help me? I don't know where I am, and I need the toilet." Well, that was it, the laughter became uncontrollable until one guy hopped out of bed and opened the room door for me. Relief.

I didn't know who let me out until the next morning, when I was sitting in the bar and a guy came up to me and said, "You were funny, last night." He walked off mimicking me, "I don't know where I am, and I need the toilet." Then Carmyn walked up and told me about the previous night's madness and how I fell out of bed. That explained the pain in my ribs. Unfortunately, Carmyn left later that day. Ah well, it happens. Still, it was another day in paradise, which meant a day in the sun by the river drinking beer.

Let me tell you about the river. The river was about 30 metres wide and just over four-foot-deep in the middle. The current was extremely strong, and this allowed a board attached to a cable, water skiing style, to be set up in the river. Balance was the key in riding this board, but it was really only the local kids that mastered it, being so much lighter than the grownups. I had a go a few times and didn't do too badly, until I'd fall off and struggle to keep my boxer shorts from coming off in the strong current.

Another great pastime, which was so fun and that we did with the local kids, was walking about 40 metres up river and jumping in and letting the current take you back down to the bathing area. The best route to take was in the middle of the river because the sides had big rocks. With the current so strong, you had to swim to shore 10 metres in advance from when you wanted to stop and get out. A game we played with the kids was swimming towards the board and trying to take out the person on it. The local kids were great, by the way. We had a lot of fun playing with them in the water or volleyball or whatever. It was good to chat with them, too, as they were the only people I was practising my Spanish with, due to all the other gringos at the lodge.

Another great use of the current was riding down the river with inner tubes. For $3.30 a head, a store outside the gates of El Retiro had for hire, inner tubes which included a drive in the back of a pickup a few miles upriver, and then you jump on the tube and enjoy the ride back down. Back at El Retiro, sometimes, people left their tubes on the river bank before returning them to the store. Kate and I commandeered one, and we jumped on together and had ourselves in stitches doing the short river run. The short river run had the most rapids, and we'd have the most exciting time, so much so, that we'd fall onto the shore rolling about in laughter. A few days passed, and it was Ben and Kate's turn to move on. It was sad to see them go, but the time we spent together was great, and through them, I'd found myself at El Retiro. They were off to Semuc Champay and beyond.

I didn't plan on leaving anytime soon; I was having a ball. I was meeting so many wonderful people and having a wild time. Because all drinks were recorded in a book to tally up people's bill when they checked-out, it was possible to see each day who had consumed the most the night before. I was regularly recorded as having drunk the most during the previous night's festivities. I liked to swap between beer and drinks of rum, including Quebec Libre—rum and lemonade. I walked into the bar, one day, and saw on the information board:

Quote of the day: Spaceman Africa—"I think I'm drunk."

Apparently, the night before, when I was playing on one of the swings at the bar, I fell off. It was obvious to blind Freddy that I'd had a drink or ten, but as I rose to my feet, I reflected out loud, "I think I'm drunk," much to the amusement of everyone around. That quote stayed up on the board for a week.

The music collection that was available on the PC behind the bar was particularly extensive. There was always some great music playing. One afternoon, 'Closer' by Nine Inch Nails came on, and I felt the urge to get up and dance in the corner by the bar, despite the vibe in the bar being low key and no one else dancing. I didn't care. I was in a good mood, and that song is a real favourite of mine. I was really going for it.

At the same time, an English couple walked into the bar. They'd only just arrived at the lodge. They walked up to the bar and surveyed the surroundings. They must have wondered what kind of crowd they were now mixing with. The guy, Jack, later told me, when he first saw me, thought, "Who's that weirdo dancing in the corner?"

Anyway, he and his girlfriend, Sam, got a drink and sat down. Jack then saw my quote on the board. "I recognise that name," he said. It turned out that Jack had met Crazy

Horse three years earlier in Tulum. Naturally, Crazy had mentioned my name in conversation, and Jack had remembered it. Thinking it was highly unlikely there was more than one Spaceman Africa in the world, Jack went to the bar to enquire of my whereabouts.

"Is Spaceman Africa here?"

Dennis, the barman, pointed to the weirdo dancing in the corner. Pretty cool, ah? I actually became rather good friends with Jack and Sam. Jack had a great sense of humour, and we shared many a laugh together.

This putting everything on your tab malarkey is dangerous. You can lose track of your spending so easily and rack up a bill larger than the amount of money you have on you. There was no access to money in Lanquin, so I had to go back to Cobán. I told the staff at El Retiro I was going, and I left my passport as security. I caught the morning shuttle, arrived in Cobán mid-morning, found a bank, and then thought I'd do a bit of sight-seeing. Come afternoon, I went back to the bus station just in time to see the 5 o'clock shuttle fill up. The driver said there was another at seven. Well, I didn't see it. I asked around, and there were no more shuttles to Lanquin until the next day. Ah well, I went to the pub and mixed with some of the locals there. They pointed me in the direction of a hotel, so I stayed there the night with the intention of returning to Lanquin the next day.

It didn't quite work out that way. I woke the next morning feeling really sick. I spent the whole day in bed, unable to move, and felt like I might spew from either end of my body if I attempted to get up. I spent another night in Cobán, and by the morning of the next day, I was capable of moving. I hadn't slept at all over the previous 24 hours but was keen to get back to Lanquin.

I made it back to El Retiro that day to find a whole new crowd there. All my friends had gone, and I was disappointed that I didn't get a chance to say goodbye to them. I paid my bill at the bar and shocked the staff by not having a beer or rum for breakfast. I decided to take a bit of a break from the booze until I felt fully recovered. I cleaned myself up and made plans to meet a friend in Guatemala City the next day. That meant it was time to go. After an entertaining and stimulating two weeks, I checked out of El Retiro and made my farewells to the lovely staff there. They joked they thought I was never going to leave. The joke was even funnier when I returned an hour later, claiming I loved the place so much I just couldn't leave. The reality was, I'd returned to collect my passport, which I'd left at reception. I was so glad I'd remembered it before getting too far down the road.

I was off again, back to Cobán, where I stayed the night with the plan to catch a bus in the morning to Guatemala City. When it came time to go to bed, I still couldn't sleep; the withdrawals were in full swing: cold sweats, constant nonsensical chatter in my head, the shakes, and paranoia. I knew the demonic nightmares were still to come. I lay in my hotel bed with the light on, in a room all to myself. I usually slept with the light on during withdrawals, as the nightmares were so terrifying.

I stared at the ceiling and noticed I could see small images. I saw little jungle natives moving at 100mph through the jungle doing acrobatics. I looked at the wall and saw the images there, too. I laughed and thought it was funny and put it down to the withdrawals. Later, I started to see three black and yellow alien-like creatures on the ceiling, dancing the can can. They were pretty funny, and I was laughing a lot. When I stared at them for more than ten or so seconds, they turned into spinning wheels, growing bigger and bigger, and came straight for me. I'd then shut my eyes, and when I reopened them, the shapes were back dancing again.

I tried my best to get to sleep, but I was kept awake by rowdy people outside my room (which I now think was all in my head) and songs playing in my mind. Not real ones, just songs made up. They didn't stop and just went on and on. It wasn't easy to make out the lyrics, but when I could, they were usually very clever and funny and always about sex.

Just as I was drifting off to sleep, I could see some people as if I was dreaming, except I was awake. I thought, "Wow, I can see people." A young redhead woman smiled at me, and then some of the others started talking to me, telling me off for all my detestable character traits, saying what a disgusting person I am and what a farce my life is. I could see them clearly, like I was watching them on a big TV screen. It was my understanding these were dead people, their spirits. I lay there motionless, in shock. I'd never experienced anything like that before during withdrawals. Their verbal abuse had been awfully aggressive and confronting. Yet, I knew their words to be true.

I started to hallucinate. I didn't know it, though; I thought it was all real. I could feel the presence of two bodies on my bed; I couldn't see anything, but later, I could hear there were two women. They were friendly, and it was quite a fun time; the tactile hallucinations were quite pleasurable, but I won't go into that. Haha.

I started to hear voices outside of my head and see and interact with fully formed people. Some of the people were dead relatives of mine, so I believed the other people to be the spirits of dead people, too. They were friendly, at first, but told me I wasn't living to my full potential and I was to go back home to Australia immediately and make something of my life.

I reluctantly did what they said and caught a bus to Guatemala City and then a taxi to the airport whilst having a friendly interaction with the hallucinations the whole time. I thought I was like Haley Joel-Osmont's character in the film *The Sixth Sense*, and I could see dead people. At the airport, I bought a ticket to Los Angeles with the intention of flying back to Australia from there. I had a five or six hour wait, however, before my flight was due to depart.

The voices became more hostile, derogatory, and commanding. A 'This is your (fuck-ups in) life' styled persecution took place. Feeling guilty, sorry, and ashamed, I did what the voices instructed me to do—anything from talking to other people to banging my fists against walls. The spirits did things, like insist I look at them when they were talking to me, but then they always changed their location in the room, making it hard for me to find them. Some of the visual hallucinations were full-bodied people; others were just miniature people, whilst some were just from the torso up, and others just their face. Some were small flying, demon, insect-like creatures of all descriptions. Often, when I made a smart-arse comment or insult, one of the insects would come and zap me. Fuckin' hurt, too. Funny how a hallucination can trick your mind into thinking you're experiencing pain.

My behaviour didn't go unnoticed. I was approached two or three times by airport security including medical staff, enquiring about my welfare. Because of my shaking, they wanted to put me into hospital, but the voices in my head were insistent that I not miss the opportunity to fly back to Australia. I assured the airport staff I was fine, despite the fact I was clearly agitated.

By the time I was on the plane to Los Angeles, the voices had me convinced I was going to die. I was told in graphic detail how the plane was going to crash at any second and I was going to end up blind, limbless, and in prison with defecated pants for the next ten years. I believed all of it. All of this was because of the way I had led my life—selfish, self-centred, drinking, and taking drugs. It later changed that I was going to be bashed by a mob on arrival at the airport and have my dick cut off. I was so scared. In the end, I was resigned to the fact that I was, indeed, going to die.

At one point during the flight, I tried to enter the cockpit of the plane. The voices instructed me to hand in my passport, because I wouldn't be needing it anymore. Understandably, that caused some trouble, and I was met at LAX by the police. They took me into custody, and I was shaking, more from fear than anything. However, I felt safer now and relieved that I hadn't been killed. The voices were swearing at me continuously for escaping their plans of my death. Immigration officers asked me several questions, and I told them what I thought was the truth. I was so delusional and, of course, had no idea what was going on. I didn't even know where I'd travelled from. I thought my journey had involved a short monorail trip past a large amusement park. God knows what the officers made of it all. They put me in a detention room at the airport, where I continued to experience the hallucinations. I couldn't escape them, and it was an extremely tormenting time.

The detainee centre was a doctor's styled waiting room, with TV, books, and snacks, and I was still there after 24 hours. Thankfully, the voices had stopped, but I was still seeing things. I spoke to the officers and asked if they could see the invisible pixie in the room. One of them asked how it is possible to see something invisible, whilst one woman said I could relax and assured me whilst I was there, nothing was going to hurt me. Anyway, they put my arse on a plane and deported me back to Australia, hallucinating the whole way.

Being deported was quite an experience. If ever you're going to get deported, I would recommend doing it at LAX. It's one of the busiest airports in the world with considerably long waiting times when you're there to catch a plane.

Not so when you're deported.

I was escorted to my flight by two immigration officers. First, I was driven to the departure terminal. The back of the van was full of apparitions dancing around me. We arrived at the terminal, and the queue for check-in was a mile long, and the queue for the x-ray machine was two miles long. But with an officer escort, I was taken straight to the front of each line and was through in no time at all. The officers organised it so I was first on the plane. I boarded right after the cabin crew. The officers walked me to my seat, next to the emergency exit with more leg room than I knew what to do with, and then waited outside until the plane took off. Nice one.

This deranged ordeal had peaked and I was starting to come out the other side of it. The hallucinations were just visual now and in the form of people. They had a more peaceful temperament, at this stage, and I still thought they were real. I was talking and playing with them the whole flight. I can only wonder what the people around me thought. Even when one of the apparitions stuck her head through the side of the plane to take a look outside; it didn't occur to me something strange was going on.

It was only after I arrived in Sydney that the 'fog' started to lift from my head, and I started to realise perhaps what I thought had happened wasn't real. But I still struggled to sort the fact from fiction regarding the whole episode. For six months or more, I kept the experience to myself. I've since learnt my delusional state was an episode of alcohol induced psychosis. I'd like to emphasise how fuckin' terrifying it was to think I was going to die and how scared and ashamed I felt having my sins put before a judge and jury in my head. The psychosis took place over a period of about 60 hours. It wasn't until I returned to Canberra, after a three hour coach ride from Sydney, that I got some proper sleep

–108 hours after I'd first woken in Cobán feeling ill. The incident concerned me for a week or two but it wasn't long before I had slipped back into my usual drinking patterns.

I was back in Canberra and in a state of shock. I'd arrived home five weeks early and just couldn't get my head around the fact I was back. Only five days earlier, I was at El Retiro with plans to travel to Peru. I was even considering blowing my flight off back to Australia in May, instead travelling until June and going to Berlin for Julia's 30th birthday. Now, I didn't even have a passport. During my psychotic episode, the voices in my head demanded I tear my passport in two, which I did. They said I wouldn't be needing it seeing as I was going to be killed. Because it was severely damaged, my passport was subsequently confiscated at immigration in Sydney. Ten years of travel had come to this. How the fuck did this happen? This wasn't in the script. Maybe I over did it with that last Quebec Libre.

It was months before the resentment of my trip being cut short subsided. Out of spite at the cards life had dealt me, I didn't make any effort to join the workforce, choosing instead to avoid the humdrum existence of the daily grind for a further six weeks. When the bitterness did subside, I was then able to look back and appreciate what a truly amazing time I had on my trip. It had a bit of everything: emotional highs and lows, beaches, jungles, affluence, hardship, stupidity, schooling, police, medical staff, and sex and drugs and alcohol. But above all, I met some incredibly friendly and kind people.

I can be a nostalgic person sometimes, as was evident when I recognised the ten year mark since I started travelling while I was in Guatemala. Looking back over the ten years, I had changed and learnt a lot. To the casual observer, I hadn't changed at all. Coincidently, I had the same long, shoulder length hair as I had ten years earlier; I still had no style when it came to my fashion sense; I was still into the same hard rock music; and on the surface, I was still the same friendly, jovial lad who liked a drink. But on closer inspection, my attitudes, morals, values and knowledge had all changed. My awareness of the world outside of my own little bubble was far greater.

    I learnt so much. I learnt powdery snow is not good for sliding a toboggan along. I learnt not to accept rides from truck drivers who have their fly undone. I learnt (the hard way) how to use a gas bottle safely. I learnt that the Shebeen Pub is trying to crack down on drug usage on their premises. And, of course, I learnt that for £28 one can buy a deed poll online and change their name. If you're thinking of changing your name, I recommend it. Life has been very amusing since I changed it. For example, Google: *Spaceman Africa Is the 2008 Name of the Year (People's Division)*. I don't think I ever learnt the pitfalls of a holiday romance and I never learnt my lesson regarding drinking. Time and time again drinking brought me undone, either financially or situationally, such as losing things. And I still haven't learnt how kangaroos have sex.

    I discovered I have an affinity for learning languages. I've realised human nature interests me; social contact and relationships are important to me. I've been able to empathise with people of other races and nationalities that are visiting or living in my own country. I learnt that one of the most important values for me is freedom—freedom of movement. Freedom to go places when and where I want, and on a whim, if so desired. And from that comes an aversion to commitment. I didn't stay with the one job or stay in the one relationship for too long. Freedom also allows for travel. For me, travel is addictive. Once I saw that there was a whole other world out there beyond my own city limits, I felt compelled to see and experience as much of it as I could. Travel became my passion and I still have that passion today. There isn't a place I wouldn't go if given the opportunity, except for a warzone. And to think, at the age of 20, I had no desire to travel overseas, except to New Zealand. Another lesson learnt from being on the road a long time is that long-term travel is not a holiday, long-term travel is life. All the hardships, frustrations, and annoyances that can occur in daily life can happen whilst out on the road. In some cases, travel is more prone to frustration and annoyances. Organising replacement bank cards is a perfect example.

From my years on the road, I took away so many special memories: working at the Shepherd's Bush Empire, seeing some great bands and making lifelong friends; running around on the Moscow metro with my mates, Dave and Brian, and mixing with the locals; the euphoria of dancing at a rave, high on drugs, and looking at my friends around me and seeing the same euphoria on their faces; talking rubbish with Niall for a week in Tullamore; Crazy Horse and I fortuitously being in the right place at the right time for the Harley Davidson 100th anniversary; the Brian Oliver story; my ongoing friendship with Julia; the New Year's parties with The Fellowship of the Ring; MJ's one liners in Cuba; and many more. So many more that I could write a book about them. Oh, hang on. Haha.

I didn't like the farewells, saying goodbye to a friend and not knowing when or if I was going to see them again. I didn't always enjoy carrying a heavy pack around on my back, especially on public transport during peak hour. Getting ripped off by tour companies or street vendors or whoever because I was a tourist never made me happy. And the jury is still out whether I enjoy air travel or not. One thing's for certain, though. Nearly two years on, Bob Rock still hadn't finished mastering the CD.

www.ingramcontent.com/pod-product-compliance
Lightning Source LLC
Chambersburg PA
CBHW071114080526
44587CB00013B/1342